T0229804

Terrorism and Homeland Security

Perspectives, Thoughts, and Opinions

Terrorism and Homeland Security

Perspectives, Thoughts, and Opinions

Edited by Dale L. June

CRC Press
Taylor & Francis Group
Boca Raton London New York

CRC Press is an imprint of the
Taylor & Francis Group, an **Informa** business

CRC Press
Taylor & Francis Group
6000 Broken Sound Parkway NW, Suite 300
Boca Raton, FL 33487-2742

© 2011 by Taylor and Francis Group, LLC
CRC Press is an imprint of Taylor & Francis Group, an Informa business

No claim to original U.S. Government works

Printed in the United States of America on acid-free paper
10 9 8 7 6 5 4 3 2 1

International Standard Book Number: 978-1-4200-9306-3 (Hardback)

Library of Congress Cataloging-in-Publication Data

Terrorism and homeland security : perspectives, thoughts, and opinions / editor, Dale L. June.
    p. cm.
Includes bibliographical references and index.
ISBN 978-1-4200-9306-3
    1. Terrorism--United States--Prevention. 2. National security--United States. I. June, Dale L. II. Title.

KF9430.T469 2011
363.325--dc22   2010011230

Visit the Taylor & Francis Web site at
http://www.taylorandfrancis.com

and the CRC Press Web site at
http://www.crcpress.com

To Nirmayla Bhomick, Dr. Michael Corcoran, and
Dr. Sheldon Greaves, fellow cofounders of Henley-Putnam University,
whose vision of the future culminated in a dream realized and opened
great opportunities in and for defense of America by addressing
educational voids in intelligence, high-level personal protection,
and counterterrorism. It is my honor to be associated with you.

This book is also dedicated to all those in the forefront of bringing peace
to a troubled world, and to those who are dedicated to the principles
of justice and freedom for all without bias or prejudice for or against
any particular religion, culture, society, race, or political affiliation.

SPECIAL DEDICATION

As this book was being prepared for publication, news was received of the death of coauthor, colleague, fellow agent, and teacher Dr. David G. Popp, a special agent with the U.S. Secret Service for twenty years before his retirement in 2002.

This book is dedicated to the memory of David G. Popp and the principles of loyalty, excellence, and service to his country and fellow man for which he unyieldingly stood.

See Chapter 10, "United States and European Union Antiterrorism Cooperative Efforts," by Dr. David G. Popp.

Table of Contents

Preface

No group or nation should mistake America's intention: We will not rest until terrorist groups of global reach have been found, have been stopped, and have been defeated.

—President George W. Bush, September 14, 2001

"Connect the dots" is a reference to a child's learning experience wherein a figure outlined in dots or numbers required the student to follow the pattern of dots or numbers to complete the picture. After the aircraft-driven bombings of September 11, 2001, the term *connect the dots* became a cliché for "think through the information and see the big picture." Connecting the dots is another way of imaginative thinking, a role of the intelligence analyst.

Prior to that horrific day in world history, there were several documented clues to the potential for what was about to happen, but unfortunately, no one was positioned to read the big picture or, as they said, connect the dots. Simply put, this was the result of a failure to communicate. Several people and agencies had snippets of information, but there was no one repository for those fragments where the whole picture of the puzzle could be assembled. Rather, it wasn't so much a lack of a storehouse or sorting depository for the information, but instead a failure to recognize the necessity of sharing the knowledge and making sense of the seemingly odd coincidences or suspicious behavior of individuals.

Terrorism begins with an act of violence in the form of kidnapping, bombing, and assassination. Students of terrorism come to research and understand how assassination can and has influenced history (or failed to change the course of history). In polite diplomatic terms, an assassination has been described as "early termination with utmost prejudice." The medieval assassins of Hassan al-Sabbah were trained in the art of "termination" with daggers, often blessed by the "Old Man" (al-Sabbah) himself at a mountain fortress at Altamut in present-day Iran. Today's most widely publicized modern assassins, under the influence of Osama bin Laden and the terror web known as al-Qaeda, operating in the same general areas as those trained at Alamut (but may move into more democratic countries in the future), are recruited and trained in the usage of self-controlled or living bombs, better known as suicide bombers, and are the weapons of choice of today's more successful terror groups. This book will introduce the reader to perspectives, thoughts, opinions, history, forms, and features of terrorism in the modern era.

Violence has always been a staple of human history. However, it was not until the tumultuous 1960s (America's decade of violence—war, riots, assassinations, cities burning, and racism, with short fuses being lit on man's intolerance for other men's race and culture) that serious studies of the causes and effects of violence were undertaken. Dr. Hannah Arendt recognized the phenomenon of violence eruptions and assumed a role of political–social investigator to attempt to analyze the causes of the manifestation of violence. Does violence beget power, or does power beget violence? War by definition is violent, but is victory accorded to only the most powerful or richest?

Dr. Arendt separated power and violence summarizing that "power and violence are opposites; where one rules absolutely, the other is absent. Violence appears where power is in jeopardy, but left to its own course it ends in power's disappearance.... Violence can destroy power; it is utterly incapable of creating it"* (Arendt). (An excellent example of violence destroying legitimate power is the novel *The Lord of the Flies*, wherein airplane crash victims, British choir boys (aged twelve and under) stranded on a forsaken island, duly elect a leader, but violence of the dissenters destroys the power of the elected leader, leading to homicidal chaos.) This thesis is also exemplified by communities or countries experiencing disintegration through a lack of political power; the more powerful an authoritarian political ruler, the less frequent the violence (i.e., the old Soviet Union and present-day China and North Korea, among others), yet this is contrary to revolutionary Chinese Communist Chairman Mao's dictum that "power comes from the barrel of a gun." Arendt stresses that "violence cannot be derived from its opposite, which is power, and that in order to understand it for what it is ... the roots and nature of violence must be examined."

Dr. Arendt concluded her study and thesis with this: "We know, or should know, that every decrease in power is an open invitation to violence—if only because those who hold power and feel it slipping from their hands, be they the government or be they the governed, have always found it difficult to resist the temptation to substitute violence for it." The substitution of violence for power is felt in every terrorist act. The powerless rising up to challenge and engage the powerful through destruction, death, and fear, is symbolic of terrorist aggression.

As a political science study of the roots of violence, Dr. Arendt was successful in making her case that violence is prone to destroying power, but it is the power of violence that eventuates in political power. Violence, if not used to foster power, eventually leads to political chaos. She effectively referenced

---

* Arendt, Hannah, *On Violence* (New York, Harcourt, Brace & World, 1970), p. 56.

sources in the political as well as philosophical spheres that reinforced her hypothesis. However, as a social science study, Dr. Arendt failed to analyze the roots or effects of violence as a source of social upheaval. But of course that was not her stated intent. Further, her book is an expansion of an essay that was originally published in European and American magazines; consequently, there was insufficient room to effectively address social causes and repercussions of violence. However, she expressly addresses rage as an instigator of violence: "Only where there is reason to suspect that conditions could be changed and are not does rage arise. Only when our sense of justice is offended do we react with rage."

Sociologists and psychologists have shown us that acts of violence are more readily engaged in while an individual is a part of a larger group, and he will commit acts that he would not otherwise even contemplate. Some have rendered this as "mob mentality."

> It is perfectly true that in military as well as revolutionary action, "individualism" is the first value to disappear; in its stead, we find a kind of group coherence which is more intensely felt and proves to be a much stronger, though less lasting, bond than all the varieties of friendship, civil or private. To be sure, in all illegal enterprises, criminal or political, the group, for the sake of its own safety, will require "that each individual perform an irrevocable action" in order to burn his bridges to respectable society before he is admitted into the community of violence. But once a man is admitted, he will fall under the intoxicating spell of "the practice of violence which binds men together as a whole, since each individual forms a violent link in the great chain, a part of the great organism of violence which has surged upward." (Arendt, p. 67, quoting Fanon and J. Glenn Gray)

Social scientist Dr. Samuel P. Huntington, who died Christmas Eve 2008, was not a man ahead of his time but a visionary who analyzed the past and present trends through sociological lenses and concluded that man's need for identity and belongingness far outstretches his viewpoints of economic politics and a world of "one." He was a man who, through simple observation and visionary conclusions, saw the consequences of "one world, one society" as the basis of major conflict as man struggles to maintain a national, religious, and self-identity through culture and ideological beliefs.

Dr. Huntington joins George Orwell and others, such as Alvin Toffler and Abraham Maslow, as forward-looking believers who painted a canvas of the future as they saw it, and who have been proven right in their controversial calculations, hypotheses, summarizations, and predictions. Every generation has soothsayers, scientists, sociologists, and visionaries who venture into the future and are often proven correct over time. But at the time of their publication of studies and predictions, these pioneers of the future are challenged, often castigated as "heretics" unwilling to move with the times or to accept the prevailing mood of those frozen in the shadow of economic, political, or religious power.

*The Clash of Civilizations and the Remaking of World Order** illustrates Dr. Huntington's (correct) belief that man's desire for belongingness far outstrips his adherence to a particular political entity, declaration, or dogma. Man's social history and future (customs, traditions, and beliefs) are as important as his political doctrines. This is the point Dr. Huntington profoundly states.

Dr. Huntington uses his vast knowledge, critical thinking, and a wide assortment of sources (political and sociological leaders and experts) to validate his belief and concerns of mankind. Relying on sociological studies and historical example, he forms a basis of thought as sustaining evidence of his thesis that change is difficult to accept, and man tends to grasp those things most meaningful to him, i.e., his culture, language, traditions, customs, etc., over politicalization or radicalization of his personal creed. The primary basis of his book was his 1993 essay "The Clash of Civilizations," wherein he first argued that the ballyhoo over a new world order was greatly exaggerated.

It seems that the course of history is determined by the mainstream of events as recorded by those who write it, and the future is locked by political and religious conservatives/liberals agreeing or disagreeing with the prognostications of futurists who attempt to forecast the future by analysis of past and present political/religious indicators, using history of the past and events of the present to build what will be.

As one who considers himself a liberal–conservative or conservative–liberal, but also a futurist and student of history, my tendency would be to throw my evaluation and support to Dr. Huntington's *Clash of Civilizations*. A clash of civilizations (cultures) has been evident throughout history from the Athens-Sparta wars (and before) to the Roman Empire versus the Barbarians, Northern Europeans versus Native American Indians, Catholics (or "The Church") versus Protestantism and others, Whites versus Blacks, etc. It's not "the economy, stupid" that brings people to war, but disagreement about ideology—political and religious. Professor Huntington was "right on" way before history's "right time."

A brief look at historical civilizations and empires reveals that the *average* length of an empire has been approximately 250 years. When the glass is turned upon an American empire (nearing its 250th anniversary) or dominant power, we see many of the same weaknesses and problems that brought down previous empires, to wit, immigration, war, failing economies, internal

---

* Huntington, Samuel P., *The Clash of Civilizations and the Remaking of World Order* (New York: Touchstone (Simon & Schuster), 1997).

dissent, corruption, lawlessness, and other various social disorders, such as fractured communities, a dysfunctional education system, and social welfare programs that fall short of expectations and needs.

A worldview of history points out many divisions of social order and creation of countries, not along cultural, geographical, or nationality lines, but by borders drawn with a pencil on a map (e.g., Africa). This has lent a great amount of disharmony, disorder, and upheaval as the "new world order" brings about distrust, envy, and resentment as each political or religious sphere competes to remain autonomous and cling to its own nationality, traditions, beliefs, and culture.

Traditionally more wars have been waged over religious dogma than any other reason. In a world where global politics are reconfigured along cultural lines a new era is being birthed. This is Huntington's fundamental thesis, which he demonstrates very well in his sustaining evidence and arguments of reasoned conclusions. Huntington was ahead of his time in his observations, but to a clear thinking pragmatist of 2009, it is obvious he was correct in his assessment.

Characteristic of the truth of human nature is that we think in terms of existence and survival; anything else is counter to that natural instinctive order. "Dying and killing seem easy when they are part of a ritual, ceremonial, dramatic performance or game. There is need for some kind of make-believe in order to inflict death unflinchingly. To our real, naked selves there is not a thing on earth or heaven worth dying for"* (Hoffer, p. 66). American philosopher Eric Hoffer, sometimes referred to as the "working man's philosopher" because of his background as a dockworker, explores the concept of self-sacrifice in the name of advancement of a social movement. His insightful presentation of, for lack of a better description, *self-sacrifice* predates what we have now come to know as suicidal murder, or to be more up to date, suicide bombing for a cause. He presents the theme that "those who would transform a nation or the world cannot do so by breeding and captaining discontent or by demonstrating the reasonableness and desirability of the intended change or by coercing people into a new way of life. They must know how to kindle and fan an extravagant hope. It matters not whether it be hope of a heavenly kingdom, of heaven on earth, of plunder and untold riches, of fabulous achievement or world domination" (Hoffer, p. 9).

Dealing with fanaticism, Hoffer looks at various motives for self-sacrifice, such as what we are witnessing today in the religious wars of the Mideast. He places an emphasis on the idea of "identification with a collective whole." It vitalizes the known that a person will do something as a member of a larger whole that he would not undertake as an individual.

---

* Hoffer, Eric, *The True Believer* (New York: Harper Perennial—A Division of Harper Collins Publishers, 1951).

"To ripen a person for self-sacrifice he must be stripped of his individual identity and distinctiveness. The most drastic way to achieve this end is by the complete assimilation of the individual into a collective body. The fully assimilated individual does not see himself and others as human beings. When asked who he is, his automatic response is that he is a German, a Russian, a Japanese, a Christian, a Muslim, a member of a certain tribe or family. He has no purpose, worth and destiny apart from his collective body; and as long as that body lives he cannot really die" (Hoffer, p. 62). In a sense, Hoffer is giving us the formula for understanding the motivations of a person wanting to join a gang, a military, a movement similar to religious fanaticism or zealotry.

He is insightful into the mind and motivations of self-sacrificing individuals and groups who are willing to go to death in the name of their cause, whether political, religious, or social. In a straightforward and common spoken manner, utilizing a long-range lens from approximately sixty years ago, he successfully argues and discusses what we consider a modern phenomenon, proving to us once again that self-sacrificing, suicidal bombers in the modern era are a powerful force to reckon with within the society of man, contrary to the truth of human nature to think in terms of existence and survival.

"What is war good for? Absolutely nothing" goes the theme of a popular song. "Generals plan for the last war" is, unfortunately, a current cynical appraisal of the state of strategic planning and preparation for war. "War is rational—a reflection of national interest and an extension of politics by other means," an often quoted Carl Von Clausewitz description of war even though he was advocating and defining war as unrestricted violence.

In *The Transformation of War* Martin Van Creveld* looks beyond these examples of phraseology to point out that the nature of war in our time is radically changing. War is no longer fought with specified fronts between "superpowers" (a term coined by William T. R. Fox in his 1950s' book *The Superpowers*). Wars are now fought through "surrogates" by guerilla armies, terrorists, common bandits, tribal factions and zealots. Lines have become blurred, challenging observable differences between civilian and soldier (i.e., a lack of uniforms or distinctive regalia, age, and sex factors), making it difficult to sort the combatants from civilian populations, common criminal activity from organized aggression, terrorism and war from patriotic behavior. Hostility and fighting between nations has given way to violent enmity of independent cells, tribal, ethnic, and religious factions fighting with the latest technology (usually funneled through neutral sources from an advanced and richer nation) or resorting to improvisation and primitive means and methods.

---

* Van Creveld, Martin, *The Transformation of War* (New York: The Free Press, 1991).

Van Creveld establishes that traditional warfare is as dated as knights in armor, with new wars being fought through smaller units and advanced technology that will literally remove the professional soldier from the battlefield. "The secret of the art consists of finding a correct balance between effectiveness and efficiency" (Van Creveld, p. 121). "Conventional war appears to be in the final stages of abolishing itself.... As war between states exits through one side of history's revolving door, low-intensity conflict among different organizations will enter through the other. National sovereignties are already being undermined by organizations that refuse to recognize the state's monopoly over armed violence. Armies will be replaced by police-like security forces on the one hand and bands of ruffians on the other, not that the difference is always clear even today. National frontiers, that at present constitute perhaps the single greatest obstacle to combating low-intensity conflict, may be obliterated or become meaningless as rival organizations chase each other across them" (Van Creveld, pp. 224, 225). As a prognosticator in 1991, Van Creveld was right on target as international events have proven in the Afghanistan–Iraq–Pakistan regions.

Viewing the above as givens, we can anticipate and come to understand that the world's relationships have evolved in a matter of three principles: (1) economic, (2) political, and (3) religious.

Economic factors influenced by several factions since the Iraqi invasion have included surges in the price per barrel of oil, thus affecting the oil consumption countries, as the world's financial basis is (or has become) based on the "oil standard." A leading question of international relations is: Did the United States invade Iraq to fight tyranny and instill democracy, to fight terrorism and insurgency, or was it to protect the oil production interests?

The second economic factor, and perhaps a leading consequence of the invasion, is the collapse of the world's most stable economic systems and banking institutions. A human element must be factored into the equation since much of the economic collapse of the world's markets can be traced to human greed for money and power. Arguably, though, man's lust for money and power predate the Iraqi invasion by thousands, perhaps millions of years.

A third aspect of economic relations has been in the fields of trade and international debt. The trade deficit, long a major world concern, at least since the President Kennedy years, has ballooned to gigantic proportions and is seemingly uncontrollable. As the late senator Everett Dirksen (D-Illinois) is reportedly quoted as saying, "A billion dollars here, a billion there, and pretty soon you are talking about real money." The inequitable trade deficit and bank–stock market collapses have put a tremendous burden on the American taxpayer, resulting in a foreign relations policy directed toward swinging the balance back toward stasis and relief of taxpayers. However, this has not occurred as anticipated, and the world continues to spiral out of economic control.

The political relations between nations considered allies and strong supporters of the U.S. policies have been strained as they pursue policies more conducive to their own domestic and international relationships. Disagreement has arisen as to the direction of the war and the desired end results. The world has shifted since the United States became the reigning superpower and the police department of the world. This has caused a loss of U.S. esteem and respect as the world's view is now more in the direction of viewing the United States as imperialist and invaders having an intention to control the oil-rich Middle East.

Political unrest and instability of governments in Africa, leftist-leaning elections in South and Central America, and (religious and political) insurgency and antigovernmental feelings and distrust throughout the world have destabilized the world, with growing concern of nations such as North Korea and Iran acquiring nuclear weapons and missile capabilities.

Other political alarms, like smuggling and enslavement of people (illegal immigration) and the "war on drugs," have caused an awakening of international political relations problems focusing on stabilization of cooperation between governments, as each government attempts to deal with the domestic causes of these problems as well as the international implications.

The third area of international relations policy is reflected in the growing strength of fundamentalist religionism. The question of "How do you fight an ideology" has been often expressed. World religious fundamentalism has seen a growing influence. The separation of church and state principle is being eroded in previously free and democratic countries. An entire province in Pakistan recently voted to follow Shireah or religious law rather than legislative law. As this was being written, Afghan President Hamid Karzai signed into law a provision severely restricting women's rights and rolling them back to the days of fundamentalist Islamic Taliban control. Under the law a Shiite woman needs her husband's or father's permission to leave the house, pursue an education, hold a job, or even go to a doctor's appointment. Only fathers and grandfathers would have child custody rights. The law also stipulates how often a husband is entitled to sex with his wife and permits martial rape if the wife refuses her husband's advances.*

The war in Iraq is being fought on three sides—economic, political, and religious—thus having a tremendous effect upon world international relationships and policies. No nation is any longer so isolated that its internal and external diplomatic, economic, and religious policies won't have an effect on the policies and diplomacies of other nations.

* "Afghan U-Turn on Women" (editorial), *Los Angeles Times*, April 4, 2009, p. A28.

A major issue in Iraq (and the surrounding countries) is stabilization of the government and the security of the people. Of course, security of the people is a responsibility of all governments, but it is taken more seriously by some than by others. International relations policies must concentrate on this most important venue. Thus, the United States is as embroiled in a war of establishing security as it is in stabilization of the government, in the theory that the government established will be as popular and democratic as willed by the people.

Will the new policies of international diplomacy and relations of the Obama administration be successful and bring stability to the distressed and political, economic, and religious upheaval in the areas in and around Iraq? One can only hope that an analytic reappraisal in international relations and policy will result in peaceful negotiations and a "return to normalcy."

How do you fight an idea, ideology, or religious movement? It is the responsibility of every free and secular country to resist, through diplomacy, intellectual analysis, and an informed public, the threats, bombings, kidnappings, assassinations, and intolerant dogma of those fanatics who would end democracy and replace it with their own version of world unification through the dictatorial establishment of draconian doctrine, canons, and religious laws. Guns and bullets don't work. For every insurgent killed, another takes his place, passed on to the next generation of terrorists. This has been proven true since the third century. Every person who believes in freedom, liberty, and democracy must be aware of the insidiousness and dangers lurking in principles of religion grounded in the ideas and ideology of a megalomaniac's self-serving pronouncements and *fatwas*.

Understanding the strength of the forces and the menace of a rigid religious movement arrayed against a free people in a secular world is the first step in developing resistance to that ideology. The primary focus of this book is directed toward bringing awareness to concerned people, and perhaps an awakening to the importance of developing particular aspects of strategic and tactical planning, responses, and preparedness of the American people in the event of a terrorist campaign in the American homeland. The strength of a nation is the education of its people. The purpose of this book is to, in some small way, afford an opportunity for learning about the potential for disruptive activity brought by those who would destroy the hard-earned constitutional freedoms of a free people in a free land.

The purpose of religion is intended to bring a code of humanity based on love, goodness, tolerance, kindness, and spiritual faith. When any religion is hijacked and corrupted by individuals who purport to speak for God, establishing rules, laws, and guidelines subjugating other people to their own fraudulent convictions, the true meaning and purpose of religion is lost, replaced by terror, death, torture, and confinement.

Abou bin Adam

Abou bin Adam (may his tribe increase!)
awoke one night from a deep dream of peace,
And saw, within the moonlight of his room,
Making it rich, and like a lily in bloom,
an angel, writing in a book of gold.
Exceeding peace had made Bin Adam bold,
And to the Presence in the room he said:
"What writest thou?" The vision raised its head,
And, with a look made of all sweet accord,
Answered, "The names of those who love the Lord."
"And is mine one?" said Abou, "Nay, not so,"
Replied the angel. Abou spoke more low,
But cheerily still, and said, "I pray thee, then,
Write me as one who loves his fellow men."
The angel wrote, and vanished. The next night
It came again, with a great awakening light,
And showed the names whom love of God had blest,
And lo! Bin Adam's name led all the rest.

—James Henry Leigh Hunt (1784–1859)

An American school student in the fourth or fifth grade during the 1950s and 1960s learned this poem as a lesson in understanding the importance of humanity and "loving your fellow man" in the sight of "the Lord" as seen through the eyes of a mortal man whose humanity placed him in highest accord.

"Write me as one who loves his fellow men" is a far cry from Osama bin Laden and his personal agenda of world dominance by the establishment of an Islamic caliphate with his al-Qaeda brethren. Even the word *caliphate* contains *hate*. Bin Laden cannot say, "Write me as one who loves his fellow man." Like all megalomaniacs of history, his beliefs center not on world peace or individual freedom, but on world dominance with him at the center. If he is not the direct center, he is spiritual inspiration for his dogmatic disciples, who, like Hydra, grow many offshoots calling for religious and secular warfare pointed toward the collapse and replacement of freedom and democracy. Bin Laden's manifesto, spelled out in "Military Studies for Those Who Would Wage Jihad [Holy War] against the Tyrants," is their blueprint.

Freedom to gain knowledge, information, and education; to move about as one wishes and pleases; and to speak freely and enjoy criminal justice safeguards is a pillar of a free world that stands in the way of those who would destroy democracy's long-standing tradition and pride of freemen everywhere.

When the editors and publisher of this book agreed to its proposed content, a call for chapter contributors went out over the Internet. The people who responded are professionals and experts in their fields with lifetime experiences, research, study, and education, which they generously agreed to share in spite of their own crowded schedules. The result is a book containing information that could easily be equal to an advanced degree in homeland security and terrorism. Contributors are a blend of recent university graduates holding bachelor's degrees and present and former (retired) government agents (master's and doctoral levels) who are highly regarded in their field for a lifetime of protecting America and who unselfishly are passing the lamp of their learning, experience, and sage advice to a new generation. Readers will find, upon concluding their reading of this book, that they have gained usable knowledge that will provide them with a well-rounded survey of homeland security and terrorism from the perspectives, thoughts, and opinions of counterterrorism and academic field agents who have seen the enemy.

Foreword

Editor's Note

In normal circumstances the author or editor of a book will write a preface as sort of an introduction to what is to follow. That was my first intent. But when I received the following essay from a recent graduate of the University of California, Los Angeles (UCLA) I scrapped the preface I had prepared. I believe she more eloquently expressed, much better than I did, what she admittedly stated is an idealist view of global terrorism, that ethnocentricity must take a backseat to world improvement and hopefully peace. As she concluded, "It all starts with a dream."

Dale L. June

Terrorism and Homeland Security

An essay by Jessica Laing

Seven years ago, if someone asked me what the Department of Homeland Security was, I probably would have given a blank stare (because it didn't exist). Today, *homeland security, terrorism,* and the *war on terror* are all phrases and words that have seamlessly integrated themselves into our vocabulary. The tragedy of 9/11 made us all aware of the threat of terrorism, and made it very clear that the United States wasn't immune. Yes, there were terrorist attacks on Americans throughout the last century: in 1979, Iranian students held 52 hostages for 444 days in a U.S. Embassy in Tehran; multiple suicide bombs and attacks in Beirut during the 1980s; two simultaneous bombs exploded near two U.S. Embassies in Tanzania and Kenya in 1998; the USS *Cole* attacked in 2000. And this doesn't include the numerous attacks committed by "home-grown terrorists" like Timothy McVeigh. Yet it was the events of 9/11 that seemed to pull all of the other events together and drop the subject of terrorism in front of everyone's face. Immediately after, the Patriot Act of 2001 was signed into law by President Bush. A year later, the Homeland Security Act of 2002 was enacted, creating the Department of Homeland Security. Since then, their effects and the effects of terrorism have in some way or another changed our lives.

For me, the worst it gets is going through airport security. Before 9/11 it was common to pack shampoo in carry-on luggage for a commercial flight. Today, there are little bottles of eye drops with the words "TSA Approved" emblazoned on the packaging to assure us and airport security personnel that we are not terrorists. I'm not saying that we don't need precautions, especially relating to air travel. The measures are necessary. In 1971 D. B. Cooper stepped on board with a bomb in his suitcase. Now we have metal detectors. But today it's a whole slew of things: belts, watches, hats, jackets, shoes, liquids have to be 3 ounces or smaller, and all containers have to fit in a quart-sized plastic Ziploc baggie. So while standing in line, waiting for my belongings to pass through the x-rays, I have the time to ponder the reasons for the heightened security and the issues related to terrorism.

First of all, terror goes back centuries, most often in the form of warfare. Thousands of years of history leave a record of bloody and ruthless campaigns ending in the pillaging and raiding of thousands of villages and countries. How is it much different today? We are still the same, only today we have long-range missiles and sophisticated technology that allow us to destroy a country from miles away. No country is immune to terrorist attacks, but neither can they say, "We've never done anything like that." It's in these times that we have airport security, new legislation, and emergency precautions as necessary tools to combat terrorism. Whether it's increasing funding for technical support at the FBI, widening the scope of search warrants to cover electronic evidence and financial records, extending Secret Service jurisdiction, or enhancing immigration laws, the U.S. government did not and will not hold back from preventing terrorist activities. While all this investigation and prevention is a good step, I can't help but think that they're already a couple of steps behind. What I mean is, when the government and law enforcement agencies obtain information of a terrorist plan, it's a race against time to stop it from coming to fruition. There are ways of uncovering plots and attacks, preventative measures to ensure public safety in the event of an attack, but there aren't ways to stop someone from becoming a terrorist to begin with. Stop it before it gets to the stage of having to arrest people for attempting to blow up the White House or hijacking a plane. Yes, I know it's a huge endeavor and extremely idealistic, but on some level, we have to take this into serious consideration. We can prepare all we want, and have the best investigative forces detaining terrorists, but the fact is, they keep coming at us. So the question is, what can we do to prevent terrorist organizations from springing up, to prevent people from feeling the need to take that route? I'm not suggesting that the laws and legislations are null or useless. They keep us safe and are a necessity, especially considering the state of current affairs. However, it seems that there could be more proactive steps the government can do, especially in terms of foreign policies, and communicating with countries that have us in their sights, not to mention home-grown terrorists. Most of the time when we find communications from terrorist organizations, they always include something about hearing their message. Does it mean that we, as a government and nation, are so bad at listening that it forces a group of people to resort to mass destruction and violence? Not necessarily. But if we changed our foreign policies to allow for more communication from countries where terrorist groups exist, that could go a long way in lessening hostilities. I mean, if my neighbor started throwing rocks at me one day, I'd try to talk to him and find out why because, unless he's just a mean or prejudiced jerk, he'll have a rationalized reason for doing it. And that way, there's some peaceable way to resolve the issue. Now, understandably international diplomacy and terrorism are harder to deal with than just a bad neighbor (unless it's the Hatfields and McCoys), but just as much as we are shoveling resources and funding into investigative operations, we should spend an equal amount of resources and funding on communicative and negotiation efforts to try to resolve some of the issues behind the hostilities. Talk is not cheap. It can be very effective in getting across an idea or understanding another point of view. In order to really prevent people from strapping on explosives and detonating themselves in a crowded public square we have only a few options: (1) tackle them before they detonate the bomb, (2) arrest them before they get to that last stage, or (3) hear their grievances before they feel like they need to join a terrorist ring in order to get their message aired.

Why do I keep going back to talks and communication? Obviously brutality isn't going to work because that's the kind of response terrorist organizations are expecting. Torturing detainees at Guantanamo isn't going to get them to talk and give up their leaders. Treating them like human beings with emotions and beliefs may get us on the right road. There is a need to understand why people become terrorists, what it is they believe so fervently that they are willing to destroy lives and cause mass destruction. Talks, treaties, understanding. We don't understand each other and may never understand each other because of the different beliefs and ideals each country holds. But a little more cultural relativity wouldn't hurt.

Okay, so all of this sounds great, but making it a reality is much more difficult, if not impossible. First of all, there is really no chance of getting Osama bin Laden and other heads of terrorist organizations to sit down and talk with world leaders. It is an idealistic thought that we'd all be able to sit down and lay out our thoughts, ideas, philosophies, and grievances without someone getting offended, and very quickly at that. Even during peace talks someone is going to get offended because each group is based on a certain set of fundamentals, and these fundamentals are the core structure of their respective society. We're all guilty of ethnocentrism. We believe our philosophy and way of thinking is the best. Again, it comes back to knowing and understanding each other. Elbert Hubbard said, "If men could only know each other, they would neither idolize nor hate." Even realizing the differences may help in coming up with a solution, but it requires a great deal of cultural relativity, which was drilled into me as an anthropology major. Then we wouldn't be so quick to judge or drop bombs on each other. Yet I have to sigh because this is all a dream, an ideal. But hey, Martin Luther King Jr. had a dream and look where things are today. There has to be a dream in order for some sort of action to follow.

Jessica Laing, BA
Los Angeles, CA

Acknowledgments

To sit here and try to thank everyone connected to this book is a monumental task unto itself. Isn't that what most authors say in their acknowledgments? Of course it is always true, and this book and author are no exception.

However, I will shorten the list by making it as brief and concise as possible, by beginning with thanking all the contributors of chapters to this book. Several chapters were written by professionals in their respective fields of expertise; some were written by recent bachelor degree college students, and some were written by nonprofessional American citizens who have no experience in homeland security and terrorism but who have their own ideas, thoughts, perspectives, and opinions. But most were written by people holding advanced degrees and a lifetime of experience.

Everyone who contributed a chapter took time out of his or her own busy schedule to help put this book together. Several preset deadlines, provided by the man whose name carries the credit for the book, were missed due to very tight personal schedules in the pursuit of methods and means to secure our world from those who would destroy it. With less than a week to go before the final deadline set by the publisher, we were still trying to gather all the material. It has been a daunting task beyond which we were all ill prepared because of our ever-expanding agendas and tightening schedules and closing deadlines.

I also must thank my brothers and sisters, Dean, Jerry, Beverly, Rosemary, and Inez, for their lifetime of support. And naturally, my wife, Muslima, and children (now all grown adults), Kelleen, Kason, Victoria, Katherine, and Mohammed, who have all been there with me when I needed them the most.

Keeping it all in the family, I want to express a special thank you to my cousin, Jesse June, who spent an entire career and well into his retirement years working dangerous assignments and missions in counterintelligence during the Cold War era. He is still very active somewhere in this country.

Working together, we can all make this world a more peaceful and wonderful place. People come into our lives for a special reason; when that mission is complete, they go out of our lives again, but their influence and impact will always stay with us. Thank you all (CRC editors, friends, acquaintances, and contributors) for coming into my life.

D. L. June

About the Contributors

Dr. Juan A. Bacigalupi is a former U.S. Army intelligence officer. Dr. Bacigalupi worked in the Defense Intelligence Agency (DIA) Imagery Analysis Section, concentrating in command, control, and communications. Additionally, while serving with the U.S. Army's Intelligence and Security Command, he was attached to First Army in support of Operation Desert Shield, and later Desert Storm. During these operations, Dr. Bacigalupi served as the chief of intelligence, during the night shift, for the Allied Ground Forces. Later, Dr. Bacigalupi served as the intelligence collection manager for VII Corps (just before the end-around sweep liberation of Kuwait). After retiring from the Army, Dr. Bacigalupi began his second career in emergency medical services, working as the assistant director of the Southeastern Massachusetts Emergency Medical Services Council. Dr. Bacigalupi currently works as a physician in the Dominican Republic. Dr. Bacigalupi holds a medical degree from the Universidad Central del Este, San Pedro de Macoris, Dominican Republic. He holds a master's degree in public administration, with a concentration in health services, from Suffolk University, Boston, Massachusetts. His undergraduate degree was in international studies, from George Mason University in Fairfax, Virginia. Dr. Bacigalupi has received specialized training in all-source intelligence analysis, threat analysis, and advanced imagery analysis techniques. While working in the emergency medical field, he received training in the Incident Command System (ICS). During his career, he participated in several mass casualty events, working in different positions. He has presented classes on ICS in international conferences.

Bart Bechtel retired in 1998 from the CIA after a lengthy career as a covert operations and counterintelligence officer throughout Europe, North America, Asia, Southeast Asia, China, Russia, and the Mediterranean. He has a broad background in domestic and international terrorism matters, crisis management, and issues related to chemical and biological weapons proliferation. He is experienced in threat assessment, analysis, and intelligence operations. He is also a lifetime member of and Outdoor Emergency Care™ instructor for the National Ski Patrol. Mr. Bechtel has been an EMT and received HAZMAT responder training. Bechtel's professional involvement in counterterrorism issues began early in his agency career, while posted in the Middle East. Additionally, he was a team leader for the U.S.

State Department's surveillance detection team training program. Bechtel is currently a director and lead instructor for the Sentinel Program, which teaches surveillance detection for public and private entities. Bechtel is a professional instructor and lecturer. He is a private consultant specializing in security, safety, management, and marketing. Bechtel was also an adjunct instructor at the California Specialized Training Institute and the National Interagency Civil-Military Institute at Camp San Luis Obispo, California. He was a founding member of and instructor for the Sheriff's Citizen Homeland Security Council in Washoe County, Nevada. Bechtel is a professor and program manager for the Center for Counterintelligence and Security Studies in Alexandria, Virginia. He has also worked extensively with federal, state, and local law enforcement, emergency services, and private security firms. Bechtel is a member of the International Association of Counterterrorism and Security Professionals, and the president of the Northern Sierra Chapter of the Association of Former Intelligence Officers. His education consists of a BA degree in history from the Monterey Institute of International Studies (1972) and an MS degree in intelligence management from Henley-Putnam University (2007).

Monte R. Bullard is a retired Army colonel who holds a PhD from the University of California–Berkeley in political science and is a graduate of the U.S. Army War College. He is now a senior fellow at the Center for Nonproliferation Studies, Monterey Institute of International Studies. He began his career in the Army Counter Intelligence Corps and served in other intelligence positions, including clandestine collection in Korea. He also commanded an interrogation center/prison in Korea. He later commanded two additional HUMINT collection organizations. He served as Army liaison officer in Hong Kong and Army attaché in Beijing. He is a graduate of the Chinese Nationalist Political Warfare College in Taiwan. He retired from the Army as commandant of the Defense Language Institute.

Debra D. Burrington received her PhD in political science from the University of Utah in 1992. Her dissertation is an ethnography titled "Balanced at the Edges: Feminist Organizing as Oppositional Practice." Between 1985 and 2002 she taught at the University of Utah for the Political Science Department, the Gender Studies Program, and the Graduate School of Social Work. While at Utah Dr. Burrington served on a number of graduate thesis and dissertation committees as well as a variety of university committees, and also functioned as codirector of the Gender Studies Program. Dr. Burrington has published a number of peer-reviewed articles and has delivered a large number of public presentations at academic conferences and other public events as part of her service to the community, as well as having appeared on a number of local and national television news programs as an expert commentator. While a political scientist by training, over the years Dr. Burrington has embraced emphases in political sociology, social movements, diversity education, qualitative research methodology, as well as organizational culture and management. More recently Dr. Burrington has returned to her interest in ethnographic methods, specifically ethnographic fiction, through the vehicle of mystery novels (one completed, one in progress). Dr. Burrington is also presently researching a book on Mormon popular culture. In 2003 Dr. Burrington joined the Los Angeles campus of American Intercontinental University, where she currently serves as vice president of academic affairs, and she has also taught in the School of Business there.

Howard Clarke is an internationally recognized law enforcement intelligence specialist with extensive experience in the areas of transnational and organized crime, and the conduct of strategic threat risk assessments for border and transportation security. He has held senior analytical posts in Australian and Canadian law enforcement organizations, including postings as chief analyst and acting director of intelligence with the National Crime Authority in Australia. Howard has extensive experience in the conduct of instructional assignments and conference presentations in international contexts, and holds adjunct instructor status with Henley-Putnam University, the Justice Institute of British Columbia, and the British Columbia Institute of Technology. He has also acquired SME status within Canadian law enforcement and federal government circles in the fields of strategic intelligence analysis and in the development of intelligence support for port and border security functions. He holds lifetime accreditation as a certified criminal analyst and is a former member of the board of governors of the Society of Certified Criminal Analysts. Howard has his own consulting practice known as the Intelligence Solutions Group (www.intelligence-solutions-group.com) and is an associate at Toddington International, Inc. (www.toddington. com).

Augusto D'Avila is a HUMINT senior instructor at Ft. Huachuca. He is a Plank Holder in establishment of DOD HT-JCOE. He served in Iraq in support of Operation Iraqi Freedom in 2003. He is an Arabic and Spanish linguist. Mr. D'Avila is also a project coordinator for development of courses for HUMINT. He has taught courses in Arab culture, Islam, militant radical Islam, culture of al-Qaeda, Iran overview, Iraq overview, and terrorist financing. Mr. D'Avila is also a mentor and instructs on cultural nuances and Arab collectivism. He has a BS in liberal arts from New York Regents University, a certificate from the U.S. Army Intelligence School, a certificate in Arabic from the Defense Language Institute in Presidio of Monterey, an AA in Arabic from Monterey Peninsula College, and a certificate in

Spanish–professional interpreting/translating from UC Riverside. He is pursuing a master's degree in counterterrorism studies.

Keely M. Fahoum is an instructor with Henley-Putnam University specializing in intelligence, counterterrorism, and close personal protection. Ms. Fahoum graduated from the University of Montana in 1998 with a bachelor of arts degree in English, specializing in creative writing, and three minors in Japanese, Asian studies, and history. After graduating from the University of Montana, she entered the U.S. Air Force, where she served as a personnel specialist for four years and a special agent with the Air Force Office of Special Investigations for five years. During her time as a special agent, she investigated and analyzed several counterintelligence and counter-terrorism cases and briefed military leadership on potential threats to military members in both domestic and deployed locations. She received her master of science degree from Embry-Riddle Aeronautical University in professional aeronautics with an emphasis on aviation safety and completed her second master's degree in national security affairs with a specialty in the Middle East from the Naval Postgraduate School. Ms. Fahoum is also a graduate of the Defense Language Institute, where she studied Arabic.

Claudia M. Huiza is an educator, activist, independent media journalist, and artist. For over twenty years, she has been a professor of Spanish literature and language, English literature and composition, Chicano studies, women's studies, critical theory, cultural studies, Latin American studies, and global studies at various colleges and universities, including UC San Diego, UC Santa Barbara, Southwestern College, and National University, where she served as lead faculty for online and on-site language arts programs. She is currently the dean of education at Platt College in California. She has published articles on women in literature and on Latinas and bilingual–bicultural literacy pedagogies in various books and encyclopedias. Her documentary work includes *Estamos Aqui* and *Producing Just Garments* with Colectivo Media Insurgente, of which the latter received the Artivist Film Festival Opening Night Honors in 2008. Her professional conferences and colloquia include: "A Report from Beijing Forum, with Bella Abzug," NGO Forum of the United Nations 4th World Conference on the Status of Women; "On the Edge: Transgressions and the Dangerous Other," Whitebox Gallery and John Jay College of Criminal Justice; and "Sewing Just Garments in El Salvador," CSU-LA Center for the Study of Genders and Sexualities Conference on Immigrant Women and Labor Organizing. She has participated in panels at the UCLA Labor Center Latino Summer Leadership School, at the Fourth International Conference on Diversity in Organizations, Communities and Nations, at the National Association for Chicana/Chicano Studies, and at the Society for Phenomenology and Media Studies, among others. Her art has been shown at the Company Gallery in Los Angeles and at Kottie Paloma Artist's Studio in San Francisco. She also cohosts and coproduces the KPFK radio show *Labor Review* with Henry Walton. She has been awarded grants by the Stuart Foundation, UC MEXUS, the American Festival Project Grants for the Arts, and the National Latino Research Center. She has been honored by the San Diego Neighborhood House Association for her community outreach, and is the proud recipient of a National University Presidential Scholar Award and the San Diego Citizen's Action May Day Humanity Award. She holds a BA, cum laude, from UC San Diego in Spanish and English literature; an MA from UC San Diego in comparative literature; and a CPhil from UC San Diego in cultural studies. She is currently working on a dissertation titled "Feminist Historiography and Transformative Politics: Alternative History in the Works of Elizabeth Martínez, Ninotchka Rosca, and Elena Poniatowska."

Elizaveta (Liza) Kirillova is a twenty-year-old 2009 graduate of American Intercontinental University (Los Angeles) majoring in criminal justice. She is from Russia and speaks six languages. She aspires to become either a CIA or DEA agent.

Jessica Laing, a graduate of UCLA and an anthropology major, with a special interest in forensic anthropology, dreams of becoming a U.S. Secret Service or FBI agent. Her love of learning continues as she is embarking on her master's level studies in forensic investigations. She speaks Mandarin Chinese and is actively training in the ancient art of Traditional Wing Chun Kung Fu.

A. K. Mohammed is cofounder and vice president of operations for a boutique firm specializing in investigative and expert testimony. This firm has affiliates across the country and worldwide and specializes in gang typology, terrorism issues, and related cases. Dr. Mohammed has an extensive background in education having taught for nearly 10 years in both onground and online platforms for a number of colleges and universities. He has consistently earned the top 1% of faculty course evaluations in classes taught and maintains a strong and strict academic code of ethics and integrity. Dr. Mohammed has extensive experience in criminal justice course development as well as curriculum development and has served as a curriculum committee member. He graduated with bachelor's and master's degrees in criminal justice and completed his doctorate in criminal justice management. He has also cocreated a clinical program that aligns government agencies, insurance, law firms, U.S. military, and others, to provide job training with the purpose for job placement of college students. He is also the co-developer of a training program that cross trains American Muslim Communities & Law Enforcement seminars to aid law enforcement and other peace officer associations to gain better understanding of the various cultural groups within the southern California region. Dr. Mohammed also serves as a member of the local police chiefs' roundtable on Muslim affairs. He is cofounder and executive director of a local nonprofit, aligning members of the law enforcement, probation and juvenile courts to promote a revolutionary education program for juveniles to help reduce the rates of recidivism. Outside of academia, Dr. Mohammed has more than 20 years' experience in business, corporate settings and management, private security and investigations, insurance, and operations.

Richard J. Niemann is an adjunct faculty member at Kaplan University School of criminal justice and Henley-Putnam University. He teaches and conducts courses in the area of homeland security, terrorism, and counterterrorism. He is the course leader in this section of the criminal justice school and has developed and designed courses for the universities. Mr. Niemann has over twenty years of experience in public safety as a criminal justice practitioner, teacher, researcher, and investigator. He continues to serve as an active police officer, tactical instructor, and consultant in the criminal justice community. Mr. Niemann is a former deputy sheriff having served in a variety of assignments, from corrections and court security to being a firearms instructor and a member of his department's SWAT team. Mr. Niemann is the managing principal of TRT Solutions, a security consulting firm. Mr. Niemann has a master's degree in homeland security with an emphasis on terrorism from the American Military University and received recognition from the International Honor Society, Delta Epsilon Tau, April 2006. He has a bachelor of science in criminal justice administration. He is certified by the American College of Forensic Examiners Institute (ACFEI) Certification in Homeland Security, CHS Level IV, and the Antiterrorism Accreditation Board (CAS). Mr. Niemann is also certified by DHS and FEMA.

Kerry Patton is an internationally recognized security, terrorism, and intelligence expert. He most recently served as an advisor for the Department of Defense within the Human Terrain Systems as the first ever Department of Defense lead social scientist throughout Regional Command East, N2KL Afghanistan. For over seventeen years he has served in the Department of Defense, Department of Justice, and as a contractor within the Department of Homeland Security. Mr. Patton has taught members of the National Security Agency, Defense Security Services agency, Alcohol, Tobacco, and Firearms agency, and numerous state and local law enforcement agencies, to name a few, in terrorism and physical security-related issues. He has served his country honorably throughout South America, Africa, the Middle East, Asia, and Europe, serving within multiple capacities ranging from human intelligence to dignitary protection of Afghan President Karzai. He has interviewed terrorists and former terrorists within Hezb Islami Gulbadine, Taliban, and the Palestinian Liberation Organization, as well as political party members in Sinn Fein. He holds an Occupation Instructor Certification through the U.S. Air Force, two associate's degrees from the Community College of the Air Force in criminal justice and instruction of technical military science, a bachelor's degree from American Military University in intelligence studies concentrating in terrorism, and a master's degree in strategic intelligence concentrating in global terrorism. Currently he is pursuing his doctorate degree in human services. His dissertation is planned to be built around the needs for sociocultural intelligence. Mr. Patton has also written a book titled *Terrorism, Intelligence, and National Security* through Authorhouse publications and has several published articles. He can often be heard as a guest on either the John Batchelor or the John Loftus radio shows. Mr. Patton is also the vice president of training and public relations for the Emerald Society of the Federal Law Enforcement Agencies (www.esflea.org). He currently teaches terrorism and intelligence courses for Henley-Putnam University.

David G. Popp, a specialist in international security issues, served for twenty-eight years in both domestic and overseas assignments with the U.S. Secret Service and the Department of Homeland Security. He was a recipient of the prestigious Albert Gallatin Award for his service to the United States. In addition, he served as an adjunct professor at several universities, including La Salle University's European Security Studies program and Henley-Putnam University's intelligence and protection programs. He was also involved in advanced postgraduate research at the University of Leicester (UK) School of Law, focusing on efforts of the United States and the United Kingdom to counter terrorism financing. Dr. Popp passed away May 27, 2009, at the age of fifty.

Jonathan Ross is a writer and business consultant who lives in Los Angeles. He is currently undergoing instructor training in Traditional Wing Chun Kung Fu under the guidance of Sifu Eric Oram, one of Si-gung William Cheung's leading instructors. He is also an American-trained instructor of Krav Maga, now affiliated with Eyal Yanilov and the International Krav-Maga Federation. His consulting website is found at www.blackrockconsult.com. Mr. Ross was recently asked by a colleague and friend that has been following his writings to devote a chapter to the topic of homeland security and the applications of the Zentropist approach toward law enforcement, counterterrorism, and private sector security consulting operations. This is actually a subject close to his heart, due to both past and current personal and professional associations that he keeps, his undergraduate studies (a two-part graduate-level thesis, developed during the autumn of 1991 and spring of 1992, was sadly somewhat prescient regarding today's global political environment, with a focus on domestic counterterrorism for Part I and counterinsurgency operations for Part II), and a close family member that works as a special agent for a federal agency that shall go nameless for now.

Michael Savasta began his military career in the U.S. Air Force as a security police officer and subsequently as an investigator attached to the OSI. While stationed at Andrews AFB, Mike worked as an intelligence officer and participated in protection service operations for high-ranking military and civilian personnel, including foreign dignitaries. This assignment also afforded Mike the privilege to serve for two years on the security detail for President Reagan. Currently, Mike is a police detective with over twenty-seven years of experience. He specializes in property crimes, including arson and explosive investigations. He teaches courses in criminology, terrorism, tactics, digital crime, and professional ethics, among other topics. Mike has been a guest speaker for the International Law Enforcement Educators and Trainers Association, the American Society of Law Enforcement Trainers, and the Florida Department of Law Enforcement. Mike has also served as a subject matter expert for the state of Florida in the areas of law enforcement curriculum. Mike has published articles in *Tactical Response Magazine*, *Law and Order Magazine*, and the *Illinois Tactical Association Magazine*. While earning his master's degree in criminal justice from Columbia Southern University, Mike's concentration was on emerging terrorism trends and global terrorism. Mike's current areas of interest include Hizballah, al-Qaeda, Hamas, and the history of terrorism.

Wayne Taylor has served with distinction as an intelligence officer and a counterintelligence officer with the Department of Defense. His assignments have been in both the tactical and strategic realms, as well as holding the position of director of the Advanced Source Operations Course at the Human Intelligence–Joint Center of Excellence for the Department of Defense. Mr. Taylor also serves as an adjunct professor with Henley-Putnam University.

About the Editor

Dale L. June, MA, university professor, corporate and police trainer (specializing in executive, close personal protection; personal and professional ethics; and topics relating to "things they don't teach at the academy") (www. thebonitacompany.com), is a former U.S. Secret Service agent assigned to the Presidential Protective Division at the White House with three presidents, and served in the Sacramento and San Diego field offices. He is also a former military policeman (110th MP Platoon, Stuttgart, Germany); city police officer (Redding and Sacramento, California); a U.S. Customs intelligence research specialist, specializing in organized crime and terrorism; a private investigator; and an executive protection specialist. He earned his MA degree in criminal Justice from George Washington University and his BA degree in public administration from California State University, Sacramento. He began his doctorial learning in strategic studies in January 2009.

He has taught executive protection classes to students from Mong Ji University in Korea, lectured similar classes in Mexico, and has been invited to be a guest lecturer in South American and African countries. He is a pioneer in private executive protection, founding and managing his own executive protection company (in San Diego), providing security for many high-ranking persons and corporations long before it became a recognized and necessary profession.

He is an adjunct professor teaching human behavior, psychology, social science, terrorism, and various criminal justice courses at two universities in Southern California. As a cofounder of Henley-Putnam University, he has been active with the university since 2001. In 2006 he was named American Intercontinental University's Criminal Justice Instructor of the Year.

He is a past member of the National Black Belt Club (Tae Kwon Do) and the Association of Former Agents, U.S. Secret Service. He holds a black belt in the Quick Defense Personal Self-Defense System, and was inducted into the U.S. Martial Artists Hall of Fame as Martial Artist of the Year in July 2005. He is training and teaching in the Surgical Strike System™ way of self-defense and is also training to become a certified instructor in Traditional Wing Chun Kung Fu.

Mr. June is the author of *Introduction to Executive Protection*, second edition (2008); *Introduction to Executive Protection* (1998); and coauthor, with Mr. Carmine Motto, of *Undercover*, second edition (1999). He also edited and assisted with Mr. Motto's book *In Crime's Way: A Generation of U.S. Secret Service Adventures* (2000), and is a contributing author and editor of *Protection, Security and Safeguards* (2000), all published by CRC Press. He has written security-related articles for international security magazines in Canada, the United Kingdom, Mexico, New Zealand, and Germany. He has written course lecture material for protective and intelligence curriculum in addition to unarmed defense and defensive tactics for protective personnel. He recently completed a 35,000-word online homeland security and terrorism lecture series, plus PowerPoint presentations and student assignments, for Career Education Corporation.

Mr. June sees himself as a "warrior" who loves to read, write, and help those who can't help (or protect) themselves, especially children, grown-ups, and dogs.

He may be contacted at 4mrusss@gmail.com or djune@henley-putnam.edu.

Gemini
Terrorism and Homeland Security

1

DALE L. JUNE

Contents

Gemini—The Twins—widely known for their dual personalities…. The twin sides of their nature perpetually pulling in opposite directions …

Introduction

Historically and characteristically terrorists put a gun to the head of their victims and negotiated; today they put a gun to their victim's head and pull the trigger (or more dramatically and ghoulishly, they put a knife to the throat and decapitate the helpless victim, then show the video on the Internet or a sympathetic television news organization). Another very popular method of spreading fear, violence, and death is the placement of bombs in crowded public places. This is a tactic first made popular during the Algerian independence movement against France in the 1950s. Taking that page from history and updating it, the current method of spreading terror is commonly the suicide bomber.*

From the early assassins and training camps of Hassan al-Sabbah at Alamut, Persia, during the first crusade, to the modern-day terrorist in the form of bombers and assassins, ideas of terrorism throughout the history

* See "The Mechanics of a Living Bomb," www.waronline.org/en/terror/suicide.htm, and "The Making of a Terrorist," www.time.com/time/worl/article/0,8599,1883334,00.

of the world have been points for consideration to bring about an equality of forces by the disenchanted, disenfranchised, revolutionaries, and fundamentalists.

Modern terrorism begins with an act of violence in the form of kidnapping, bombing, and assassination, all of which can and have influenced history. In polite diplomatic terms, assassination has been described as early termination of life with utmost prejudice. The medieval assassins of al-Sabbah were trained in the art of "termination" with daggers, often blessed by the Old Man (al-Sabbah) himself. Today's most widely publicized modern assassins, under the influence of Osama bin Laden and the terror web known as al-Qaeda, operating in the same general areas as those trained at Alamut (but may move into more democratic countries in the future), are recruited and trained in the usage of self-controlled or living bombs, better known as suicide bombers.

There are words that typify motivation for growing unrest in religiously conservative areas of the world. The first word is *globalization*. A shrinking world unified by commerce and political alliances undeniably has great advantages to the economy of the world. Advanced technology, speed of communication, and international travel have brought the world to the brink of becoming one community. The countries of Europe have come together to form the European Union, sharing a universal currency, flexible border regulations, and common markets. The western hemisphere has forged an agreement (the North American Trade Agreement) for trade between the nations in that hemisphere.

Another very common word that is bringing nations closer is *outsourcing*. Industrial nations send certain types of work to third world countries, where the cost of labor is much lower and adequately available for manufacturing, assembly, or telemarketing.

Lesser known or not commonly used words that are finding their way into the language and having a profound effect are *McDonaldization* and *Disneyization*. *McDonaldization* is a generic term to describe proliferation of fast food, instant gratification, and consumerism in a "throwaway" society. *Disneyization* connotes fantasy, amusement parks, and consumption merchandizing.

All four terms succinctly describe what is seen as major aggravations to conservative religious fundamentalist philosophy. From American right-wing radically conservative religions advocating bans against music, dancing, and intermingling of the sexes, to the correspondingly, yet militantly centered forms of Islamism, there is a sense of moral decay in the world. Driven even further, the conservative and militant right-wing Islamists foresee a dilution of their religion and decomposition of their culture. Given the nature of the strict religious code combined with militancy, the formula is in place to create factions that will engage in horrific acts to destroy what they deem as heretical and claim the right to destroy the infidels, or unbelievers who are responsible for modernization.

Encyclopedic length verses, chapters, and books have been written about terrorist incidents in the United States and abroad. It is not within the scope of this chapter to discuss individual historical terrorist acts that have been defined elsewhere. However, it is intended to discuss certain selected terrorist incidents of the modern era (since 1970) that have played important roles in the direction of the current mainstream thinking and policy formation that has altered the course of human affairs.

History of Terrorism*

> In the beginning there were two brothers, Cain and Abel....
> Terror—Unforgiving and uncontrollable fear.

Early History

The history of the earth is synonymous with violence, fear, and terror; earthquakes, floods, fires, volcanic eruptions; creatures large and small living in fear of what manner of being or living thing preyed upon the lesser and weaker. It was simply, in the words of Charles Darwin, survival of the fittest—and only the strongest and most adaptable survived.

For whatever reason, flora and fauna that flourished in the very earliest time periods died and became extinct thousands and millions of years before man made his first appearance. No matter what position a person takes on the conception of man, either evolution or creation, one thing is certainly true: man adapted better than any other creature on earth. He was to become the master of his universe. But there were faults in the fragile creature of Man. He was possessed with jealousy, anger, and rage; the only mortal thing willing and capable of killing simply for one purpose—for the sake of killing. Man's history is illuminated with instances of conquest, terrorism, assault, vandalism, and assassination.

At the first beginnings of man's time, man ruled through brute strength, fighting as an animal with tooth, nail, and muscle. Then someone picked up a stick or stone and struck his stronger opponent with it, and thus weapons were born. Man's history is a direct parallel with the development of weapons. Slings replaced the throwing arm, bows and arrows gave man the advantage of fighting from a longer distance, and the arms race proceeded through history with the most capable, well armed, and stronger dominating.

---

* Hundreds of volumes have been written about this topic. Here we will attempt to highlight only the news magazine or *Reader's Digest*™ rendition.

Along the continuum of time, someone somewhere developed a logic that the weaker and less equipped, with fewer weapons, weaker numbers, limited supplies, etc., could strike fear into their enemies by using stealth, surprise, and terror. Even the story of *Beowulf*, the hundreds-of-years-old Anglo-Saxon epic, tells of fear generated by Grendel, a lone terrorizer against the army of a king. Grendel would suddenly strike out of the darkened night and slay the soldiers who lived in fear of the surprising attacks.

Terrorist attacks have been successful because of their violence, surprise, and suddenness of initiation. They usually begin with bombings, shooting, hostage taking, and assassinations. Assassinations are the quintessence of terror because they usually strike a powerful leader or public figure, leaving the populace to wonder about their own safety and security.

Assassination

One of the very first political assassinations of historical significance occurred with the stabbing death of Julius Caesar by members of the Roman Senate on March 15 of 44 B.C., as they feared his rising power and his declaration that he was a god.

The holy books of religion (descriptions and recipes for living in a God-fearing world) are ripe with descriptions of sudden attacks, death, and destruction. Trickery, treachery and shadows of the night brought fear to the strong and strength to the weak. In an early recording of a religious-political assassination, Ali, the son-in-law, cousin, and successor to the prophet Mohammed, was struck down by an assassin (a former Ali supporter) who waited in the darkened shadows while Ali was praying and killed him with a poisoned sword. This act was but one of several that led to the bloodshed between Sunni and Shiite Muslims to this day.

The Middle Ages

Toward the end of the eleventh century, a mysterious man of the desert, Hassan al-Sabbah, established his headquarters high atop a mountain near Alamut, Persia (approximately a hundred miles from the modern city of Tehran, Iran). Here he founded a school for young men and a few very select women to train in the deadly art of deceit and murder.

Al-Sabbah selected and recruited (often kidnapping) young vulnerable boys to his training camp. Through the use of drugs (reportedly hashish), he placed the boys in a well-kept garden and supplied them with the favors of women, food, and anything else they would desire. He convinced them they were in paradise. After keeping them in the garden for approximately two weeks, he would again have them drugged and returned to the outside world. Al-Sabbah told them that if they wanted to return to paradise, they would have to train and act according to his word.

Because of their use of hashish, they became known as *assassins*, a term derived from a medieval Latin word, *assassinus*, taken from the Arabic word for "hashish eaters," *hashishin*. It is unknown for sure if the assassins used hashish before making their attack, but the reputation is that they did. Assassins trained in the use of several methods of killing, including poison. Primarily the weapon of choice was the dagger (sometimes blessed by the master, al-Sabbah himself). Knowing they were on a mission of murder-suicide but rejoicing in the belief they would be returned to paradise, the assassins would go as far as working for years in a trusted position within the household of the one projected to be killed. Acting on orders, the trusted killer would attack with his dagger, expecting to be killed following his act. Those who actually committed the assassinations were called *Fedai*, a name now used by Arab guerillas as *Fedayeen*.

The assassins operated under the direction of al-Sabbah and his successors for nearly two hundred years, selling their services to whomever hired them throughout the entire Muslim territories, targeting whoever opposed their own extremist faction of Islam. Specifically, their enemies were rival Muslim caliphs and the Christian crusaders who invaded and traveled in the Muslim countries of the Middle East to spread the Christian gospel and to wage war for Christianity with the specific intent to destroy the "godless" and barbaric Muslims. In an ironic twist of history, Muslim terrorists have expressed a worldwide goal of forming one *caliphate* of universal Islamic control. Thus, the present intent is to kill all infidels unless they convert to Islam. The favorite current method to force conversion is by an act of terrorism.

The sect of the assassins was eventually defeated in the late thirteenth century, when thousands were slaughtered by the invading Mongol hordes of Mangu Khan, the third successor to Ghengis Khan, as they swept toward future conquests in Europe.

At about the same time in another part of the world, in feudal medieval Japan, assassins moved with the shadows of the night to deal a hand of death for a singular purpose: to make a political statement or deliver a religious message. These highly trained, black-dressed, martial artists, practitioners of nin-jitsu and being one with the darkness and the night, the mysterious ninja, trained for only one purpose: to assassinate rivals of their master shogun. They would appear suddenly, commit the act, and disappear as quickly and quietly into the darkness. Their campaign of assassinations spread terror through the hearts of nobles and peasants alike. Even the professional soldiers in the army of shoguns, the highly trained and skillful samurai, held the ninja in fearful and deadly respect.

The Age of Revolution

The term *terror* comes from the Latin word for "to tremble," as in total fear. Modern historians trace the common usage of the word terror to the French Revolution and the *reign of terror* led by Robespierre. Vivid hopes of the French Revolution in 1789 contained dreams of liberty, equality, fraternity and popular sovereignty, representative democracy, rights, and happiness.

Thousands of French citizens, including the king, were sent to their death on the killing platform of the guillotine. Eventually Robespierre himself was seized and led to his death on the bloody stage. He was dead, the reign of terror came to an end, but the word *terror* came into practical and common usage to describe the feelings of total and uncontrollable fear. Terrorism became an equalizing weapon of the weak against the powerful. Of course, the powerful often used terrorism to intimidate the weak or disenfranchised (an example is the Ku Klux Klan in America).

By modern standards and definitions, the use of terrorism has been prevalent on American soil for over five centuries. The Spanish, French, English, and Dutch used fear and superstition (as well as overwhelming force and torture) to force Native Americans into submission. Moving forward, the American colonists used guerilla warfare and terrorist tactics against the British during the American Revolution. Prior to the revolution, colonial patriots, dressed as Indians, raided three ships in the Boston harbor and tossed the cargo of tea into the bay. An act of terrorism by "patriots." Here we encounter the double conundrum: patriot or terrorist?

Modern Terrorism

Modern terrorism's opening page came in Algeria in the 1950s. As Algeria was fighting for independence from France, "freedom fighters" or "patriots" began a campaign of terror by placing bombs in crowded public places.

Guerilla warfare and terrorism differ only by degrees and definition. Guerillas target and attack strategic military installations and personnel. Terrorists aim their attacks at the noninvolved citizenry. But the often hit-and-run tactics of guerillas lead to terror and fear among the soldiers of the military forces. There is a story coming from the Vietnam War of the 1960s and 1970s telling of a soldier awakening one morning and finding the head of his tent-mate on a pole outside the tent, placed there by the enemy, the Viet Cong. True or not, the story illustrates the power of terror.

For the sake of brevity, we begin the discussion with modern terrorist trends in the late 1960s and early 1970s. International terrorism combined with political assassinations, rioting and burning, and civil disobedience and upheaval in the United States and abroad highlighted these two decades in violence, death, and destruction.

Sociologists have labeled the 1960s in America as America's decade of violence. It could as well be named America's decade of assassination, as there were six major assassinations on America's landscape that decade, from 1963 to 1968. And violence reigned. With such enormity as riots, assassinations, social protests, fire bombings, etc., the land of America became psychologically unhinged. In 1969 the Charles Manson family savagely and brutally attacked and killed movie actress Sharon Tate and five others in their home. The next night the bloody scene was recreated in the home of Mr. and Mrs. La Bianca, a randomly selected house in the Los Angeles area. Until the murders were solved (initially blamed on drugs by the LA police), people across the nation were frozen in their disbelief of the horror, fear, and terror.

Various groups took active participation in antigovernmental policies (especially the war in Vietnam). Most organizations followed a protocol of shouting, picketing, and demonstrations that were usually very loud, expressive, and unruly, but for the most part there was little, if any, direct violence, such as kidnapping, arson, or bombing. Violence was not a part of their message, and their medium was demonstrations aimed at a peaceful solution to the civil rights movement and the war in Vietnam. During all the turmoil and havoc of the antiwar movement, there were also nonpeaceful and violent organizations, for instance, the Weather Underground and the Symbionse Liberation Army (SLA). The tactics they engaged in were certainly capable of being defined as terrorism.

The SLA was an assembly of social misfits that considered themselves a revolutionary army to conduct urban guerrilla warfare, though at its zenith it numbered no more than a couple dozen members. They committed bank robberies, two murders, and other acts of violence, but gained their greatest share of international notoriety for their brazen kidnapping of Patty Hearst, whom they mentally and physically mistreated through demeaning tactics until she participated with them in an armed bank robbery.

The Weather Underground was perhaps the most violent of the revolutionary groups in the United States during the 1960s and 1970s, with participation in riots and several bomb placement attacks against an assortment of banks (especially the Bank of America) and the government, with bombs located in the U.S. Capitol building, the Pentagon, and the Department of State.

They went as far as declaring war against the United States and advocated a classless world. As the Weathermen, they adopted the slogan "You don't need a weatherman to know which way the wind blows" from a line in a Bob Dylan song, and were responsible for participation in the riot during the 1968 Chicago Democratic National Convention and loud protests, termed the days of rage, during the trial of the Chicago Seven, who were instrumental participants during the riots.

Terrorism came into sharp focus in the 1970s, with such names as Abu Nadal, Black September, and the Jackal, and incidents such as airplane skyjackings (in 1972 President Nixon initiated a program called sky marshals to stop the flood of skyjackings), kidnapping of representatives of the oil-producing countries (OPEC), public building takeovers by a group of Hanafi Muslims, Black September's 1972 attack on the Munich Olympics, bombs detonated in crowded restaurants and public buildings, including the U.S. Capitol building in Washington, D.C., and other incidents of a nature designed to bring fear and terror.

On the international stage, "the name of the game" was a long series of airliner hijackings. The operation usually consisted of several hijackers, with smuggled weapons, finding their way aboard an airliner (usually an international flight). Somewhere after reaching cruising height and speed, they would take over the plane using force and violence. After making their demands known, usually demanding the release of imprisoned comrades, the plane was flown to a neutral site in a country that was sympathetic to their cause. There, after lengthy negotiation, the hostages and the plane would be released. In several instances, the plane was blown up.

One very frightening change of terrorist tactics regarding an airline incident where there was no hostile takeover or negotiation was the December 21, 1988, bombing of Pan American Flight 103 over Lockerbie, Scotland. The flight bound from Heathrow Airport (London) to John F. Kennedy Airport in New York exploded in the air over Lockerbie, killing all aboard the plane and several on the ground. Investigation eventually disclosed that a Libyan terrorist had placed a bomb in a cassette recorder in unaccompanied luggage that had been loaded onto the flight from another connecting flight.

The 1980s brought a period of relative calmness, but as historically shown, terrorism, like other aspects of human endeavor, is recyclable. The 1990s brought a new and larger framework of terrorism to the United States and the world.

On February 23, 1993, a massive bomb exploded in the basement of the World Trade Center in New York, killing six and injuring over a thousand. The intent was to bring the North Tower down and crash it into the South Tower, causing the destruction of both.

In April 1995, a new element was introduced to Americans. Timothy McVeigh, a former American soldier, placed a large, homemade improvised explosive device (IED) made from common farm fertilizer and diesel fuel in a rented van and parked it near the Alfred P. Murrah Federal Building. The resulting explosion destroyed the building, killing 168 men, women, and children while injuring over 800 others. This was a very serious jolt to America. McVeigh could not have chosen a more practical target if his intent was to spread terror throughout the country (this is an example of one-incident terrorism). He selected a city in the heartland of America where terrorism would seemingly be far removed, and by targeting a federal building, he demonstrated his rage against the government.

Knowing the formula of takeover and negotiation and being trained to cooperate with airline hijackers, the passengers and crew of the doomed airliners on September 11, 2001, reacted in exactly the way they were informed and trained, which in this case was a very serious mistake. No one anticipated that the people taking over the plane were going to make this a murder-suicide flight. Though bombings of public places and suicide bombings had been a historical fact for many years, this one day began a new era in terrorist attacks. It was also the birth of a new type of warfare and the end of traditional war.

The intent and spirit of those long-deceased followers of the philosophy and decree of Hassan ibn al-Sabbah is ever present and operative to this very day in the person of Osama bin Laden and his fanatical believers, as evidenced by the number of terrorist attacks and assassinations promulgated by groups of dissident fundamentalist Muslims and insurgents. Favored weapons of assassins and terrorists have evolved from crude sharp instruments such as arrows, spears, daggers/knives, and poison, to guns and explosives and suicide bomber vests and belts containing explosives with nails, marbles, and ball bearings and the "mother of all bombings"—fuel-laden passenger commercial airplanes turned into suicidal dive bombers piloted into the World Trade Center and the Pentagon.

Following hard on the heels of the twin tower and Pentagon bombings was the spread of the anthrax virus via U.S. postage and the activities of the Washington, D.C., area snipers, who killed at random spots from a hidden location (in the trunk of a car).

Making each terrorist act more heinous than the last, new words have crept into our language: roadside bombs, hostage takeover, workplace violence, suicide bombers, stalker, serial killer, sniper, shoe bombs, dirty bombs, anthrax and small pox viruses, weapons of mass destruction, and improvised explosive device.

Globalization, Modernization, and Terrorism: Interlocking Roles

Globalization and modernization are identical twin factors in the ongoing evolution and changing face of terrorism. Religiously based terrorist groups use terrorism as a vehicle to protest what they believe are threatening social movements to replace their culture and conservative religious lifestyles. Leading edges of globalization are represented by fast food restaurants, amusement parks, and what are seen as decadent examples of moral decay, for example, music, movies, DVDs, Western seductive and provocative clothing, association with the opposite sex, and activities that have been judged to violate moral codes and their draconian explanation of the intent of their God. A loose examination of what are seen as rigid guidelines of religious precepts leaves one to wonder if specific sects of religion are antimodern, believing it sinful to enjoy the present life in anticipation of a better life in paradise.

In previous paragraphs we discussed topics similar to the section currently under consideration. Here we will delve deeper into globalization, modernization, McDonaldization, Disneyization, and religious fundamentalism, all of which are, or may be, closely related to motivations of several generalized forms of terrorism.

Globalization and modernization impact the technological and communication advances in the war on terrorism, with instant fact finding, gathering and dissemination of intelligence, surveillance from satellites far in space, and placement of cameras, monitors, and surreptitious listening devices. It is possible to read files deleted from computers and to record every computer keystroke. The advancement of technology brings people and events directly into living rooms in real time. This may be a boon to counterterrorism, but at the same this double-edged sword also feeds valuable information to terrorists while providing them an up-to-the-minute stage for their atrocities.

We will begin with deeper definitions and understanding of these special terms and examine how the modern world is seemingly on a collision course with traditional cultures in what can be considered third world countries, or in more polite and modern terms, developing countries.

The Role of Globalization on Terrorism

Globalization is a formalized term for bringing the peoples of the world into one village for economic, technological, sociocultural, and political advantages. Certainly there are advantages to globalization in the sense of greater opportunities for the nations involved and the people of those nations. However, globalization must be recognized as a major factor in denationalization of what had been constructed as national. This includes culture, legends, traditions, customs, and political jurisdiction. American political scientist Dr. Samuel Huntington* recognized the disintegration of national unity and the spirit of those who resist the onrushing change. He saw the consequences of "one world, one society" as the basis of major conflict as man struggles to maintain a national, religious, and self-identity through culture and ideological beliefs.

---

* Huntington, Samuel P., *The Clash of Civilizations and the Remaking of World Order* (New York: Touchstone, Simon & Schuster, 1997).

Humans have a serious resistance to change, especially if it is too rapid and sudden. In the current rush of the world to embrace globalization, certain factions of Man enact their resistance to it by methods contrary to the rules of civilization, i.e., terrorism, death, suffering, and exploitation of the masses.

Modernization

In the same token and spirit of globalization is its twin consequence of modernization. Modernization historically has evolved over a lengthy period of time, allowing the people to adapt to changes on a very subtle transition. However, modernization and change have occurred in the world of the twentieth (especially after the Second World War) and twenty-first centuries at an ever-quickening pace, disallowing people ample time to adjust. As social change transforms nations and societies from agrarian to industrial ones and into an age of technology, it is important to see and recognize all the consequences, beneficial and harmful, brought to the people of the affected societies.

A primary motivation for the Iranian Revolution of 1979 that dislodged a forward- and progressive-thinking shah from office and replaced him with a strict form of conservative Shiia Islamism was a generalized belief that the shah was adapting Western methods, lifestyles, and products too quickly for the people to readily adapt. To protest the American influence in Iran at the time, American embassy employees were taken prisoner and held hostage for 444 days. Looking back over the past, one could conclude that the Iranian revolution was the genesis of the new era of terrorism. Within a few short years after the revolution, the nature of terrorism escalated to suicide bombings and execution of hostages.

McDonaldization

In 1967 Mr. Ray Kroc opened the first McDonald's fast food hamburger restaurant. Thus was created a consumer throwaway society demanding immediate personal satisfaction and faceless impersonal service. Expanding rapidly, McDonald's soon went global, and today the McDonald's golden arches are easily recognized in nearly every major city in the world. To a world community of tradition and conservatism this encroachment on values may be too sudden a change and is but one reason for rejecting Westernization.

The McDonald's formula of success emphasizes four elements of management operation that can be translated into similar components of a terrorist organization: efficiency, calculability, predictability, and control.

Efficiency
McDonald's set the standard for efficiency by setting up an assembly line type of operation where each employee has only one job to produce the hamburger.

It takes several operations to produce one hamburger, but if each person in the process is assigned one job only, the burger can proceed to completion and be handed to the consumer within seconds. This process is much more efficient and quicker than if one person completed one burger. Efficiency in a terrorist operation is also of equal importance where speed and timing are extreme considerations. The first aspect of planning a terrorist operation is calculating the percentage of success, which consists of utilization of a minimum number of personnel and resources, tactical planning, rehearsal, and timing. The theme for a terrorist could be "efficiency and speed—get in, get the job done, and get out!"

Calculability

As an operator of a McDonald's franchise can attest, it is important to understand that to avoid waste and to serve as many people as possible, he must be able to calculate the average number of hamburgers he expects to sell daily and plan accordingly. A terrorist must calculate every aspect of the operation and consider all consequences in advance; to be considered are the number of persons involved, their special area of expertise, equipment and logistics, plus the statement they want to make and what is expected as a result of the operation.

Predictability

It is predicted that from the moment a customer enters a McDonald's restaurant his order will be taken, he will be served, and he will exit the restaurant all in a matter of fifteen minutes or less. To ensure this timetable, the restaurants arrange uncomfortable seating to encourage the customer to leave after he has eaten his meal. A terrorist rehearses and practices his operation well ahead of time and will not engage it unless he is satisfied with the timing and that his prediction of success will be equal to the effort.

Control

In a McDonald's, everything is strictly controlled: waste, timing, cleanliness, spoilage, even the menu and customer flow. In a terrorist takeover the first item on the agenda is to take control of all people and their environment. All during the operation, every aspect of the target of the terrorist action or every piece of the life of the hostage is controlled by the terrorist.

Disneyization

Disneyland is recognized as "the happiest place on Earth." Here, reality is suspended in a sanitized world of fantasy with its glitzy light shows, a panorama of merchandising, and consumer consumption. Through a marketing strategy that has made Disney Company one of the most successful in the world, Disneyland and many imitators have sprung up in unlikely places, including emerging countries. To say this has had an adverse affect on the populace, especially the ultra-conservative religious factions who have forbidden music, computers, VCRs, television, movies, commingling of men and women, etc., would be a gross understatement. To not consider the insult to those particular religions or traditional third world countries is to invite a protest action. As we have seen, a common protest action comes in the form of terrorism.

Religious Fundamentalism

We must realize that much of the religious trauma of today has historical roots going back at least over two hundred years. When we compare modern Islamism with Christianity, it is easy to see that Islam is going through the same throes as Christianity of approximately six hundred years ago with the Catholic and Protestant reformations. What we see are two primary sects fighting against each other and more conservative factions, with incursions of terrorism from each.

Loosely interpreted, the word *fundamentalism* refers to a strict adherence to basic principles, usually in a strict traditional religious sense. Though the word was not a common reference until the later part of the twentieth century, fundamentalism (austere and narrow interpretation of the Bible or other books, such as the Quran) was the form of religious practice followed by the early 1600s. Conservative religious fundamentalist doctrine adheres to the following type of thinking:

> Man was not built for happy living. He must learn to give up the pleasant dream, at least so far as this life and world are concerned. Let him cultivate a thick skin, to endure the hardships and adversities of life! Let him kill all his natural cravings and aspirations for the good things of this flesh! All these philosophies and religions which have drawn to their standards the masses as well as the classes have taught self-denial, self-suppression, a killing of the personal will, a surrender to those dark powers of the universe called Fate, or Nature, or the Gods and either mild contentment or resignation or the apathy of despair. Never happiness!*

The Tyranny of Fundamentalism

Since the takeover of Iran during the Iranian revolution of 1979 by Shiite Muslims, the term *fundamentalism* or *fundamentalist* has become an adjective attached to stringent adherence to Quranic verses and Sharia law. Living

---

* Pitkin, Walter, *The Psychology of Happiness* (New York: Simon and Schuster, 1929).

under Sharia law eliminates governance under legislative law, or laws of man. Followers of Sharia adhere to "God's word"; thus, there is no separation of church and state because the church is the state. What man places in the words of God becomes the law of the land. Thus, men empowered by their religious precepts control the law, often in draconian and outdated manners and enforced by harsh penalties, including beatings, maiming, decapitation, and stoning to death for even the slightest infraction.

It is a mistake to assume that the conflict is only between fanatical religious factions and modernization through globalization. There are terrorist blocs who engage terrorism for a plethora of other reasons, including personal grievances (real or imagined), specific topics such as antiabortion, political change, better living conditions, and recognition for specific groups, and causes of distress and revenge or settlement of injustices.

The two foremost terrorist groups operating against the United States are the Taliban and al-Qaeda, whose proclaimed mission is to destroy the "decadent" West, primarily the United States, and replace democratic separation of church and state government with an all-inclusive Islamic caliphate and institute the harsh rules of Sharia law. The threat is real, and battles against these antidemocratic religious fundamentalists must be continued and won where they are breeding—in the hotbeds of fanatical beliefs.

Taliban Background

The Taliban is a form of Islamic Wahabbism, a strict fundamentalist Islamic sect adhering to an unwavering, absolutist interpretation of the Quran. They follow an extremely strict and antimodern ideological form of Sharia (religious) law, which may explain recent movements toward a return to restrictive practices and to eliminate globalization, outsourcing, McDonaldization, and Disneyization.

Sharia law or religious laws interpreted and issued by the all-male Ministry for the Promotion of Virtue and Suppression of Vice (PVSV) and enforced by its "religious police" call for a harsh ban on certain objects, activities, and personal dress of a "provocative nature," and restricts employment, education, and sports for women, movies, television, videos, music, dancing, hanging pictures in homes, clapping during sports events, kite flying, and an endless list of other prohibitions that are deemed to be modern and contrary to interpretation of the Quran by Taliban leaders. Men must be unshaven with beards extending longer from the chin than the width of a doubled fist.

Women especially are targeted by Sharia restrictions. They are prohibited from working, except in the medical fields because male doctors are restricted from viewing the female body. They cannot wear clothing the religious or vice police regard as stimulating and attractive. Girls are not allowed to attend school, and females are not allowed on public streets unless accompanied by a close male relative. Home windows must be darkened to prohibit women from being seen from the outside.

The Growing Power of the Taliban

After their capitulation to Allied forces in Afghanistan in January 2002 the Taliban appeared defeated. But the Coalition's victory was more heliographic than actual because Taliban suicide bombing attacks continued and new troops trained and recruited at madrasas (Islamic schools) rallied to the call to join the Taliban's fight, and by mid-2009 the Taliban reformed stronger and more determined than before. Tactics, however, have begun to more resemble guerilla warfare than terrorism. While guerilla warfare participants target military personnel and facilities and terrorists aim at the noninvolved citizen, the Taliban has incorporated both aspects in their crusade. In May 2009 an American military patrol delivering school supplies to schoolchildren aged five to twelve was ambushed by a small strike force of Taliban fighters.

Threats and Appeasement

This same year, 2009, Pakistan ceded a major victory to the Taliban when it approved a Taliban takeover of the Pakistan Swat Valley Region, only 90 miles from the Pakistani capital of Islamabad. Sharia law was immediately installed with very restrictive rights and curtailment of everyday freedoms previously enjoyed by the inhabitants. Within days, however, because of Taliban encroachment beyond the Swat area, Pakistani troops began an active campaign to push back the Taliban.

Pakistan has learned that appeasement of the Taliban fails, as the surrender of the Swat Valley can attest. For several years Pakistan turned a blind eye to the enclaves of Taliban hiding in the mountains between Afghanistan and Pakistan. The Pakistani government knew of the presence of the Taliban in their country for a long time but failed to act against the conservative fundamentalists for various political reasons and threats of terrorist type retaliation.

Appeasement of the Taliban by the Pakistani government by surrendering the Swat Valley to the Taliban led to further bloodshed and extension of the Taliban reach, up to nearly 60 miles from the capital. The government then had to reengage the Taliban in physical combat in attempts to dislodge the Taliban from the annexed areas.

Appeasement didn't work in 1938, despite British Prime Minister Neville Chamberlain's declaration of "peace in our time" upon conclusion of a summit meeting with Adolf Hitler surrendering to Hitler Germany's intent to invade Poland in exchange for no further aggression. Appeasement didn't work then, it didn't work in Pakistan in 2009, and it never will work when surrendering to bullies and megalomaniacs. Appeasement as a political policy is doomed to failure.

Taliban Tactics

The Taliban has utilized terrorist tactics including suicide bombings, public executions of kidnapped victims, and other assorted strategies generally associated with terrorism. However, in their recent resurgence, their tactics have more resembled guerilla tactics, as their forces have used ambushes and hit, strike, and retreat methods of attack. That is not to say tactics have completely evolved from terrorist attacks, especially suicide bombings, roadside attacks, and placement of explosive devices, because they continue unabated and with success.

Assessment

While the resurgence of the Taliban is growing stronger in the Afghanistan-Pakistan areas, it would appear their fighting is being restricted to those areas, but their influence throughout the region is growing in popularity as young men rush to join their ranks.

Looking at the Taliban and its potential for terrorist attacks in the United States and the rest of the secular world, a conclusion can be reached that for the immediate future the Taliban will concentrate on winning military victories in Afghanistan and Pakistan. As the power of its Sharia law is consolidated in those contested areas, the Taliban may attempt to spread its influence on a wider frame and assist the al-Qaeda network to realize its stated goal of overcoming secular nations and bringing them all under one unified Islamic rule.

There has been no confirmation or rumored location of the spiritual leader and mastermind of al-Qaeda, Osama bin Laden, in spite of the $50 million reward offered for his capture, but his influence is felt through every string of the al-Qaeda web. His declared war on the United States and the modern decadence of the Western nations will continue long after his death. Modernization brought him wealth and power, but his strict religious fundamentalism has brought him to the delusional belief that he will one day become the caliph heading an international Islamic caliphate.

What of al Qaeda?

The international loosely framed network of terror cells called al-Qaeda (meaning "the base") has been held responsible for the majority of major terrorist attacks against the United States and other nations (i.e., Great Britain, France, Germany, and Spain). The most recent major attack having alleged al-Qaeda ties was the November 2008 attacks in Mumbai, India. Al-Qaeda is a very loose organization; in reality, it isn't even an organization in the commonly accepted definition of the term—it is a number of independent cells brought together through common terrorist activities, interests, and methods. Each cell operates on its own with little or no communication between them. They may share a common training background and adhere to the al-Qaeda terror manuals with a common defined purpose of establishing one worldwide Islamic caliphate.

Al-Qaeda is like a large snake, sitting quietly in the bushes planning and waiting. When the time is right, a sudden strike designed to bring death, fear, and far-ranging publicity will reawaken a world that falls into the trap of a delusionary feeling of false security. This snake of al-Qaeda is such that if one part is cut off, another will take its place.

Major al-Qaeda attacks against the United States include the marine barracks suicide bombing in Beirut, both World Trade Center bombings, the attack against the USS *Cole*, and bombing attacks against U.S. embassies in Kenya and Tanzania. Other international attacks include an attempted subway bombing in London and a railway bombing in Spain. It may be conjectured that all these attacks may be a prelude or "dress rehearsals" for what may be planned for a future attack in the United States.

Other Terrorist Threats

Though the Taliban and al-Qaeda are perhaps the foremost known terrorist threats on the world stage, there are terrorist groups acting independently to fight for whatever cause they espouse. It may be a lone right-to-life advocate or snipers (Washington, D.C., area snipers) hiding in the trunk of a car frightening an entire portion of the country, nearly closing down businesses and interstate travel. A terrorist may mail pipe bombs or anthrax powder to an unsuspecting recipient. A hate group or neo-Nazi white supremacist organization may attack the person or persons of its particular focus of interest. Terrorist threats come from semimilitary organizations training to "retake" the United States from far left-wing radical liberals. Whatever the cause or supposed cause, there will always be those who will accept the responsibility to fight for or against it and be willing to embrace terrorist methods to engage the battle.

Homeland Security

Response to Potential and Actual Terrorist Threats

> An evil exists that threatens every man, woman and child of this great nation. We must take steps to insure our domestic security and protect our homeland.
>
> **—Adolf Hitler, 1922, upon establishing the Gestapo**

Words similar to these were spoken by President George W. Bush in response to the devastating World Trade Center and Pentagon bombings by an ensemble of nineteen suicide-murderers carrying out a plan originated in the mind of radical apocalyptists.

The President proposes to create a new Department of Homeland Security, the most significant transformation of the U.S. government in over a half-century by largely transforming and realigning the current confusing patchwork of government activities into a single department whose primary mission is to protect our homeland. The creation of a Department of Homeland Security is one more key step in the President's national strategy for homeland security.*

Homeland is variously defined as "one's native land. A state, region, or territory that is closely identified with a particular people or ethnic group. Security is best defined as state or feeling of safety: the state or feeling of being safe and protected—freedom from worries of loss: the assurance that something of value will not be taken away—something giving assurance: something that provides a sense of protection against loss, attack, or harm."

The creation of the Department of Homeland Security by the Homeland Security Act of 2002:

- Established a single department whose primary mission is to protect the American people and their homeland
- Unified principal border and transportation security agencies
- Coordinated a cohesive network of disaster response capabilities
- Created a central point for analysis and dissemination of intelligence and other information pertaining to terrorist threats to protect America's critical infrastructure
- Joined research and development efforts to detect and counter potential terrorist attacks

---

* http://www.dhs.gov/xabout/history/publication_0015.shtm (accessed December 7, 2009).

The primary mission of the department is to:

- Prevent terrorist attacks within the United States
- Reduce the vulnerability of the United States to terrorism
- Minimize the damage, and assist in the recovery, from terrorist attacks that do occur within the United States
- Carry out all functions of (twenty-two disparate) entities transferred to the department, including acting as a focal point regarding natural and man-made crises and emergency planning
- Ensure that the function of the agencies and subdivisions within the department that are not related directly to securing the homeland are not diminished or neglected except by a specific explicit act of Congress
- Monitor the connection between illegal drug trafficking and terrorism, coordinate efforts to sever such connections, and otherwise contribute to efforts to interdict illegal drug trafficking.*

By creating the Department of Homeland Security, President Bush and Congress established a more efficient means to "insure domestic Tranquility, provide for the common defence, promote the general Welfare, and secure the Blessings of Liberty,"† and keep alive the dream sculpted on the Statue of Liberty: "Give me your tired, your poor, Your huddled masses yearning to breathe free, The wretched refuse of your teeming shore. Send these, the homeless, tempest-tost to me, I lift my lamp beside the golden door!"‡ Unfortunately an extension of providing for common defense and the war on terror has resulted in a prolonged shooting war, bleeding the United States of its finest men and women and billions of dollars, weakening the economy.

Arguably, however, it can be stated that with the creation of the Department of Homeland Security and the ongoing war in Afghanistan and Iraq further acts of terrorism on American soil have been prevented. Thus, it can be concluded that the challenge of the existing evil threatening every man, woman, and child of this great nation has been met and the steps taken to ensure our domestic security and protect our homeland, to this point in time, have been successful.

Barbarians at the Gate

From about 100 B.C. to approximately 400 A.D. the Roman Empire was threatened by a force they could not defeat in war or social context: the Huns, Visigoths, and others considered barbarians. Eventually the gates of

---

* Ibid.
† Preamble of the U.S. Constitution.
‡ Lazarus, Emma, "The New Colossus."

Rome itself opened as the "outsiders" poured into the capital of the empire. Of course it was not the end of the empire, but the glory of Rome was in a serious steep decline as the cultures blended and intermarriage changed the complexion of politics and society.

Unfortunately that is how the modern exodus into the United States is viewed by many. Illegal immigration into the western hemisphere actually began on that historic October day in 1492 when Admiral Columbus and his crew landed in the New World. Forgotten is the fact that as a nation of immigrants, the United States has been and always will be the bright star in the sky for those seeking a new beginning. But among those immigrants who enter the United States for the potential of earning a living and gaining an education for better positioning on the socioeconomic scale, there are those whose sole purpose is to destroy the very same opportunities, freedoms, and civil rights granted to all Americans. They will penetrate our borders and hide behind the same constitutional guarantees they seek to destroy. Being educated in America and learning trades, settling and working in low-profile neighborhoods and jobs, they "sleep" until called upon to carry out missions of destruction and chaos. These are the current barbarians at the gate.

Home-Grown Terrorist

Unfortunately, however, "the number, variety and scale of recent U.S. cases suggest 2009 has been the most dangerous year domestically since 2001."[*] This *Los Angeles Times* article of December 7, 2009, highlighted several instances wherein the number of major arrests of Americans accused of plotting with al-Qaeda and allies to deploy bombs in New York and elsewhere showed a steady increase. Homeland Security Secretary Janet Napolitano provided some insight in a strongly worded speech about the threat of radicalized homegrown terrorism. "We've seen an increased number of arrests here in the U.S. of individuals suspected of plotting terrorist attacks or supporting terror groups abroad such as Al Qaeda.... Home-based terrorism is here. And, like violent extremism abroad, it will be part of the threat picture that we must now confront."[†]

Response to Terrorism: Homeland Security

Governmental response to terrorist acts has had one very major consequence: the resulting actions have lost Americans many of the freedoms they famously

---

[*] Rotella, Sebastian, "A U.S. Strain of Extremism May Be Rising," *Los Angeles Times*, December 7, 2009, p. A-1.
[†] Ibid., pp. A-1, A-12.

enjoyed, for instance, weapons searches and screenings for entrance to all governmental and public buildings, the freedom to privacy due to acts like the Patriot Act (enacted immediately after the Pentagon and World Trade Center bombings), the ability to take certain items aboard a plane, warrantless interception of communications, and movements for establishment of a national identification card that would be required to be carried at all times. As each terrorist act is played out, the primary response has been to increase security measures, which in the long run has created an erosion of personal freedoms and choices. Thus, perhaps, the terrorists are actually winning the war on terrorism.

In the world, terrorist activity continues on a near daily basis. Suicide bombings in the troubled areas of Iraq, Afghanistan, and Pakistan have kept the fires of horror and destruction burning. In common terms, the bombings are terrorism, but in the new vernacular of the war, the proper wording has become *insurgents*. The war on terrorism continues, but no longer by that name. Airliner hijackings have disappeared since the September 11, 2001, assault on America, and the world tightens security around airports and aircraft, sporting events, public buildings, and any place a bomb can be placed, a person kidnapped or assassinated, and arson spread. As long as people in the world are willing to kill themselves to kill and maim others, to hide behind the democratic freedoms they are attempting to destroy, and to embrace ideologies spouted by megalomaniacs, terrorism will be a nightmare wrapped in reality.

Preparedness and Response in Terrorist Acts

The best time to prepare for an emergency is before it happens. A common-sense approach to modern living is preparedness, but how easy it is to make excuses for not being prepared for an emergency, even something simple like a medical emergency or a home fire. One could conservatively estimate that only one in ten people (most likely the percentage is much lower) are trained in CPR, the ABCs (airway, bleeding, and circulation) of medicine, and even fewer are aware of procedures to follow and what to expect in a large natural disaster such as an earthquake, fire, or flood. Beyond personal concerns, response, and action, what of the larger-scale emergencies, such as evacuation of a major city and the treatment of casualties, or perhaps food, clothing, shelter, and medical attention for those injured or displaced?

Most public buildings have evacuation plans and guidelines, including drawings depicting routes and directions for quick and easy evacuation, posted somewhere near elevators and other obvious locations. But who takes the time (even while waiting for an elevator) to read and understand them? As a guest in a hotel, how many people actually read the emergency evacuation instructions or even bother to note the location of fire alarms and extinguishers? Surprisingly, or not surprisingly, the quick answer would be few. The public mind-set is a collective "it won't happen here" or "it won't happen to me." But obviously, emergencies, natural and man-made, do occur "here" and to "me."

A very quick search of the Internet revealed a wide range of state laws and terror-related preparedness programs, including training. This is evidence of a governmental concern about preparation for emergencies related to terrorism and the ability to respond in a timely and appropriate manner. However, it must also be recognized that plans and procedures must trickle down to local and individual levels.

Training

Recognizing the Problem

A "playbook" or course lesson plan should begin with an analysis or definition of the problem. Framing the problem in terms of "trends" leads the trainee to look at the whole scope of the matter from historical perspectives to present day, and to look at and anticipate the future of terrorism with the evolution of accompanying violence attendant on an act of terrorism.

Reflexes and Rehearsals

Once the background and framing of the problem is complete and solution examples are explored and ratified, testing of the models must be undertaken to determine the degree of workability and whether government and individuals can react as intended. Since the bombings of 9/11, municipalities have rehearsed planned scenarios to gauge readiness and capabilities of resources such as first responders, medical facilities, and evacuation procedures.

Preparation and rehearsals by official agencies is a giant step, similar to the civil defense programs during the Cold War era of the 1950s, but there is a glaring difference. The civil defense preparedness programs stored food, water, blankets, medical supplies, etc., in strategic locations while schools and businesses practiced building evacuations, "drop and cover" exercises, and received information about responding to emergencies.

Preparedness Exercises

Prepare, Prepare, Prepare

How does a government or municipality prepare for a "what if" scenario? It begins with imagining and preparing reasonable and probable scenarios and formulating a relevant plan to deal with the problem. How do we evacuate a large city that has only two or three main traffic arteries, is crisscrossed with bridges or railroad tracks, or perhaps there is a large body of water (an ocean) on one or two sides? What if one of those traffic arteries or the bridge is demolished by explosives beginning the terrorist emergency?

How about a suicide bombing in a large and heavily populated shopping center, nightclub, or amusement park where there are several fatalities and injuries? Can the governmental response handle all the elements of such a heinous action? Are there sufficient medical facilities available for response to care for the injured, dying, and dead? Can the police set up a "crime scene" for investigation and search for evidence while keeping out the onlookers, the curious, and the souvenir hunters? Is there a policy and procedure for handling the local and national news media, who will be flocking to the scene? Are there public information facilities and personnel capable of handling the news media rush for information? How about the public, who will be rushing to the scene to look for loved ones or perhaps jamming the telephone circuits attempting to contact someone who may have fallen victim? How will crowd and traffic control be directed?

Practice, Practice, Practice

After constructing the scenario and defining its parameters (not overlooking all possible contingencies), the plan must be rehearsed with a self-examination critique as an after action report detailing what was right and how to improve what went wrong. The plans should be reviewed and updated at least quarterly and rehearsed at least annually. Of course the funding for rehearsals will be limited, but a well-rehearsed plan and response will save perhaps thousands of lives.

Individual Preparation, Planning, and Practice

Individual preparation begins with making a survey of a home, checking for sufficient fire alarms and fire extinguishers, planning escape routes in the event of fire, including relocation and family meeting sites, preparing an evacuation bag, and storing medical equipment and food and water for a minimum of three days for each person living in the home. (There is insufficient space in this unit to fully explore all the preparation and needs of a household preparing for an emergency. However, there are a number of Internet sites available for emergency preparation checklists. See Yahoo.com, Google.com, or other search sites with key words *emergency preparedness*.)

Planning for an emergency is finding a solution to a problem before it becomes a problem. Once the emergency checklist is complete, the next phase is planning. The plan should be simple (complemented with all the necessary resources) and easy to implement in the event of an unexpected evacuation or response. The people occupying a house or building should know exactly where all emergency equipment and supplies are stored for quick access. Critical telephone and contact numbers—police, fire, medical, and relevant persons to contact—should be available and within reach. (It is a good idea to have such a list laminated to protect it from weather, tearing, etc. It might also be minimized in size to fit into a wallet or pocket.) Some items usually overlooked on checklists for preparation and planning for an emergency are an availability and access to cash, vehicle fuel, and solar or cranked power radio.

Practice means refining reflexes and eliminating any unforeseen difficulties while completing a task with minimal room for error. A family must rehearse its response and preparations through alarm drills and practicing specific scenarios of home evacuation.

Government Response to Emergency Situations

Planning

It has often been repeated that a terrorist attack happens with surprise and violence. Prime examples are the bombings of the World Trade Center in 1993, the Murrah Federal Building in 1995, and of course, the Trade Center and Pentagon bombings in 2001. Let us not forget the bombing of Pearl Harbor in 1941 (although it was an aggressive act of war). All these events required instant and efficient governmental response, as did the hurricane striking the Louisiana Delta area in 2005 (Hurricane Katrina).

From the smallest hamlet to the largest mega-urban complex in America, city supervisors and planners at all levels of government, including local, county, state, and federal, must consider every type of emergency imaginable. Drawing upon the experiences of New York, Oklahoma City, Washington, D.C., and the victims of Hurricane Katrina, planners can anticipate problems related to mass evacuation, massive injuries, fires, flooding, looting, and numerous logistical problems, like supplying food, water, and shelter, and the predicament associated with saving as many lives as possible and dealing with the human elements of search and rescue plus maintaining a stable government.

During the planning phase, rapid response teams consisting of military (and National Guard), police, fire, medical, Red Cross, Salvation Army, and other support units should be included, readied, and prepared for any type of live-saving emergency, including the surprising and violent terrorist attack.

Preparation

To quote American forefather Benjamin Franklin; "For the want of a nail, the shoe was lost; for the want of a shoe the horse was lost; and for the want of a horse the rider was lost, being overtaken and slain by the enemy, all for the want of care about a horseshoe nail." Proper planning and preparation can save the day (lives).

A page of history from the Civil Defense (CD) preparedness days of the 1950s and 1960s Cold War-era should be revised and updated through local, state and federal government crisis management planning. The CD program consisted of identifying relocation buildings and sites and arranging deposits of food, clothing, water, blankets, and other emergency supplies necessary for survival. The cached equipment was inspected, updated and rotated on a routine basis. To engage a similar program will require major funding, allocation of resources, and determination of safe relocation sites such as were provided by the civil defense program.

The government (local to federal) should have regular programs of informing and educating the public in the planned practices and procedures of the political entity (city, county, state, federal) for reacting to emergency. This can be done through public meetings and news media outlets like the local newspaper and television. The old civil defense programs also featured dedicated radio frequencies for issuing instructions during an emergency crisis. The frequencies were tested regularly so the public would be aware of which frequency on which to focus their attention. This program should also be revised and include television and mobile telephones (through flash and text messaging) as immediate instruction resources.

The first order of business in preparing for a response to a terrorist attack is in prevention. Counterterrorism units of the government (city, county, state, and federal levels) must develop data and information that can be analyzed to provide strategic and tactical intelligence to detect, deter, and disrupt a planned terrorist activity. This intelligence should be shared among all levels of government (in spite of the inborn organizational egos of being the first and only agency having the information)—a lesson well learned from the 2001 bombings and the 9/11 Commission Report.

Another important aspect of the 9/11 Commission Report stated, "There was a significant lack of imagination" (on the parts of the intelligence community and enforcement agencies; the terrorists certainly exercised their imagination in conceiving and carrying out the attacks). In the planning and preparation phases (especially when dealing with the element of human terrorist), imaginative approaches—both from what the terrorist may do and to ways of countering it—must be explored, considering the likelihood of an event occurring and the means and ways of preventing or reacting to it.

An old cliché has become a standard guide for a terrorist-generated emergency, especially with the assistance of advanced technology: "If it can be imagined and paid for by the terrorist, it can be done." Therefore, a corollary or consequential cliché would be: "If a defense force can imagine and pay for an anticipated action, it can be prevented or minimized." Consequently, emergency planners have to consider all possible types of emergencies (perhaps the demolition of a major dam and resulting flooding), and sufficient funding must be banked or appropriated to respond to whatever the esti-mated cost of the emergency and restoration to normalcy.

Response

The better planned and prepared individuals and governments will be able to respond in a timely manner, quickly, and efficiently to any imagined and anticipated real emergency, whether it is by natural occurrence (fire, flood, or storm) or man-made by a group of ideological terrorists (a semimilitary mili-tia) or an individual. The entire emergency response community, from an individual to the most highly trained organization and political body, must have an agenda-placing response to an emergency situation at the top of their priority lists.

Emergency response is a responsibility of the governmental jurisdiction in which the emergency occurs. However, it is also important for the indi-vidual on each team to be able to react appropriately in a crisis situation. The appropriateness can only come through planning and practice or rehearsal.

Benjamin Franklin was correct in his assumption and analogy. Overlooking something as minor as a small nail (tidbit of information) and failing to properly plan and prepare will result in the failure to respond to the advancement of the enemy (or terrorist encroachment and attack). An educated public is the best defense against man-man emergencies, and a pre-pared public practiced in the ways of response can minimize overall physical and psychological damage.

Terrorism and Counterterrorism at Political and Operational Levels

Don't use an elephant gun on a gnat. A gnat is a pesky little fly-like bug that flits and buzzes around and in the eyes of its host. An elephant gun, of course, is a large-caliber firearm packing enough power to stop an elephant. After the 9/11 surprise sky liner bombing attack by a small group of operatives rep-resenting a faction of dedicated ideologists willing to die for their cause, the United States and a coalition of allies responded with the "shock and awe" of all the firepower at their disposal. The munitions expended in the opening hours of the rebuttal created an unprecedented firestorm of rockets, bombs, gunfire, and destruction.

"No group or nation should mistake America's intention: We will not rest until terrorist groups of global reach have been found, have been stopped, and have been defeated," said President George W. Bush on September 14, 2001. Thus began America's war on terror.

On May 1, 2003, President Bush grandly expressed: "Mission accomplished." The Taliban in Afghanistan had been defeated and Saddam Hussein captured, but there was no sighting of Osama bin Laden, the leader of the so-called terror network al Qaeda. He has since, however, been heard from in audiotapes supplied to the Arabic television news network Al Jazeera. It is noted that Hussein was not captured as a result of the bombings but as a result of analytical work done by intelligence analysts working far from the immediate war zone.

After eight years of "mission accomplished" (a political miscalculation), as declared by President Bush, the war on terror continues. The measurable progress on that war is such that the Obama administration declared in April 2009 that the phrase "war on terror" will no longer be used in spite of the ongoing wars in Afghanistan and Iraq. British officials stopped using the phrase in 2006 and said it has been a mistake that may have caused "more harm than good."

British Foreign Secretary David Miliband said (January 2009), "The concept of a war on terror is misleading and mistaken. Historians will judge whether it has done more harm than good," adding that, in his opinion, "the whole strategy has been dangerously counterproductive, helping otherwise disparate groups find common cause against the west.

"The more we lump terrorist groups together and draw the battle lines as a simple binary struggle between moderates and extremists or good and evil, the more we play into the hands of those seeking to unify groups with little in common; we should expose their claim to a compelling and overarching explanation and narrative as the lie that it is.

"Terrorism is a deadly tactic, not an institution or an ideology." He argued that "the war on terror implied a belief that the correct response to the terrorist threat was primarily a military one—to track down and kill a hardcore of extremists." But he quotes an American commander, General David Petraeus, saying the western coalition in Iraq "could not kill its way out of the problems of insurgency and civil strife."

Instead of trying to build Western solidarity against a shared enemy, Miliband argued it should be constructed instead on the "idea of who we are and the values we share." He went on to say that "democracies must respond to terrorism by championing the rule of law, not subordinating." It is an argument he links directly with the Guantánamo Bay detention camp. "That is surely the lesson of Guantánamo and it is why we welcome president-elect Obama's clear commitment to close it."*

Looking back over the last eight years, we can see many political and unwise mistakes made by the Bush administration that may have seemed

---

* Borger, Julian, "'War on Terror' Was a Mistake, Says Miliband," *The Guardian*, January 15, 2009.

appropriate at the time. A very serious mistake was the president's reference to the war and invasion of Afghanistan and Iraq as "a crusade" to defeat the terrorist. Politically, this was a very poor choice of words referring to the unsuccessful Christian crusades during the middle ages to defeat and eradicate the Muslim religion and to reclaim the holy lands for Christianity. The term *crusade* inflamed the Muslim world even further and cast the United States as invaders with the intent to conquer Islam (as well as terrorists) and to control the oil-rich nations.

A serious flaw in the political and operative levels of thinking was resorting to the use of torture to interrogate prisoners of war, dubiously referred to as "enemy combatants." The United States was founded on the ideals of the rule of law respectful of the dignity of individuals and the human person. Subjecting another human to such inhumane features as waterboarding (a near drowning experience) or Chinese water torture (constant dripping of water on the nose of the person being tortured), and placing insect-phobic persons in small cage-like enclosures heavily populated with vermin and insects such as cockroaches (reminiscent of the tactics used in Room 101 of George Orwell's *1984* and the tactics of the interrogator for "Big Brother," threatened to place a rat on the chest of the protagonist, Winston Smith, who was deathly afraid of rats) are tactics that were long forbidden by the Geneva Convention and other rules of war for the treatment of prisoners of war.

Were the tactics and battle plans successful? There have been no international terror attacks on U.S. soil since the invasion of Afghanistan and Iraq. So in that frame we can, in fact, answer yes. But that may be a subjective conclusion. The economic consequences have stripped the U.S. Treasury and caused excessive financial burdens upon the people, and huge numbers of soldiers and civilians have been killed. The political fallout has been enormous as the Bush administration quickly fell out of favor and was factually ineffective in political arenas around the world.

On the ground, fighting has evolved to attempting to establish a stabilized government built along the lines of a democracy and to build a solid infrastructure for security and civilian living. However, nearly on a daily basis, terrorists (now, perhaps euphemistically, referred to as insurgents) place roadside bombs of improvised explosive devices (IEDs) to attack convoys and supplies, and sponsor and become suicide bombers, killing tens and hundreds of innocents, and the Taliban (a very religiously conservative faction) has resurged and resurfaced from its defeat in Afghanistan to become a serious force to be reckoned with in Pakistan.

Framing the war on terrorism in more logical terms, we could conclude that politically and operatively speaking, the war has gained nothing more than a temporary lull in international terrorist attacks. This can dictate an alternative approach in our crusade against those who engage in terrorist tactics.

First, we must define the problem of terrorism in the words of British Foreign Secretary David Miliband, "Terrorism is a deadly tactic, not an institution or an ideology." Following this reasoning, counterterrorism on both the political and operative levels can remove the elephant gun and resort more to tactics of intelligence gathering and analysis, attack terror cells with small strike forces, and utilize psychological and propaganda (education) sources as countertactics informing the public of the dangers and risks of terrorism to espouse the causes of terrorism as the lies they are and to strike out the public's belief in "not here, not in my backyard apathetic attitude."

The escalation of commitment against terrorism must take into consideration the risks and favorable consequences. First, political factors must be considered. Is the definition of terrorism framed in terms of political and religious ideological rhetoric, or is it merely an enactment of a violent criminal threat posed over the heads of a particular political platform or religious ideology? Defining the problem in specific terms will dictate the political and counterterrorism operations. Framing in these terms will allow proper allocation of resources and appropriate actions.

Risk assessment of a counterterrorist operation will define the strategic and tactical plans and programs that will best fit the problem. Gains and losses should be weighed against the costs and the urgency of the problem. Tactics of the past, similar to the threats of nuclear warfare during the Cold War, cannot be expected to be successful in a new kind of threat. New threats call for new methods for combating them.

A reevaluation of the political fallout should be a consideration when specific inflammable words such as *crusade* are considered insensitive and threatening. Political rhetoric should be limited to directly addressing the causes and terms of terrorism, and to form coalitions for imaginative solutions and to drop their stubborn attachment to existing views, beliefs, and approaches to the problem. As in the words of General David Petraeus, we "could not kill [our] way out of the problems of insurgency and civil strife." This analysis pleads for new political and operational approaches to political and religious dogma and ideology justified as causes for terrorist campaigns.

There is an old saying, popular with professional law enforcement agents: "You catch more flies with honey than you do with vinegar." To wit, to win the hearts and minds (gain the confidence) of the person being interrogated, it is better to treat a prisoner (or suspect) with dignity and respect. Somewhere in the political front of the current war, torture was rationalized as being an important and effective agent for ferreting out information and was carried out on the operational level.

In many agencies the term *interrogation* was long ago replaced by the word *interview*. We interview rather than interrogate because interrogate has connotations of torture, psychological breaking, and dark rooms with one electric light hanging from the ceiling in which a connection can be made for administering electrical shock to the person being interrogated. *Interview*, on the other hand, connotes a one-on-one or more friendly basis and atmosphere in which a rapport has been established between the interviewer and the interviewee. On an operational level, the interview approach has been found to be more successful and should be more widely implemented in the course of information gathering.

Operationally, the first line of defense against terrorism is intelligence. Gathering data, making an analysis, forming inferences and hypotheses, reaching conclusions, making recommendations, and dissemination of the final material provide decision makers (politically and operationally) with grist for discussion, planning, and implementation.

There are two types of intelligence and decision making: strategic for long-range planning and tactical for immediate use. Strategic is a primary tool for the high-ranking planners, decision makers, and political offices. Contingency planning and preparations, including potential political ramifications, are serious considerations that must be anticipated for time distances from the present into the future and must be made by those who are responsible for policy making.

Tactical use of intelligence and planning is for organizations and personnel responsible for implementation of the policies and programs formulated by the policy and decision makers (the political connections). When policy is set, it is up to the operational organizations to accept the mission and carry it out. Operationally, it is the "boots on the ground" assets who use various means and methods to conduct the assignment in the best way possible to achieve success and to ensure the policies and programs of the political aspects are concluded as planned.

An analysis of the remarks of British Foreign Secretary Miliband leads to an easy conclusion that his outlook and opinion are the recipe for a political solution to one of the world's oldest problems: how to deal with small numbers of faces that strike at established governments and organizations in manners that bring death, destruction, and terror to the hearts of innocents.

Looking at terrorism as the pesky gnat flitting about the head of a much more powerful force, we want to swat it away, but in its hit-and-run existence it continues to thrive and breed new generations of pesky flies. All the firepower, bombs, and rockets of the most awesome military arsenal in the world can continue to swat at the small factions of terrorists who are willing to make every sacrifice, including their own life, to engage the giant. But unless the appropriate political policies and decisions (including talk, not torture) are made, the operational arm will continue to be ineffective regardless of the size of the gun and its explosive power.

Conclusion

Current and Changing Trends of Terrorism

Weddings, funerals, schools, restaurants, and indiscriminate locations such as buses and other points of public transportation and gatherings are all targets of insurgents, small in number but large in arranging and making "body count."

The primary weapons in this new style war are suicide bombers and improvised explosive devices made with low-cost materials countering the billions of dollars and highly sophisticated weaponry and technology of the coalition forces who are better trained and equipped for war against a matching force with designated lines, an enemy in uniforms, and similar tactics. The smart bomber has replaced the smart bomb. The lessons of war learned in Vietnam, that an enemy follows an amorphous plan, often blurring the line between combatants and civilians, were hard lessons that didn't go unnoted. However, the tactic of blowing up oneself in the act of destroying the enemy, or people who have no connection with the hostilities other than being in the wrong place at the wrong time becoming victims of a bomber who sees himself as a martyr, attacks and destroys more than lives. It also attacks and breaks the morale of the people, forcing concessions from the government and military forces.

The New Era: A New War

The United States and a coalition of allies amassed and responded to the airplane bomb attacks of September 11, 2001, with one of the largest armed forces in the history of the world. Eight years later, the coalition is showing signs of cracking, and the strength of organizations like the Taliban and the al-Qaeda network of terrorists appears to be gaining. This has happened through a series of strategic and tactical suicide bombings taking the lives of hundreds, if not thousands, of civilians that clearly indicate that old methods of war and the rules of war no longer apply.

A primary example is the April 2009 concession of the Swat Valley by the government in Pakistan to the Taliban and the institution of Quranic or religious law. This compromise quickly led to a draconian religious government limiting the rights and movement of women and girls, strict religious obedience, and empowerment of tribal warlords. It also led to expansion of the Taliban into other areas not covered by the compromise. Pakistan failed to learn the lesson of Neville Chamberlain of Great Britain, who after conceding Poland to Hitler declared, "Peace in our lifetime." Appeasement did not work then and it does not work now when dealing with a ruthless enemy who utilizes tactics so bloodthirsty and heinous that the Mongol hordes of centuries past could not comprehend.

War as it has been carried out for centuries, with soldiers charging across a field or up a hill screaming out a war cry and assaulting the enemy with concentrated firepower, with bullets flying like bees around a honeycomb hive, is no longer the way a war is discharged. Since man first picked up a stick or a rock to attack an interloper or enemy, he has continually evolved newer and more powerful weapons; the long bow replaced the crossbow, gunpowder and guns (pistols, rifles, and cannon) replaced the bow. Years later, rockets and bombs, airplanes and ships equipped with the latest technology, such as satellite surveillance and drone aircraft, became the ultimate in war materials and killing machines. In contrast to all this, with a flick of a power switch connected to a vest armed with explosives crammed with marbles, ball bearings, screws, and nails, one person, willing to sacrifice himself or herself (female suicide bombers are a new trend), has been proven capable of trumping all the advanced technology of huge military complexes.

Improvised weaponry is actually nothing new. Historically, smaller and less equipped factions have fought with whatever could be used to kill and destroy an enemy. In 1956, the people of Hungary rose against and fought the Soviet Union's armored tanks with glass bottles filled with gasoline and a burning fuse (Molotov cocktails). When thrown against the tanks, the glass would break, causing an explosive fire. Unfortunately, the uprising was eventually controlled by the overwhelming forces of the Soviets. In defeat, the Hungarians showed the world that a small force, using the simplest methods, could resist a larger and stronger force. That is the principle behind the current trend in terrorist tactics.

Terroristic tactics of the Weather Underground, the SLA, and groups like the Ku Klux Klan and paramilitary organizations of self-styled minutemen appear to be ancient history as the new profile of terror has been exemplified by the first World Trade Center bombing in 1993, Timothy McVeigh, the Washington area snipers, and others who have moved to more sophisticated methods of bringing terror and chaos. The terrorist acts of subway and railroad bombing, kidnapping, and use of poisonous gas in other parts of the world may be only dress rehearsals for the terror storm to be released on the American population.

Future Trends

To identify a trend, indicators must lead the analyst to recognize patterns based on a set of events or timings, geographic locations, and specific protocols, unspoiled by bias and prejudice, to prognosticate possibilities, options, and a series of a set of potential or actual consequences. One or two events do not a trend make. It takes several instances, events, or occurrences over an indeterminate time to create the patterns the analyst must recognize and identify.

Founded on what has been witnessed in the terror trends of the past forty years, we can recognize patterns of destruction and force as small affiliations armed with the simplest or even primitive weaponry become forces to be reckoned with. We can conclude that traditional warfare has become obsolete, replaced with individuals and small organizations determined to fight the "giants" with charismatic and influential leaders, imaginative and improvised arms, determination, and a willingness to die for the cause.

In the future we can foresee a widening ripple of suicide bombers in the United States and the placement of bombs in public places and along highways, in places like bridges and overpasses. The psychological impact of such an event would be traumatic to the American people, who would be willing to concede more power to the government and police agencies for the sake of security.

There are current movements getting louder and gaining strength to repeal the Second Amendment of the Constitution (the right of the people to keep and bear arms) because of the violence and killings with guns in the streets, schools, churches, and workplaces of America. Disarmament of the populace would be conceding defense of the nation to the government and police agencies. If this trend of forfeiting power and the institution of a surveillance society continues, freemen everywhere will come to rue the day. Perhaps at that time, an individual or group of individuals will rise up, utilizing makeshift weapons, and carry out a campaign of terror against a far more superior force to regain the freedoms guaranteed by a Constitution diluted by erosion of people's rights, liberty, and freedom.

Recommendations and Conclusions

Counterterrorism efforts should recognize that terrorism is carried out by small groups striking swiftly and violently. A hard lesson learned is that a like reply to terrorism is more effective than large military forces. The backbone of counterterrorism is the development of an efficient and reliable intelligence apparatus that can rapidly gather, analyze, and disseminate terrorist intelligence to responsible mobile teams who can respond to the terrorist effort with their own strike of swift and violent force.

Homeland security is an important issue for everyone, not only the governmental agency named Homeland Security. There are many issues involved in homeland security, such as a widening concern about illegal immigration into the United States, readiness and response to emergencies, and growing movements toward creating a society under constant surveillance. It is the responsibility of every free person to be alert for potential terrorist planning, surveillance, and activity. Further, every person should adapt a lifestyle that includes preplanning and preparation for his or her own personal response to a terrorist-generated emergency.

Care must be taken when defining terrorism because what one side sees as a movement toward freedom, self-government, religious ideology, or support of any particular cause, another can take as insurrection or rebellion. It is all in the eye of the beholder. What must be recognized is that warfare as previously conducted is obsolete; small groups or individuals can wage a new war in the guise of terror and sabotage, and the weapons of choice are bombs, which spread fear, distrust, death, and destruction in an indiscriminate manner.

Care must also be taken when implementing security measures designed to thwart or deter an adverse attack because the resulting consequences may be a concession of individual rights, freedom, and liberty, all of which are given to the people by the government and guaranteed by the Constitution. What the government gives, it may take away in the name of security.

Recommended Historical Reading

Altamut by Valdimir Bartal
The Assassin Legends: Myths of the Ismai'lis by Farhad Daftary
The Assassins by Bernard Lewis
Assassins: The Story of Medieval Islam's Secret Sect by W. B. Bartlett
The Clash of Civilizations and the Remaking of World Order by Samuel P. Huntington
Fatal Purity: Robespierre and the French Revolution by Ruth Scurr
History of the Order of the Assassins by Enno Franzius
The McDonaldization of Society—An Investigation into the Changing Character of Contemporary Social Life by George Ritzer
The Mini-Manual of Urban Terrorism by Carlos Marighella
My Forbidden Face: Growing Up under the Taliban; A Young Woman's Story by Latifa
The Secret Order of Assassins: The Struggle of the Early Nizari Ismai'lis against the Islamic World by Marshal G. S. Hodgson
Secret Societies of the Middle Ages: The Assassins, The Templars, and the Secret Tribunals of Westphalia by Thomas Keightley
The Templars and the Assassins: The Militia of Heaven by James Wasserman

Recommended Videos

100 Years of Terror from the History Channel
The Battle of Algiers
Munich

Terrorism in the Twenty-First Century
How Are Governments Coping?

2

MICHAEL SAVASTA

Contents

What Is Terrorism?

Academics, politicians, experts in the security field, and journalists have struggled for years over the definition of terrorism. According to the Congressional Research Service, there are over a hundred different definitions of terrorism (Schmidt and Youngman, 1988). In their book *Political Terrorism*, Schmidt and Youngman cited 109 different definitions of terrorism, which they obtained in a survey of leading academics in the field. These definitions contained certain recurring elements, to include violence against civilians or civilian targets; a political aim; fear; emphasis on terror; psychological effects and anticipated reactions; and the planned, systematic, and organized action of the terrorists (Schmidt and Youngman, 1988). According to the U.S. Department of Defense, terrorism is defined as the unlawful use of, or threatened use of, force or violence against civilians or property to coerce or intimidate governments or societies, often to achieve political, religious, or ideological objectives (U.S. State Department, 2006). While there is no hope that people will ever all agree who is a terrorist and who is not, one point cannot be argued. Nonviolent innocent civilians are being targeted and killed by groups of individuals linked to terrorist organizations.

What Is the Root Cause of Terrorism?

While there are many reasons that may explain why a young Palestinian girl would blow herself up in order to kill as many Jews as possible, or why an Arab man would kill himself while murdering thousands of American civilians, the most frequently mentioned root cause of terrorism is poverty. Some experts believe if more money were spent to alleviate poverty, terrorism would disappear (Meir-Levi, 2005). In March 2002, during a global antipoverty conference in Monterey, President George W. Bush stated: "We will challenge the poverty and hopelessness and lack of education and failed governments that too often allow conditions that terrorists can seize." Conference attendees commented that the president's suggestion that the poor will become terrorists unless their plight is addressed is insulting (Tripathi, 2005). While poverty is widespread in most of the world, you do not see these areas producing terrorist organizations. Former British Prime Minister Tony Blair has stated that the root causes of terrorism were the lack of democracy, the Middle East conflict, and poverty (Simonsen and Spindlove, 2007).

The mistreatment and killing of Muslims by Americans is also mentioned as a root cause of terrorism. For someone not familiar with Muslim society, this would sound like a reasonable cause. Especially in light of the present turmoil in the Middle East (Meir-Levi, 2005). In determining the root cause of terrorism, it may be better to identify conditions and circumstances that give rise to terrorism. For example:

1. Extremist ideologies that permit the devaluation of innocent civilian lives are at least a beginning cause of terrorism. At the moment, the world's leading ideology is clearly extremist Islamism (Bjorgo, 2003).
2. Corrupt governments may give rise to opposition that may turn to terrorism as a means of overthrowing the government.

People who do not have a legitimate way of dealing with the corrupt government may turn to terrorism in an attempt to overthrow the regime. In most of these cases, you will see a charismatic leader emerge who is able to take a political agenda and transform it into a program for violent action (Meir-Levi, 2005). The leader is a very important part of this process.

What Role Should International Groups or Agencies Play in Combating Terrorism?

The war on terrorism is not a war that is fought by one nation. The United States needs assistance from the international community. After a terrorist attack, a response from the United States by itself is understandable and probably unavoidable. But if a U.S. response results in too much pressure on any one government or state, these states may collapse, with radical Islamists left to pick up the pieces (Terrorism, 2005). This is where U.S. allies need to play a part. There has to be a unified world system in place in which the world's leading states are partners, not enemies—in other words, an international community to combat terrorism. This community is based on shared adherence to Western-led modernity. The international community must understand that combating the causes of terrorism has to involve some kind of economic and social programs, not simply military strikes (Terrorism, 2005). The United States cannot occupy and police the Muslim world in the struggle against Muslim terrorism. It is essential to have the cooperation of leading Muslim states and the rest of the international community (Terrorism, 2005). Actions by the General Assembly of the United Nations also play a big part in combating terrorism. Resolutions like protection of human rights and fundamental freedoms, preventing the risk of radiological terrorism, and measures to prevent terrorists from acquiring weapons of mass destruction are all important (United Nations, 2006).

What Impact Do Communications and the Media Have in the War on Terrorism?

It is important to understand the effects of the media on the war on terrorism. It has been argued the media has an obligation only to the reader/viewer. Report the news and only the news. Others say the media must deny the terrorists publicity, and to give in would only add fuel to the fire (Hamblen, n.d.). Nobody would argue that after a significant event such as a terrorist attack, the media provides much-needed information, makes announcements, and gives instructions regarding specific services available to the victims and the families (Hamblen, n.d.). These may include food, shelter, health-related services, transportation, or the status of availability of emergency personnel (U.S. State Department, 2005). However, terrorist acts are intended to create terror, fear, or chaos among the public. The spread of public terror, fear, and feelings of chaos depends largely on the images and messages being carried by media reports about the terrorist acts and threats (Perl, 2006). The presence of the media at these global events may at times exaggerate the effects out of proportion. It is important to keep in mind the media competes for their audience, and is constantly under pressure to be first with the news (Hamblen, n.d.). They want to provide more information, excitement, and entertainment than their rivals. If the media remains somewhat objective, it is the only way people can see what is happening in the society, good and bad (Perl, 2006). The more objective the media is, the better, because what one press fails to report, a competitor will. The only justification for forbidding a particular press to publish is when it loses it objectivity so much that its articles are lies by any standard, or at least gross distortions from the truth by any standard (Hamblen, n.d.).

We all remember the blunder by Geraldo Rivera during a Fox News broadcast. Rivera began to disclose an upcoming operation, even going so far as to draw a map in the sand for his audience. We know the media is not going away. With this in mind, maybe a solution would be to come up with a number of options for enhancing the effectiveness of government media-oriented responses to terrorism and for preventing the media from further-ing terrorist goals as a by-product of vigorous and free reporting (Perl, 2006). Some of these options may include (Perl, 2006):

1. Financing joint media-government training exercises
2. Establishing a government terrorism information response center
3. Promoting use of media pools
4. Promoting voluntary press coverage guidelines
5. Monitoring terrorism against the media

What Solutions Are Effective in Dealing with Terrorists?

The events of September 11, 2001, shocked people around the world. American politicians and journalists rarely go a day without discussing the attack. While new to American soil, acts of terrorism have been prev-alent in other nations for many decades (New Counter Terrorism, 2006). Governments in these countries have tried, sometimes successfully, to address them. Solutions for dealing with terrorism will not come from one country or government (New Counter Terrorism, 2006). It must be a collec-tive undertaking by many people and nations. Terrorists are versatile these days, and often, as soon as a counter to a specific threat is found, they'll find a new method to wreak havoc. According to Ken Brigden, "Unless we understand them we can't defeat them. Understanding where the terrorists came from, how are they structured, how do they communicate and where is the threat coming from?" Ken Brigden is the director for the new Counter Terrorism Science and Technology Center in the United Kingdom (New Counter Terrorism, 2006).

Science and technology, including information technology, are clearly a vital part of overcoming the terrorism threat. Information technology is essential to virtually all of the nation's critical infrastructures, which makes any of them vulnerable to a terrorist attack (Making the Nation, 2002). IT plays a critical role in managing and operating nuclear power plants, dams, the electric power grid, the air traffic control system, and financial institutions (Making the Nation, 2002). Information technology can be categorized into four major elements:

1. Internet
2. Telecommunications infrastructure
3. Embedded/real-time computing
4. Dedicated computing devices

Each of these plays a different role in national life and each has different vulnerabilities. The Internet, for example, has numerous unprotected areas where terrorists can infiltrate (Making the Nation, 2002). Weak or no passwords, not running backups, and keeping a large number of open ports and outdated software are just a few of the vulnerable areas of the Internet (Making the Nation, 2002). Terrorists can use these weaknesses and vulnerabilities to plan attacks, raise funds, collect resources, spread propaganda, or recruit new members.

The telecommunications infrastructure is extremely vulnerable to a terrorist attack. In early March 2005, the *New York Times* reported that "government agents have recently uncovered numerous calls from difficult to track pre-paid cell phones, internet-based phone service, pre-paid phone cards and public pay phones in the U.S. to known al Qaeda locations overseas (Bedi, 2005)." Terrorists may use mobile phones to detonate explosive devices. In certain parts of the world, when a bomb is exploded, and terrorist activity is suspected, cell phone networks are shut down to prevent secondary attacks (Bedi, 2005). If a terrorist group succeeded in shutting down a telecommunications network in a particular region, it would have a devastating effect on the area.

If you believe the root causes of terrorism are poverty, illiteracy, and unemployment, solutions would be easy. They would include education, financial assistance, and job placement. However, it is clearly evident that it is hard to come up with solutions to terrorism (Bedi, 2005). Even the long-awaited Iraq Study Group Report has failed to come up with a viable solution to the quagmire in Iraq. The study group's mandate is to provide a positive, forward-looking assessment of the Iraq War, including relevant changes in policy (Burns, 2006). Among the group's 70 recommendations were (Burns, 2006):

1. The U.S. should reduce political, military, or economic support for Iraq if the government in Baghdad cannot make substantial progress toward providing for its own security.
2. President Bush should put aside misgivings and engage Syria, Iran, and the leaders of insurgent forces in negotiations on Iraq's future, to begin by year's end. The report urged the president to revive efforts at a broader Middle East peace.
3. The number of U.S. troops embedded to train Iraqis should increase dramatically, from the 3,000 to 4,000 currently to 10,000 to 20,000, in order to accelerate the date when Iraqis can provide for their own security.

In conclusion, the war on terrorism is not going away. Terrorism itself is not going away. If we look back at the September 11 attacks, was the bombing of Afghanistan a solution? If the United States did not bomb, it would be considered weak and more terrorist attacks would take place. By waging a war on terrorism, some people believe you are putting people at risk (Making the Nation, 2002). That if we kill terrorists, we will anger them and they will retaliate and kill more innocent people around the world. Some people talk about seeking peace by instilling pacifist ideas into people. By doing this we may be telling the terrorists they are free to attack nations because they will not suffer any retribution. Terrorism has existed for centuries. Solutions to it may take just as long.

What Progress Has Been Made in Protecting Nations and Individuals from Terrorism?

Immediately after September 11, our government mounted a strong campaign against terrorism. The aim was to make Americans feel secure. The government of the United States took steps to help reestablish safety within this country (National Strategy, 2006). Americans needed to feel safe and secure in their homes. Over the short term, some of these steps involved strategies for securing our borders from potential terrorists. Denying our enemies the tools to travel internationally and across and within our borders significantly impedes their mobility and can inhibit their effectiveness (National Strategy, 2006). The government also took steps to defend potential targets from attacks. Our enemies are opportunistic, exploiting vulnerabilities and seeking alternatives to those targets with increased security measures. The targeting trend since at least September 11 has been away from hardened sites, such as official government facilities with formidable security, and toward softer targets, like schools, restaurants, places of worship, and nodes of public transportation, even large sports venues (Strategies, n.d.). These are places where innocent civilians gather and which are not always well secured. Specific targets vary, but they tend to be symbolic and often selected because they will produce mass casualties, economic damage, or both.

Long-term strategies employed by the U.S. government to deal with terrorism revolve around advancing effective democracy (Strategies, n.d.). The long-term solution for winning the war on terror is the advancement of freedom and human dignity through effective democracy. Effective democracies honor and uphold basic human rights, including freedom of religion, speech, assembly, association, and press. Long-term strategies also include effective counterterrorism activities (National Strategy, 2006). Governments need to employ a three-tiered response to terrorism: preparedness, prevention, and response. First, they need to be prepared. Nations must have the ability to detect and disrupt terrorist activity (National Strategy, 2006). This may mean spending significant money to strengthen law enforcement agencies to enable them to not only investigate but also to prevent terrorist activity. They need to increase their intelligence gathering capabilities and strengthen the infrastructure, to include food supplies, banking, and health care systems (National Strategy, 2006). The second tier is to prevent terrorist attacks by increasing border security and maintaining a tighter control of the people and goods entering and leaving the country (Strategies, n.d.). Organizations like the Department of Transportation are responsible for security at airports and establishing minimum standards for security (National Strategy, 2006). The last tier of the protection from terrorism is the response. Nations must have rapid and effective capabilities to reduce the impact of a terrorist incident, should one occur. They need to be able to manage chemical, radiological, or biological attacks as well as conventional attacks (Strategies, n.d.). The training of emergency personnel is a very important part of the response as well. In addition, it is very important to support the victims of an attack through regular crisis management and recovery exercises and activation of emergency response personnel and national health services (National Strategy, 2006).

Law Enforcement Fight against Terrorism

Before the attacks on the twin towers on September 11, 2001, police agencies around the country were busy preparing for what would be a very unlikely terrorist attack. Nobody believed that terrorism could ever be present in this country, especially downtown New York City. However, since that very chaotic and deadly Tuesday morning, law enforcement has not stopped preparing for the next attack. Law enforcement agencies around the country are committed to ensure the safety of the people they serve. In order to do this, they need to prepare for future terrorist attacks (Fight Against Terrorism, 2004). This preparation includes:

1. **Terrorism working groups:** These groups are formed both locally and regionally to address concerns regarding resources such as first responders, public/environmental agencies, hospitals, and volunteer groups.
2. **Joint terrorism task force:** With help from Homeland Security, law enforcement has set up high-tech surveillance centers around the country in an attempt to uncover future acts of terrorism.
3. **Law enforcement mutual aid:** Local law enforcement agencies, along with government agencies, need to combine forces in order to combat terrorism. Areas like training and mutual aid agreements will reduce the cost and establish procedures in the event of another terrorist attack.
4. **Access to data and information:** The main idea of sharing information between law enforcement agencies is to prevent future attacks. The access to pertinent information is sometimes hindered by rules and procedures and the culture of the agencies. For example, the FBI may not want to share information with local municipalities because they feel they are the recognized authority and above sharing information with police officers. This lack of cooperation must stop if we are to prevent future terrorist attacks (Fight Against Terrorism, 2004).
5. **Public education:** Law enforcement agencies, whether local, state, or federal, need the help of the public in order to fight the war on terrorism. According to a paper published by the University of New York at Albany in 2003, the public's assistance in the fight against terrorism is critical. Areas such as detection, identification, and prevention are mentioned as the primary tools and activities where the public could have an enormous effect on terrorism. Without help from the citizens of this country, law enforcement efforts to prevent terrorism will fail (Terrorism and Health, 2003).

While the vast majority of communities in this country will never experience a terrorist attack, law enforcement officials can never drop their guard. It is critical that officials plan for the possibility of such an event taking place.

Conclusion

Have we made any progress as far as stopping terrorism, or has it actually increased? Are we any closer to bringing the terrorists' leaders to justice? In today's society, and especially in the future, terrorism cannot or will not be tolerated. Wanting to defeat terrorism is a goal for many nations. Actually doing so may be more difficult than expected. In order to eliminate terrorist organizations, several things must occur. First, the United States and its allies need to hunt down terrorists and destroy their networks, make it known that any state that assists or harbors any terrorist will be dealt with accordingly, and then carry out the penalty. Second, nations need to launch both a political and an economic attack on the terrorist organizations (Simonsen and Spindlove, 2007). If the terrorists have no home, no money, and nowhere to train, we may be able to defeat them. The U.S. government and its allies should freeze any and all suspected assets and shut down the flow of money to the terrorist organizations. Finally, if all these steps fail, any and all terrorists, especially the Muslim extremists, must be eliminated by a very precise military plan. Although this might not be agreeable to many, it is necessary for the safety of democratic societies like the United States, and even more essential for Muslims.

References

Bedi, R. 2005, September. Telecom—The terrorism risk. http://www.pvtr.org/ (accessed December 7, 2006).

Bjorgo, T. 2003, June. Root causes of terrorism. http://www.nupi.no/IPS/filestore/ Root_Causes_report.pdf (accessed November 30, 2006).

Burns, R. 2006, December. Iraq study group to testify on report. http:// www.sun-sentinel.com/news/nationworld/ats-ap_top10dec07,0,17521. story?page=2&coll=sns-newsnation-headlines (accessed December 6, 2006).

Fight against terrorism. 2004. http://ue.eu.int/uedocs/cmsUpload/15523.04.pdf (accessed August 4, 2007).

Hamblen, J. n.d. The effects of media coverage on terrorist attacks. http://www.ncptsd. va.gov/facts/disasters/fs_media_disaster.html (accessed December 1, 2006).

Making the nation safer: The role of science and technology in countering terrorism. 2002, September. http://newton.nap.edu/books/0309084814/html (accessed December 4, 2006).

Meir-Levi, D. 2005, November. Terrorism: The root cause. http://www.frontpagemag. com/Articles/ReadArticle.asp?ID=20117 (accessed November 30, 2006).

National strategy for combating terrorism. 2006, September. http://www.whitehouse. gov/nsc/nsct/2006/ (accessed November 26, 2006).

New counter terrorism centre aims to provide solutions. 2006, August. http://www. mod.uk/defenceinternet/home (accessed December 4, 2006).

Perl, R. F. 2006. Terrorists, the media and the government. http://www.fas.org (accessed December 1, 2006).

Schmidt, A. P., and Youngman, A. I. 1988. Political terrorism, 5. Amsterdam: SWIDOC and Transaction Books.

Simonsen, C. E., and Spindlove, J. R. 2007. Terrorism today: The past, the players, the future. Upper Saddle River, NJ: Prentice Hall.

Strategies for winning the war on terrorism. n.d. http://www.whitehouse.gov/nsc/
    nsct/2006/Section V (accessed December 5, 2006).
Terrorism and Al Qaeda. 2005. http://www.defenselink.mil/ (accessed November
    26, 2006).
Terrorism and health threats. 2003. http://www.albany.edu/2003/jan2003/healthter-
    ror.htm (accessed July 27, 2007).
Tripathi, S. 2005, February. Economics and politics: Debunking the poverty-terror-
    ism   myth.   http://www.saliltripathi.com/articles/povertyterrorismmyth.htm
    (accessed December 6, 2006).
United Nations action against terrorism. 2006, January. http://www.un.org/terror-
    ism/res.htm (accessed December 7, 2006).
United States Department of Defense Strategic Plan. 2006. http://www.defense.gov/
    pubs/pdfs/2006-01-25-Strategic-Plan.pdf (accessed November 5, 2006).

A Manifesto of War and Hate
A Look Inside an al-Qaeda Manual

3

DALE L. JUNE

Contents

> We think in terms of existence and survival.
>
> **—Unknown**

> The confrontation that we are calling for with the apostate regimes does not know Socratic debates ..., Platonic ideals ..., nor Aristotelian diplomacy. But it knows the dialogue of bullets, the ideals of assassination, bombing, and destruction, and the diplomacy of the cannon and machine-gun.
>
> **—Shi'i Ayatollah Baqer al-Sadr***

> We have the right to kill four million Americans—two million of them children.
>
> **—Suleiman abu Ghaith, al-Qaeda spokesman†**

To a majority of Americans, living in the most liberal, open, and free democracy in the history of the world, it is undreamed of that a growing and menacing "dark force" has one intent, and one intent only, to destroy the freedoms and liberties of this land for their own purposes wrapped in the mantle of "doing God's will." Yet that is the expressed direction of al-Qaeda and the followers of this terror-centered system of belief. Dogmatic and chilling as it is, an al-Qaeda manual spells out the specifics and intentions of replacing democracy with an Islamic caliphate that would suspend modern progression and destroy all freedoms as currently enjoyed in a free world.

---

* Al-Qaeda manual.
† *Military Guide to Terrorism in the 21st Century, U.S Army Training and Doctrine Command* (Ft. Leavenworth, KS: Deputy Chief of Staff for Intelligence, Assistant Deputy Chief of Staff for Intelligence—Threats, 2005).

This chapter will closely examine many of the features and directives of an al-Qaeda training and propaganda manual. Naturally, it is impossible and impractical in this chapter (or book) to address every issue in the manual because the greater portion speaks about procedures, policies, and personnel. However, the portions of the book giving a narration to ideology, beliefs, and philosophy are examined because they should serve as caveats or warnings of the intention, objectives, and purpose of the militant Islamic fundamentalist who would destroy all Western cultures, modernization, and democracy and replace them with very strict medieval era-minded regimes governed under a form of religious caliphates, tribal sheiks, or sultans.

The objective will be to not only provide a counter to many of the characteristics that spell out the goals of al-Qaeda, but also to alert the reader to the warlike mongering logic behind the production of this training manual. It is a very serious mistake to downplay the importance of it and to underestimate the enemy, for that is exactly what al-Qaeda is—an enemy whose mission statement is to destroy all secular governments and democratic ways of life and replace them with a religiously intolerant government bent upon returning the world to the backward eras of the dark ages when the world was ruled by "the Church" and "God's word."

It is not for God, as proclaimed by the fanatical leadership (they work to cleanse the world of the ungodly or unbelievers), but for the power it will render to them as the autocratic leadership of an anarchist empire where only the most powerful and influential will rule.

The term *al-Qaeda* literally means "the base." Its original reference was to a terrorist training camp. The name stuck and became the designation for a "solid base for the creation of a perfect Islamic society."* Abdullah Azzam, a mentor of Osama bin Laden, referred to the solid base as advocating "a concept of jihad that was essentially a traditional fundamentalist interpretation of the nature of the jihad: the reclamation of once-Muslim lands from non-Muslim rule in places such as Palestine, what was then the former Soviet Union, and even southern Spain which had been under Muslim rule five centuries earlier."†

A split occurred between bin Laden and Azzam, eventually resulting in the assassination of Azzam because Azzam wanted nothing to do with creating conflict between Muslims. Along with several other extremely militant religious ultra-jihadists, bin Laden advocated a solid-base organization of zealots advocating spreading the rule of Islam by violent overthrow of apostate governments across the Muslim world. In time, the advocacy grew to

---

* Bergen, Peter, *The Osama bin Laden I Know* (New York: Free Press, a division of Simon & Schuster, 2006), p. 75.
† Yungher, Nathan I., *Terrorism: The Bottom Line* (Upper Saddle River, NJ: Pearson/ Prentice-Hall, 2008), p. 74.

include a worldwide movement, resulting in a loosely organized worldwide web of al-Qaeda and warfare between the two main hubs of Islam, the Sunnis and the Shiites.

"Bismillaah shir Rahmaanir Rahiim": "In the name of Allah, the beneficent, the merciful." This phrase, calling upon God and praising him for his mercy and compassion, begins every chapter in this captured manual, prepared as "Military Studies for Those Who Would Wage Jihad [Holy War] against the Tyrants,"* and seems to be counter to the activities of blood, terror, and fear being called for in the manual—the essence of which makes "killing in the name of God justified if done to 'unbelievers.'" Of course unbelievers (or infidels) are anyone not following certain strains and beliefs of this brand of Islam.

It is not the intent of this chapter or book to raise issues for or against any religion. Each has its own majesty, mystery, symbols, martyrs, and rituals. The commonality is a belief in God as a strong and pure all-powerful being whose purpose is to guide man through the many pitfalls and temptations that are traps set by the devil to capture the souls of man. Whether you believe that, or you believe in God as a politicized organized religion or in the spirituality of goodness, kindness, and love, or if you don't believe in God at all, one thing is certain: more people have been killed by wars of religion than for any other purpose.

In what seems to be a major contradiction at the source of armed religious confrontation throughout history is an ideology or dogma of monotheism as believing in one God expressed thusly: "There is but one God and he is God. My God is more pure, merciful and compassionate than your God. If you do not believe in my God, you must be an 'unbeliever,' therefore you are evil and a follower of Satan. God has commanded to eradicate evil. Therefore 'unbelievers must be killed in the name of God.'" The contradiction lies in the fact that if there is "but one God and he is God," how can "your God" be more powerful, pure, merciful, and compassionate than mine?

Perhaps the answer lies in the belief of the beholder. Not that any one belief is stronger than another or more correct but in the answer to the reckoning. The reckoning is that good must triumph over evil and followers of another faith are often considered unreasonable and poorly informed. Therefore, it can be concluded (reckoned) a lesser faith is born from the devil (thus is evil) and must be destroyed to protect God and goodness. It is true that you cannot reason with an unreasonable person. It is also always true that it is the other fellow who is unreasonable. But then again comes the parable "which belief is the correct belief?"

* Al-Qaeda manual.

The word *Islam* in itself is of little significance when considering the dialogue of God to render death to the unbelievers and to destroy their evil. The word *Islam* simply means "peace." It is the mongers of conflict and self-righteousness who have hijacked the meaning and objective of true Islam, which is to bring peace and to join the world in the belief in one God regardless of the name of a religion (Christian, Jew, Muslim, Buddhist, etc.) or the basis of it. By calling upon war to join the world, the extremists have forsaken spirituality, goodness, kindness, and fellowship of man.

Explaining why the use of violence to spread Islam all over the world was divinely sanctioned, Shi'i Ayatollah Baqer al-Sadr wrote, "the world as it is today is how others shaped it … we have two choices: either to accept it with submission … or to destroy it, so we can construct the world as Islam requires…. We are not fighting within the rules of the world as it exists today. We reject all those rules."*

> The confrontation that we are calling for with the apostate regimes does not know Socratic debates …, Platonic ideals …, nor Aristotelian diplomacy. But it knows the dialogue of bullets, the ideals of assassination, bombing, and destruction, and the diplomacy of the cannon and machine-gun…. Islamic governments have never and will never be established through peaceful solutions and cooperative councils. They are established as they [always] have been by pen and gun … by word and bullet … by tongue and teeth.†

Nothing could be clearer than that simple paragraph telling the world of plans for a confrontation not with diplomatic dialogue, debates, reasoning, or logic, but armed conflicted through the entire cache of terrorist tools: gun battles, assassinations, kidnappings, bombings, and general destruction. Targets of assassination and kidnapping are world leaders, spokespersons for democracy, free thinkers, professional and business leaders, and others who oppose a strict theocratic "the church is the state" government where there are no free elections or independent representation. Bullets and bombs don't discriminate, and as the above paragraph vividly states, they will be heavily relied upon to bring forth the form of government the usurpers so vividly describe following historical precedent.

On October 19, 2007, former Pakistani prime minister Benazir Bhutto returned to Pakistan after eight years of self-imposed exile. She was greeted in Karachi by large crowds who cheered and welcomed her. Suddenly a grenade exploded in the crowd, followed very shortly by a much larger bomb

---

* Al-Qaeda manual.
† From this point forward, the quotations, unless otherwise noted, are taken from the al-Qaeda manual.

ignited by a suicide bomber, killing at least 125 people and injuring upwards of 300 more.

In a speech referencing the bombing, Bhutto said, "The attack was not on me. The attack was on what I represent. It was an attack on democracy and it was an attack on the very unity and integrity of Pakistan. We believe democracy can save Pakistan from disintegration and a militant takeover." (The next day, the *Los Angeles Times*, quoting the *Daily Times*, reported, "The bombing made it starkly clear that unless the streets are made safe, no free and fair elections can be held in January 2008.*) "This bombing was not done by Muslims. It is against our religion to kill others. It was done by Islamic militants for their own purposes." In her statement, Bhutto (a Muslim) referred to knowing of several threats to her safety, including warnings that several suicide bombers had been dispatched to kill her and her followers.

"There was one suicide squad from Taliban elements, one suicide squad from Al-Qaeda, one suicide squad from Pakistan Taliban and one, I believe, from Karachi."

This attack and several hundreds of others serve to emphasize the means and lengths al-Qaeda, and others, will go to bring anarchy and their creed to the world. According to news accounts of the follow-up investigation of the Bhutto attack, "A head thought to be the bomber's was recovered. A bomber's injuries usually include decapitation and generally differ from those of others in the vicinity because of the blast pattern." It was estimated that the bomber had at least 45 pounds of explosives on his body, plus ball bearings and marbles to exaggerate the intensity of the blast. "Some Pakistani newspapers printed graphic photographs of the man's severed head, his facial features clearly identifiable."†

On December 27, 2007, another assassination attempt upon Bhutto, after she finished speaking at a political rally in Rawalpindi, Pakistan, was successful. Mrs. Bhutto stood up through the open top of her armored vehicle to acknowledge the cheering crowd of thousands of supporters. There were shots from a small firearm, followed closely by an explosion set off near the car by a suicide bomber. Mrs. Bhutto was shot in the neck and chest by the bomber and killed by the force of the explosion, which also killed twenty others.

In mid January 2008 an American CIA assessment agreeing with the official Pakistan government investigation concluded that a Pakistani tribal leader with ties to al-Qaeda was responsible for the killing, which set the Pakistan political scene and the best interests of Western governments into chaos.

Quranic verses quoted in the al-Qaeda manual continue the call for true believers to die in the arms and in the name of Islam: "O ye who believe! Fear

---

* Los Angeles Times, October 21, 2007, p. A3.
† Los Angeles Times, October 20, 2007, p. A5.

Allah as He should be feared, and die not except in a state of Islam." This verse may be viewed in two perspectives: (1) be God fearing (but naturally the age-old philosophical question might be asked: If you have a good, just, beneficent, merciful, and compassionate God, why must you fear Him?) and die as an Islamist—everyone who is not a Muslim must convert to Islam, and (2) wherever you die, it should be in a state of Islam, meaning that Islam becomes a worldwide state encompassing the entire population of the world.

> O mankind! Fear your guardian lord who created you from a single person. Created, out of it, his mate, and from them twain scattered [like seeds] countless men and women; fear Allah through whom ye demand your mutual [rights], and be heedful of the wombs [that bore you]: for Allah ever watches over you.
> O ye who believe! Fear Allah, and make your utterance straight forward: That he may make your conduct whole and sound and forgive you your sins. He that obeys Allah and his messenger, has already attained the great victory.

Reading these paragraphs, one must wonder about the source of a belief in killing, terror, and control. Where is the rationalization except for seeking forgiveness for mortal sins by attributing such actions as commands of God who must be obeyed? By knowing he will be cleared of sin, the God-fearing Islamist can easily and readily go forth and commit atrocities and be guiltless and feel no fear of God's wrath. In other words, no action is so heinous that he will be held to account by his God. Herein lies a very clear example of religious fanaticism validating what in other societies and religions would be considered immoral behavior.

Historical Perspective

We stand from afar and wonder: "Why do they hate us?" After all, the Western world has brought progress, technology, convenience, education, medical advances, and numerous other features, including water irrigation to an uninhabitable desert and people that are only three and a half generations removed from desert-dwelling wanderers living under the rule of various tribal leaders. "The most truthful saying is the book of Allah and the best guidance is that of Mohammed, God bless and keep him. [Therefore,] the worst thing is to introduce something new, for every novelty is an act of heresy and each heresy is a deception." In the words and in the viewpoint of al-Qaeda, modernization historically has also brought chaos, and a turning from the true religion and death.

Martyrs were killed, women were widowed, children were orphaned, men were handcuffed, chaste women's heads were shaved, harlots' heads were crowned, atrocities were inflicted on the innocent, gifts were given to the wicked, virgins were raped on the prostitution altar.

After the fall of our orthodox caliphates on March 3, 1924 and after expelling the colonialists, our Islamic nation was afflicted with apostate rulers who took over in the Moslem nation. These rulers turned out to be more infidel and criminal than the colonialists themselves. Moslems have endured all kinds of harm, oppression, and torture at their hands.

Those apostate rulers threw thousands of the Haraka Al-Islamyia (Islamic Movement) youth in gloomy jails and detention centers that were equipped with the most modern torture devices and [manned with] experts in oppression and torture. Those youth had refused to move in the ruler's orbit, obscure matters to the youth, and oppose the idea of rebelling against the rulers. But they [the rulers] did not stop there; they started to fragment the essence of the Islamic nation by trying to eradicate its Moslem identity. Thus, they started spreading godless and atheistic views among the youth. We found some that claimed that socialism was from Islam, democracy was the [religious] council, and the prophet—God bless and keep him—propagandized communism.

Colonialism and its followers, the apostate rulers, then started to openly erect crusader centers, societies, and organizations like Masonic Lodges, Lions and Rotary clubs, and foreign schools.

They aimed at producing a wasted generation that pursued everything that is western and produced rulers, ministers, leaders, physicians, engineers, businessmen, politicians, journalists, and information specialists. [Koranic verse:] "And Allah's enemies plotted and planned, and Allah too planned, and the best of planners is Allah."

They [the rulers] tried, using every means and [kind of] seduction, to produce a generation of young men that did not know [anything] except what they [the rulers] want, did not say except what they [the rulers] think about, did not live except according to their [the rulers'] way, and did not dress except in their [the rulers'] clothes. However, majestic Allah turned their deception back on them, as a large group of those young men who were raised by them [the rulers] woke up from their sleep and returned to Allah, regretting and repenting.

The young men returning to Allah realized that Islam is not just performing rituals but a complete system: Religion and government, worship and Jihad [holy war], ethics and dealing with people, and the Koran and sword. The bitter situation that the nation has reached is a result of its divergence from Allah's course and his righteous law for all places and times. That [bitter situation] came about as a result of its children's love for the world, their loathing of death, and their abandonment of Jihad [holy war].

Unbelief is still the same. It pushed Abou Jahl—may Allah curse him—and Kureish's valiant infidels to battle the prophet—God bless and keep him—and to torture his companions—may Allah's grace be on them. It is the same unbelief that drove Sadat, Hosni Mubarak, Gadhafi, Hafez Assad, Saleh,

Fahed—Allah's curse be upon the non-believing leaders—and all the apostate Arab rulers to torture, kill, imprison, and torment Moslems.

These young men realized that an Islamic government would never be established except by the bomb and rifle. Islam does not coincide or make a truce with unbelief, but rather confronts it.

The confrontation that we are calling for with the apostate regimes does not know Socratic debates …, Platonic ideals …, nor Aristotelian diplomacy. But it knows the dialogue of bullets, the ideals of assassination, bombing, and destruction, and the diplomacy of the cannon and machine-gun.

The young came to prepare themselves for Jihad [holy war], commanded by the majestic Allah's order in the holy Koran. [Koranic verse:] "Against them make ready your strength to the utmost of your power, including steeds of war, to strike terror into (the hearts of) the enemies of Allah and your enemies, and others besides whom ye may not know, but whom Allah doth know."

I present this humble effort to these young Moslem men who are pure, believing, and fighting for the cause of Allah. It is my contribution toward paving the road that leads to majestic Allah and establishes a caliphate according to the prophecy.

A call to the young and impressionable that the only way back to God's divine kingdom (paradise) and to right the wrongs brought by the *apostate rulers* is to reestablish the rule of a caliphate (like the rulers of medieval times) through holy war and to destroy all who do not follow. Forget diplomacy and negotiation, war is the answer through bringing terror and destruction to the enemies of God. (As mentioned earlier, if the religious faith and following is not commensurate with what they believe is God's word for his chosen—the fanatical Islamists—then the only way is to strike suddenly, with surprise, shock, and violence, through assassination and bombings, striking terror in the minds and hearts of those who do not conform.) In other words, "if you are not part of the solution, you must be part of the problem."

We cannot resist this state of ignorance unless we unite our ranks, and adhere to our religion. Without that, the establishment of religion would be a dream or illusion that is impossible to achieve or even imagine its achievement. Sheik Ibn Taimia—may Allah have mercy on him—said, "The interests of all Adam's children would not be realized in the present life, nor in the next, except through assembly, cooperation, and mutual assistance. Cooperation is for achieving their interests and mutual assistance is for overcoming their adversities. That is why it has been said, 'man is civilized by nature.' Therefore, if they unite there will be favorable matters that they do, and corrupting matters to avoid. They will be obedient to the commandment of those goals and avoidant of those immoralities. It is necessary that all Adam's children obey."

It is interesting to discover that the apostate rulers and their modernization programs are referred unambiguously to as "this state of ignorance" in the above paragraph. This is an obvious use of subtle propaganda meant to demean and perhaps dehumanize those who believe in modern ways, lifestyles, society, and culture, and that the contemporary course must be resisted (which is the stated objective) "unless we unite our ranks, and adhere to our religion." In the very next sentence the point is made that their own form of religion cannot be established unless modernization is halted and replaced by the ideology of traditional morality.

The following paragraph should bring grave concerns to everyone who believes in separation of church and state. From the time religion was "discovered" until the late eighteenth century (with the adoption of the American Constitution), the Church ruled over all, including the kings and emperors of the world. No king or emperor would dare to question the Church as represented by popes, cardinals, priests, monks, etc., for fear of excommunication. There were exceptions: French king Charlemagne traveled to Rome to crown himself emperor in spite of opposition from the pope, and King Henry VIII of England, for example, wished to be granted a divorce from very Catholic Catherine of Aragon. The King was excommunicated but formed his own religion—the Church of England. As the ruling entity, the Church, represented by the pope, or similar figure, set the standards for living (and dying) according to the wishes of God.

> He [Sheik Inb Taimia] then says, "It should be understood that governing the people's affairs is one of the greatest religious obligations. In fact, without it, religion and world [affairs] could not be established. The interests of Adam's children would not be achieved except in assembly, because of their mutual need. When they assemble, it is necessary to [have] a leader. Allah's prophet— God bless and keep him—even said, 'If three [people] come together let them pick a leader.' He then necessitated the rule by one of a small, non-essential travel assembly in order to draw attention to the remaining types of assembly. Since Allah has obligated us to do good and avoid the unlawful, that would not be done except through force and lording. Likewise, the rest of what he [God] obligated [us with] would not be accomplished except by force and lordship, be it Jihad [holy war], justice, pilgrimage, assembly, holidays, support of the oppressed, or the establishment of boundaries. That is why it has been said, "the sultan is Allah's shadow on earth."

It cannot be put in better, or stronger, words than these, the meaning of which is "the church is the state—the state is the church." Gone are free elections, democracy, education, and other accoutrements of a free state, such as music, dancing, freedom for women, and constitutional law with its safeguards and guarantees. "God wishes it" is all the leaders of a church state ("the sultan [a]s Allah's shadow on earth") need for justifying anything they wish to offer when the ruling party is the "representative of God." A mandate here, a *fatwah* there, issued by the priests and high lords of the religion who profess to speak for God and enforce his law serves their own purpose and eliminates opposition and free thinking.

Here ends the philosophy of al-Qaeda in the manual. The remaining portion iterates the responsibilities, duties, and requirements of the military faction, some of which are universal standards for military everywhere. Yet one can easily see the emphasis given to the call to form a worldwide fanatical and militant Islamic caliphate united under the flag of oppression and denouncement of everything modern or Westernized. It doesn't take much analysis to realize the direction of the military responsibility, according to al-Qaeda, follows the path of urban or guerrilla warfare targeting civilian populations through suicide bombings, assassinations, and created chaos.

Principles of Military Organization

Military Organization has three main principles without which it cannot be established.

1. Military Organization commander and advisory council
2. The soldiers (individual members)
3. A clearly defined strategy

Military Organization Requirements

The Military Organization dictates a number of requirements to assist it in confrontation and endurance. These are:

1. Forged documents and counterfeit currency
2. Apartments and hiding places
3. Communication means
4. Transportation means
5. Information
6. Arms and ammunition
7. Transport

Missions Required of the Military Organization

The main mission for which the Military Organization is responsible is the overthrow of the godless regimes and their replacement with an Islamic regime. Other missions consist of the following:

1. Gathering information about the enemy, the land, the installations, and the neighbors.
2. Kidnapping enemy personnel, documents, secrets, and arms.
3. Assassinating enemy personnel as well as foreign tourists.
4. Freeing the brothers who are captured by the enemy.
5. Spreading rumors and writing statements that instigate people against the enemy.
6. Blasting and destroying the places of amusement, immorality, and sin; not a vital target.

7. Blasting and destroying the embassies and attacking vital economic centers.
8. Blasting and destroying bridges leading into and out of the cities.

Importance of the Military Organization

1. Removal of those personalities that block the call's path—All types of military and civilian intellectuals and thinkers for the state.
2. Proper utilization of the individuals' unused capabilities.
3. Precision in performing tasks, and using collective views on completing a job from all aspects, not just one.
4. Controlling the work and not fragmenting it or deviating from it.
5. Achieving long-term goals such as the establishment of an Islamic state and short-term goals such as operations against enemy individuals and sectors.
6. Establishing the conditions for possible confrontation with the regressive regimes and their persistence.
7. Achieving discipline in secrecy and through tasks.

Necessary Qualifications for the Organization's Members

1. *Islam*
   The member of the Organization must be Moslem. How can an unbeliever, someone from a revealed religion [Christian, Jew], a secular person, a communist, etc. protect Islam and Moslems and defend their goals and secrets when he does not believe in that religion [Islam]? The Israeli Army requires that a fighter be of the Jewish religion. Likewise, the command leadership in the Afghan and Russian armies requires any one with an officer's position to be a member of the communist party.

2. *Commitment to the Organization's Ideology*
   This commitment frees the Organization's members from conceptional problems.

3. *Maturity*
   The requirements of military work are numerous, and a minor cannot perform them. The nature of hard and continuous work in dangerous conditions requires a great deal of psychological, mental, and intellectual fitness, which are not usually found in a minor. It is reported that Ibn Omar—may Allah be pleased with him—said, "During Ahad [battle] when I was fourteen years of age, I was submitted [as a volunteer] to the prophet—God bless and keep him. He refused me and did not throw me in the battle. During Khandak [trench] Day [battle] when I was fifteen years of age, I was also submitted to him, and he permitted me [to fight].

4. *Sacrifice*
   He [the member] has to be willing to do the work and undergo martyrdom for the purpose of achieving the goal and establishing the religion of majestic Allah on earth.

5. *Listening and Obedience*

In the military, this is known today as discipline. It is expressed by how the member obeys the orders given to him. That is what our religion urges. The Glorious says, "O, ye who believe! Obey Allah and obey the messenger and those charged with authority among you." In the story of Hazifa Ben Al-Yaman—may Allah have mercy on him who was exemplary in his obedience to Allah's messenger—Allah bless and keep him. When he [Mohammed]—Allah bless and keep him—sent him to spy on the Kureish and their allies during their siege of Madina, Hazifa said, "As he [Mohammed] called me by name to stand, he said, 'Go get me information about those people and do not alarm them about me.'"

6. *Keeping Secrets and Concealing Information*

It was said in the proverbs, "The hearts of freemen are the tombs of secrets" and "Moslems' secrecy is faithfulness, and talking about it is faithlessness." [Mohammed]—God bless and keep him— used to keep work secrets from the closest people, even from his wife A'isha—may Allah's grace be on her.

7. *Free of Illness*

The Military Organization's member must fulfill this important requirement. Allah says, "There is no blame for those who are infirm, or ill, or who have no resources to spend."

8. *Patience*

[The member] should have plenty of patience for [enduring] afflictions if he is overcome by the enemies. He should not abandon this great path and sell himself and his religion to the enemies for his freedom. He should be patient in performing the work, even if it lasts a long time.

9. *Tranquility and "Unflappability"*

[The member] should have a calm personality that allows him to endure psychological traumas such as those involving bloodshed, murder, arrest, imprisonment, and reverse psychological traumas such as killing one or all of his Organization's comrades. [He should be able] to carry out the work.

10. *Intelligence and Insight*

When the prophet—Allah bless and keep him—sent Hazifa Ben Al-Yaman to spy on the polytheist and [Hafiza] sat among them, Abou Soufian said, "Let each one of you look at his companion." Hazifa said to his companion, "Who are you?" The companion replied, "So-and-so son of so-and-so."

11. *Caution and Prudence*

In his battle against the king of Tomedia the Roman general Speer sent an emissary to discuss with that king the matter of truce between the two armies. In reality, he had sent him to learn about the Tomedians' ability to fight. The general picked, Lilius, one of his top commanders, for that task and sent with him some of his officers, disguised as slaves. During that mission, one of the king's officers, Sifax pointed to one of the [disguised] slaves and yelled, "That slave is a Roman officer I had met in a neighboring city. He was wearing a Roman uniform." At that point, Lilius used a clever trick and managed to divert the attention of the Tomedians from that by turning to the disguised officer and quickly slapping him on the face a number of times. He reprimanded him for wearing a Roman officer's uniform when he was a slave and for claiming a status that he did not deserve.

The officer accepted the slaps quietly. He bowed his head in humility and shame, as slaves do. Thus, Sifax men thought that officer was really a slave because they could not imagine that a Roman officer would accept these hits without defending himself.

King Sifax prepared a big feast for Lilius and his entourage and placed them in a house far away from his camp so they could not learn about his fortifications. They [the Romans] made another clever trick on top of the first one. They freed one of their horses and started chasing him in and around the camp. After they learned about the extent of the fortifications they caught the horse and, as planned, managed to abort their mission about the truce agreement. Shortly after their return, the Roman general attacked King Sifax' camp and burned the fortifications. Sifax was forced to seek reconciliation.

B. There was a secret agent who disguised himself as an American fur merchant. As the agent was playing cards aboard a boat with some passengers, one of the players asked him about his profession. He replied that he was a "fur merchant." The women showed interest [in him] and began asking the agent—the disguised fur merchant—many questions about the types and prices of fur. He mentioned fur price figures that amazed the women. They started avoiding and regarding him with suspicion, as though he were a thief, or crazy.

12. *Truthfulness and Counsel*

The Commander of the faithful, Omar Ibn Al-Khattab—may Allah be pleased with him—asserted that this characteristic was vital in those who gather information and work as spies against the Moslems' enemies.

13. *Ability to Observe and Analyze*

The Israeli Mossad received news that some Palestinians were going to attack an Israeli El Al airplane. That plane was going to Rome with Golda Meir—Allah's curse upon her—the Prime Minister at the time, on board. The Palestinians had managed to use a clever trick that allowed them to wait for the arrival of the plane without being questioned by anyone. They had beaten a man who sold potatoes, kidnapped him, and hidden him. They made two holes in the top of that peddler's cart and placed two tubes next to the chimney through which two Russian-made "Strella" missiles could be launched. The Mossad officers traveled the airport back and forth looking for the Palestinians. One officer passed the potato cart twice without noticing anything. On his third time, he noticed three chimneys, but only one of them was working with smoke coming out of it. He quickly steered toward the cart and hit it hard. The cart overturned, and the Palestinians were captured.

14. *Ability to Act, Change Positions, and Conceal Oneself*
Nothing could be more clear as spelled out in this manifesto of War and hate; Osama Bin Laden and his network of Al-Qaeda, with threads like a world-wide web, have strategic goals of dominating the world that does not conform to his vision of adherence to "God's will."

The Concept of Martyrdom

4

DR. A. K. MOHAMMED

Contents

Martyrdom in Islam

Small philological observations can sometimes introduce us to larger histori-cal problems. No one familiar with Christian martyrdom will be surprised to learn that the Arabic words that Muslims use for *martyr* and *witness* are identical. The terminology is unmistakably Christian. By the fourth century, the Greek martyrs (witness) had acquired a technical sense and had come to denote one whose suffering and death bore witness to the truth of Jesus' passion and resurrection. Witnessing, suffering, death, and heavenly reward have since been intimately connected in Christian life and thought.

Given the parallel terminology, one might expect to find a similar under-standing of martyrdom in Islam. At the level of reward, Muslim martyrs are not far from their Christian counterparts. Both are promised remission of sin and immediate life in paradise; the souls of both reside at the highest level of para-dise, near the throne of God; both are given the privilege of interceding with God on behalf of their coreligionists. Overall, the benefits accorded Muslim martyrs closely resemble those in Syriac Christianity (Wensinck, 1921).

Whatever the similarities, there is one major difference in conception between Muslim and Christian martyrdom: for Muslims, one earns the title of martyr without any apparent act of witnessing. The martyr's sacrifice does not generally attest to anything specific, nor does it symbolize much beyond the obvious sense of death in the service of God's plan. The awkward fit between witnessing and martyrdom is further suggested by the strained attempts of some Muslim authorities to make sense of the word. For example, in one tradition, the martyr is called witness because his soul is alive and able to behold directly the abode of peace, while the souls of others see paradise only on the day of resurrection.

Furthermore, elsewhere, the martyr is a witness because he undertook to testify to the truth until his death; or because he will serve as a witness against the ancient communities who rejected God's prophets; or because the Prophet will be a witness on the day of judgment for those of his followers slain in the way of God. With respect to their burial, there are suggestions that one reason for not washing the bodies of martyrs is so that their wounds might continue to testify to their status in the afterlife (Ayoub, 1987). In short, the Muslim tradition had to invent for itself a connection between witnessing and martyrdom, since none was immediately apparent.

All this points out the unique attitude toward sacrifice and struggle among Muslims, an attitude forged by a political experience quite different from that of the early Christians. Martyrdom achieved its religious significance for Christians in the period before the faith had enjoyed any political success. Asserting an ultimate, heavenly victory was at least in part a way for Christians to face down political failure, represented in the first instance by the career of Jesus himself. Islam, by contrast, had more success from the beginning; it emerged not as a persecuted sect, but in the course of military conquest and political victory. While there had been persecutions in Mecca during Muhammad's early career, early Muslim martyrs did not enjoy any special cultic visibility in the later tradition.

The religious value of suffering and death was never the obvious lesson to draw from the experience of the early Muslim community. What struck Muslims more naturally was the prophet's call for active struggle against injustice and idolatry. Even the dramatic accounts of Hussain's (Prophet Mohammed's grandson at Karbala in present-day Iraq) martyrdom tend to emphasize righteous struggle against worldly injustice more than patient endurance of suffering and death. Where the early Christians mourned, the Muslims strove. According to Hodgson (1960), Muslims sought not so much consolation as guidance from their faith. The ideal was less to die for the faith than to struggle actively for it, and to enjoy the fruits of victory here on earth. However ambiguous its use of the term *witness*, the Qur'an is absolutely clear on the Muslim's duty to struggle in the service of God, and on the rewards enjoyed by those slain in the course of jihad: "And those slain in the way of God, He will not send their works astray. He will guide them, and dispose their minds aright, and He will admit them to Paradise, that He has made known to them" (47:4–6).

The earliest Muslims knew who was destined for heaven. Members of the community were by definition people of paradise or *ahl al-janna*; all others were people of the fire or *ahl al-nār*. Although individual piety was not irrelevant, for most Muslims it was membership rather than piety that marked one out for paradise (Van Ess, 1997). Those who fought "in the way of God" had a special status beyond the promise of paradise: they were "mightier in rank with God" (9:20); their sins were forgiven (61:12); whether slain or victorious they received a vast reward (4:74). The Qur'an generally offers such rewards to all warriors, not simply to martyrs. The one reward unambiguously associated with martyrdom is immediate life in paradise: "Do not say of those slain in God's way that they are dead; they are living, only you do not perceive" (2:154). Beyond this, the Qur'an is not terribly concerned with battlefield martyrs as a group apart from other Muslims.

One can find in the hadith material the clear distinction between martyrs and ordinary Muslims. They not only enter paradise immediately, skipping both the punishment of the tomb and the final judgment (Smith and Haddad, 2002), but they also ascend to the highest level, their souls alive and inhabiting the white birds in the lanterns hanging just beneath the throne of God. Martyrs occupy a special place in paradise reserved otherwise for prophets, righteous men, just imams, and those who choose death over unbelief by refusing to renounce their faith under torture. In another hadith, the prophet is made to reassure a grieving mother that her son is in the highest garden, the *jannat al-firdaws*.

Moreover, martyrs are also spared the pain of death. God is even said to have spoken face-to-face with one of the martyrs of Uhud, the prophet's first major military defeat. The prophet lists seven blessings from God to the martyr, as narrated in hadeeth of al-Miqdaam ibn Ma'di Karb:

1. He is forgiven from the moment his blood is first shed.
2. He will be immediately shown his place in paradise.
3. He will be spared the trial of the grave.
4. He will be married to 70 houris.
5. He will be secure on the day of the greatest terror (the day of judgment).
6. The crown of dignity will be placed on his head, one ruby of which is better than this world and all that is in it.
7. He will be permitted to intercede for seventy of his relatives.

Considering these blessings that await martyrs, it is doubtless why martyrs are so pleased with their situation that they want nothing more than to return to earth to be martyred a second time. The afterlife benefits accorded martyrs are thus straightforward. Less so is the issue of just who qualifies for them. Not all casualties of war will receive a martyr's reward from God: most jurists require first of all that the war be fought against unbelievers and second, that the warrior himself be properly motivated. Intention is central to the performance of all acts of piety in Islam; prayer or pilgrimage done without proper intention may be sufficient to qualify one as a Muslim in the social sense, but they do not fulfill the ritual requirement in God's eyes and will not earn one afterlife benefits. Martyrdom in jihad works precisely the same way.

As several hadith remind, those who fight hypocritically, or chiefly in search of earthly reward, or out of zeal for fighting itself, or simply to display their bravery, are not in the final scheme of things martyrs. Only those who fight desiring the face of God, or seeking to make the word of God supreme, are martyrs in any ultimate sense. And yet even the hypocritical warrior, should he die at the hands of the enemy, is to be buried as a martyr. As we ourselves lack access to the intention and sincerity of others, we are to treat all battlefield deaths as martyrdom.

If death in battle is the only way to gain a martyr's funeral, the heavenly rewards themselves are more widely distributed. The hadith and jurisprudential literatures stretch the category of shahid to encompass far more than battlefield martyrdom. According to one frequently cited report, the prophet granted the title of shahid to victims of drowning, pleurisy, and plague, as well as to the innocent victims of accidental building collapse. Other ways to acquire direct access to paradise include the following: death in defense of one's property, death in childbirth, and death by accident while engaged in jihad.

In some of these cases, particularly those involving violent, sudden, or exceptionally painful death, the special rewards accorded the victims might reflect the continuing survival of ancient folk beliefs and their power to shape the lettered tradition. These forms of death had long been felt to deserve recompense; now, God shows Muslims his special favor by considering such deaths atonement for sin, and thus as entitling these people to special treatment in the afterlife (Wensinck, 1921). The inclusion of plague in the prophet's list of martyrdoms is perhaps in part theologically inspired: God has sent plague as a mercy and martyrdom to the believers; those who die while remaining steadfast in their belief in God's decree are classed with the battlefield martyrs. In at least one report, the plague victim's boils are directly equated with the fallen warrior's wounds (Dols, 1977).

One might understand all this as an attempt to make martyrdom available to more and more people in the postconquest world. The prophet himself would apparently agree: in reply to a companion's claim that only those killed in war are properly considered martyrs, the prophet is reported to have said, "In that case the martyrs of my community would be few," before going on to enumerate the other types of death that likewise earn one martyr status. This represents an expansion of the category of martyr without any fundamental change in its nature. It is still through death that one earns a martyr's reward, even if battling unbelievers is no longer a central feature of the process. But the religious scholars also go further and positively equate particular religious activities with martyrdom. Such a tendency is clear, for example, in the assurance that the soul of the pilgrim who dies on hajj goes immediately to paradise.

It is thus not merely death while fulfilling religious duties that earns one martyrdom; the very fulfillment of such duties might in some circumstances bring one to that level. Interpreting one of his companion's dreams, the prophet explains why the believer who died in bed after two colleagues had died on jihād was in fact given priority at the gates of paradise: "No one is more virtuous in God's eyes than the believer who lives long in Islam, and is able to go on praising and glorifying God, and making the profession of faith" (Ahmad ibn Hanbal, *Musnad*, i, 163). A similar logic lies behind those traditions in which, for example, the Qur'an reciter is promised a martyr's reward, or the prayer caller is said to receive the reward of forty thousand martyrs (Ahmad ibn Hnbal, *Musnad*, iv, 437). More than simply an expansion of the category, this amounts to a change in the very conception of martyrdom.

In their revaluation of martyrdom, the legal scholars were driven chiefly by a quietist impulse. While there was often no love loss between the scholars and the rulers of the day, the former were no rebels. Despite the activist model of the prophet, the scholars were as a whole distinctly uncomfortable with sedition and political upheaval, lest the moral life of the community be endangered. As the collective bearers of religious authority in the Muslim world, they were generally willing to tolerate far from ideal political arrangements, as long as these arrangements did not jeopardize the private, scholarly elaboration of religious law. Even dissenting movements, at least those that managed to survive beyond the first three centuries of Islam, came eventually to reconcile activist ideals with quietist necessity (see, e.g., Lewis, 1986). It was generally the idealistic dissenters, those who insisted on actively resisting the ruler's armies at the cost of their lives, that Sunni and sectarian religious scholars had in mind when seeking to demilitarize martyrdom.

Battlefield martyrdom was a potent tool for forging loyalty within dissenting groups. Perhaps the single most important martyrdom in this sense was that of Hussain ibn 'Āli, whose death at Karbal' in 680 helped create a deep emotional loyalty to the 'Alid house, and to this day has helped Shī'ites sustain what is the chief sectarian divide within Islam. Other dissenters also made much of their martyrs. Those rebels, known as seceders, also called themselves vendors; that is, those who sell their lives in exchange for paradise, with apparent reference to Qur'an 4:74 and 9:112. It is easy to see a notion of martyrdom behind this designation.

One sees in Kharijite circles the cluster of practices against which the religious scholars would aim their fire: activism, asceticism, and the deliberate seeking of martyrdom in battle. The first is represented by the Kharijite practice of hijra, exodus from the society of unbelievers to one of the group's own camps. It was, in the first Islamic century, through hijra to the garrison towns that one generally acquired a place in Muslim society; Kharijite encampments would similarly serve as hijra sites, from which active resistance to state power could be launched. For Kharijites, as for other Muslims, it was through hijra that one became a member of the community, that one joined the people of paradise. Hijra and jihad are closely linked in the Qur'an, in Kharijite teaching, and in anti-Kharijite polemic. It is the Kharijites, in fact, who are most commonly associated in our sources with *talab al-shahada*, the deliberate seeking of martyrdom on the battlefield (see Crone, 1994).

The practice of asceticism is relevant not only because it helped cement the collective identity of these groups but also because of its connection to hijra, jihad, and the deliberate seeking of martyrdom. In a speech just before launching an attack, the Sufrit Salih ibn Musarih commended his followers: "Fear of God, austerity in this world, desire for the afterlife, [and] frequent pondering of death.... Do not fear being killed for the sake of God, for being killed is easier than dying naturally." He added: "Natural death comes upon you when you least expect it, separating you from your fathers and your sons, from your wives and from this world" (quoted in Rowson, 1989, p. 33). Moreover, he states, "If your anxiety and aversion to this is too strong, then, indeed, sell your souls to God obediently, and your wealth, and you'll enter Paradise in security and embrace the black-eyed houris" (quoted in Rowson, 1989, p. 33). That asceticism, battle, and martyrdom are connected should be of no surprise; they went hand in hand in the Near East long before the Islamic period, and the connection is well attested outside of Kharijite circles in early Islamic times (Wensinck, 1921).

To summarize, the Muslim understanding of martyrdom was not static in the early period. It evolved along with Muslim society itself and was significantly shaped by the tension between the activist model of the prophet and the later pragmatic quietism of the scholars. As a rule, the hadith expresses the values of the religious scholars, even if in form it preserves the words of the prophet. Here, the prophet appears as the chief spokesman for a view of martyrdom consistent with the quietist outlook of classical Islam and of the scholars who made it. This is brought home strongly in those hadith where the prophet ranks the scholars higher than the martyrs and declares that on the day of judgment, the ink of the scholars will weigh more heavily with God than the blood of the martyrs (Goldziher, 1971).

Martyrdom and Suicide Bombing

Islam provides that involvement in jihad grants the reward of heaven to Muslims willing to sacrifice themselves in the course of defending religion. Orthodox Muslims endorse the idea that the devout believer, who has a task of serving God, can accomplish the service during one's life or through death (Ajami, 2001). Death in the service of God is considered holy or martyrdom rather than suicidal; it is a product of unwavering faith that leads the individual toward self-mortification (Strenski, 2003).

Although there is a dispute about whether Islam condones or calls for suicide in the service of God (e.g., Hafez, 2004), in the Palestinian–Israeli

Figure 4.1 A 64-year-old grandmother and martyr. (From http://www.canada.
com/topics/news/world/story.html?id=323bef98-71e7-4602-b211-83e78bb83230
&k=97958.)

context, both secular and religious militant organizations have invoked
Islamic texts and symbols on martyrdom and jihad to motivate individuals, and to justify their recruiting and dispatching suicide bombers (Hafez,
2004).

The sixty-four-year-old Palestinian grandmother in Figure 4.1 blew herself up near Israeli troops sweeping through northern Gaza on November
23, 2006.

Martyrdom in Islam forms an intrinsic component of the concept
of jihad; hence, it does not lend itself to Western definitions of suicide.
According to Islamic teachings, *intihar* (suicide) designates despair and
violent withdrawal from society, whereas *shahadat* (martyrdom) represents
the ultimate form of giving for the well-being of the community. Suicide
is essentially a characteristic of individualist societies, mainly resulting
"from lack of integration of the individual into society" (Durkheim, 1951).
Primarily collectivist Arab populations record very low suicide rates for
males and virtually none for females. On the basis of 1987 statistics, Maris
et al. (2000) report two suicide cases per million for males in Syria and
none in Egypt. These statistics become extremely significant, especially
when compared with 661 suicide cases per million in Hungary and 197
cases per million in the United States.

The inappropriateness of Western concepts of suicide necessitates a new
venue for understanding the motives of suicide bombers. Durkheim's notion

of altruistic suicide inspired by "religious sacrifice or unthinking political allegiance" (1951, p. 15) may shed light on kamikaze missions, but certainly not on Palestinian human bombs. As fervent Japanese nationalists, the kami-kazes died for the sake of imperial Japan without expectation of personal reward. Palestinian suicide bombers, on the other hand, feel they comply with the highest form of Islamic worship, for which they have specific spiritual expectations.

In the Qur'an, several verses deal directly with the concept martyrdom: "Think not of those who are slain in Allah's way: They are dead, nay; they live, finding their sustenance in the presence of their lord" (Surat al-Imran, verse 169), implying that martyrs or shahid do not really die. In fact, they are to receive reward in the afterlife: "Verily he will admit them to a place with which they shall be well pleased: for Allah is All Knowing, Most Forebearing" (Surat al-Hajj, verse 59).

Al-'Amad (2000) explains the religious foundations of martyrs: "In Islam the martyr is a rebel, he is a fallen hero on the road to the target" (p. 68). Al-'Amad (2000) adds: "the martyr as a role model ... held in high esteem, close to sainthood. Heroes of Islam and its martyrs are symbols of the umma's survival and a label for its national and religious dignity. Blood becomes a symbol, a meaning, a significance, and turns into an ideology ... blood relations" (p. 68). Those who participate in suicidal missions or self-martyring operations in the cause of Islam will be rewarded with a place in Jenna, the Muslim paradise:

> Allah hath purchased of the believers their persons and their goods; for theirs in return are the gardens of Paradise: they fight in his cause, and slay and are slain: a promise binding on him in truth, through the law, the Gospel and the Qur'an: and who is more faithful to his covenant than Allah. Then rejoice in the bargain which you have concluded: that is the achievement supreme. (Surat al-Taubat 9:111) (6)

Donner (1991) suggests that the numerous Qur'anic verses calling for jihad, in abnegation of the luxuries of life, reveal the apocalyptic nature of Islam. He detects a sense of moral urgency in the Qur'an, and a perception of the approaching day of judgment. Placed in this context, earthly life loses its worth, and the merits of jihad become exceptionally easy to discard.

Ali Shari'ati defines two distinct types of shahadat. The first type of sha-hid is one who gives up his life through jihad: he is chosen by shahadat. The second type rebels and consciously welcomes death; he chooses his own sha-hadat. The most revered of the shahids that chose shahadat was Husayn. He was killed after refusing to avoid a confrontation with a regime, which though illegitimate, vastly outnumbered Husayn's forces. Husayn's example, which only involved injury and death to combatants, has been used to legitimate martyrdom that has inflicted many collateral deaths on noncombatants. The reason that some willingly choose this new type of self-martyrdom is that shahadat is seen as a way to draw attention to injustice so that action can be taken against it.

In the area of jihad, suicidal attacks are acts of martyrdom. They assume a special importance because of their symbolism as well as the other effects they have. According to Abu-Amr (1994), "Perhaps it is the blessing of God almighty bestowed upon one mujahid or two mujahidin, enabling him or them to charge against the enemy position, or against a concentration of enemy military forces on a martyrdom mission" (p. 102). He adds that "inflicting heavy losses, breaking the enemy's morale and determination in the face of this Islamic spirit of martyrdom ... it increases fear of the Muslims after a long period of weakness and humiliation" (p. 102).

References

Abu-Amr, Z. 1994. *Islamic fundamentalism in the West Bank and Gaza: Muslim brotherhood and Islamic Jihad.* Bloomington: Indiana University Press.

Ajami, P. 2001. *The Arab predicament.* Tel Aviv: Maskel.

Al-'Amad, S. 2000. *The martyr imamin history and ideology: The Shi'i martyr versus the Sunni hero.* Beirut: Al-Mu'assasa al-'Arabiyya lid-Dirasast wan-Nashr.

Ayoub, M. (1987). Martyrdom in Christianity and Islam. In *Religious resurgence: Contemporary cases in Islam, Christianity, and Judaism,* ed. R. Antoun and M. Hegland. New York: Syracuse University Press 569–74.

Crone, P. 1994. The first-century concept of higra. *Arabica* 61:352–87.

Dols, M. 1977. *The black plague in the Middle East.* Princeton, NJ.

Donner, F. M. 1991. The sources of Islamic conceptions of war. *Just war and Jihad: Historical and theoretical perspectives on war and peace in Western and Islamic traditions,* ed. J. Kelsay and J. T. Johnson. New York: Greenwood Press 113–21.

Durkheim, E. 1951. *Suicide,* trans. J. A. Spaulding and G. Simpson. New York: The Free Press.

Goldziher, I. 1971. *Muslim studies.* Vol. 2. London: Allen & Unwin.

Hafez, M. 2004. *Manufacturing human bombs: Strategy, culture, and conflict in the making of Palestinian suicide terrorism.* Paper presented at the National Institute of Justice Conference, Washington, DC.

Hodgson, M. 1960. A comparison of Islam and Christianity as a framework for religious life. *Diogenes* 32:49–74.

Lewis, B. 1986. On the quietist and activist traditions in Islamic political writing. *Bulletin of the School of Oriental and African Studies* 10:141–47.

Maris, R. W., Berman, A., and Silverman, M. M. 2000. *Comprehensive textbook of suicidology.* New York: The Guilford Press.

Rowson, E., trans. 1989. *The Marwanid restoration.* Albany, NY: SUNY Press.

Smith, J., and Haddad, Y. 2002. *The Islamic understanding of death and resurrection.* Oxford: Oxford University Press.

Strenski, I. 2003. Sacrifice, gift, and the social logic of Muslim 'human bombers.'
    Terrorism and Political Violence 15:1–34.

Terri Harris, R. 1998. Nonviolence in Islam: The alternative community tradition.
    In *Subverting hatred: The challenge of nonviolence in religious*, ed. D. L. Smith-
    Christopher.

Van Ess, J. 1997. *Theologie und Gesellschaft im 2. und 3. Jahrhundert Hidschra*. Berlin:
    Walter de Gruyter.

Wensinck, A. J. 1921. *The oriental doctrine of the martyrs*. Amsterdam. Mededeelingen
    der Koninklijke Akademie van. Wetenschappen, Afdeeling Letterkunde 53:6.

Zentropism and Homeland Security

5

JONATHAN ROSS

Contents

Mastery is a path and not a destination.
The fluent blade cuts cleanly.

—The creed, or motto, of the Zentropist

Zentropism

The Zentropist Defined: The First Attribute*

A Zentropist is someone who "harnesses the potential for work and creativity available within a system and through enlightened application of knowledge and skills, and the alignment of carefully considered goals and objectives, achieves a desirable and harmonious outcome." In order for this to actually be meaningful and actionable, those that embrace this philosophy need to possess the capability to bring measurable value to their interactions, whether in the professional or personal arena.

There are seven primary attributes that must be cultivated in order to become a Zentropist. These are willingness, discipline, adaptability, knowledge, character, courage, and understanding. It should be understood that the primary attributes are all interrelated and connected, although the order

---

* Adapted from http://zentropist.wordpress.com/2009/02/02/the-zentropist-defined-the-first-attribute/. With permission.

of presentation is no accident. There is a natural flow to the order, which, as with many things in nature, takes the shape of a circular structure. From the expression of the will, as defined below, the Zentropist learns discipline. Through the disciplined approach, rather than fall into regimented, inflexible modes of thought or behavior, the Zentropist learns the value of adaptability. With the understanding that force can have but one direction at a time in a given moment, the Zentropist gains insight into knowledge in its myriad forms. With knowledge, the Zentropist builds character, with the end goal to share the wisdom, as it has been shared with him or her, and to bring light to the darkest recesses. As the Zentropist solidifies and forges character, courage manifests itself, expressed in the choices that are made, the actions and paths taken (or not), the measure of the things that the Zentropist holds dear. From courage springs understanding, the ability to see things for what they are; the realization that despite the chaos and confusion that roil the surface, we operate in a world that seeks to find stasis or balance, and as an agent of change, the Zentropist is responsible for restoring equilibrium. This brings the Zentropist full circle to the power of the will.

Although resistance, both internal and external, may be encountered on the journey of expanding one's mastery of each of these attributes, it is a part of the process whose value cannot be understated. Resistance ultimately makes the mind, body, and spirit stronger, and all of these must continuously evolve, for the alternative is stagnation.

As a Zentropist, willingness signals a commitment to growth in all its forms. The Zentropist must display "the willingness to engage in lifelong learning and exploration to hone one's knowledge to a razor edge." There are simply no shortcuts to this path. It involves the application of one's curiosity, thirst for information, and quest for continuous improvement over time. It is a lifelong journey whose destination always lies over the next mountain, or across the next swift-moving river or vast body of water, or across the seeming barrenness of the desert.

Learning over the course of the Zentropist's lifetime may take many forms, from formal instruction and schooling to impromptu observations of others; from apprenticing or shadowing those in possession of a desirable skill set to transmitting one's knowledge as a teacher or instructor; for the wise teacher acknowledges that the student, inadvertently or not, may impart lessons every bit as important as those that he or she desires to communicate.

The Zentropist Defined: The Second Attribute*

The second attribute is focused on discipline and is expressed by the Zentropist as follows: "The discipline to commit to a course of action deci-

---

* This section is adapted from http://zentropist.wordpress.com/2009/02/04/the-zentropist-defined-the-second-attribute/. With permission.

sively and with a fullness of intent." So what does this mean in practice? It is an acknowledgment that decisive action, unlike the equivocating, faltering steps that many choose to take, is always preferable. Now what is unspoken in this premise, and critical to understand, is that decisive action is not rash, or entirely emotional, nor is it always purely based on endless analysis or complete disclosure of every factor that may influence a given situation. The truth is, sometimes decisions must be undertaken with limited information available, within a compressed time frame, when waffling or seeking compromise or consensus is simply not possible. This does not, however, as we will discuss, suggest that the path or course taken in the moment is one that we are locked into. This concept of adaptability, or interruptibility, forms the third attribute of the Zentropist.

That being said, by virtue of taking decisive action, we must always act with a fullness of intent. It is not acceptable to adapt half-hearted measures or a noncommittal and cavalier attitude toward problem solving. The Zentropist respects the process too much, yet does not fall in love with the process, for it is but a solution-seeking mechanism—in other words, a tool, akin to the arrow in an archer's quiver. One can have a fullness of intent, a commitment to strive with every fiber of the being while serving as the conduit of a solution to a problem, or presenting the means to bypass or overcome an obstacle, yet still retain flexibility and adapt to ever-changing feedback and energy. There are times when the energy resisting a course of action is too great, when applying greater force is apt to introduce unintended consequences, which might be mitigated by deflecting or releasing the opposing force, thus exposing an alternative solution to the problem or obstacle at hand.

I think it best to remember a quote from Theodore Roosevelt, one of the great American Presidents in my book (an opinion shared by a number of historians as well). He remarked, "In any moment of decision the best thing you can do is the right thing, the next best thing is the wrong thing, and the worst you can do is nothing."

Indeed ...

The Zentropist Defined: The Third Attribute*

The Zentropist must adapt to changing circumstances by remaining keenly attuned to all senses. Upon first impression, this may seem a virtual impossibility, for how can one commit yet not commit? This can be expressed by invoking the mental image of an antenna that can transmit or receive signals depending on how it is wired. The Zentropist, even while in transmission mode, must always reserve sufficient bandwidth to continuously

* Adapted from http://zentropist.wordpress.com/2009/02/06/the-zentropist-defined-the-third-attribute/. With permission.

receive, to be able to process the data stream arising from his or her interaction with the surrounding environment and make necessary adjustments without fail. Newtonian physics teaches us that every action has an equal and opposite reaction, which, again, is nature's way of finding and achieving balance.

In order to operate effectively, the Zentropist accepts that one must maintain "the adaptability to operate in fluid environments and to remain interruptible."

The Zentropist acknowledges that if a course of action is not producing the desired results, it is foolhardy to blindly continue on the course without making some adjustment. In certain circumstances, the adjustments may be relatively minor; yet these seemingly small acknowledgments can have significant cumulative effect. Conversely, there are times when a particular tactic or stratagem is simply untenable, even if they have worked previously, and to stubbornly refuse to see this creates unnecessary hardship and stress on the enterprise in question. In these instances, the Zentropist must be prepared to find new solutions, which may reflect a change in objectives (the short term) or signify a change in goals (the long term).

Again, one must be cautioned against falling into the trap of interpreting resistance as an indication that a course of action is misguided or incorrect; change of any kind produces stress, and stress must not always be looked at in a pejorative light. What is critical is maintaining a careful alignment of both the objectives and goals and seeking to move continuously toward their resolution.

In Lao Tzu's classic work *Tao Te Ching*, the expression "to be like water" appears. Water is a natural element that is at once fluid and powerful; given sufficient time, water will erode the mightiest rock and can even defeat metal. It does this, however, not through brute application of force or imposition of its will, but by remaining fluid, chipping away at the obstacle as it continues on its journey, whether as drops falling from the sky or a stream, river, or sea that is constantly in motion. In this deceptively compliant manner, it imposes the "death of a thousand cuts." And the Zentropist does well to remember that "the fluent (or fluid) blade cuts cleanly."

I'll leave the third attribute of Zentrophy with a passage from Lao Tzu, as translated by Chao-Hsiu Chen:

> The greatest good is like water:
> It benefits all life without being noticed.
> It flows even to the lowliest places where no one chooses to be
> and so it is very close to the Tao.
> It settles only in quiet locations.
> Its deepest heart is always clear.
> It offers itself with great goodness.
> It keeps its rhythm as it keeps its promises.

It governs tributaries as it governs its people.
It adapts to all necessities.
It moves at the right moment.
It never flaunts its goodness
and so it never attracts any blame.

The Zentropist Defined: The Fourth Attribute*

We now turn to the fourth of the Zentropist's primary attributes, which is centered on knowledge in all its myriad forms. There is a natural tendency for some to seek to flaunt their accumulation of knowledge, to prove to the world that they are "expert" or somehow all-knowing when it comes to a particular subject. This is the course of fools and charlatans. On the other hand, there are those who revel in their ignorance, or worse, do not comprehend how dramatically their lack of knowledge impacts their journey through this life, which is a tragedy in of itself.

The Zentropist walks the middle path. The Zentropist seeks "the knowledge of when to speak, and when to listen." For as with force, which can only have one direction in a given moment of time, one can be speaking or one can be listening. One cannot, however, be doing both simultaneously.

Knowledge can be highly esoteric or highly technical; it can be mundane, it can be revolutionary; it can change the course of human events or it can simply be a part of the greater flow of life. The Zentropist must selectively continue to evaluate his or her body of knowledge, to seek to broaden it where appropriate, and to plumb the depths of the subjects to which he or she is drawn, for knowledge calls out to those who seek it and takes on a life of its own. Possessing knowledge for knowledge's sake may not be productive in our fast-paced modern world, but encouraging the curiosity and thirst that lead one down a path, so long as that path is not one of self-destruction or harmful to the well-being of others, is to be admired.

Let us also be clear on an important point. A Zentropist is not someone who knows a little about a lot of things, a dilettante masquerading as a subject matter expert. In fact, a Zentropist must have a command of a number of subjects, and certainly should demonstrate expertise or substantial capability in specialized fields. That being said, a Zentropist should also have the wisdom to consult with those more knowledgeable when the situation warrants, and must never overstate or overestimate his or her abilities. To do so would invite the very disharmony and chaos that we seek to overcome.

---

* Adapted from http://zentropist.wordpress.com/2009/02/09/the-zentropist-defined-the-fourth-attribute/. With permission.

The Zentropist exhibits qualities of both the generalist and specialist, which some in the business world have termed a versatilist. Per a press release statement in 2005 regarding the IT sector by Diane Morello, VP of Research at Gartners, Inc., "Versatilists are people whose numerous roles, assignments and experiences are enabling them to synthesize knowledge and context to fuel business value." In many respects, the versatilist as defined by Ms. Morello is a prototypical Zentropist.

It has been famously said that "to know is to know that to know is not to know." This is something that is rather profound on several levels. In admitting our ignorance, our knowledge is revealed, and in seeking to address the very deficiencies that we all know to exist, we discover new things about ourselves that lead to our continued evolution.

And the more a Zentropist evolves, the better he or she can serve not only his or her own needs, but those of others.

And that, ultimately, is what it is all about…

The Zentropist Defined: The Fifth Attribute*

It is perhaps ironic given the times in which we live that we will speak of Character and its crucial role as the fifth of the seven Primary Attributes of the Zentropist. It should come as no surprise to those reading these postings that the world has been in an economic crisis for some time, arising from both individual and collective failings of character, arising from those who seek only to take more than they contribute, and who lack the fortitude to "do the right thing" simply because it is, well, the right thing.

From the Zentropist standpoint, one must seek to develop, "*The character to remain humble while maintaining the confidence, bearing and integrity to transmit the wisdom gained from experience.*" It's a tall order, I realize, and only a liar will tell you that he or she has never fallen short of the mark. As has been observed, we often learn more from our failures than we do from our successes; perhaps this is simply hardwired into the human psyche, some feature set of our genetic programming, whether you view this as a product of some larger Creation guided by a "Great Architect of the Universe (to borrow a Freemasonry expression) or simply the result of random mutations and natural selection over time.

Humility and humbleness are traits that some interpret as weakness, and this is a terrible mistake. The moment we start believing in our own infallibility is the moment that we architect the beginning of our personal disaster. No one has all the answers, and the true Zentropist will accept this without reservation. It is not about faith, or lack thereof. The Zentropist must pursue

---

* http://zentropist.wordpress.com/2009/02/11/the-zentropist-defined-the-fifth-attribute/. With Permission.

Truth as guided by his or her conscience, fully aware that the path one walks is seldom as straight as one might initially believe. For that path will intersect with others, and by different routes the same destination may very well be reached, although the journeys will by definition be different for all.

What is most critical at this juncture for the budding Zentropist is that as the journey progresses, in spite of mistakes made (and some may be whoppers), and for whatever successes both great and small are celebrated, one must draw confidence in his or her ability to make a difference. The Zentropist does not aspire to be some "Superman" as defined by Nietzsche, but rather, seeks to set an example of persistence and perseverance by overcoming shortcomings, by turning former weaknesses into strengths, by leveraging strengths to achieve some greater good.

By moving forward and maintaining one's integrity, by living true to the Primary Attributes which form the code and creed of the Zentropist, one will acquire wisdom which may be used to the benefit of one's self and others.

Some may believe that our journey through life is walked on the precipice of a Great Abyss, which we may choose to acknowledge or not, and that our actions will indeed "echo through time" whether we realize this or not. Whether we gaze into the abyss, and whether or not it looks back are inconsequential; the Zentropist has a responsibility to share his or her gifts, however humble they may be perceived, for in doing so he or she will be rewarded one thousand-fold.

The Zentropist Defined: The Sixth Attribute*

Courage is a trait often spoken of, and perhaps as commonly misunderstood. Courage, or the lack thereof, may or may not expose one to physical harm, but its absence will almost certainly expose one to psychological harm.

John Wayne once famously remarked that "courage is being scared to death and saddling up anyway." Some might debate the Duke's courage off-screen (there's no denying that he embodied it in spades on celluloid), but that little nugget does certainly encapsulate physical courage. Yet this is but one expression of the term.

It is acknowledged by the Zentropist that one must develop "the courage, both intellectual and physical, to seize the initiative, to act in a moral and ethical manner, to inspire others, to exercise good judgment and to endure whatever is necessary to prevail."

Far too often, we lack the courage of our convictions, and find ourselves shirking from a course of action because we perceive it to be unpopular or possibly exposing us to undue ridicule, risk, or danger. The true Zentropist

---

* Adapted from http://zentropist.wordpress.com/2009/02/13/the-zentropist-defined-the-sixth-attribute/. With permission.

cannot abide such shortcomings, at least for long, and will find the inner strength necessary to rise to the occasion. In doing so, guided by a moral compass that is not swayed by the court of public opinion or the self-serving lodestones of greed and selfishness that warp the navigation of some, the Zentropist will serve as an inspiration to those who understand the value of the path taken.

Ernest Hemingway had a great deal of courage, yet ultimately, this was perhaps his undoing, for courage without good judgment becomes needless sacrifice, and this is to be avoided whenever possible. Still, it is instrumental to look at the foreshadowing of his ultimate fate in a passage he famously composed in the classic *A Farewell to Arms*:

> If people bring so much courage to this world the world has to kill them to break them, so of course it kills them. The world breaks every one and afterward many are strong at the broken places. But those that it will not break it kills. It kills the very good and the very gentle and the very brave impartially. If you are none of these you can be sure it will kill you too but there will be no special hurry.

The Zentropist seeks to bend rather than break, but understands that sometimes we must be broken to rebuild ourselves more strongly. In the practice of working on behalf of others, the Zentropist must always have the courage to do right by one's charges, to find the solutions to the best of one's abilities, and to produce results that deliver tangible and hopefully long-lasting value.

I'll leave you with some final words from Mark Twain, one of my favorite authors, who said, "Always do right—this will gratify some and astonish the rest."

So get out there and astonish the masses.

The Zentropist Defined: The Seventh Attribute*

We finally reach the last of the Zentropist's primary attributes. In doing so, we travel full circle, reflecting an observation made by the Lakota medicine man Black Elk, who said, "The power of the world always works in circles, and everything tries to be round."

For those that choose to walk the path of the Zentropist, every day presents new challenges and new opportunities, with the possibility of uncovering fresh insights as well. Although many in the West are more familiar with the Japanese term *Zen* in reference to a particular strain of Buddhist philosophy,

---

* Adapted from http://zentropist.wordpress.com/2009/02/17/the-zentropist-defined-the-seventh-attribute/. With permission.

its origin and roots lie somewhere to the West of Nippon, perhaps in India, although it rose to prominence in China, particularly in its adaptation (along with Taoist teachings) by the monks of the now world famous Shaolin Temple order. In China, it goes by the name Ch'an Buddhism, and is spoken of as "the middle path," which provides some clue to its essential nature.

Many are familiar, at least superficially, with the concepts of Yin and Yang, of opposing forces that cannot exist independently and must operate in harmony and balance each other; for one in excess of the other leads to chaos and disharmony. If the Zentropist is to realize the overarching goal of the path, one must come to terms with the seventh attribute, "the understanding that amid the seeming chaos of the world lies balance and we must seek to maintain this."

There are many who would suggest that it is the very imbalances that manifest in our world that lead to the greatest discord and suffering. Such issues are perhaps best left to another discussion, but there is an underlying truth that our world is one filled with contrasts that operate in apparent harmony regardless of our efforts to change them or otherwise impose our will or desires.

The Zentropist must remain aware at all times that when pursuing a desired outcome, there will be consequences, intentional or not, and these must be carefully monitored, so the net result of our efforts is beneficial rather than harmful. If one accepts the notion that entropy is but a measure of the order and disorder existing within a system, and the premise that chaos is invariably present to one degree or another, finding constructive means to channel the available energy into productive work is paramount.

In many respects, the Zentropist is not unlike the director on a film set, providing the unifying creative vision that is influenced by the collaborative actions of many others, ideally working in harmony but upon occasion, deliberately or not, operating at cross-purposes. It is the responsibility of the Zentropist to intercede in these instances so that balance is restored and that progress continues with as little interruption as possible. The Zentropist, by virtue of working on behalf of others, does not operate in a vacuum, and all actions and behavior must be governed accordingly.

The Zentropist is also wise to keep the following axiom close at hand and to diligently practice it, for the Zentropist by definition must assume the mantle (and burden) of leadership and, in exercising this responsibility, may need to delegate his or her authority. *However, while a leader may delegate authority, a leader can never delegate nor abdicate responsibility or accountability.* As a general rule, Corporate America has shirked this philosophy for years, and the results are all too apparent in the current global financial crisis. Those that pursue personal financial enrichment and material rewards at the expense of all else will inevitably suffer the consequences and reap the whirlwind that their selfish and self-serving desires have spawned.

The leader that embraces the simple yet vital principle above may very well have what it takes to walk the path of the Zentropist.

Do you?

The Creed of the Zentropist*

I believe that this concise phrase, the creed, or motto, of the Zentropist—"The fluent blade cuts cleanly"—penetrates to the essential core of the Zentropist. I also want to pay tribute to the source of this inspiration, which is the novelist Takashi Matsuoka, from a passage in *Cloud of Sparrows* (Dell Publishing, 2003), which reads:

> Words can damage. Silence can heal. Knowing when to speak and when not to speak is the wisdom of sages.
>
> Knowledge can hinder. Ignorance can liberate. Knowing when to know and when not to know is the wisdom of prophets.
>
> Unimpeded by words, silence, knowledge or ignorance, a fluent blade cuts cleanly. This is the wisdom of warriors.

"I believe that the constant practice of the art of Wing Chun will enable me to transcend to a higher mental and physical level." So begins the pledge that has been handed down within Traditional Wing Chun Kung Fu. *Gung Fu* literally means "work performed over time," signifying a lifetime commitment to self-improvement, self-mastery, and the full realization of one's potential.

Practitioners of various martial arts traditions quickly learn that the physical aspects of such training are but one level of understanding, and that the real value of such practice is to embrace the moving meditation, discipline, and life lessons that are intertwined with the physical expression of the art.

For one without the other is an empty vessel, regardless of whether one studies a traditional Eastern system or more modern Eastern or Western variant. Invariably, in the hours spent honing one's physical skills, a transformation occurs, particularly when sparring, when failure to "live in the moment" and "flow like water," to borrow a famous quotation from Bruce Lee, results in the unpleasant consequence of getting hit.

Life is like that. Since we cannot know the future, and we cannot defend without fail from every possible angle of attack, it is inevitable that we will take our hits, and from this reality must spring an attitude that no matter what, we'll keep going and persevere. We all get knocked about and sometimes even knocked down in life, but what separates those who are most

---

* Adapted from http://zentropist.wordpress.com/2009/02/11/the-creed-of-the-zentropist-preview-of-coming-attractions/. With permission.

successful from those who have given up is their willingness to wade back into the fray and apply the lessons learned.

Some of these lessons are embodied in Wing Chun's core principles.

Guard your centerline. Whether in a physical fight or simply going about one's daily routine, you must always be aware of what is most vital to you, and avoid allowing your center to be compromised. If you don't know what is important, and you don't have a solid sense of your center, you will be vulnerable and ultimately directionless.

Don't fight force with force. All too often, our first instinct is to meet strong energy with the same. If we're stronger than the energy we are encountering, we may overwhelm it, but sometimes it is better for us to deflect or release that energy instead and counter on a different path. Within every crisis lies opportunity.

Remain interruptible. While it's important that we commit to a course of action, if we overcommit we lose our balance, unnecessarily exposing our center. We must retain the ability to shift quickly to another path, so when one gate is closed to us, another one opens. The destination does not necessarily change; how we get there does. The ability to adapt to adversity, to turn failure into ultimate success, is what keeps us going in our darkest hours.

And, finally, when obstacles seem most daunting and we question our most basic assumptions, we would do well to remember that "mastery is a path and not a destination."

Zentropism's Applications for Homeland Security*

Needless to say, I firmly believe that the seven primary attributes that are fundamental to the Tao of the Zentropist have a direct bearing on the ability of a civilian (including sworn law enforcement personnel, who in my opinion should *not* be separated out from this grouping) or military operative/agent/ officer to improve the skills necessary to effectively predict, identify, and disrupt potential terror operations. If one thing is abundantly clear, the shocking (at least in the eyes of most Americans) events of September 11, 2001, were caused not only by a colossal failure of intelligence gathering and information sharing among myriad often competing and dangerously bureaucratic civilian and military governmental agencies, but also by an inexcusable failure of imagination. Quite simply, folks that should have known better simply could not fathom the unconventional means that could be employed to

* Adapted from http://zentropist.wordpress.com/2009/02/26/zentropisms-applications-for-homeland-security/. With permission.

sow terror and strike at the "soft underbelly" of a target, namely, the United States, which in the case of the fundamental and malignant interpretations of Islam existing in certain Sunni and Shi'ite traditions, is the very manifestation of corruption and decadence.

One of the most important constructs of the Zentropist approach to life, whether as a tool used in the pursuit of one's occupation or as a guide to self-improvement and mastery, is an appreciation for unconventional thought and the necessity of not becoming beholden to rigid interpretations of data, as well as a marked aversion to bureaucratic group-think and "passing the buck," which, sadly, seem to be the hallmarks of far too many institutions. Those who work in the security consulting/personal protection field understand that the moment one has to draw a weapon to protect a client (arguably one of the last lines of defense), there has already been a certain amount of failure in the system; because if proper planning, including threat assessment and analysis and the resultant preventative measures, was performed prior to the assailant(s) breaching the "inner ring" of the protection circle, then the best efforts to circumvent the undesired action were obviously flawed.

As those who follow such things now know, the 9/11 hijackers could have been disrupted at several junctures in their ramp-up to operational status had the right people been able to put the pieces together. Occam's razor, which states that "all other things being equal, the simplest explanation tends to be the correct one," is a very useful axiom to keep in mind. It is absolutely mind-boggling, for example, that a flight school would not find it odd that students were interested in learning how to take off and fly commercial aircraft, but had little interest in landing. I've been around aviation long enough to hear pilots (at least those that intend to live to fly another day) remark, "Take-off is optional but landing is mandatory."

As much as I personally find the expression "thinking outside of the box" to be repeated *ad nauseam* by those that don't grasp its implications, so as to begin to lose any meaning, it is important to acknowledge that we must never let our preconceived notions, cultural biases, or ignorance and underestimation of the commitments of others deter us from seeing through their eyes, so we might better understand likely behavioral patterns. We must never become so blind to the fact that when our antenna is clearly telling us that the other party is doing X, we fail to address this threat because in our worldview, X is unfathomable and therefore, we falsely conclude that the other party is surely doing Y.

While Sherlock Holmes is a fictional character (to our great loss, in my opinion), his creator, Sir Arthur Conan Doyle, was a keen observer that made Holmes's deductive reasoning and ability to read his environment based on subtle clues feel so real as to border on the preternatural. Yet these skills, and more important, the *attitude* and *discipline* necessary to develop them, are well within the realm of the possible and align quite fittingly with the capabilities of the Zentropist. As the fictional Holmes commented to his fictional friend/companion/biographer John Watson, "When you have eliminated the impossible, whatever remains, however improbable, must be the truth."

One of the challenges of the Zentropist is deciding where the line of impossible begins and accepting that even the improbable must be given credence when all available evidence points in that direction.

You don't build a hypothesis, much less a theory, by manipulating the facts (which includes errors of omission) or observable phenomena to fit your conclusions; you must collect, parse, and analyze all available data and then seek to deduce patterns that explain that which you're witnessing.

This is made all the more important, with the stakes dangerously high, when it comes to maintaining the security for human life, whether individual or collective. Because when you play on the defensive, you need to be right 100% of the time, while the offense potentially only needs to be right once.

Many societies, both Eastern and Western, demonstrate an almost pathological need to classify and categorize things, perhaps in an effort to impose some social order, or at the very least, the artifice of one.

It is hardly breaking news that as I write this, the global economy is undergoing an enormously painful correction or transition, or perhaps even a complete meltdown of the existing order, with all the attendant consequences, ramifications, and "bad juju" that this entails. People at virtually all levels are feeling the impact (and those that have not, as of yet, perhaps should beware of being smug, as the stage is becoming fertile for more contentious expression of dissatisfaction, namely, peaceful or even violent revolution from certain quarters), and the accompanying disharmony and chaotic energy unleashed is not inconsequential.

With job security being an illusion for all but a fortunate few, many people are finding themselves having to actually give meaningful thought to the career paths and choices that they have made, engage in "personal branding" and really try to develop a longer-term career strategy. In doing so, and performing such frank soul searching, those in the working world will often have to contend with being labeled by others as a specialist or generalist, although in recent years, as I previously referenced ("The Zentropist Defined: The Fourth Attribute"), the term *versatilist* has entered the lexicon among savvy workers.

Of these various existing labels, the Zentropist is closest in relation to the definition of a versatilist, although characteristics of both the generalist and specialist will be found. If we examine the concept of Zentropism as a philosophical and ethical framework, the inevitable realization that should follow is that anyone, no matter how lofty or humble his or her occupation is perceived to be, can embrace the primary attributes and utilize these not only for occupational growth, but personal development as well.

By imposing labels of "generalist" or "specialist" on a person, whether this is done by one's self or others, we immediately limit the potential of that human being to evolve and transform. If we dig deeply enough, even the individual widely perceived as fitting the traits of a generalist is apt to have command of some subset of knowledge, no matter how arcane, narrow, or useless, to encroach on the domain of a specialist in that particular field.

It is probably self-evident, but perhaps not to all, that one of the primary criticisms of the generalist is that while this individual knows a little about a lot of things, he or she is unable to go beyond the surface when deeper understanding or command of certain skills or knowledge is called for, and perhaps is even perceived as a bit of a dilettante that flits from one thing to the next, without mastering anything.

Of course, the Zentropist can only smile at the notion that mastery has a fixed goal line that once crossed, can never be exceeded or improved upon.

Conversely, the specialist can be in high demand and well regarded in his or her field, so long as this knowledge is perceived as being valuable to others, but as soon as that knowledge becomes (or is perceived to be) outdated, commonplace, or simply no longer relevant, that individual is seen as a dinosaur or one unable to change with the times and adapt to new circumstances.

Humans should not have expiration dates, beyond the time when our journey in this world is finished. Up until that moment, as the Zentropist understands, barring deterioration of our minds/body/spirit, we retain the capacity to learn and to grow. The Greeks spoke of *gnosis* ("knowledge") and *sophia* ("wisdom") as being highly desirable for individual cultivation, and these are indeed highly worthy goals for us to pursue, so long as we understand that we will never reach the finish line. It is a journey without end, in which the road we travel will reveal many things about ourselves and others.

So rather than allow yourself to be branded by others or, worse, to perceive yourself as falling into the generalist or specialist camp, accept where you are today and commit to embarking upon the path of the Zentropist. If you expand your thinking and refuse to accept the limitations that are often self-imposed or even (all too often unfairly) placed on you by others, you may surprise yourself with what you can accomplish if you "get your mind right" and commit to the path that beckons.

We all have something of value to contribute to this world, and if we accept this not as a burden, but as a sacred or simply meaningful statement of fact, our lives, and the lives of those that intersect with us, no matter the duration of such contact, will be richer for it.

The Elephant in the Room

6

Homeland Security and the Unresolved Challenge of Insider Threats

HOWARD CLARKE

Contents

Introduction

What is the greatest unresolved challenge on the homeland security agenda?
This question sounds like the recipe for an energetic discussion, or a vigorous argument perhaps. I suggest that the following discussion points toward a worthy candidate for "top challenge" status—the problem of insider threats. We might describe this as an elephant in the room type of problem*—difficult to ignore and hard to deal with. Consider the following:

---

* The expression "elephant in the room" refers to a situation where something major is going on; it's on everyone's mind and impossible to ignore—like an elephant in the room. But nobody talks about the elephant because nobody knows what to do about it.

In February 2001 Robert Hanssen, a veteran FBI agent and counterintelligence specialist, was charged with spying for the former Soviet Union, and then Russia, over a fifteen-year period. During this period Hanssen compromised vital intelligence secrets, and provided the Soviet (and later Russian) intelligence service with a large volume of highly classified material detailing aspects of U.S. defense strategy and weapons technology, as well as other highly sensitive information on U.S. espionage and counterintelligence efforts.

In the decades preceding the Hanssen arrest, as well as in the decade following, the media and the courts have continued to document the prolific history of internal conspiracy cases at America's airports, seaports, and land borders. This insider subversion of port and border security mechanisms has facilitated a seemingly endless flow of illicit products and undesirable persons through U.S. ports and borders. At the same time, in recent years and in contemporary headlines, we read of growing concerns over cyber threats and the associated risks to the nation's critical infrastructure (CI).*

Initial reflection will quickly alert us to the obvious fact that threats, whether directed against national interests or particular corporate interests, will be either of the *insider* or the *outsider* variety—or some combination of the two. However, our focus in this chapter is on the insider threat variety.

Further reflection will move us beyond this fairly obvious point—and give us pause to consider not only the serious nature of insider threats, but also the unique advantages that an inside adversary holds and the major ramifications for homeland security of a successful insider attack. Further, we might well consider what viable risk mitigation options are open to us: *What can we do about such threats?* First, though, we need to address important matters of definition and terminology.

Exploring Definitions: What Are Insider Threats?

Insider threats are posed by persons within an organization who choose to exploit the situation by attacking the organization's interests, assets, or other stakeholder interests. This attack does not typically come via bombs and airplanes,† but involves other sinister modes of attack or exploitation. Insiders can include current, former, or contract employees of an organization. Examples of insider threat can be as diverse as the following:

---

* In this chapter, the CI abbreviation denotes critical infrastructure rather than counterintelligence.
† The Fort Dix plot, which had an insider threat component, was envisioned by the conspirators to involve in effect bombs and bullets. Refer to *U.S. v. Duka* (D. N.J.), No. 1:07-CR-00459-RBK, complaint, filed May 7, 2007.

- A worker within a corporation who provides proprietary information to a competitor
- A foreign intelligence agent who has penetrated a U.S. intelligence agency for the purpose of conducting espionage from within the agency
- A spouse who leaks insider information about a partner's business assets to a competitor for some perceived advantage
- A port worker who collaborates with a criminal organization in order to facilitate the smuggling of contraband into the United States

From a security perspective, an insider can be anyone with knowledge of operation or security systems who has unescorted access to facilities or security interests (Biringer et al., 2007). In this sense, an insider threat will likely develop with the involvement of a person(s) who has authorized access to particular information and infrastructure assets or resources.

Insider threat development might involve a relatively passive role (only provides information), or it may result from a more active insider involvement (facilitates entrance or exit of goods or persons, or improperly interferes with business or security processes). A more extreme version of active involvement is also possible (for example, active participation in a violent attack).

We can define the key elements of insider threat as (1) a situation of *trust*, which provides the basis for the rights and privileges accorded an insider, (2) employee *access*—privileged access to knowledge, assets, and systems, in combination with (3) *malevolent intent* of some sort.

Insider threats directed against critical infrastructure and key resources (CIKR) represent a particular concern. In their consideration of the insider threat to critical infrastructure the National Infrastructure Advisory Council (NIAC) recently arrived at the following definition:

> The insider threat to critical infrastructure is one or more individuals with the access and/or inside knowledge of a company, organization, or enterprise that would allow them to exploit the vulnerabilities of that entity's security, systems, services, products, or facilities with the intent to cause harm.

Insider Threats Represent a Crucial Issue in the Homeland Security Agenda

The nexus between homeland security and insider threats is readily apparent. Insider threat agents represent actual or potential adversaries, and they can also function as attack vectors that may be utilized by an outsider.

Insiders with malevolent intent have the capacity to do serious damage to the state, economy, and health and safety of the American public. Even when insiders do not act directly at the bidding or in the interests of terrorist organizations, their activities can undermine the integrity of security arrangements, and they may create or facilitate the exploitation of security vulnerabilities. In any of a number of ways they can also increase the likelihood of a successful terrorist attack against the U.S. homeland or against U.S. interests.

To make this suggested nexus more explicit, consider the definition of homeland security presented in the National Strategy for Homeland Security (2002):

> Homeland security is a concerted national effort to prevent terrorist attacks within the United States, reduce America's vulnerability to terrorism, and minimize the damage and recover from attacks that do occur.

When insider threats manifest themselves in vital spheres such as border security, supply chain security, transportation security, information technology, and telecommunications, the implications can be very serious indeed. The National Strategy for Homeland Security illustrates this point when it states:

> In the food processing and distribution industry, disgruntled or former employees have caused nearly all previous incidents of food tampering, providing a glimpse of what terrorists with insider access might accomplish.

As has been identified in numerous studies and official inquiries, within the realm of border and transportation security, *internal conspiracies** linked to smuggling represent a serious and ongoing threat to homeland security. In these environments, insiders have, and can provide, access to loading docks, cargo shipments, and restricted areas in seaports and airports.

"The transportation organization that is paid to smuggle cocaine today may very well be contracted to smuggle instruments of terror or terrorists tomorrow. Historically these smuggling organizations have easily adapted to law enforcement efforts to detect their activity."

—John P. Clark, Office of Investigations, Bureau of Immigration and Customs Enforcement, Department of Homeland Security, May 2003

Insider Threats and Espionage

The linkage between espionage and utilization of insiders working for government and the military is statistically very strong. Research conducted

---

* An internal conspiracy is a particular manifestation of insider threat and involves collusion between an insider and outsiders in order to achieve some mutual benefit using an unlawful way or unauthorized means. This is a significant problem within border control and transportation sectors.

by Herbig and Wiskoff for the Defense Personnel Security Research Center (PERSEREC) on the subject of espionage against the United States by American citizens for the period 1947–2001* found the following:

- between 1950 and 1975 most cases of espionage by American citizens involved military personnel, involving enlisted military personnel and civilians working for the military
- among civilian spies approximately 25% were employees or government contractors
- one-third of all espionage against the U.S. since 1945 was conducted by persons with security clearances who worked in either the intelligence or communication fields.
- the most successful American spies who have acted against the U.S. came from most of the civilian agencies and military services, and included persons who reflected the full range of access to classified information from the highest security clearance down to no clearance at all.

A second PERSEREC study found that, while there is evidence of persistent attempts by foreign intelligence services to infiltrate US government organizations and to recruit cleared employees for illegal activities, the greater concern is self- initiated espionage activity involving insiders.

Utilization of government agency insiders for espionage purposes can be a relatively cost-effective method of intelligence collection, as it obviates the need for more expensive, resource-intensive collection methods. This factor makes it particularly attractive for those nations that lack satellite and other high-technology collection resources or the budgets to support those resources.

We need also to remember that not all espionage is conducted by agents acting on behalf of nation-states, or on behalf of adversary states, and not all espionage is concerned with national security secrets. Both corporate espionage and economic espionage represent covert endeavors in which insiders represent prized assets.

PERSEREC research also found that seventeen neutral or nonadversary countries had received information from American spies. Herbig and Wiskoff (2002) speculate that this suggests the model of espionage "as a contest between adversaries" is simplistic, and that the value of information obtainable from insider sources is too attractive for even so-called allies to resist.

In 2006 IBM's Global Business Security Index report concluded that as software becomes more secure, computer users would continue to be the

---

* Consider the national security implications if terrorist groups were able to establish control over the thousands of computer networks already infected with the Conficker computer worm.

weak link for companies and organizations. Interestingly, this report also suggested that future trends are likely to include insider attacks in which criminals will persuade users to execute attacks on their organizations rather than rely on external attacks against increasingly secure software.

Case Study: Robert Hanssen—Espionage Insider Threat Personified

On February 20, 2001, Robert Hanssen, a twenty-seven-year FBI agent, was charged with spying for the former Soviet Union, and then Russia.

According to court documents, Hanssen provided the Russian intelligence service with information on "some of the most sensitive and highly compartmented projects in the U.S. intelligence community" as well as details on U.S. nuclear war defenses. In return, the Russians paid him $1.4 million over the period of his espionage activities, including over $600,000 in cash and diamonds and $800,000 deposited in a Russian bank account. Hanssen was finally identified after U.S. authorities obtained his file from a covert intelligence source.

Although Hanssen's motives are unclear, they seem to have included ego gratification, disgruntlement with his FBI employment, and financial need.

Hanssen exploited the FBI's computer systems for classified information to sell and monitored the possibility of investigations that might target him by accessing FBI computer files.

Hanssen's Insider Threat Activities and Modus Operandi

Hanssen's modus operandi included the following:

- Downloaded large quantities of data from the FBI's Automated Case Support System
- Searched within FBI systems to see if they had identified his drop-site locations, and to see if his name had surfaced as an investigation subject
- Installed unauthorized software on his office computer
- Hacked into the computer of a FBI colleague
- Photocopied sensitive FBI documents and walked out with them
- Borrowed a Top Secret document, photocopied it in the backseat of his vehicle, and returned it

With one exception, all his activities involved either technical access, for which he was authorized, or nontechnical methods, such as unauthorized removal of classified material.

Source: Adapted from *Espionage Cases 1975–2004*, Defense Personnel Security Research Center, Monterey, California, December 2004, and RAND Proceedings of March 2004 Workshop: Understanding the Insider Threat, "Presentation: The Robert Hanssen Case."

Insiders, Cyber Threats, and Critical Infrastructure

Major components of the nation's essential and emergency services, as well as its critical infrastructure, rely on the uninterrupted use of the Internet and communications, data, monitoring, and control systems. A successful cyber attack could cripple the highly interdependent critical infrastructure and key resources (CIKR) and trigger cascading effects far beyond the targeted sector and the physical location of the incident. Such an event would also severely disrupt the effective functioning of government and business and would represent a serious threat to national security and the economy.

The previously mentioned NIAC report outlined some of the potentially serious consequences that could arise from a successful CI–level insider threat. These include:

- Disruption of CI services within a particular geographic area or sector
- Large-scale economic loss associated with physical damage and financial loss, financial failure of a CIKR service provider, loss of critical intellectual property or technology, and reduced ability to maintain delivery of CI services
- Adverse psychological impacts, including loss of public confidence, which could trigger further large-scale economic loss, and loss of life or compromise to public health

A variety of state and nonstate actors threaten the security of the nation's cyber infrastructure. These include terrorists, who are known to exploit the Internet for communication, recruitment, training, and propaganda purposes, as well as hostile foreign governments that have the capability to launch attacks on the informational and physical elements of the cyber infrastructure. The additional member of this unholy trinity of threat groupings is cyber criminals who threaten the economy, the profitability of corporations, and the personal information of individuals. These cyber criminals could well pose a heightened threat if wittingly or unwittingly recruited by foreign intelligence or terrorist groups.*

---

* Consider the implications if terrorist groups were able to establish control over the thousands of computer networks already infected with the Conficker computer worm.

In 2006, IBM's Global Business Security Index report concluded that, as software becomes more secure, computer users would continue to be the weak link for companies and organizations. Interestingly, this report also suggested that future trends are likely to include insider attacks in which criminals will persuade users to execute attacks on their organizations rather than rely on external attacks against increasingly secure software.

A congressional panel warned in November 2008 that China had stepped up its cyber espionage efforts against the U.S. and was stealing "vast amounts" of sensitive information from U.S. computer networks. Soon after, in December 2008, the Commission on Cyber security reported: "Cybersecurity is now one of the major national security problems facing the United States." Then, in April 2009, The *Wall Street Journal* reported that the U.S. power grid was vulnerable to cyber attack and had been 'infiltrated' by foreign spies. The report claimed that software had been left behind that could shut down the electric grid.

Insiders and Threats to the Integrity of Ports and Borders

Phil Williams has argued that "while the insider threat has received a lot of attention in the world of computer or cyber crime, it requires similar attention in the world of freight-forwarding, shipping and even government" (Williams, 2007). Insiders in government or security agencies, working at ports of entry, can provide false authentication that goods and persons have been checked when in fact they have not.

There is a long history of such insider threats at U.S. ports and borders (as illustrated in the boxed text below). In 2000 the Interagency Commission on Crime and Security in U.S. Seaports reported that internal conspiracies "present the most serious challenge to drug interdiction efforts at seaports because they can thwart traditional Customs Service targeting and examination processes."* These conspiracies involve illicit activities committed by organized criminal groups working in concert with corrupt individuals employed in seaports or within the transportation industry.

"Staff can be bribed to ignore criminality or paid large sums to assist in drug trafficking or theft. Once compromised, such employees may be unable to stand up to terrorists. Any airport staff who are not thoroughly background checked and routinely searched are potential weak links."

—An independent review of airport security for the Government of Australia (The Wheeler Report), September 2005

---

* ICCS, 2000, iv.

The insider threats at ports and borders are not by any means restricted to governmental and security agencies. Transportation sector employees involved in the movement of people and goods, as well as other workers within the logistics supply chain, also feature in internal conspiracies.

A key element of the cargo security challenge is the fact that an insider or front company can simply establish as a procedural norm that complies with Customs requirements or border and transportation security rules. Contents aside, a malevolent or illegitimate shipment that does not deviate from this norm is unlikely to raise red flags. Williams comments that "when compliance becomes both routine and expected, the prospects for exploiting the trust that has been established are heightened" (Williams, 2007). Adversaries can also readily acquire knowledge of Customs risk profiling methods and priorities, particularly if there is insider involvement.

Case Study: Internal Conspiracies at Ports and Borders

Corruption and internal conspiracy activities have long been associated with port and border control activities. The problem is *not* unique to the United States—it is a universal phenomenon, due largely to the nature of transactions involved with processing people and goods at the ports of entry. Having said this, and given the enormous investment in funds, technology, and human resources at the nation's borders, one hopes that this problem can be resolved to an acceptable degree.

In fall 2000 the Interagency Commission on Crime and Security in U.S. Seaports published a damning report on the level of criminality and associated security vulnerabilities in the nation's seaports. The commission examined crime and security at nineteen major U.S. seaports and concluded in one of its key findings that internal conspiracies presented the most serious challenge to drug interdiction at seaports because they can thwart Customs efforts.

An earlier project conducted at the Port of Miami found that narcotics smuggling involving port workers accounted for roughly 70% of the total of seaport drug seizures during the period under study, and further, that internal conspiracies involving port employees were responsible for 60% of the cocaine and 80% of the marijuana smuggled into the United States through the Port of Miami.

The preceding examples, while historically dated, do highlight a major homeland security vulnerability that has not yet been effectively resolved, despite enhancements in port security, more rigorous background screening of port employees, and the instigation of proactive investigations to target these activities. Although security at all U.S. ports of entry has been tightened considerably in recent years, there is ample evidence that the internal conspiracy threat at U.S. seaports remains an active concern.

In 2004, the State of New Jersey Commission of Investigation Report on Organized Crime found that internal conspiracies involving airport employees continued to be a problem at Newark Liberty Airport, particularly with regard to drug and contraband smuggling. This report also commented that smuggling groups had penetrated Customs brokerage operations—a particular concern given that these "are the people who are … legitimately involved in getting cargo on the pier and through Customs" (State of New Jersey Commission of Investigation, 2004).

In March 2007 a high-profile security breach at the Orlando International Airport in Florida introduced an even higher level of public and governmental scrutiny to the issue of insider threats at airports. The breach involved two airline employees who smuggled fourteen firearms and 8 pounds of marijuana onboard a Delta Airlines aircraft bound for San Juan, Puerto Rico.

The situation is little better at the land borders. Corruption has become increasingly pervasive on the U.S. border with Mexico. There have been convictions of corrupt officials on the southwest border who had accepted bribes to facilitate the passage of people or drugs (Pomfret, 2006). It was also reported in October 2006 that since 2004 at least two hundred public employees had been charged with helping to move drugs and people across the border while thousands more cases of corruption were reported to be under investigation (Vartabedian et al., 2006).

Insider Threats and the Global Economic Downturn

Recent reporting has highlighted the increased risk posed by insider threats driven by the worsening global economic situation. The faltering U.S. economy has resulted in increased jobs cuts and other manifestations of corporate downsizing. Consequently, security analysts are warning companies to be especially vigilant about protecting their data and networks against disgruntled employees.

> "That threat greatly increases at times when companies are laying off staff, cutting back on raises and bonuses, deferring promotions, consolidating operations and outsourcing work to save money."*

Companies surveyed in a recent McAfee study estimated that they lost an average of $4.6 million worth of intellectual property in 2008. The research also found that more and more vital digital information, such as intellectual

---

* Australian Homeland Security Research Centre, Recession impacts on the security industry and crime.

property and sensitive customer data, is being transferred between companies and continents—and lost. Of the companies surveyed, 42% assessed laid-off employees as the single biggest threat to their intellectual property and other sensitive data that they faced in the current economic climate.*

A recent edition of the Australian Homeland Security Research Centre's National Security Briefing Note reported that the economic downturn is having an impact on the nature and size of IT crime. This report refers to the increase in white collar crime associated with the increased layoffs of IT professionals who it suggests are:

- stealing data and selling it online
- setting up botnets which are rented out
- producing hacking toolkits for sale
- setting up criminal sites for information sharing and commercial sale[†]

Which Manifestations of Insider Threat Should Concern Us Most?

It is difficult to give a definitive answer to this question—and the answer depends on how we measure the adverse consequences from an insider betrayal and key variables in a successful insider threat incident, such as identity of the target, level of attack success, etc.

It is obvious, however, that an effectively operationalized insider threat action in any of the preceding spheres of national life could have a devastating impact—whether measured in terms of direct public harm, economic damage, severe impairment in the functioning of government, or other harm to national security or the national interest.

In gauging the severity of insider threat actions, conventional wisdom suggests that we might take into account such factors as:

- Adverse public safety impacts, harm to persons
- Damage to national security and the integrity of government functions
- Business disruption and loss of business assets
- Damage to the economy—national, regional, local
- Adverse impact on CI and key resources
- CI interdependency impacts and disruption of vital services
- Loss of public confidence in government

---

* McAfee, Unsecured Economies.
† Australian Homeland Security Research Centre, Recession impacts on the security industry and crime.

If, for discussion purposes, we use these particular measurement criteria, and depending on the severity of a particular insider threat attack, we can readily see how insider threat manifestations such as espionage, cyber threats, and terrorist-driven port and border penetration incidents could have a devastating impact on the nation and on vital aspects of national life.

The Challenge of Dealing with Insider Threats

As is well illustrated by the Robert Hanssen case, insider threats are difficult to guard against because the perpetrators are *on the inside and are trusted*. Insiders are well positioned to exploit vulnerabilities—typically having both knowledge and access advantages. As such, they pose a greater threat compared to outsiders, given their freedom to choose the time, place, and method of attack.

Mitigating the risk posed by the insider threat is problematic for a number of reasons. We can agree with Biringer et al. (2007), who observe that the challenges include:

> social and labor union sensitivities, and the legitimate access rights granted to authorized insiders, which can allow access to critical assets, sensitive business processes and security infrastructure.

There is also a real danger, in corporate environments, of underreporting or nonreporting of insider offenses. Concerns over corporate reputation and associated commercial considerations can adversely impact preferred reporting and risk mitigation outcomes. This can also result in a lowered awareness within affected work environments and the development of false perceptions regarding the risk posed by insider threats.

The NIAC study, previously mentioned in this chapter, developed an extensive list of additional factors that make insider threat mitigation difficult. These include:

- *More research needed on insider threats*: Need for more research on insider threat mitigation options, particularly in the technology field.
- *Inadequate education and awareness*: Current levels of critical infrastructure owner-operator understanding and awareness of the insider threat are uneven, and in many cases inadequate.
- *Challenges in management and maintenance of employee identification*: It has become increasingly difficult for operators, particularly those with global operations, to conduct effective identity management, and the growth in business outsourcing is an added complication.

- *Uneven background screening practices*: There are varying levels of acceptance and implementation of employee background screening across the critical infrastructure sectors.
- *Technology challenges*: Technology systems that manage physical and cyber security often function as silos and not interoperably. There is inadequate fusion of insider incident data, and there is a rapid proliferation of technology-based threat avenues open to insiders.
- *Cultural and organizational obstacles*: These include disconnects between key internal stakeholders (security, IT, legal, corporate management) and corporate mind-set challenges (e.g., tendency to unquestioned trust in long-term employees).

As we will see, an awareness of the nature and extent of insider threats, in addition to an enhanced understanding of motivational factors and facilitating conditions, can contribute to risk mitigation.

Insider Threats: Lessons Learned

According to the PERSEREC studies, "one-fourth of known American spies experienced a personal life crisis (such as a divorce, death of someone close, or a love affair gone awry) in the months before they decided to attempt espionage." In many cases of insider espionage, colleagues or friends of the perpetrators *failed to act* on indicators and the espionage activities went on for longer then necessary before detection. This finding demonstrates a key indicator that can be constructively addressed. As suggested by other researchers this "failure to act" risk factor can be mitigated to some extent through appropriate awareness and education initiatives.

The Insider Threat Study conducted by the U.S. Secret Service in conjunction with Carnegie Mellon University's CERT Coordination Center (Cappelli et al., 2005) (USSS/CMU-CERT) developed a number of important insights regarding insider threats related to CI sectors. Pertinent points from that research included:

- *Motivational issues*: Negative work-related events triggered the majority of insiders' actions.
- *Indicators*:
  - The majority of the insider attacks were only detected when a noticeable irregularity had developed in the information system or when a system became unavailable.
  - Most insiders however had previously "acted out" in a concerning manner in the workplace and some warning signs were evident to either co-workers, family or friends

- *Modus operandi*:
  - The majority of insiders planned their activities in advance.
  - Insiders used unsophisticated methods for exploiting systemic vulnerabilities in applications, processes, and procedures, but relatively sophisticated attack tools were also employed.
  - The majority of insiders compromised computer accounts, created unauthorized backdoor accounts, or used shared accounts in their attacks.
  - Remote access was used to carry out the majority of the attacks.
- *Precipitating conditions*: When hired, the majority of insiders were granted system administrator or privileged access, although less than half of all of the insiders had authorized access at the time of the incident.
- *Consequence and impact*: Insider activities caused organizations financial losses, negative impacts to their business operations, and damage to their reputations.

The preceding insights emerged from a study that had its focus on computer system sabotage. Can we, however, correlate them with lessons learned in other spheres of insider threat activity?

The NIAC study had two phases—the first being to define the insider threat to CI, and to explore the scope and dynamics of this threat. The second phase specifically examined opportunities for risk mitigation through enhanced employee-screening processes. While personnel security is a well-established field within sensitive areas of government employment, for example within the defense and national security sectors, this is not the case in the CI sectors, which are largely controlled by private operators.

Consequently, having considered the nature and dynamics of insider threats, the NIAC study reviewed options for improving employee-screening processes.

The close linkage between public and private sectors is particularly evident at this point. CI operators require a capacity to place appropriate trust in their employees and the means to ensure that this can do done effectively. Given the crucial significance of CIKR for U.S. homeland security, government and the public depend upon the operators in this field to place this trust carefully as well.[*] The potential for cascading failures across CI sectors is particularly troubling, and extends the implications of a security failure beyond a single operator.

With the seriousness of the stakes clearly identified and articulated, the NIAC report then proceeded to identify common elements in a quality screening approach that might be applied within CIKR sectors. The report noted the crucial importance of legislative impediments and enablers.

---

[*] NIAC, 26.

In brief, the NIAC found the following to be the case for employee screening within CIKR sectors:

- current legislation in the U.S. enables some sectors to screen their employees effectively while leaving other vulnerable
- CIKR sectors vary so widely that an across-the-board, government-applied screening process would not adequately address the problem
- CIKR operators have a need to be able to access criminal history records in order to be able to make effective risk determinations and associated determinations.

More broadly, the NIAC study identified opportunities to reduce insider threats to CIKR operators by implementing constructive changes in the following areas:

- education and awareness: including the key role of government in providing leadership, enabling and subject matter knowledge in these areas
- employee screening
- technology policies
- information sharing
- more research and development of guidance products

A heightened awareness of the nature and extent of insider threats, and an enhanced understanding of key motivational factors and facilitating conditions behind these threats, can contribute to enhanced risk mitigation efforts. Further to comments by NIAC on this subject, Shelley Kirkpatrick, in her research on insider threats, pushes the "more research" button firmly. Her point is that we do not have enough quality case study material on the varying insider threat motivational factors which impact different sectors and that more research is needed on this.[*]

Shelley Kirkpatrick has suggested that chief security officers need to develop more detailed insider threat profiles based on incidents, motives and people.[†] We caution to add however, that for this suggestion to bear fruit there needs to be a more effective integration of data on insider threats, so that these profiles are based upon the complete and up-to-date information.

Kirkpatrick's analysis provides an interesting perspective on the variability of insider threat motivational factors across different sectors. She has observed:

---

[*] Shelley Kirkpatrick, Refining Insider Threat Profiles, 2.
[†] Ibid, 1.

- conventional wisdom equates insider threat with employees who are driven either by disgruntlement or greed, however she argues that this is only part-truth
- certain sectors are more prone to attacks by disgruntled insiders
- in contrast to findings in the banking and finance sectors, the most frequently reported motive in insider attacks in the CI sector was revenge, triggered by some negative work-related event

Kirkpatrick's findings provide a useful roundup of the key thoughts we can derive from the collective research conducted on insider threats. She comments*:

> By increasing awareness that numerous types of insider threats exist, practitioners and researchers can begin to identify indicators or "red flags" of each type. Examples of new indicators of potential threats may include an awareness of employees, whose career aspirations have not been met, frequent trips to foreign countries, and requests to work late shifts. Companies need to reconsider their pre-employment screening practices and managerial awareness training practices as well as how their human resources, legal and security functions can best work together to effectively address insider threats.

Concluding Remarks

Much progress has been in understanding the dynamics of insider threats in recent years. As suggested in the preceding discussion, progress has been uneven and certain areas of vulnerability are difficult to effectively address. Significant challenges remain in key areas such as IT-related insider threats and internal conspiracies at ports and borders. The rapid rate of technology change, the increasing reliance of modern organizations on high-tech processes and the growing sophistication of technology use by employees will continue to place demands on security management and insider threat mitigation in this field. The significant criminal activity drivers behind internal conspiracies at ports and borders will continue to make this a problem that is difficult to manage.

On a more positive note, the studies that we have highlighted in this discussion, along with other similar research, do provide hopeful signs for a way forward. Valuable insights and opportunities have been identified in regard to mitigating the insider threat challenge. These include:

- Organizational and cultural impediments that need to be addressed
- Awareness and educational initiatives

* Ibid, 9.

- The vital importance of public-private partnership collaboration and development of key initiatives in this direction
- Legislative initiatives
- New-employee screening initiatives

As an example of the effective utilization of insights developed through insider threat studies, the Defense Intelligence Agency developed a guide* to help its staff understand potential espionage indicators by insiders and their responsibility in reporting issues that cause concern in this area. These guidelines were informed in part by the PERSEREC studies referenced in this chapter and they address two important problem areas: lack of employee understanding as to what constitutes "suspicious" and reportable activities, and the precise nature of required reporting procedures.

The protection of American cyberspace has become a national priority. A number of key government pronouncements have emphasized the importance of public-private partnerships in securing the nation's CI and improving national cyber security.

The emphasis on informed, whole-hearted collaboration between key public and private partners in addressing insider threats is vital. Perhaps we can get this particular "elephant" out of the room and into a setting that is suitable, safe and comfortable for all concerned.

Suggested Reading

Cappelli, D., Keeney, M., Kowalski, E., Moore, A., and Randazzo, M. 2004. *Insider threat study: Illicit cyber activity in the banking and finance sector.* Pittsburgh, PA: Carnegie Mellon University.

Department of Homeland Security. 2006. *National infrastructure protection plan.* Washington, DC: U.S. Government Printing Office.

Fussell, E. 2004, March. Security breaches are real. *InTech.*

IBM. 2006, January. Press release on Global Business Security Index report. http://www-03.ibm.com/press/us/en/pressrelease/19141.wss (accessed April 22, 2009).

Interagency OPSEC Support Staff. 2004. *Intelligence threat handbook.* Operations Security Information Series. www.fas.org/irp/threat/handbook (accessed April 22, 2009).

McAfee, Inc. 2009. *Unsecured economies: Protecting vital information.* Santa Clara, CA.

McNicholas, M. 2008. *Maritime security: An introduction.* Burlington, MA: Butterworth–Heinemann.

Noonan, T., and Archuleta, E. 2008, April. *The National Infrastructure Advisory Council's final report and recommendations on the insider threat to critical infrastructure.*

* Accessed at www.ncix.gov/archives/docs/Your_Role_in_Combating_the_Insider_Threat. pdf

Office of the Inspector General. 2007, September. *Review of the FBI's progress in responding to the recommendations in the Office of the Inspector General Report on Robert Hanssen*. Special Report.

Purpura, P. P. 2007. *Terrorism and homeland security: An introduction with applications*. Burlington, MA: Butterworth-Heinemann.

RAND National Security Research Division. 2004. *Understanding the insider threat: Proceedings of a March 2004 workshop*.

Rasmussen, Gideon T. 2006, August. Insider Risk Management Guide. *TechTarget*. http://www.gideonrasmussen.com/article-13.html.

White House. 2003, February. *The national strategy to secure cyberspace*.

References

Australian Homeland Security Research Centre. 2009, March. Recession impacts on the security industry and crime. *National Security Briefing Note*.

BBC News Online, February 10, 2009, http://news.bbc.co.uk/2/hi/technology/7880695.stm

Biringer, B. E., Matalucci, R. V., and O'Connor, S. L. 2007. *Security risk assessment and management*. Hoboken, NJ: John Wiley & Sons.

Cappelli, D., Keeney, M., Kowalski, E., Moore, A., Shimeal, T., and Rogers, S. 2005. *Insider threat study: Computer system sabotage in critical infrastructure sectors*. Pittsburgh, PA: Carnegie Mellon University.

Defense Personnel Security Research Center. 2004, September. *Espionage Cases 1975–2004*, Monterey.

Herbig and Wiskoff, 2002, July. *Espionage Against the United States by American Citizens*, 74.

Interagency Commission on Crime and Security in U.S. Seaports. 2000. *Report of the Interagency Commission on Crime and Security in U.S. Seaports*. Washington, DC.

Kirkpatrick, S. 2008, September. Refining Insider Threat Profiles.

National Infrastructure Advisory Council. 2008, April. *Final report and recommendations on the insider threat to critical infrastructures*.

Office of Homeland Security, 2002, July. *National Strategy for Homeland Security*.

Pomfret, J. 2006. Bribery at border worries officials. *Washington Post*, July 15.

State of New Jersey Commission of Investigation. 2004, May. *The changing face of organized crime in New Jersey: A status report*.

Vartabedian, R., Serrano, R. A., and Marosi, R. 2006. The long, crooked line: Rise in bribery tests integrity of U.S. border. *Los Angeles Times*, October 23.

Williams, P. 2007, August. Terrorism, organized crime, and WMD smuggling: Challenge and response. *Strategic Insights*, Vol. VI, Issue 5.

Thinking Locally, Acting Globally

7

Resurgent Islamism, Transnational Objectives, and Regional Instability

KEELY M. FAHOUM

Contents

The resurgence of Islamism has traversed a path of local, regional, and global interaction. The current nature of resurgent Islamism is the product of an evolutionary process adapting and responding to stimuli from local and global sources. In order to understand the trajectory of contemporary Islamism, it is necessary to address the historical context in which particular Islamist groups molded objectives, strategy, and tactics.

The challenge in addressing Islamism is that it is not a monolithic ideal that can be broken down into clear moving parts. It is a conglomeration of personal and political motivations, religious framing/narrative building, and spotty organizational opportunities challenged by a lack of wider Arab or Muslim unity. As Islamism developed within its own local enclaves, the world was simultaneously connecting and the local space in which Islamists could organize was rapidly shrinking.

In this chapter, I will first discuss the role of resurgent Islamism in historical context, examining the emergence of anticolonial Islamism, the rise of secular nationalism (and subsequent repression of religious resistance), and the reemergence of Islamism as a transnational anti-Western effort. Second, I will argue that resurgent anti-Western Islamism has moved away from local and transnational concerns and has become a regional effort to reshape the Middle East and, in effect, has eclipsed both local and transnational grievances.

The Rise of Anticolonial Islamism: The Islamic Revival and Resistance against the West

Nineteenth-century colonialism shaped economic, social, and political development throughout the world, but particularly within the Middle East. Anti-imperialist movements took shape under the cloak of Islam as a reaction to what was seen as complete public sector domination by British and French colonialists. European colonizers pressed ideals of secularism, pluralism, individual liberties, human rights, and to some extent, democracy on their colonized territories with little thought of how to assimilate them into the society in terms the given population would understand.* Khurshid Ahmad argues that there are four consequences directly related to the impact of colonial rule that are necessary for an understanding of contemporary Islamic resurgence.† First was secularization of the state and its political, economic, and social institutions. Second was a new pattern of Western dominance, not just by political rule but through basic institutional changes within the colonized countries and their relationship with the outside world, resulting in a dependency on the West. Third, the dissection of education into secular and modern versus religious and traditional resulted in the division of society into two groups: modern, secular elites and traditional, religious leadership. The fourth consequence was a crisis of leadership. Ahmed asserts that the traditional leadership of the Muslim society was "systematically destroyed" and replaced by a foreign political leadership who did not possess the confidence and trust of the people.‡ These four consequences can all be observed in the case of Egypt before World War II.

Egypt became a *de facto* British colony (protectorate), and although they allowed Egyptians to maintain some level of day-to-day control, British

---

* Aslan, Reza, *No God but God: The Origin, Evolution and Future of Islam* (New York: Random House, 2005), 222–23.
† Ahmad, Khurshid, "The Nature of Islamic Resurgence," in *Voices in Resurgent Islam*, ed. John L. Esposito (London: Oxford University Press, 1983), 218.
‡ Ahmad, 218–19.

officials, military members, teachers, and civil affairs personnel dominated the Egyptian government. The disproportionate representation and institutional control created a separate and unequal environment that fostered resentment by the Egyptian population against what they viewed as the British colonialists' cultural superiority.* The blended political system was viewed by many Egyptians as corrupt and driven primarily by selfish interests.† Although religion played an important role in society, Egyptian political and intellectual elites began to move away from customary practices and beliefs associated with Islam and instead adopted Western modes of dress and social interaction. To anticolonial Islamist thinkers such as Muhammad Abduh, Rashid Rida, and Jamal al-Din 'al-Afghani, this Westernization of the Egyptian elite generated a desire to bring the true Islam back to Egyptian social and political life. Jamal al-Afghani developed a strong sense of anti-imperialism and became the first voice of anti-imperialism in the Muslim world. To understand the character of anticolonial Islamism, it is necessary to review the contributions of one of its most influential pioneers, Hasan al-Banna. He is credited with starting the Muslim Brotherhood, an organization that has had an enormous impact on contemporary, postnationalist era Islamism.

Al-Banna gave a voice and identity to the early Egyptian Islamist movement. He attributed Muslim weakness and vulnerability to several issues: struggles for power, divisions within the religion over benign issues, indulgence of the elite in the decadence of the West, rule by non-Arabs (Turks or Persians) who never experienced or lived by true Islam, lack of interest in practical science, and complete submission to authority.‡ He mobilized a population of disenchanted Egyptian Muslims and brought Islam in from the cold, secular niche it had been relegated to as a result of the Europeanization of Egypt. Al-Banna bore witness to the struggling nationalist ideologies and the subjugation of Islam to more secular positions within the Egyptian society.

From al-Banna's perspective, since the time of Prophet Muhammad's death in 632, Muslim society was sliding further away from its true role as the axis for political, economic, and social life. He was frustrated by what he interpreted as de-evolution of Islamic ideology at the hands of Western influence. He believed that the subjugation of Muslims to European powers was an outgrowth of a departure from the straight path of true Islam. Al-Banna demonized the economic ties between European powers and Muslim societies and felt that the yoke of indebtedness to Western countries had choked

---

* Cleveland, William, *A History of the Modern Middle East* (Boulder, CO: Westview Press, 2004), 105.
† Commins, David, "Hasan al-Banna, 1906–1949," in *Pioneers of Islamic Revival*, ed. Ali Rahnema (London: Zed Books Ltd., 1994), 127.
‡ Ibid., 133.

the breath of Islam out of Egyptian life. He did not lay the entire weight of blame at the feet of the foreign invader; rather, he also placed responsibility with the scholars of al-Azhar University in Cairo, who were committed to teaching Islam and its true meaning to Muslims.[*] He felt that they did not arm Egyptian citizens with the knowledge and moral rectitude to withstand the assault by Western immorality. Al-Banna's Islamic ideology permeated all aspects of Egyptian life. His ideas were most influential because they integrated politics and religion into a digestible equation for Egyptians who were frustrated and bitter at the Europeanization of their country. For al-Banna, the evolution of Islamic ideology progressed through two main avenues: politics and religion. Islamism established "pillars of communal identity" for the Arab public to rally around as a strategy to resist European colonization and to create a unified, positive identity.[†]

The dominance of the West and secularization of Egypt propelled Muslims to ask themselves why and how the West could contribute to the decay of their pious life and deprive them of their past heritage. Change was perceived as a dangerous prospect and was resisted vehemently by most anticolonial Islamists. Their strategy in dealing with Western encroachment on Muslim values can be described as "protective resistance."[‡] There were efforts to isolate and withdraw from any process of Westernization and an effort to preserve and protect the Muslim legacy, including cultural, intellectual, and institutional strategies.[§] These same elements can be seen in contemporary Islamist efforts to resist Western influence.

The Decline of Anticolonial Islamism and the Rise of Secular Nationalism

As secular nationalism rose, anticolonial Islamism fell. The caliphate had been removed from power in 1924 and the institutions of Islam were constantly bombarded by secularism. Regionalism struggled to establish legitimacy by linking a constructed nationalist mythology to a pre-Islamic past.[¶] In Syria, Antun Sa'adah, a Lebanese Christian who founded the Syrian Social Nationalist Party in Beirut, reminisced about Greater Syria's tie to Phoencia and resisted unification with other Arab states.[**] For Sa'adah, a separate non-Arab identity transcended pressure from other Christian or

---

[*] Ibid., 134.
[†] Cleveland, 234.
[‡] Ahmad, 21.
[§] Ibid.
[¶] Ibid.
[**] Ibid.

Muslim Arab states and secured itself firmly to the chosen historical narrative of the Phoenicians.

Islamism was shunned and marginalized in favor of symbols of Arabness. The idea of Arab nationalism was vague and indeterminate. It served more as a feeling and survived the eventual decline of nationalism. Islamic solidarity was not completely lost but took a backseat to the pursuit for a wider Arab identity. The struggle, it seemed, was to find the best vehicle by which to resist Western domination and imperialism, yet still propel Arab society forward into the same modern playing field as the rest of the world. The connection between Islam and Arab unity had not yet surfaced. Nationalism spread as an idea of "imagined community" by which people identified themselves as members of a theoretical society that in some way joined them to strangers.* Pan-Islamism encountered problems overcoming sectarian differences to achieve religious solidarity. Groups of nationalists in the Middle East argued that religious revival was incompatible with modernization.† Nationalists sought to battle European colonizers with pan-Arabism rather than pan-Islamism. However, Islam was never completely removed from nationalism; it was still a fundamental part of being a Muslim.

Secular nationalism was the context in which Arab rulers under European mandates attempted to fashion separate identities between regimes, establishing flags, anthems, and symbols that emphasized the inimitable nature of the new states. State formation within the Middle East was not an organic response to the growth of capitalism but an inorganic process based on the needs of colonial powers. The policies of the mandates were not looking to enable democracy but instead facilitated dependence and created situations that benefited the colonial nation and hindered independent development of agriculture or industry beyond that which they could control. The process of state formation occurred by, with, and through colonialism.

Three types of colonialism affected the Middle East: direct (French in Syria, Lebanon, and Tunisia), indirect (British in Jordan and Iraq), and settler (Israeli in Palestine and French in Algeria). All colonialists used minorities in key positions and built up respective armies that would enter the equation later on to destabilize the postcolonial government. In the end, colonialism weakened the process of state formation and set the new states of the Middle East on the course for conflict and susceptible to future manipulation. Power was solidified and a large-scale peasantry was created. The rise of landed elites was a process that occurred only after state formation. The local elites wanted to consolidate their own local bases of power while consistently striving to please the Europeans. For these elite, the idea of pan-Arabism did not

---

* Ernst, Carl W., *Following Muhammad, Rethinking Islam in the Contemporary World* (Chapel Hill, NC: University of North Carolina Press, 2003), 203.
† Aslan, 233.

overthrow their own determination to retain control or power and carefully positioned local allies as a safety net in case the Europeans withdrew. It was during the 1950s that monarchies were replaced by military officers who emerged from the lower or middle social classes and who were motivated by nationalism and a desire to gain military superiority over Israel.* Political affiliations were no longer based on religion or internal village dynamics. Instead, nationalism emerged from a feeling of being threatened, the absence of a felt identity, and lack of state-consolidated institutions. Nationalism in the Middle East preceded state building, which was opposite of what occurred in Europe.

Even when the Europeans finally left the Middle East, they did not give up complete control or influence over the governments they left in power. When the world entered the Cold War, the Middle East became a staging ground for by-proxy wars and covert support for Arab regimes in the form of economic assistance and military weapons. The United States and Soviet Union effectively split the region into areas of influence, and countries that chose to avoid another linkage to the West sided with the Soviet Union.† Regimes became more and more authoritarian and state bureaucracy expanded prolifically to the point that it hindered any form of growth or true democracy.

Islamism, although not dominating the political scene, quietly grew in strength and influence. By the late 1940s, the Muslim Brotherhood boasted that membership exceeded five hundred thousand.‡ The Egyptian government began repressing and killing Islamist leaders, and eventually the two came to loggerheads over violence against foreigners and an Islamic vision for the state. A military coup in the early 1950s put Gamal Abd al-Nasser in power and initiated an era of pragmatic nationalism and unaffiliated ideological orientation. The Free Officers organization existing in secret within the Egyptian military envisioned an end to British colonialism and removal of Egyptian sympathizers. The goals of the Free Officers were not strikingly different than those of the Islamists; however, the two groups began to compete for public support, and eventually Nasser outlawed the brotherhood after an assassination attempt. The new Egyptian government under Nasser balked against the old social, economic, and political order. Land reform became the cornerstone of his rule, but also abrogated the old constitution in favor of a document that called for a strong army and an end to imperialism and feudalism.§

Syria also played an important role in the development of nationalism and Islamism. The Muslim Brotherhood in Syria developed from the middle class, who kept themselves separated from any economic dependence on

---

* Gerges, 274.
† Ibid.
‡ Ibid., 302.
§ Ibid., 308.

the government and who worked as tradesmen by day.* Students and members of the intellectual class also joined the brotherhood, and the nature of the organization varied with its respective geographical centers. The group in Aleppo became the most active center for the movement and was the foundation for grievances against the French. Post–World War I brought a significant change in the nature of the trading class because of the influx of Armenians and the detachment of the port city of Alexandretta, which caused the Muslim trading class great difficulty while the Christians were able to prosper through connections with European markets.† With the rise of pan-Arabism, support for the nationalist movement rivaled that of the brotherhood. The Islamist group garnered success in the urban areas of the country, but lacked widespread support from the rural areas. The Syrian Ba'athists enjoyed support from the countryside and organized the peasants into a more class-conscious group, bringing the peasants into the political life of the country.‡ Arab socialist leaders worked to align the interests of the peasants with the struggle for a nation under Arab unity. Akram Hurani argued that the welfare of the Arab people was tied to the fate of the peasants, and thus the latter's emancipation was necessary to cement the future of a wider Arab movement.§ He saw value in the theory that the Arab defeat in the 1948 conflict against Israel was attributed to social influence over the military and solidified a theoretical link between the agrarian class and the national movement. Hurani encouraged his sympathizers to enter the military, which would become a protectorate of the peasant movement and which would propel the Alawis to a strategically important position within the Syrian government.¶

Relations between Arab states fomented an effort at expanding the "Arab circle of identity" and the creation of the United Arab Republic (UAR) in 1958. Egypt and Syria united under the banner of Arabness and established the Republic capital at Cairo. Citizenship was changed from Syrian or Egyptian to simply, Arab, and the states were referred to as Arab Territory. Yemen also joined for a short time. This was the first time the new states worked to form a solidified identity based on a secular distinctiveness rather than a broader religious-based character. For Syria, the UAR provided an opportunity to escape domestic political competition and an economic opportunity within Egypt. The Egyptian leadership of the UAR and the perceived arrogant attitude of the military and administrative

---

* Batatu, Hanna, *Syria's Muslim Brethren*, MERIP Reports 110, *Syria's Troubles*, (November–December 1982) 14.

† Batatu, 16.

‡ Batatu, Hanna, *Syria's Peasantry, the Descendants of Its Lesser Rural Notables, and Their Politics* (Princeton, NJ: Princeton University Press, 1999), 124.

§ Ibid., 127.

¶ Ibid., 158.

personnel working in Damascus garnered resentment from the Syrian elite. The desire to connect with the Egyptian market failed, and Syria left the UAR after groups within the country began jostling for control of the government.

While Arab nationalism was never solidified as a lasting physical union, the concept continued to hold sway among secular and religious populations. The main stumbling block for nationalists was overcoming postcolonial authoritarian governments that held tightly to the reins of power, repressed opposition parties, and slowed the liberalization of Arab economies. Militaries were kept weak and at a distance for fear of overthrow, and when faced with external challenges, failed miserably. There were also barriers to achieving a strong concept of unity, primarily due to ethnic differences and a tendency to cling to pre-Islamic greatness.* The creation of Israel and subsequent military losses to the new Jewish state ushered in a feeling of disappointment, disillusionment, and realization that strength would come with unity. But the face of unity was yet undecided. Would it be religious or secular?

The Broken Promises of Nationalism and Search for the Nature of Arab Unity

Throughout the rest of the 1950s and early 1960s, the idea of secular pan-Arabism spread through the Middle East within Ba'athism and Nasserism. Both political ideologies advertised themselves as genuine powerful Arab government systems capable of delivering on social and political issues, to include the existence of Israel. Israel became synonymous with the concept of colonialism. As a result of the 1967 war, nationalism failed in a humiliating and devastating manner. The resounding question became: Where was all the power that was supposed to come from pan-Arabism? If there was a perception that the pan-Arabist state was a force to be reckoned with, all that was left after the war was the image of a paper tiger. Some scholars consider this the beginning of the end for the secular state. When the opportunity came to keep its promise on the international front with Israel, it failed miserably. For some Egyptians, the Arab secularist movement failed to produce a hybrid secularism that blended some medieval Muslim secularism and the Western type it tried to reproduce.† In addition, the type of secularism fed to the Egyptians was a direct influx from the West to European-educated Arab intellectuals born and raised in Egypt.

---

* Aslan, 234.
† Abu-Rabi, Ibrahim M., *Contemporary Arab Thought: Studies in Post-1967 Arab Intellectual History* (Sterling, VA: Pluto Press, 2004), 95.

Nasser had not only failed on the authoritarian nationalism front, but in agrarian reform, industrialization, and firm control of the state apparatus and bureaucracy.* The loss to Israel, however, served as the primary catalyst for the revival of Islamism. Arabs began looking for another ideology to help them recuperate from the humiliating loss against Israel. The Muslim Brotherhood, among other Islamist groups, saw the tide turning and realized they were no longer pigeonholed behind Marxist secular divisions. It was their opinion that Egypt lost the war because they had abandoned God. They blamed the morally corrupt officials for the loss of battles and territory. Islamists began seeing that the values of Islam had power loaded in them. Their argument became more assertive and cited Israel as an example of a country that built its nation in the name of religion. For Islamists, the failure of nationalism was in labeling religion as backwards. They argued if Nasserism was right and secularism was the answer, then why was Egypt beaten so badly? Throughout the rest of the 1960s and early into the 1970s, this argument began to gain momentum. Islamists in Egypt emerged as a serious threat to the Nasser regime.

The Arab socialist and nationalist pan-Arab state idea was characterized by authoritarianism, a command economy, and dominating society. It was able to diminish the influence of Islamism but eventually began to fall apart. The reasons for the fall of nationalism derive from a failure to deliver on a social promise. Nationalists could blame some of their failure on Israel, but there was a social fatigue settling in. There was a rise in the number of people who were highly educated, but not enough jobs to fill. In addition, the economies were inefficient, infrastructures were overburdened, and social demands were increasing rapidly. The failure of the Arab armies during the 1967 war with Israel was the proverbial tipping point for Arab nationalism. Whatever promises were made by the nationalists to stand up to the colonialists (Israel) were empty. The humiliation and loss of symbolic (and real) territory illustrated the lack of progress once promised by nationalists. It was at this point that some began to hold up Israel as an example of what rallying behind religion could do. The failure of Arab nationalism was not in the idea itself, but in the implementation. Nasser sold his idea of unity as the answer to all the nations' problems, but when nationalism broke apart, the belief didn't shatter, just the idolization of the leadership. The desire for a cure-all ideology was still present, and Islamists were ready on the periphery to step in.

---

* Picard, Elizabeth, "Arab Military in Politics: From Revolutionary Plot to Authoritarian State," in *The Arab State*, ed. Giacomo Luciani (Berkeley: University of California Press, 1990), 191.

Radicalization of Islamist Groups and the Rise
of Transnational Anti-Western Islamism

Many of the anticolonial Islamist thinkers influence contemporary Islamism and its resistance to Western domination. Qutb, Mawdudi, and al-Banna's writings are still distributed, meditated upon, and their vision for a strong Muslim entity woven into the tattered threads of nationalism. Between the 1970s and the 1990s, Islamists began to focus their efforts on dislodging the "near enemy," to establish *Shari'ah* and create a wider Muslim community.[*] Imperialism, as it was, created a dependency through economic expansion and political domination, and contemporary Islamists did not miss an opportunity to present it as one of their grievances with the West.[†] They argued that the West kept Muslims "militarily impotent" and politically and economically dependent.[‡] Representatives of the transnational concept of Islam gave priority to the "imagined communities" of nationalism despite their respective ethnic, cultural, or linguistic differences.[§]

Between the 1970s and 1990s Islamists focused on the domestic agenda citing four goals: overthrowing the impious ruler who had abandoned Islam, fighting against any Muslim community that deserts Islam, reestablishing the caliphate, and liberating the religious prisoners in order to spread ideology to a lost nation.[¶] The happenings outside the border were of little importance compared with the mission of righting a wrong that had derailed religious discourse for decades.

The idea of nationalism did not die out; Islamists viewed the state as a "strategic tool to restructure society and politics" that placed them under a new designator: religious nationalists.[**] The goal of overthrowing the despotic state was not ideologically driven; rather, it was more from practical capability. They were not ready to face the West on the battlefield, nor had they yet marshaled significant support behind their cause. Ideological activism "requires the transformation of Islam into a very political tool, objectifying it into a thing that is instrumental to the attainment of other ends."[††]

There were significant events that occurred during the 1970s and 1980s that added credibility to Islam as a force to be reckoned with. Iran's monarchy

---

[*] Gerges, Fawaz A., *The Far Enemy: Why Jihad Went Global* (New York: Cambridge University Press, 2005), 43.

[†] Evans, Peter, "Imperialism, Dependency, and Dependent Development," in *Dependent Development: The Alliance of Multinational, State and Local Capital in Brazil* (Princeton, NJ: Princeton University Press, 1979), 16.

[‡] Gerges, 44.

[§] Ernst, 203.

[¶] Ibid.

[**] Ibid., 49.

[††] Ernst, 204.

was overthrown by a revolutionary movement represented by an Islamic façade that gave credence to the role of Islamism as a competitor with the West. Many observers in the Middle East were flabbergasted that a religious movement could topple a Western-controlled authoritarian government that seemed practically invincible.

During the same year, the Russians invaded Afghanistan to stop the fall of the communist puppet government in Kabul but faced a particularly lethal form of religious resistance (*jihad*) of the *Mujahideen,* Afghans and foreign fighters who had traveled to Afghanistan to fight against forces trying to destroy Islam. The victory of the resistance created a momentum for the foreign fighters, brandishing the zeal of anointed battle with them as they traveled back to their home countries. There was a sincere problem facing home governments who had to reabsorb the holy fighters: How could they be demobilized and reintegrated into their societies?[*] What Islamists had now was an operational example of the power of *jihad.* Whereas Arab nationalists promised resistance and reform through modernization and emulation of the West, jihadists and transnational Islamists had two victories against it and gained stature and followership as a result. Claiming Islam and using religious rhetoric had become a symbol of political power and legitimacy.[†] Afghanistan provided an ungoverned physical space in which foreign fighters could congregate, train, strategize, and build networks to employ in their future battle with their respective local rulers.

Islamists on a large scale were not ready to commit to a global battle. Their grievances were primarily local, and they desired to take what they had learned and use it to benefit their own people. They went into the battles thinking locally but acting globally. A small group of jihadists began to discuss the idea of shifting their target from the near to the far enemy. Local governments began to see the threat posed by these returning fighters and subsequently participated in indiscriminate repression, jailing, and torture. These actions had two consequences: they radicalized the Islamists and redirected their efforts to the influential authority over the local governments, the West.

The 1990s witnessed a split between Islamic nationalists and transnational anti-Western Islamists. Although the transnational activists evolved out of the religious nationalist movement, their emergence was marked by radicalization and a significant shift toward violence. The targets of their efforts were American interests in Africa, the Middle East, and eventually inside the United States. The stationing of U.S. military members inside Saudi Arabia during the 1991 Gulf War became a pivotal moment that reinforced

---

[*] Gerges, 73.
[†] Kepel, Gilles, *Jihad: The Trail of Political Islam* (Cambridge, MA: Belknap Press, 2002), 121.

jihadists' suspicions that the West had strategic designs on the Middle East. The rebuffing of Osama bin Laden's Mujahideen fighters only emboldened and inflamed the religious sensibilities of many Islamists and crystallized the United States as the ultimate "head of the snake," which they felt must be decapitated in order to facilitate widespread Islamic change.

The transnational anti-Western Islamist effort was not monolithic; competition and a desire to control the direction of the fight festered among the groups. Ideology was not enough to sustain the movement; there had to be resources to facilitate operations and recruitment. The one element that was lacking among the transnational groups was organization; they fell victim to the same problems Arab nationalists did: complex bureaucracy and a lack of unity among Arabs or Muslims beyond local concerns. Ethnicity created a particularly difficult problem for al-Qaeda, and Osama bin Laden has struggled to control infighting among his own cadre.[*] Distance became a significant problem for Islamists; even with modern communication devices, links between the underground operatives and tacticians in a different country were vulnerable to interference and manipulation.[†]

Bin Laden's theories brought together two political forces: Saudi Islamist dissidence based on the Wahhabist teachings, and the call for jihad to eliminate the foreign occupation, which was modeled after the preachings of Abdallah Azzam in Pakistan.[‡] His decision to attack the far enemy was a huge gamble; he risked alienating the large moderate class of Muslims who feared they would be persecuted for his spectacular and gruesome actions. While most Islamists hold local concerns and intend to remove local regimes from power, bin Laden and his fighters targeted the United States in order to attempt to discredit the world's only superpower.

The Origins of Anti-Western Islamist Concerns: Local, Transnational, or Regional?

The important factor to extract from the evolution of the Islamists is that in the most basic form, it is rooted in local concerns. Colonialism, identity, and modernization all applied significant pressure to social, economic, and political nodes within separate Middle East states, fostering similar pressures within local political and private spaces. Because the transnational anti-Western Islamist efforts were hamstrung by internal squabbles and an inability to organize into a cohesive group, they never formed a solid movement. Although anti-Western Islamist concerns can

---

[*] Ibid., 70.
[†] Kepel, 316.
[‡] Ibid., 319.

be derived from both local and global grievances, neither cause can be held in *absolutum*. The globalization of the anti-Western Islamist efforts stemmed largely from

> a deep structural, developmental crisis facing the Arab world, in both socio-economic and institutional terms; it is a crisis of governance and political economy, not of culture or foreign policy. At the heart of this structural crisis lie entrenched authoritarianism and a vacuum of legitimate political authority fueling the ambitions of secular and religious activists.[*]

The transnational Islamists attempted to fill the spaces of legitimate political authority with promises of salvation and widespread social service support to the areas abandoned by government. From the very beginning, the jihadist effort was a response to the political and social order at home, not against the wider world order. Scholars assert that one cannot confuse the rhetoric of the transnational anti-Western Islamist; his true goal is local change. While the primary theme of Islamic opposition groups includes first igniting change within the political system before ushering in an Islamic order, there was a generous amount of confusion about what the actual political structure should be: toleration or rejection of democracy.[†]

I argue that there is a tertiary concern that has motivated anti-Western Islamism and, in fact, may relegate transnational Islamism to the periphery—that of regional concerns. Although prenationalist thinkers pushed for action against the West and eventually against the representatives of the foreign colonizer who sat in power at the head of the local government, rarely did they incite violence or action within the Muslim population itself. Granted, there were disagreements and some sense of antipathy toward sectarian minorities within certain Middle Eastern states, but most of the discomfort between Sunni, Shi'a, and Sufi religious sects was the product of the postcolonial government left in place, which favored minorities or those of notable family lineage rather than those who held significant and real influence over the population.

The decline of the transnational Islamist during the late 1990s and early twenty-first century was attributed to a lack of organization, internal rivalries, and the inability to form a cohesive, committed movement. Al-Qaeda represented a minority population of various ethnicities who collected irredentist *jihadis* who had no larger political ambition to wage local or global war against the West. They were simply foot soldiers for the cause and lacked a broader goal of Arab or Muslim unity.[‡] The attack on the United States in September 2001

---

[*] Gerges, 273.
[†] Faruki, Kemal A., "The Islamic Resurgence: Prospects and Implications," in *Voices of Resurgent Islam*, ed. John L. Esposito (New York: Oxford University Press, 1983), 278.
[‡] Ibid., 81.

represented a dramatic effort to reach out to the larger Muslim community and show that a great superpower can suffer a blow from the Islamist soldier and to collect global support for a transnational jihad against colonial powers. Al-Qaeda faced significant blowback from the operation and plunged into underground networks that were primarily aided by geographically impossible terrain and shifting ethnic loyalties they were able to co-opt along the way. But without grounded communication systems and with significant fragmentation, the different transnational jihadi groups began to weaken. Internal rivalry and bickering, crumbling hierarchies, increasing autonomy among different groups, and the emergence of increasingly violent "lieutenants" representing al-Qaeda began to weaken the group. It seemed the fault lines within al-Qaeda were deepening and downgraded the group significantly.

The U.S. decision to invade Iraq in 2003 provided al-Qaeda and their transnational counterparts with a renewed sense of vigor. The amount of pressure and resources being applied to Afghanistan was reduced, which allowed bin Laden and his associates, at the minimum, a boost of morale. Iraq provided al-Qaeda a well-defined and confined region in which to employ their foot soldiers and supported the anti-Western Islamist credo that the West was just looking for opportunities to assert their hegemonic intentions over Muslims. The images of uniformed American soldiers rolling over Iraqi neighborhoods in their tanks, allowing looting and pillaging within cities, and abusive and humiliating behavior in detention centers and prisons, were splashed across newspapers and television screens around the world, and ultimately, the inability to protect Iraqi civilians against violence provided ample fodder for recruitment efforts across the world. Al-Qaeda had a grand opportunity to marshal *ummah* support against the foreign invaders and to reassemble their vision for a resurgence of Islamic greatness as a global effort, but this time regionalized within the state of Iraq. Local concerns were railroaded by the golden opportunity presented in Iraq and the battleground provided the space in which Islamists of all colors could connect and network as they had within Afghanistan during the Russian invasion. One of the most important results of the invasion of Iraq was the alienation of politically secular and religious Muslim groups that had previously rejected al-Qaeda's global jihad and who had favored local efforts instead of tackling bigger concerns.* The deck was being stacked in the transnationalists' favor, and it looked as if al-Qaeda was gaining strength and influence throughout the world. Al-Qaeda planned to use a regional war as the example for displaying the fallibility of the world's last superpower.

The momentum that al-Qaeda was building began to decline alongside an increase in violence against Iraqi civilians and the sectarian targeting

---

* Ibid., 271.

that began with Abu Musab al-Zarqawi's efforts to initiate a divide between Sunnis and Shi'as within Iraq. I argue that within this effort to divide Muslims, the methods of the transnational Islamist went too far and have now eclipsed their goal for victory against the United States. By focusing the violence and disruption on regional sectarian divisions, Zarqawi effectively usurped the transnational goals and relegated them to regional concerns. The sectarian fight is regional and has the potential to reach out beyond Iraq's borders to involve a wider conflict between Sunnis and Shi'a spread throughout the Middle East. Prior to the invasion of Iraq, regional concerns were isolated among individual states dealing with internal social pressures related to sectarian divides; however, if the violence within Iraq seeps out to surrounding states, regional stability may then be at stake. Whether this was part of al-Qaeda's overall strategy to ignite global instability in an effort to unseat the Western powers, or simply a rogue lieutenant with his own selfish ambitions, the local and transnational concerns of anti-Western Islamists have now taken a backseat to regional concerns of a sectarian war and wider instability in the Middle East.

Conclusion

In order to explain resurgent Islamism in light of local and transnational concerns, I examined the historical causes of anticolonial Islamism, the rise and fall of secular nationalism, and subsequent growth of anti-Western contemporary Islamism. It is through analyzing evolving religious resurgence that we see the different concerns of nationalistic ideologies play out in local, regional, and global politics. Colonialism and foreign mandates contributed to weak economies, dependency on foreign aid and guidance, a tendency to use authoritarian tactics to control the population, and a weak military to prevent coups—all constructs that contributed to the rise and fall of secular Arab nationalism.

Islamism arose as a response to colonization and the expansion and domination of economic, social, and political aspects of local life. It resisted cultural manipulation and clung tightly to traditional values to prevent undue influence from outside forces. Islamists perceived attempts to secularize the population as a threat to their moral and religious rights and looked outside their borders for assistance from the larger Muslim community. Arab nationalism failed to deliver what it promised. Contemporary Islamists are "enthusiastic about the possibility of restructuring their society, individual and collective life and rebuilding socio-economic life on the foundations of Islam."[*] The impact of colonialism on Muslim society inspired the level

---

* Ahmad, 225.

and significance of the response to external forces. The prospects for Islamic resurgence within the Muslim world are subject to certain unknown factors: revolutions, counterrevolutions, pressure of external events, emergence or death of a charismatic leader—all factors that could either speed up or slow down the process.* Islam's appeal was that it offered "solid community attachments, a network of religious and charitable institutions to answer members' spiritual and material needs and an alternative form of governance."†

Resurgent Islamism is characteristically local, although it has been manipulated and employed on a global scale. Recently, transnational anti-Western Islamists have grown weak, unable to organize and mobilize a meaningful membership. Infighting, rivalries, and ethnic divisions have hindered groups such as al-Qaeda, but the group was given new life after the United States invaded Iraq in 2003. For a moment it appeared that the global group would gain strength and demonstrate to the world *ummah* that jihad was a useful tool to fight superpowers. As a result of its lack of organization, some of al-Qaeda's lieutenants began inciting and provoking sectarian violence in an effort to create instability within the region. The effort to take jihad global has failed as a result of its own momentum and could just as quickly become a regional battle between Sunni and Shi'a populations. Although some scholars relegate the Islamic movement to simply a reawakening of faith, there is a sense of idealism and hope for the future. Other scholars assert that the West must stop trying to fight against the resurgence of Islamism and instead come to terms with it.‡

---

* Faruki, 289.
† Harik, Judith Palmer, *Hezbollah: The Changing Face of Terrorism* (New York: I.B. Tauris, 2004), 9.
‡ Ibid., 228.

Suicide Bombing as an Ultimate Terrorist Tool

8

DR. A. K. MOHAMMED

Contents

Heinous and unprecedented acts of terrorism occurred during the last decades of the twentieth century. These attacks ranged from hijackings of airplanes, boats, buses, and other means of transportation, to the kidnapping of civilians for political blackmail or ransom. Atrocities also ranged from the blowing up of restaurants, malls, buildings, resorts, airports, airplanes in mid-air, and trains and buses, to gun attacks on individuals or groups of people.

Notwithstanding their different goals, motivations, diffusion, scope of action, means, and targets of action, all these terrorist groups seek either to sow fear upon their enemies and humiliate and intimidate them into surrendering to their demands, or to undertake a long-term military struggle in order to weaken the enemy by guerrilla warfare and constant bleeding. They also try to either capture the attention of the world media in order to air their grievances and attain their redress, or simply obtain by terrorist means objectives that they could not achieve in the arena of the battlefield.

This chapter reviews the production of suicide bombing and its economy, i.e., why this tactic is fast becoming the most common tool for spreading terror; in other words, how suicide bombings maximize the resulting terror and how suicide bombing is fast becoming the ultimate terrorist weapon.

The Production of Suicide Bombing

Becoming a suicide bomber is a social process; it involves socialization, and it is subject to rules and exhibits patterns. The opportunity to engage in it is likewise socially determined. Research has shown that suicide bombing requires three major elements: motivated individuals, access to organizations whose objective is to produce suicide bombing, and a community that extols perpetrators as heroes and embraces their acts as a noble form of resistance (Oliver and Steinberg, 2005). Studies addressing motivation to commit suicide have focused on the psychology of perpetrators, inquiring whether suicide bombers exhibit measures of psychopathology or are abnormal (e.g., Merari, 2004). Most observers agree that suicide bombers are rational individuals, whose resort to suicide is based on reason or a result of specific cost–benefit analysis (Hafez, 2004).

Motivations to engage in suicide bombing include national or religious ideologies, and collective/altruistic and individual/fatalistic reasons (Pedahzur et al., 2003), although motivation is not always accompanied by ability to perpetrate violence on individual or organizational levels (Ganor, 2003). Some observers have identified three major types of suicide bombers: those who act out of religious convictions, those who have the need to retaliate or avenge the death of a family member or loved ones by the enemy, and those who are exploited by an organization, being led to agree to perpetrate an attack for minor economic rewards or promises for the afterlife (Kimhi and Even, 2004). Research has addressed the role of religious convictions or culturally based motivation to propel suicide bombing (Oliver and Steinberg, 2005). Frustrations from political conditions have also been listed as motives, referring to suicide as oppositional terrorism (Crenshaw, 2002), a measure employed to exact revenge, retaliate for group humiliation, or restore national honor (Rosenberger, 2003).

The role of social groups—family, peer, ethnic, religious, or national—in shaping perpetrators' social identities, and in internalizing collective memory of injustice, defeat, or dishonor, has been noted (Oliver and Steinberg, 2005). Some have argued that suicide bombing is not an act of desperation but of struggle (Merari, 2004), as content analysis of the farewell messages recruits videotape prior to the mission suggests (Hafez, 2004). Suicide bombing has been explained as a means to achieve self-empowerment, redemption, and honor for individuals who experience powerlessness, downfall, and humiliation (Hassan, 2003). Others have called attention to the suicide as a guaranteed access to worldly pleasures forbidden in this life, and a hope for an attractive afterlife (Berko, 2004).

Exposure to and contact with facilitating organizations is critical in becoming suicide bombers (Bloom, 2005). The organizations that produce suicide bombings provide a complete framework: wherewithal, finances, equipment, contacts, and support personnel throughout the journey. These resources comprise the infrastructure without which successful missions cannot be executed. Familiarity with prospective targets, area residents' routines, and security personnel schedules are also important, as is access to and information about desirable targets, including the propitious time to execute a mission. Selecting candidates who can blend in the surrounding environment, have language skills to communicate with local people, exhibit confidence, wear appropriate clothes, and other amenities that provide them a Western look so as not to attract suspicion, is also the organization's responsibility. Without the support network, organization, and infrastructure, an individual cannot become a suicide bomber.

The symbolic value of suicide in the service of religion or nation, and the honor bestowed on the suicide bomber and his or her family are also critical in the production of suicide bombing. Both secular and religiously based terrorist organizations have invoked religion when launching suicide bombing. Perpetrators who were dispatched through both types of organizations referred to one's religiously based obligation to be involved in the struggle and listed the Garden of Eden as a reward for the suicide mission.

Following the 9/11 terrorist attacks, it seems that any place is not safe. In malls, buses, cafes, convenience stores, beaches, and commercial areas, people are exposed to pictures of shattered establishments and scattered bodies. Every place today is a potential target for suicide bombing. According to Hoffman (2003): "First you feel nervous about riding the bus. Then you wonder about going to a mall. Then you think twice about sitting for long at your favorite café. Then nowhere seems safe. Terrorist groups have a strategy—to shrink to nothing the areas in which people move freely—and suicide bombers, inexpensive and reliably lethal, are their latest weapons" (p. 1).

A suicide bombing is a bomb attack on people or property, delivered by a person who knows the explosion will cause his or her own death. It redefines basic cultural relationships and merges private, psychological motivations with public, ideologically charged actions. According to Davis (2003), terrorists, including suicide bombers, share several characteristics: "oversimplification of issues," "frustration about an inability to change society," "a sense of self-righteousness," "a utopian belief in the world," "a feeling of social isolation," "a need to assert his own existence," and "a cold-blooded willingness to kill" (p. 37). In addition, Bandura (2004) observes that "Islamic extremists mount their jihad, construed as self-defense against tyrannical, decadent infidels who seek to enslave the Muslim world" (p. 121), a view that allows them to "redefin[e] the morality of killing, so that it can be done free from self-censuring restraints" (pp. 124–25).

Although the concept predates the label, the term *suicide bombing* was only popularized in the 1980s, in the middle of the Lebanese civil war (1975–1990). Inspired by Iran's Islamic revolution and supported by Syria, the Hezbollah militants, claiming legitimacy in their nationalist struggle, led a suicide attack against the U.S. Embassy in Beirut in December 1981, killing sixty-nine. Two years later, Hezbollah fanatics crashed an explosives-laden pickup track into a Beirut facility housing U.S. Marines, killing 241 U.S.

marines and 58 French airborne troops. This led to the eventual withdrawal of all U.S. and French troops from Beirut.

While suicide bombings have been used by some secular terrorist movements in the past, such as the Tamil Tigers in Sri Lanka and the Kurdistan Workers' Party (PKK) in Turkey, generally it is religiously inspired terrorist movements that have employed this as a tactic (Rich and Mockaitis, 2003, p. 9). In the Middle East, the contemporary phase of suicide bombing is rooted from the Hezbollah movement since 1982 among the Shiite population in southern Lebanon during the Lebanese civil war. A decade later, it came to the Palestinians, a group of whom formed the al-Aqsa Martyrs Brigades in late 2000 and adopted suicide bombing as a tactic in contrast to the mass casualty attacks by Hamas and Islamic jihad. Suicide bombing in Israel has been a regular security problem ever since. Almost two-thirds of all such incidents in Israel have occurred since September 2000. Indeed, suicide bombers are responsible for almost half of the approximately 750 deaths in terrorist attacks since then (Hoffman, 2003, p. 42).

Suicide bombing was a tactic that al-Qaeda took one dramatic stage further with the 9/11 attacks, ensuring a major dramatic impact on global public opinion. It takes martyrdom to a new and rather "purer" level than the suicide bombing on the West Bank or South Lebanon, since the collective suicide of the nineteen plane hijackers on 9/11 was purely in the cause of a global Islamic jihad rather than more immediate political demands of local ethnic or nationalist movements. However, it is likely that the basic impulses behind the suicide terrorism of al-Qaeda remain the same as they were in other movements—it is largely an individual decision, and there is little or no evidence to suggest that the influence of a charismatic religious or political leader is sufficient by itself to drive a person to commit terrorist suicide (Merari, 1990).

Suicide bombers pack together nuts and bolts, screws and ball bearings, any metal shards or odd bits of broken machinery with a homemade explosive and then strap them to their bodies. They then go to any place where people gather and detonate the bomb.

Suicide bombing has the advantage of being relatively cheap as a tactic since the cost of each bomb is around $150 (Hoffman, 2003). At the same time, it is an effective response given the relative lack of success in smuggling in large-scale weapons onto the West Bank, and also confirms the apparent Islamic commitment of the movement's adherence to martyrdom (Shaher, 2004). Moreover, terrorists do not need sophisticated and expensive technologies to make bombs; they can make bombs in their headquarters or in their houses (Figure 8.1).

The symbolic value of suicide in the service of religion or nation, and the honor bestowed on the suicide bomber and his family, is also critical in the production of suicide bombing (Post et al., 2003). Both secular and religiously

Figure 8.1 The explosive belt of a Palestinian suicide bomber, captured by the Israeli police. (From http://www.mfa.gov.il/MFA/MFAArchive/2000_2009 /2001/6/Palestinian%20Terrorism-%20Photos%20-%20Tel-Aviv%20sui-cide%20b, accessed December 19, 2006.)

based terrorist organizations have invoked religion when launching suicide bombing (Hafez, 2004). Perpetrators who were dispatched through both types of organizations referred to one's religiously based obligation to be involved in the struggle and listed the Garden of Eden as a reward for the suicide mission (Berko, 2004).

Suicide Bombing in Cost-Benefit Terms

Although radical in nature, insurgents see advantages and strengths in the tactic of suicide bombings. From a cost–benefit analysis, suicide bombings seem to be a perfect tactic for the manpower-deprived insurgents. Suicide bombings sacrifice a small number of insurgents to cause damage to a much larger number of targets. As an instrument of broadcasting a political message, no other kind of attack better demonstrates an insurgent's dedication to a political agenda, and no other kind of attack has sparked as much fear. The greatest strength of suicide bombings is the fact that they are extremely hard to detect and stop.

Carrying out this terrorist act is cheap since the cost of each bomb is around $150 and draws considerable international media attention to the conflict (Rich and Mockaitis, 2003, p. 9). A tactical advantage of suicide attacks over conventional terrorist tactics is the guarantee that the suicide bombing will be carried out at the most appropriate time and place with regard to the terrorists' objectives. This ensures the maximum number of casualties, which most likely would not be achieved via other means, such as the use of a remote-controlled charge or timer bomb.

As "thinking bombs," suicide bombers make sure that the attacks are carried out at the most appropriate circumstance. In other words, suicide bombings strike at the right place and at the right time. This maximizes the number of casualties.

Suicide bombings also draw considerable international media attention to the conflict, since the act indicates a display of great determination and inclination for self-sacrifice on the part of the suicide bomber (Ganor, 2003). The advantages of suicide bombing for terrorist organizations do not stop here. High-profile and much publicized suicide bombings can trigger additional, imitative suicides (Mazur, 1982). This suggests that mass media play an important role in terrorism (Figure 8.2 and Figure 8.3).

In a traditional terrorist insurgency, the exposure of an individual terrorist could be devastating for the terrorist organization. In suicide bombing, however, rather than being captured, bombers blow themselves up. This saves the organization from being exposed to authorities. This is also economical in the sense that there is not a need for an escape plan, and that cost for treatment of injuries is virtually nonexistent, since bombers in this tactic kill themselves in the process.

Another advantage of suicide bombing for terrorist groups is that there is a steady supply of suicide bombers. In addition to the monetary incentives for the family of the suicide bombers, they believe that bombing is not a suicide, but rather a form of martyrdom; these terrorists are looking forward to the rewards that will await them if they sacrifice their lives (Shuman, 2001). Suicide bombers view themselves as martyrs fighting a jihad against their heretic, apostate opponents (Rapoport, 1990, p. 103). Terrorist organizations are never out of a supply of suicide bombers since there are many individuals who strive for martyrdom, as well as economic incentives.

Monetary rewards for terrorist organizations can be large. Suicide bombers sometimes draw sympathy from sources distant from the location of the attacks, especially donors who are willing to enable others to die as martyrs in the service of a cause. For example, following a supermarket bombing by an eighteen-year-old Palestinian girl, a Saudi telethon reportedly raised more than $100 million for the Palestinians (Hoffman, 2003). Also, support from the Diaspora is common. According to one estimate, the Tamil Tigers have been funded by eight hundred thousand Tamils living abroad, in Australia, Canada, and elsewhere, who have sent back as much as $150 million annually. Payments and other benefits are given to the individual families of the dead Palestinian attackers.

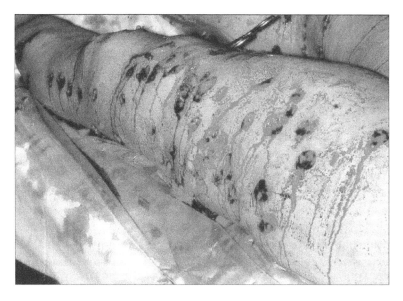

Figure 8.2 The left lower limb of a fourteen-year-old female who sustained multiple shrapnel injuries. (From Almogy, G., et al., *Ann. Surg.*, 239, 295–303, 2004.)

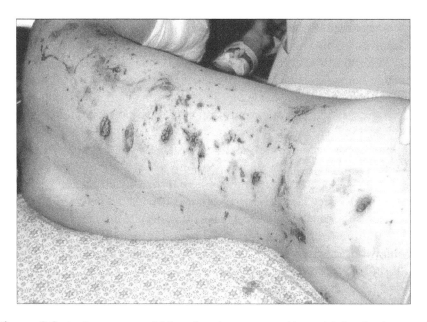

Figure 8.3 A sixteen-year-old female who was standing with her back toward the attacker. The girl sustained a penetrating rectal injury. (From Almogy, G., et al., *Ann. Surg.*, 239, 295–303, 2004.)

In order to understand the threat of suicide bombers, it is helpful to examine the insurgent attacks on January 4, 2006, January 5, 2006, and January 9, 2006. On January 4, a suicide bomber snuck into a funeral packed with Iraqi mourners in Miqdadiya and detonated a bomb strapped to his torso. In the commotion that followed, a car bomber drove into the midst of the crowd and exploded, killing even more (Oppel, 2006). About thirty-two people died (Straziuso, 2006) and thirty-six were wounded (Oppel, 2006). Apparently, the funeral was for the nephew of a local political leader. Elsewhere on the same day, insurgents set off a stationary car bomb in Khadhamiya as an Iraqi police patrol passed by, killing five and wounding fifteen. Before the day was done, another car bomb exploded in Dora, killing a policeman and two civilians and wounding eleven more. Note that the latter two attacks occurred near the capital, which was tightly monitored by coalition forces (Oppel, 2006).

Suicide bombings are efficiently fatal: they result in many casualties and cause extensive damage. Suicide attacks on average kill four times as many people as other terrorist acts. According to the U.S. State Department's latest annual report on global terrorism, the number of suicide bombings increased exponentially in 2005: an estimated 3,000 deaths were attributed to 360 suicide bombings last year, more than the 472 suicide attacks in the five years from 2000 to 2004 documented in a study by the Center for Strategic and International Studies (Sands, 2006, para. 3). While the 9/11 terrorist attacks remain the deadliest of their kind, there are indications of an increase in the number of suicide bombings. Among the most lethal were the fifty-four persons killed in the July 2005 subway bombing in London and nearly sixty fatalities blamed on Iraqi suicide bombers targeting hotels in Amman, Jordan, four months later (Sands, 2006, para. 4).

Suicide bombing is an effective response given the relative lack of success in smuggling in large-scale weapons onto the West Bank, and it also confirms the apparent Islamic commitment of the movement's adherence to martyrdom (Shaher, 2004). It does not come as a surprise, then, that suicide bombing has become increasingly popular. From 1980 to 2001, suicide attacks worldwide reportedly represented only 3% of all terrorist attacks but accounted for 48% of the total deaths due to terrorism (Pape, 2003, p. 5). In the Palestinian-Israeli conflict, suicide attacks carried out between 2000 and 2002 caused about 44% of all Israeli casualties, despite only representing 1% of the total number of attacks during the period (Moghadam, 2003, p. 65).

Similarly, it is extremely difficult to counter suicide attacks once the terrorist is on his way to the target. Even if the terrorists are apprehended, the explosive device can still be detonated.

Another benefit of suicide bombing to terrorist organizations is that it requires a small number of people to kill hundreds of people. Once again, highlighting suicide bombing's brutal efficiency, 241 marines were killed by a single suicide bomber in October 1983 in Lebanon; a single driver plowed his truck into a makeshift army camp in Sri Lanka in 1987, killing 40 soldiers. On September 11, 2001 almost three thousand died at the hands of just nineteen hijackers (Madsen, 2004, p. 3). In Bali, more than two hundred tourists died at the hands of two bombers on October 12, 2002, while murder on this scale is unlikely to have been achieved by conventional terrorist means.

Moreover, martyrdom operations are cheap, with the bomb ingredients widely available, as they also fill a civilian use. One Palestinian official's prescription for a successful mission includes: "a willing young man (or woman) … nails, gunpowder, a light switch and a short cable, mercury (readily obtainable from thermometers), acetone…. The most expensive item is transportation to an Israeli town. The total cost is about $150" (Atran, 2003, p. 1537).

Acetone peroxide is a widely available explosive and the simplest in preparation. Its components can be easily bought in any household store without provoking suspicion—hydrogen peroxide is used for bleaching hair, and acetone is used for nail polish, as a solvent, or as an electrolyte. Acetone peroxide has one definite advantage over other types of explosives: it cannot be discovered by dogs. Specially trained dogs can discover explosives such as ammonal, plastic explosives, and hexogen, but not acetone peroxide (Mechanics of a Living Bomb, n.d.).

In addition to entailing closely related economic and strategic benefits for the terrorist organization, suicide bombing minimizes the costs that it incurs in its armed struggle against its enemies. On the contrary, the economic costs that Israel has sustained as a result of suicide terrorism have been proportionally much greater. According to the Bank of Israel, the damage to the Israeli economy from just one year of intifada (2002) was estimated at 3.8% of the GDP. Following its conceptual framework and assuming the intifada had ended by the end of year 2000, the accumulated three-year loss is enormous: one-fifth of one year's gross domestic product. Also, the absolute number of poor people, since the intifada started, increased by 22%. Finally, the number of poor children rose by 30% (Palestinian Gets Saddam Funds, 2003).

Yet another reason why suicide bombing is fast becoming the ultimate terrorist weapon is that there is no need for an escape plan. From an operational perspective, suicide bombing is appealing, as the terrorist organization does not have to plan an escape route, which is considered one of the most difficult and complicated parts of the terrorist plan.

There is a great risk of the terrorist group being exposed if members of the organization are apprehended. However, suicide bombings disenable authorities to get any information about the organization. For example, after the Madrid atrocity, when police raided an apartment to arrest others in connection with the terrorist attacks, the four inside the apartment blew themselves up, rather than being captured and having to assist police in their inquiries. Likewise, Tamil Tiger rebels have traditionally carried one cyanide pill, which they can swallow in the event of imminent capture.

According to a former Hamas leader, suicide bombing is the most important strategic weapon of the Palestinian resistance. In addition, a secretary-general of the Palestinian Islamic Jihad described suicide bombing's utility as follows: "Our enemy possesses the most sophisticated weapons in the world and its army is trained to a very high standard.... We have nothing with which to repel the killing and thuggery against us except the weapon of martyrdom. It is easy and costs us only our lives ... human bombs cannot be defeated, not even by nuclear bombs" (Sprinzak, 2000, p. 66).

In general, suicide bombing remains a weapon of the "weak" in relation to a much stronger and superior enemy. Martyrdom operations have gained popularity as the ultimate terrorist instrument because terrorist groups are able to benefit from the death of a member, conferring a sense of legitimacy on it (Madsen, 2004). Terrorist organizations glorify suicide bombing, infusing a culture of martyrdom that may include posters, songs, and flyers; this inspires others to join the organization. Indeed, even before the suicide bomber has struck, he or she is in many ways a living martyr.

In the Qur'an, several verses deal directly with martyrdom: "Think not of those who are slain in Allah's way: They are dead, nay; they live, finding their sustenance in the presence of their lord" (Surat al-Imran, verse 169), implying that martyrs do not really die, but in fact, they are to receive reward in the afterlife: "Verily he will admit them to a place with which they shall be well pleased: for Allah is All Knowing, Most Forebearing" (Surat al-Hajj, verse 59).

Finally, terrorist organizations are able to capitalize on widespread media coverage that suicide bombings attract. The fate of the martyr is part of the story, and the large number of victims, again, ensures public attention. Since the gruesome effect of the violence is intended to be impressed upon an audience, the shocking nature of the attack is part of the calculation (Madsen, 2004, p. 2). The media coverage conveys an image of extreme discipline, dedication, and skill on behalf of the terrorists in carrying out such an audacious and incomprehensible act (Taarnby, 2003, p. 8). This conversely instills a feeling of fear and helplessness among the target population in the face of a supposed invisible and unstoppable enemy.

Suicide Bombing as an Act of Martyrdom

As suggested in the previous section of this chapter, suicide bombing is becoming an ultimate terrorism tool because of the many men and women, young and old (mostly between the ages of twelve and twenty-five), who are willing to give up their lives for the sake of their beliefs. In terrorism studies, scholars have been examining why Islamic radical suicide bombers give up their lives freely in pursuit of achieving their ultimate goal. In tackling this problem, one must contextualize the actions of suicide bombers within the jihad concept of *shahada* (martyrdom).

What drives suicide bombers to sacrifice their own lives for a cause? Traditional explanations suggest that economic problems result in terrorism. The Palestinians' turn to suicide bombing results from the desperate situation of the populace, particularly among young people growing up angry and hopeless, some of them naively idealistic and some of them manipulated for political ends by the group's military strategists. There is a great deal of truth in these claims. The Palestinian populace is desperate. Its young people are angry and hopeless. The idealism of some is manipulated by military strategists, and families respond to inducements like large cash payments.

In addition, many argue that globalization leads to economic insecurity, and that this insecurity breeds fundamentalism, fear, and ultimately terrorism and violence. Some scholars also argue that terrorists are relatively uneducated, and marginal in their societies. For example, Stern (2003) points out that terrorists are drawn from a large pool of volunteers who tend to be from the poorest segments of societies. She quotes a jihadist (holy warrior): "Most of the peoples who join these groups are from the poorest classes. Eighty-five percent come from below the poverty line; twelve percent are from the middle classes, and around three percent from the rich" (p. 214).

Furthermore, Saleh (2004) considers that the emergence of Palestinian suicide bombers is a direct consequence of the weakening of social and economic conditions.

Following this logic, an increase in income per capita and in the employment rate would reduce the incentive for suicide bombers to perform violent acts. According to Azam (2003), "Economic factors are a major compelling reason why young men seek opportunities in the bombing sector" (p. 1). Low levels of education, poverty, and meager living conditions create despair, which results in anger, hatred, frustration, and ultimately terrorism.

However, some scholars have stressed the inadequacy of the social and economic variables in accounting for suicide bombings. Krueger and Maleckova (2002) conclude that "suicide bombers clearly are not motivated by the prospect of their own individual economic gain, although it is possible that the promise of larger payments to their families may increase the willingness of some to participate in these lethal missions" (p. 29). Krueger and Maleckova (2002) suspect that suicide bombers' major motivation "instead results from their passionate support for the ideas and the aims of their movement" (p. 29).

Berrebi (2003), who explored the details of 285 Hamas and Islamic jihad suicide terrorists, concurs with earlier findings that terrorists "are completely different than the classic characteristics of a suicidal individual" (p. 1), and finds that suicide bombers "tend to be younger, of higher economic status,

and higher educational attainment than their counterparts in the population" (p. 4). Likewise, Berman (2003) notes that those selected for suicide
bombing missions tend to be those most committed and the most capable of
handling the complexities and difficulties that might arise.

The myth that suicide bombers are driven to their actions by the frustration stemming from poverty and ignorance is exploded by the actuality that
today's Palestinian bombers tend to be well educated and relatively economically stable (Atran, 2003). While cash payments from abroad to families of
suicide bombers continue, now all levels of the economic and educational
spectrum are represented (Stern, 2003).

Despite well-publicized photos of families holding checks for as much
as $25,000, the bomber's family may receive little direct financial incentive
(Reuter, 2004). Therefore, the factors of economic hardship and poverty that
frequently invite Western scholars to interpret suicide bombing in their light
fail to account for the intensity and agenda of political Islam. The Islamic
literature points to the presence of concepts related to political struggle in
Islam, which have been used over centuries in countless conflicts. While suicide bombings are not exclusive to either religious groups or religious culture (Pape, 2003), such acts are becoming more religiously motivated. Atran
(2003, p. 69) notes that at least 70% of suicide attacks that occurred between
2000 and 2003 were religiously motivated.

It can be said that religion is thus the primary motivation why extremists
launch suicide bombings. Following the July 2001 suicide bombing attack
in Netanya, unnamed sources from Hamas admitted that suicide bombers
undergo a process of indoctrination that lasts for months. In the view of
Islamic radical suicide bombers, killing oneself is no longer an act of self-
destruction (intihar), but rather divinely commanded martyrdom (istishad)
in defense of the faith (Stern, 2003). In other words, suicide bombing is not
a suicide but rather a form of martyrdom; it does not violate religious prohibitions against killing oneself (Reuter, 2004). According to a BBC report,
suicide bombers are recruited from mosques, schools, and religious institutions. They are likely to have shown particular dedication to the principles of
Islam. They are taught the rewards that will await them if they sacrifice their
lives (Shuman, 2001).

Suicide bombers are not suffering from clinical depression or emotional difficulties; they perceive themselves as fulfilling a holy mission that
will make them martyrs. Religious suicide bombers believe their goals and
activities are sanctioned by divine authority. Martyrdom, the voluntary
acceptance of death as a demonstration of religious truth, is a concept central to Islam.

Suicide bombers view themselves as martyrs fighting a jihad against their
heretic, apostate opponents (Rapoport, 1990, p. 103). Transforming oneself
into a living bomb is perceived as the equivalent of using a gun against one's

enemies. The struggle is much the same, the only difference being one of chronology: the bomber dies while killing several enemies rather than after doing so (Kramer, 1990, p. 131).

Virtually all major world traditions involve conceptual tension over the issue of self-caused death. In what is known as the Judeo-Christian tradition, suicide comes to be rejected as sinful, but is often conceptually difficult to distinguish from voluntary martyrdom—death accepted and in many cases sought or embraced to attest to one's faith. Martyrdom in Islam forms an intrinsic component of the concept of jihad; hence, it does not lend itself to Western definitions of suicide. According to Islamic teachings, *intihar* ("suicide") designates despair and violent withdrawal from society, whereas *shahada* ("martyrdom") represents the ultimate form of giving for the well-being of the community.

Suicide is essentially a characteristic of individualist societies, mainly resulting from lack of integration of the individual into society. In collectivist Arab societies there are very low suicide rates for males and virtually none for females. The inappropriateness of Western concepts of suicide necessitates a new venue for understanding the motives of suicide bombers. The notion of altruistic suicide inspired by "religious sacrifice or unthinking political allegiance" (Durkheim, 1951, p. 15) may shed light on kamikaze missions, but not on Palestinian human bombs. Whereas the kamikazes died for the sake of imperial Japan without expectation of personal reward, Arab suicide bombers feel they comply with the highest form of Islamic worship, for which they have specific spiritual expectations.

The dynamics of the terrorist group shape individual behavior, giving many members a strong sense of belonging, of importance, and of personal significance. Suicide bombers often articulate a sense of personal, sacred mission. When Hezbollah introduced suicide bombing as a tactic, it soon became clear that the religious fervor of the bombers could help the organization compensate for its small numbers and inadequate military capabilities.

Resentment and self-righteousness are often considered to be the underlying motivators for engaging in terrorism. Perceiving themselves as victims, the terrorists hone a hypersensitive awareness of slights and humiliations inflicted upon themselves or their particular group, and picture themselves as part of an elite heroically struggling to right the injustices of an unfair world. Typical suicide bombers are persuaded to join the movement because of both pragmatic and ideological reasons: the allure of martyrdom and the very tangible economic and social benefits his or her family will receive after his or her actions.

It is, of course, difficult to ascertain what terrorists are really thinking or what really motivates them, especially considering the tendency of terror organizations to maintain high levels of secrecy and the contextual situation of long-standing sociocultural conflicts. Similarly, it is easy to misinterpret the happy expressions often seen on the faces of suicide bombers. A smile may mean contemplation of eternal paradise, or it may represent satisfaction that the individual has helped the organization advance its goals one step forward (Kramer, 1990, p. 131).

Perhaps inevitably, one cannot know with certainty the extent of the suicide bomber's ideological fervor, nor can one pinpoint his or her emotional and cognitive responses to engaging in terror. Scholars and analysts are only left with observations of behavior in public, i.e., the actual suicide bombing or attempt, and the postdetonation interpretations of family and friends, and so must extrapolate all manner of important background as we reconstruct the influences leading up to the suicide bombing.

Summary

To summarize, the previous section has shown why suicide bombings will become the ultimate instrument in achieving terrorist organizations' ultimate goal. This is because suicide bombings can be carried out at very low cost. Bombs are inexpensive, can be made in the comfort of the home, and some cannot be detected. In addition, suicide bombing does not require escape routes. As bombers kill themselves, there is no fear of surrendering information. Moreover, terrorist groups capitalize on the promise of martyrdom. Suicide bombing also enhances likelihood of mass casualties and extensive damage on the economy of the target. Lastly, it affects the public and media, due to the overwhelming sense of helplessness. Thus, this research explores both socioeconomic and religious factors in explaining why suicide bombings or martyrdom operations will become the greatest terrorist tool.

Suicide bombing is largely economic in nature; every human act is economic. In this vein, suicide bombers make their own choices, which involve costs and benefits. Their acts and the increasing popularity of suicide bombing among terrorist organizations can be examined using an economic perspective. Basically, economics is based on normal, rational human action; thus, if suicide bombers are deranged and irrational, economists cannot say anything about them. Instead, they send them to the department of abnormal psychology. However, sociologists who have studied suicide bombers find and conclude that these persons are normal and rational, not crazy or irrational. Indeed, if individuals or organizations want to hire a suicide bomber, they do not want a crazy person, as he or she may not follow directions.

Iannaccone (2003, p. 10) sees a supply and demand for suicide bombings. Organizations that conduct such acts of terror can be regarded as firms. So the economic theory of firms and supply and demand is applicable to suicide bombings. The supply of persons willing to sacrifice themselves for a cause is more than enough. It only requires a small number of suicide bombers to inflict terror, and there is a supply, mostly young people, men and women, who are willing to give up their lives for a cause. On the other hand, the demand for suicide terrorism comes from the firms or terrorist organizations whose leaders feel hatred and anger toward the enemy target. Palestinians and Iraqis can be considered demanders of suicide bombing because the sentiment of hatred and anger and the desire for revenge are shared by many of their people.

The fact that violence is counterproductive does not matter, since those who demand suicide bombing feel glad when their enemies are hurt, even if they also get hurt. Indeed, there is a market for martyrs and firms that organize terrorist suicide bombing. Iannaccone (2003, p. 18) concludes that, in order to reduce suicide bombing, demand, rather than supply, must be reduced.

The following are problems that may be encountered if the deterrence focuses on reducing the supply: (1) terrorist firms can function effectively even if the supply of suicide bombers is very small; (2) standard criminal penalties have little or no impact on the expected costs and benefits confronting a rational suicide bomber; (3) there are many different sources of supply and methods of recruitment, and thus if enemies block one source or method, terrorist firms can readily substitute others; and finally, (4) reducing the rate of suicide bomber success may not yield comparable reductions in the net expected benefits associated with suicide missions and may actually increase the net benefits (Iannaccone, 2003, pp. 13–14).

In the end, suicide bombing will continue to become the ultimate terrorist tool. The situation of supply-side deterrence can be likened to illegal drugs. Much of the campaigns against illegal drugs are a futile attempt to limit supply, but that just drives the cost up while doing little to reduce the quantity, since the quantity demanded is rather unresponsive to changes in price (Foldvary, 2004, para. 6). Likewise, targeting suicide bombers only shoots up the price while not doing much to reduce such activity; simply stopping or killing suicide bombers will not stop terrorism, since those who die will be replaced by others.

In order to reduce the demand for suicide bombing, the market conditions must be altered. According to Iannaccone (2003): "Changing market conditions provides the only true solution to the problem of suicide bombing and militant religious radicalism. Other approaches (such as targeting firms, leaders, and recruits) raise operating costs and induce substitution but leave in place the underlying demand, and hence the underlying profit opportunities, associated with this line of business" (p. 18).

Consider the Arab citizens of Israel who do not engage in suicide bombing; on the other hand, many Palestinian Arabs in Gaza and the West Bank aspire to be suicide bombers. According to Foldvary (2004), the difference is that "Israeli Arabs have much more economic opportunity, and they don't feel as much resentment, anger, grievance, and hatred toward Israelis" (para. 7). By itself, poverty does not directly cause violence.

However, poverty mixed with a sense of humiliation, defeat, injustice, and outrage against human rights violations is a potent source of the demand to inflict damage on the hated occupier and violator—and so the terror continues.

References

Atran, S. 2003. The moral logic and growth of suicide terrorism. *The Washington Quarterly* 29(2).

Bandura, A. 2004. The role of selective moral disengagement in terrorism and counterterrorism. In *Understanding terrorism: Psychological roots, consequences, and interventions*, ed. F. M. Moghaddam and A. J. Marsella, 96–99, 113–117. Washington, DC: American Psychological Association.

Berman, E. 2003, September. *Hamas, Taliban and the Jewish underground: An economist view of radical religious militias.* National Bureau of Economic Research, Working Paper w10004. www.nber.org/papers/w100004 (accessed June 1, 2006).

Berrebi, C. 2003. Evidence about the link between education, poverty and terrorism among Palestinians. http://www.cprs-alestine.org/polls/94/poll (accessed July 27, 2006).

Davis, P. B. 2003. The terrorist mentality. In *Violence and terrorism*, ed. T. J. Badey. 6th ed. New York: McGraw-Hill.

Durkheim, E. 1951. *Suicide*, trans. J. A. Spaulding and G. Simpson. New York: The Free Press.

Foldvary, F. E. 2004. The economics of suicide bombing. http://www.progress.org/2004/fold353.htm (accessed July 28, 2006).

Ganor, B. 2003. The first Iraqi suicide bombing: A hint of things to come? ICT. http://www.ict.org.il/articles/articledet.cfm?articleid=477 (accessed October 2, 2006).

Hoffman, B. 2003, June. The logic of suicide terrorism. *The Atlantic Monthly*, 40–47.

Iannaccone, L. R. 2003. The market for martyrs. Paper presented at the 2004 Meetings of the American Economic Association, San Diego. http://www.mercatus.org/repository/docLib/MC_GPI_WP35_040807.pdf (accessed July 28, 2006).

Kramer, M. 1990. The moral logic of Hizballah. In *Origins of terrorism: Psychologies, ideologies, theologies, states of mind*, ed. W. Reich, 131–57. Cambridge: Cambridge University Press.

Krueger, A. B., and Maleckova, J. 2002. Does poverty cause terrorism? The economics and the education of suicide bombers. *The New Republic* 24:27–34.

Madsen, J. 2004. Suicide terrorism: Rationalizing the irrational. *Strategic Insights* 3(8).

Mechanics of a living bomb. n.d. http://www.waronline.org/en/terror/suicide.htm (accessed July 27, 2006).

Merari, A. 1990. The readiness to kill and die: Suicidal terrorism in the Middle East. In *Origins of terrorism: Psychologies, ideologies, theologies, states of mind*, ed. W. Reich, 121–125. Cambridge: Cambridge University Press.

Moghadam, A. 2003. Palestinian suicide terrorism in the second intifada: Motivations and organizational aspects. *Studies in Conflict & Terrorism* 26:65–92.

Rapoport, D. C. 1990. Sacred terror: A contemporary example from Islam. In *Origins of terrorism: Psychologies, ideologies, theologies, states of mind*, ed. W. Reich, 103–30. Cambridge: Cambridge University Press.

Reuter, C. 2004. *My life is a weapon: Modern history of suicide bombing.* Princeton: Princeton University Press.

Rich, P. B., and Mockaitis, T. R., eds. 2003. *Grand strategy in the war against terrorism.* London: Frank Cass.

Sands, D. R. 2006. Suicide bombing popular terrorist tactic. *The Washington Times.* http://www.washtimes.com/world/20060507-102037-9660r.htm (accessed July 27, 2006).

Shaher, Y. 2004. The al-Aqsa martyrs brigades. *International Policy Institute for Counter Terrorism,* March 24.

Shuman, E. 2001. What makes suicide bombers tick? http://www.israelinsider.com/channels/security/articles/sec_0049.htm (accessed July 27, 2006).

Sprinzak, E. 2000. Rational fanatics. *Foreign Policy* 120:66–74.

Stern, J. 2003. *Terror in the name of God: Why religious militants kill.* New York: Harper Collins.

Taarnby, M. 2003. *Profiling Islamic suicide terrorists,* 76–82. http://www.jm.dk/image.asp?page=image&objno=71157 (accessed July 27, 2006).

The Battle of Ideas
Political Warfare versus Psychological Operations

DR. MONTE R. BULLARD

Contents

National security today depends as much on success in the battle of ideas as it does on military combat. Whether the conflict of ideas is based upon ideology or religion, understanding the methods employed by nations in that struggle is critical. Today's conflict between America and terrorism or radical Islam is a test of whether the United States can adjust to this threat by including more focus on the struggle of ideas under conditions of asymmetric warfare.

Historically the United States has not fared well in that aspect of international conflict. In Vietnam American troops won every contest on the battlefield, but lost the war. In the current Middle East conflict the battle of ideas is clearly a problem for U.S. forces. Part of the solution to this problem is to develop a little deeper understanding of how our potential antagonists handle the issue. A clear articulation of the just and logical side of the debate just does not work. There must be a more comprehensive strategy, and we can learn a great deal from the Russian and Chinese systems.

While it is not possible to name names, it is almost certain that key members of some Middle East enemies have trained in Russia or China. While they may not have adopted the same methods, there is little doubt that their approach to many aspects of the battle for ideas came from that training.*

---

* When the author was stationed in Beijing in 1980 it was known that one entire compound, formerly that of the U.S. Embassy, was being used by the PLO while they were being trained.

This chapter is designed to explain how the Chinese and Russian political warfare systems work and to compare them with the relatively superficial approach taken by the United States.

One of the most important tools of war (hot or cold) is the political/psychological component of the conflict. Before this complex topic can be discussed, it is necessary to examine some of the key terms, particularly political warfare and psychological operations (Psyops), because in nearly all the literature these terms are not defined in the same way. This topic is extremely complicated, and to gain a good understanding, it is useful to place the concept into a broader context of the psychological and political aspects of national strategy. This section will define some of the terms in detail and contrast the Russian/Chinese approach, called political warfare, with the American approach, called Psyops.

Generally in warfare, of whatever type, there are two main goals: (1) kill or destroy the enemy and its war-making capability, and (2) change the minds or allegiances of those who believe in the cause of that enemy. Once an enemy has been conquered, it is still necessary to persuade everyone that the defeat is in the best interests of all for the future.

If we were to examine the first goal we would be looking at air, land, and sea strategies, tactics, and weapons systems. We would include organization, logistics, and all the other aspects of military warfare. What must be understood is that while political warfare or Psyops is part of the general strategy for winning a war, it must be in complete harmony with the military activity at the strategic, operational, or tactical level.

The psychological/political effort is more important in today's war on terrorism than it has been at any time in history. We see examples daily in the mass media of individuals and groups so loyal to their cause they are willing to sacrifice and die. We wonder what makes an eighteen-year-old girl eager to die as a suicide bomber and her family and friends support it. Part of the answer is that the political warfare activities of America's enemies have been extremely successful. The example of anti-American zealots is something we must pay close attention to and understand what drives their feelings.

A key lesson we must learn is that the American effort, called Psyops, and our adversaries' approach (Russia, China, al-Qaeda etc.), called political warfare, are different. The two concepts are currently in conflict in the war on terror, and the U.S. side has little appreciation for the concept of political warfare. The most important difference between the two approaches is that the United States prepares subordinate Psyops activities to support a military operational plan while the adversaries prepare military activities to support a larger political plan.

Political warfare actions used by our adversaries are perhaps the most dangerous threat to America now. The success of those actions is manifested in their ability to influence the American media, the American public, and the U.S. Congress to oppose war efforts.

The political warfare concept or system is far more complex than the concept of Psyops. Historically, the United States has rejected the concept of political warfare because it is closely associated with the Russian and Chinese political commissar systems, which challenge the idea of unity of command.

Political warfare actually began in France in the 1790s as part of the way loyalties of commanders and troops were monitored. The concept spread to Russia as part of the Bolshevik organization. In the 1920s it continued into China, where it became a key component of both the Communist and Nationalist armies.

The point here is that both Russia and China have honed the concept of political warfare to the point of establishing national-level military colleges (parallel to and at the same level as the National Defense Universities) exclusively for the topic of political warfare and separate from their war colleges that focus on military strategies. The courses in these universities study how to integrate the political messages into the national military strategy at all levels. What is also important is that both Russian and Chinese political warfare colleges have trained thousands of foreign students, particularly in the Middle East and Southeast Asia, in this art. They have specially trained officers at all levels to add the "political consequences" factor to operational plans and to subordinate military actions to a larger political plan. Whenever any military action is taken, someone is thinking about the political consequences on different target audiences. These target audiences will be explained in much more detail below.

Prior to the Vietnam War nearly every war in history was between sides of relatively equal strength—at least in the perception of the participants. The wars started when one side believed it was a bit stronger and could win a military conflict. The Chinese Civil War ending in 1949 and Vietnam were the conflicts in which the combatants were clearly not equal in military power, and both sides knew it. It was asymmetrical warfare. The North Vietnamese and Viet Cong knew from the beginning, especially after the entry of the United States with its B-52s and other advanced weapons systems, that they would have to use a special strategy, and that strategy included a significant political warfare component.

Ho Chi Minh, the leader of the Communist Vietnamese revolutionary forces, had traveled a great deal, including to the United States. He even asked President Woodrow Wilson to help him throw the French out of Indo China. More important, he served as a lecturer at Whampoa Military Academy in China and as a political commissar in the Chinese army. He worked on the topic of youth education—part of the political warfare system.

One of the most effective aspects of that system is the preparation of military operational strategic and tactical plans. When a military operations plan is written, it must include a political warfare annex; that is, how can political work enhance the war fighting capacity and what are the likely political consequences of any military action? The political warfare annex was as important to the operations plan as the intelligence annex and, of course, was closely related. Part of the planning had to include what political or military activity could be undertaken to weaken the will of the other side, especially when it had an enormous military superiority. In many cases the political plan is given priority and the military actions are the supporting element. For example, al-Qaeda attacks in Baghdad were often more for political impact than military gain.

What American military leaders failed to understand in Vietnam was that when the Viet Cong attacked a hill, it was not to kill American troops or to capture the terrain (traditional military thought). The attack was designed to make the front page of the *New York Times* (and other mass media) and weaken the will of the American people and the U.S. Congress to support the war. America's withdrawal in Vietnam was the signal to revolutionary groups all over the world that they could go up against the world's strongest military power if they thought out the political warfare part of the strategy.

The current conflict in the Middle East is similar. It is not a coincidence that al-Qaeda selected a strategy that would kill just a few Americans every day over a long period of time, rather than wait and marshal forces to kill many Americans in a single battle. It was not just out of military necessity. They recognized the asymmetric nature of the conflict and designed a political warfare strategy from the beginning. They knew, after studying Vietnam and Somalia, that the key was to weaken the will of the American people and ultimately the U.S. Congress, since they could never defeat the U.S. forces on the battlefield. They knew that if they could kill even one or two Americans every day, the action would be reported in the American mass media. They have proven very effective at this strategy to the point that they made their cause an issue in U.S. politics, where one of the political parties began to call for total withdrawal of American troops.

Unfortunately, this is one aspect of warfare in which the U.S. military has not done well. Usually the focus of American propaganda efforts are on means of dissemination more than the content, and that has proved to be a disaster over the years. The United States has paid less attention to the political consequences of military action. The American military knows and understands the propaganda techniques of producing leaflets, loudspeakers, and radio or TV broadcasts, but it has not done well at preparing the appropriate content or paying attention to the consequences of particular military actions.

During the Vietnam War it was often said that the Americans dropped enough leaflets onto the country to cover the entire nation 3 feet deep in paper. It may be an exaggeration, but not by much. It was also said, particularly in the field of Psyops, that the American military did not gain ten years' experience, but one year's experience ten times—because the length of tour was about one year. Another criticism was that the personnel who engaged in Psyops were generally those who did not do so well in one of the other basic branches of the Army. Many were reservists, though, and that did provide, in many cases, an excellent knowledge base of the enemy culture and perhaps language, but they really had little understanding of how to integrate the activity into the overall military effort.

In Vietnam one tactical-level program was known as Chieu Hoi and was designed to encourage enemy troops to defect to the other side. The leaflets, loudspeakers, and broadcasts tried to convince the Viet Cong or even the North Vietnamese troops that they would be better off if they crossed over and surrendered. They guaranteed safe passage and good treatment. The idea was good, and worked to a certain extent. But the lack of language and cultural understanding often caused the message to be counterproductive.

One leaflet showed pictures of scantily clad women and promised a good girl to everyone who defected. The cultural impact was serious—and reinforced the North Vietnamese propaganda that America was a land of decadent cultural values. There were many examples of leaflets prepared by soldiers who had studied Vietnamese at the Army Language School (now Defense Language Institute) and who knew the language quite well. But they did not understand the culture well enough to avoid traps that caused their message to support the enemy more than the American effort. In many cases, the language in the messages was technically correct, but it was clear that they were not written by native-born Vietnamese—another example of American dominance over the Vietnamese.

Another example of how the effort could be counterproductive was the use of large airplanes to drop the leaflets in remote areas. That often reinforced the enemy propaganda that the South Vietnamese were being controlled by and had become puppets of American imperialism.

There have been some academic attempts to understand this issue. One is an excellent example of scholarly academics, not practitioners (with one exception), scrutinizing the notion of propaganda.* It is a clear attempt to show that this topic is important and needs examination using a more scientific method, as only scholars can do. The central problem, of course, is that this topic is not the central research topic of any of the contributors. In fact, none of those living are associated with one of the elite universities, such as Harvard, Yale, Stanford, or Berkeley. We must give credit, however, for the attempt, but not for the results. In some cases the writings are examples of overanalysis. Common sense might tell us more about the topic than the application of a rigorous academic theory. Nonetheless, good questions are asked.

---

* Jowett, Garth S., and O'Donnell, Victoria, *Readings in Propaganda and Persuasion: New and Classic Essays, 4th ed.* (Thousand Oaks, CA: Sage Publications, 2006).

A second book, although a bit outdated (1989) and too focused on the Soviet Union as an enemy, provides some excellent discussion about past attempts to employ Polwar and Psyops.* It provides insights into real problems at the national level as well as at the application level. Although it does focus on the Soviet Union before its demise, it is possible in many cases to visualize similar problems today. Just substitute the Middle East for the Soviet Union as an adversary. This book identifies critical U.S. weaknesses in 1989, and not much has changed. It is important to note that the authors are mostly senior academics who have served in high positions in the intelligence or policy-making community, or are senior military officers who have been engaged in the practice of Psyops. Historically the solution to weaknesses in the U.S. approach has been to reorganize and rewrite some doctrine—a very simplistic approach.

A third book is useful because it is the result of insiders writing and explaining "fundamental PSYOP roles, principles, and methods."† It is useful because it includes many who have been working in this field at the operational level. It exposes many of the weakness in the U.S. approach.

There is not much written about the use of political warfare (Polwar) or Psyops in Iraq and Afghanistan from a lessons learned perspective, but it is almost certain that when those wars are dissected, a lot will be learned about those aspects of the conflict.

When literature about Polwar or Psyops is read, it is important to pay close attention to each author's background and approach. Many authors come from managerial, technical, or purely academic backgrounds, so their knowledge of the big picture and some components of the field is limited. Some writers are political scientists or sociologists, so they describe the actors (terrorists in today's conflict) very well and how they fit or don't fit into various societies. There are even a few articles written by military persons, but they usually focus on field techniques. It is critical that we understand how political warfare and Psyops fit into broader military or conflict strategies of our enemies and our own troops to find ways to cope with this relatively new type of warfare.

Polwar and Psyops are topics that require an interdisciplinary approach. They cannot be studied in a vacuum by looking only at case studies and then trying to formulate generalizations that apply to the future. History, political science, sociology, military strategy, law, and even geography make important contributions to the thinking about this topic.

---

* Lord, Carnes, and Barnett, Frank R., eds., *Political Warfare and Psychological Operations: Rethinking the US Approach* (Washington, DC: National Defense University Press, 1989).
† Goldstein, Frank L., and Findley, Benjamin F., Jr., *Psychological Operations: Principles and Case Studies* (Maxwell AFB, AL: Air University Press, 1996).

Definitions

Psyops, sometimes called propaganda, is considered by most scholars and critics as bad and immoral under any conditions—even wartime ("dysfunctional and negative activity").* In some cases it is described as "dirty tricks." This means that if Psyops is to be employed, it will be necessary to explain the activities in terms acceptable to critics. It is not unlike war. There are many who believe that war is not the solution, that one should never resort to the use of force. While many will never accept the use of Psyops in wartime or peacetime, it is critical that the activity be placed into context and an explanation be made of why it is considered a valuable national security tool.

When the writings of scholars or even experienced bureaucrats are reviewed, there is a general condemnation of propaganda use—even during periods of war. Part of the condemnation results from ineffective or even counterproductive use, and part is a result of general moral indignation. Often a key to the conflict in thinking is in the writer's difference in definitions. Propaganda, political warfare, and Psyops are discussed by scholars or former practitioners with specific definitions in mind, but those definitions are often understood differently by different readers. To define the terms and some of the subtopics, it is necessary to begin with general definitions and then by identifying target audiences.

The *Department of Defense Dictionary of Military and Associated Terms* (Joint Pub 1-02, December 1, 1989) defines strategic psychological activities as

> planned psychological activities in peace and war which normally pursue objectives to gain support and cooperation of friendly and neutral countries and to reduce the will and the capacity of hostile or potentially hostile countries to wage war.

Another contribution to the definition is by Angelo Codevilla, where he defines political warfare as

> the marshaling of human support, or opposition, in order to achieve victory in war or unbloody conflicts as serious as war.[†]

This definition misses a lot and assumes political warfare as an alternative to violent battle. Another broad definition comes from Jowett:[‡]

---

* Jowett and O'Donnell, xii.
† Lord and Barnett, 77.
‡ Jowett and O'Donnell, ix.

The central and simple purpose is to alter and manipulate public attitudes, perceptions and ultimately behavior in such a way as to benefit those employing such techniques.

It is possible to isolate a number of elements from these definitions and look for them in future definitions:

1. Target audiences
2. Wartime or peacetime
3. Strategic/tactical level (national strategy or battlefield techniques)
4. Organization and persuasion techniques
5. Goals (ideology or content of activity)

Target Audiences

While most authors use the term *propaganda*, they are writing about completely different concepts. For example, Russia or Nazi Germany's use of propaganda deals primarily with influencing Germany's own population.[*] Even the United States had a program during World War II that was aimed at its own population.[†] In all these examples of "immoral" or "ineffective" uses of propaganda, the target audience was one's own troops or civilian population. At the other end of the scale, the chapter on Korean "brainwashing" focuses only on enemy troops.[‡] Nearly all doctrine prepared by U.S. organizations focuses exclusively on enemy troops and populations.

Defining the target audience makes a major difference in the approach to any psychological effort, as it complicates any discussion or definition of terms.

Generally there are eight possible target audiences:

1. One's own citizens (military and civilian)
2. Enemy citizens (military and civilian)
3. Allied citizens (military and civilian)
4. Nonaligned citizens (military and civilian)

Within these broad categories of target audiences, each of which requires a different approach and usually a different content to the message, there are a number of potential target audiences at lower levels, for example, youth groups, mass groups (unions), political party elements, etc.

---

[*] Ibid., chaps. 5–7.
[†] Ibid., chap. 8.
[‡] Ibid., chap. 10.

The targets of psychological operations makes a huge difference in the type of techniques used and the general approach to the activity. A major problem occurs when an effort against one target audience has a negative impact on one of the other target audiences, which in the long term could be counterproductive to the overall war effort.

Political Warfare

Authors and government writers are not consistent in their definition of any of these terms—the most important of which are *political warfare* and *psychological operations*. The one place where consistency does exist is in the doctrine that comes out of the Russian and Chinese systems. Much of that doctrine has been passed on to their surrogates in Southeast Asia and the Middle East. For that reason, it is important to be clear on the meaning of the terms. It is not just so we can sort out our own activities, but we must also be able to understand the activities of our adversary that are aimed at us if we are to develop effective counterefforts.

Political warfare is the most comprehensive term and includes a wider scope of activity than psychological operations or propaganda. This is not a loose or fuzzy term. It has a specific meaning and a well-defined body of literature, especially in Russia and China. They give much more prominence to political warfare than does the United States.

Perhaps the worst example of a weak definition of the term is by a scholar, Angelo Codevilla, who defines political warfare only by its methods: gray and black propaganda, support for foreign groups, and agents of influence. It is not likely that any other author uses the term this way, and once we understand the global meaning of the term, we can see how Codevilla's approach, while useful in discussing some low-level techniques, is extremely misleading when examining the broad concept of political warfare.

Political warfare is the total effort used by one government to change the attitudes and behavior of *anyone* who might disagree with it. Political warfare includes programs against all the target audiences, although in the case of Russia and China, the nation's own military and civilians receive the most attention. The government must build loyalty to the incumbent political party and the military first; then it can look outward. The methods principally used for this effort are a form of the Leninist organizational method. The organizational techniques extend to every citizen in the society, and some receive much more attention than others (party, military, youth groups, mass media, and education system).

Another unique characteristic of political warfare is that it places high priority on integrating the political effort into all military operational plans. For every military plan at every level a military unit political officer (commissar) must anticipate the political consequences on each target audience of every military action. So before any military attack, there is an annex to the operations plan that tries to determine the likely consequences of the military action plan. Will it adversely or positively influence the people in each of the target audience groups? This is quite different from an American Psyops officer looking at an operations plan and preparing his or her own plan to supplement the attack with leaflets or loudspeakers.

Quite often, mostly at higher levels, the military operations plan is a part of a broader political plan. That is, the political goal is defined first, and then the military is asked to take action to further that plan. This is quite different from the U.S. approach, where the military plan is always first and the Psyops efforts are an adjunct.

The Chinese and Russian political warfare organizations and doctrines are extremely complex, as is what they have passed on to their surrogates in the Middle East and Southeast Asia. Historically, political warfare systems passed on to other nations or groups have been adapted to fit the conditions of the receiver.

Political warfare is far more than indoctrination of a population and control by a political party over a military. It includes organizational and manipulation techniques that allow those in control of the system to control the whole society. It includes a defined, but adjustable structure, and special indoctrination techniques. The substance or content (Russian or Chinese Communism, Chinese or Vietnamese Nationalism, Islam) of political warfare can be different. The potential effectiveness depends on the structure and functions of the system.

The following is a brief description of how a small part of the Leninist organizational techniques work in different groups. The concepts and principles were carried to the logical extreme in China during the Great Proletarian Cultural Revolution. The organization and techniques were used in every organization in the society (military, civilian bureaucracy, factories, schools, newspaper offices, mass groups—youth, agriculture, women's), and sometimes even in neighborhoods.

The best example of how it is supposed to work is at the level just above the grassroots level, and it is from the Chinese People's Liberation Army (PLA).*

In the PLA every commander at every level has a political commissar on his staff. The same has been true for factories, schools, and any other type of organization, but in the civilian organizations they are called party secretar-

---

* For a more comprehensive view of a political warfare system in action, see Bullard, Monte, *The Soldier and the State: The Role of the Military in Taiwan's Development* (Armonk, NY: M.E. Sharpe, 1997). Much of the information on political warfare in this section was taken directly from this book.

ies. Depending on the level, each commissar has a staff of his own. These are the full-time party cadres (*apparatchik*).

This system actually began in France during the French Revolution and was designed primarily as a means to watch over the commander to ensure his political reliability and loyalty to the nation's center. In China it was a way to prevent regionalism or warlordism. Later, the system evolved into an excellent means of social control over all military, economic, and political activity in the country. It is effective at controlling the people at the grassroots level as well as civilian and military leaders when it is implemented properly.

The system reached China through the Soviet Union in 1927. It was actually used by the Nationalists before the Communists, but when they split, the system was adopted by both and evolved differently in each army.

The key to this system is the ability of the commissar (or party secretary in the case of a factory or school) to circumvent the normal chain of command, even though he is listed as a subordinate of the commander.

What we must see is a powerful control mechanism that can be used effectively by whichever interest group controls the top. It is what maintains a Leninist system. It is extremely effective, and the primary way to ensure total loyalty to whomever is in charge.

The basic philosophy of the system comes in part from Mao's dictum that "political power grows out of the barrel of a gun." He also noted that the party must control the gun. What that says is that whoever controls the military controls the nation. There is little doubt that with this very effective political commissar system, the military can be controlled. There is no guarantee, though, as to whom the controllers are.

We must not fall into the trap of believing this control is necessarily sinister or oppressive. For the most part, it is a very positive control, so its very existence can be rationalized to its participants. There are mechanisms built in to detect dissent quickly and to pacify the organization by making the participants happy with their role—both psychologically and materially happy.

The best way to examine the pervasiveness of this system is to describe how it works at the company level in the military. The description below is how it is ideally supposed to work. It doesn't always work that way, though.

First, examine the parallel structure. At every level there is a parallel party structure. In Western armies, that is contrary to the Prussian principle of unity of command. The party leaders at each level can report up the chain of command through the party structure only. Instructions can go down to the party leaders, bypassing the commander of the unit. One of the major changes in this system made by the Taiwanese and South Vietnamese was that the commissar was subordinated to the commander and everything had to go through the commanders (Figures 9.1 and 9.2).

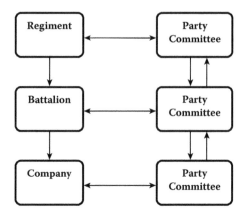

Figure 9.1 Organization for company level Polwar meeting.

The commissar is concurrently the secretary (key man) of the parallel party organization. The committees are made up of appointed soldiers. Sometimes they are elected in open elections and then co-opted into the party later.

The welfare committee is charged with ensuring that the soldiers eat well, have good living accommodations, good clothing, etc. They are also responsible for entertainment and recreation of troops. They organize events and serve as a sounding board for problems. Problems are brought by the committee members to the attention of the commissar, who discusses them with the commander. The commander must either accommodate the demands or explain why he cannot.

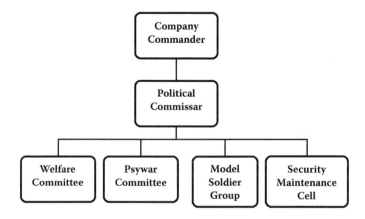

Figure 9.2 Within the company the relationships might be diagrammed as shown (the names vary with the particular system, Russian, Communist Chinese, or Nationalist Chinese).

The Psywar committee is responsible for indoctrinating the troops with the appropriate attitudes and beliefs. Note that in this system the main focus of the Psywar effort is one's own troops. They organize newspaper reading or radio listening periods. They teach current events with the correct party message. The make sure all the troops get whatever the party message of the day is. They are used to teach the current behavior norms and to provide the attitudes that ensure compliance with national and organizational directives. It is political socialization at its best.

The model soldier committee is usually elected—a means of identifying natural leaders at the lowest levels. They are then trained to be the first to volunteer for everything and are the opinion formers for the group. This has proven to be a very effective way of co-opting the natural leaders into the Communist system. Once the natural leaders are identified, there are a number of techniques to eventually co-op them into the Communist system.

The security maintenance cells are secret informants, not known to their fellow troops, and they report directly to the political commissar.

The political commissar meets with these committees and the security maintenance cells on a regular basis so he knows what is on the minds of every soldier. He gets feedback on conditions from the welfare committee, and he tries to provide the commander with good advice as to what will solve the problem. If the commander cannot solve the problem, he uses the commissar and the Psywar committee to persuade the troops why he cannot solve it and why they must sacrifice for the good of the motherland.

For example, if the welfare committee determined that the food was not good, they would bring the matter up to the commissar. They might tell him that there is not enough meat and they don't have enough energy to do their job. The commissar would tell the commander, who would probably make a genuine attempt to get more meat. If, for budgetary or other reasons, he could not, he would initiate an indoctrination session with the commissar to explain to the troops that at this time they are very poor or that no meat is available in the area. The point is that they do try very hard to accommodate the troop's wishes or explain why they can't respond.

Another interesting point is that in most units the commissar is considered the mother of the unit, and the commander the father, or disciplinarian. That means that when there is trouble, the troops are not really reluctant to go to the commissar because he usually has a record of solving all kinds of personal problems. He is particularly sensitive about each soldier's family, and if a soldier complains that his parents aren't getting enough to eat at home, the commissar will take action through the party organization to get them more food.

We can see in recent reports from the Middle East that there is a concern by Hamas, for example, for the families of the suicide bombers, and each gets a stipend of $3,000 to $5,000. This is a clear characteristic of a political warfare system in action. It also encourages the next round of suicide bombers, and it is really much more practical than, as the Western press reports, doing it to meet seventy-two virgins in heaven.

The commissar meets with his security maintenance cells or informants in secret. They inform on their fellow troops. When they spot one of their fellow soldiers who does not go with the flow, they report him. The commissar then singles that soldier out for special indoctrination. At first he tries to apply peer influence. He may even tailor the indoctrination periods to target the individual's attitude problem. He allows the model soldiers to try to convince him he is wrong. If that doesn't work, he has many other options, the most extreme of which is to remove him from the group so he won't contaminate the others. He might be sent to a special farm for "learning through labor" or some other type of more strictly monitored unit.

The commissar or party secretary in a factory keeps dossiers on each worker. Based on that dossier, which is filled from notes from informants or from firsthand observation at meetings or from political tests, all promotions and assignments are determined. This is a principle from the bottom to the top, and this is what has given the commissar or party secretary so much power. This is especially true when the principal criterion for promotion or assignment is political reliability, but that can be extended to include general attitudes and how that person relates to his group.

It is critical to understand that the Leninist system is not strictly a negative sanction system. It does make the life of the troops more comfortable and helps them to solve their personal problems, which in turn creates an environment that makes them more efficient at their job and loyal to their unit. It is a major contributor to combat effectiveness.

For broader problems the commander can create or manipulate a consensus using small or large group meetings.

There are two categories of unit meetings that recur frequently, usually once a week, but as much as daily during times of political tension. One is the criticism/self-criticism session. It usually occurs in a squad-size group, about ten people. Each soldier must stand up and criticize himself and others for not having the proper attitude, as learned from the current materials prepared by the Psywar committee, or for not exerting his maximum effort to get a job done for the "people." He is not free to be silent or passive. He must participate, and someone is always taking notes on what he says. This places tremendous peer pressure on each individual to conform.

In China at the height of the Great Proletarian Cultural Revolution nearly every citizen, in the ideal, was also under extreme supervision and social control. Every citizen belonged to a small group (*Xiao Zu*) and was required to meet five or six times a week for long struggle or self-criticism sessions. The purpose of the meetings was to change the basic personality (attitudes and behavior) of each individual to be a selfless contributor and conformist to the Socialist society. The meetings were extremely diabolical and oppressive. Each member of the group was required to stand up and confess his weaknesses or mistakes to the other members of the small group. He or she was also required to criticize himself and his or her friends.

A sample of a session is as follows. Picture a work team on a pig farm. Three members, good friends, are going out to fertilize the fields after cleaning out the pig manure trough. All are carrying their buckets. The second from the end was feeling bad that day and decided to dump some of the manure along the way to lighten his load. That night at the struggle session the person who was behind the shirker went through a self-criticism by saying only that he had tried to work hard that day but was lazy for an hour or so. He did not mention that his friend had dumped part of his load on the way back. The shirker then stood up for his turn. He mentioned that he had not been feeling good and that he had dumped part of his load and therefore had not made his fair contribution to the motherland and the great Chinese Socialist society. He then said, "And my friend who just spoke saw me dump my load, and he did not report me." That friend then is in great trouble. The mutual surveillance system was all-pervasive. Everyone was compelled to spy on everyone else. No one trusted anyone.

Based on this description, what did nearly all Chinese consider to be the "freedom" they missed most under this system? It was the freedom of silence. At these meetings no member was allowed to pass—there was no freedom of silence. Members had to find something wrong with themselves so they could show improvement and that they were good members of the Socialist society. So they began to make up things that were not viewed as too damaging and things they could easily correct. Sometimes it was only wrong thoughts.

These sessions had a profound effect on the political culture of China, the attitudes that affect political activity. First, a distrust of everyone developed. Second, individuals began to live in their own little world. Third, everyone learned to lie, and lying became an acceptable social act justified by self-survival.

The second type of meeting is a consensus-forming meeting. It is a meeting of the company in the PLA or a work unit in the outside. It is usually about one hundred people. Before each meeting, the commissar calls together his model soldier committee and perhaps the Psywar committee separately. He tells them the school solution to a problem to be presented to the committee. Once the main group meets, the commander presents the problem and asks for recommendations from the group. This is the "mass line" at work (see Figure 9.3).

As soon as the commander presents his problem, one of the prompted model soldiers in the 1st platoon would say: "I think we should do it this way." Another soldier from the 3d platoon would say: "That's a great idea."

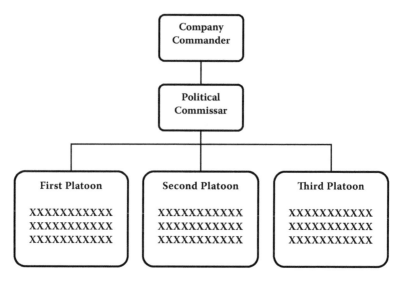

Figure 9.3 Command structure parallel party organization.

Others would chime in, including nonprompted passive people who then believe it is a true consensus.

Often after the commander presents his problem one of the soldiers who is not clued in will offer a suggestion. That suggestion is noted, and if it has merit it may be included in the solution. This happens often enough that the group doesn't always know which are prompted and which are not, so the whole process is believable. Furthermore, each member of the group feels he or she is a part of the solution. They are willing to exert all their effort because they have a stake in the outcome.

This whole process of manipulating a consensus is quite different from the style used by Western commanders, where the commander stands in front of the group and issues orders, or worse, stays in his office and issues orders. It is easy to contrast preparations for going into battle—to include against the students in Tiananmen. In the United States when a company (about one hundred men) was tasked to capture a hill, the company commander would gather his platoon leaders and some squad leaders, but not the troops. He would tell the first platoon to flank left and the third platoon to flank right. He would explain who takes the frontal assault and who is in reserve. He would explain the timing of the attack. He would then issue the orders to go. The fighting troops would not be present at the meeting.

In the Chinese system the company commander would gather all the troops. He would explain the task for attacking the hill and ask for suggestions. He would then manipulate the system using the approach discussed above. As a result, all the troops would have a psychological feeling that they are part of the solution. They had a stake in the outcome, and they could not blame the leaders if something went wrong. They then become very fierce as fighters. For years our intelligence reports in Vietnam told how the morale of the Viet Cong was terrible and going down. Yet every time they attacked they were tremendously brave, disciplined, and dedicated soldiers. There was no "fragging" in their army (trying to kill the platoon leader on the way to battle because you didn't believe in his orders). We never did understand why this phenomenon occurred. This method probably partially explains how suicide bombers are made.

Under this system there is no possibility for resentment to build to a point of a subversive organization developing. The system knows what is on every individual's mind, and if there is dissent, they can change the minds or get rid of the dissenter. This, of course, also represents a tremendous defense against U.S or allied propaganda efforts.

As mentioned earlier, it is important to be very careful not to fall into the trap that this Leninist Party system is totally sinister and oppressive, or that it is used only to control the military. It does accomplish many good things for the group, and it can make the group much more combat effective or, in the case of a terrorist cell, more efficient. One of the most important things it provides is stability within the group and predictability of actions between its members—and that is a powerful management tool.

There are many problems with the system. The main problem is that it is not always implemented well. In times of crises the commissar has the authority to approve everything the commander does. He gets totally involved in the operational aspects of the unit. He becomes an intermeddler. When that happens, he often picks up resentment from everyone because most commissars are not technically competent. The commissar is responsible only for the mental attitudes of the troops, and the commander is responsible only for the operational competence. The system works fairly well. This dichotomy is often called the "red" versus "expert" conflict and exists in every organizational unit that uses this system.

When China went through a period of reduced party control, it meant that this mechanism would break down. It meant, for example, that the criteria for promotion emphasized technical skill instead of political reliability. The importance of the commissar was then diminished. Another thing that reduced his importance was the phasing down or out of the frequent political meetings.

Other problems with the system have been discussed frequently. Sometimes the message being passed down is so unbelievable that even the true-believing party cadres have a hard time with them. This is especially true when they are forced to convince the troops that a new policy is correct when it is 180 degrees from an earlier policy that they put an equal effort into—and that happened a lot.

A final problem with the system is that the commissar becomes too powerful, and as Lord Acton said, "Power corrupts and absolute power corrupts absolutely." Commissars are usually true believers, but many of them take the job for personal advancement only. They usually milk the system, and it becomes obvious to the troops.

The above description is only a minor part of a political warfare system and the type of thinking that goes into it. Of course, in such a system the central authority is the highest level of the Communist Party, and whatever ideology or party line they introduce into the system is carried out very well. It should also be noted that this system is really good at identifying those individuals who do not comply with the system, and they are reeducated or eliminated.

In addition to the Leninist organizational system for society, political warfare also includes total control over the mass media and education system. It also includes a number of organizations responsible for political warfare to be conducted against foreign target audiences, but the primary target audience for Russian and Chinese political warfare is their own troops and populace, and that is what sets them apart from the American system.

Political warfare efforts against foreign target audiences have two basic characteristics. First, they are extremely centralized in the Communist Party, as opposed to the government. How it works in organizations such as al-Qaeda is not clear. In the case of the Soviet Union, a small group at the top of the Communist Party, the International Department of the Communist Party Central Committee,* enlists the aid of the most senior professional specialists to develop programs targeted against the United States. It is critical that as we see these types of active measures (forgeries, agents of influence, international fronts) we recognize them and are prepared to counter them as part of a Psyops effort.

Second, military force is subordinated to political ideology (Communism or radical Islam). It is quite unlike the U.S. approach in which a Psyops officer or organization becomes aware of the military attack plan and then conjures up ways to support that action. It is the reverse in a political warfare system. A political plan is prepared and then military actions are employed to support that plan.

The efforts at political warfare toward each of the audiences are significantly different. It is also an extremely important concept of political warfare that no military action is taken for military purposes only. All military action, no matter how small, must be considered in the light of the political consequences.

Another major difference between the U.S. system and the political warfare system is in preparation of the cadres. In the political warfare system

* Goldstein and Findley, Chap. 10.

most political cadres serve in that position for their entire career. They also attend several schools in their development. There are years of training. In the U.S. system it is a major problem to find officers to serve in Psyops, they have little formal training, and one of the recommendations is to get people to be away from their unit for a week or two for training. It is really pros versus amateurs.

Political warfare includes all of the methods used to change the minds of all target audiences and for political warfare, one's own citizens and soldiers have the highest priority. The Communist's and probably radical Islam's approach to this effort is clearly more complex and refined than that of the United States. We see it daily in the news reports from Iraq, where attacks are clearly for the psychological impact more than for any military advantage.

Psyops

Political warfare is a much more comprehensive term and includes a well-defined structure, techniques, and doctrine. The next term to understand is *psychological operations* (Psyops), which is the principal American term to describe this type of psychological activity.

The term *psychological operations* is important because it is formally and officially defined by the U.S. government, particularly the military. It is not just a term that many people use.

Psychological operations (PSYOP) are planned operations to convey selected information and indicators to foreign audiences to influence the emotions, motives, objective reasoning, and ultimately the behavior of foreign governments, organizations, groups, and individuals.*

The definition goes on to divide Psyops into three levels:

Strategic Psyops are international information activities conducted by U.S. government (USG) agencies to influence foreign attitudes, perceptions, and behavior in favor of U.S. goals and objectives during peacetime and in times of conflict. These programs are conducted predominantly outside the military arena but can utilize Department of Defense (DOD) assets.

Operational Psyops are conducted across the range of military operations, including during peacetime, in a defined operational area

---

* Joint Publication 3-53, *Doctrine for Joint Psychological Operations*, Joint Chiefs of Staff.

to promote the effectiveness of the joint force commander's (JFC) campaigns and strategies.

Tactical Psyops are conducted in the area assigned a tactical commander across the range of military operations to support the tactical mission against opposing forces.

Similar definitions appear in the earlier *U.S. Army Field Manual 30-3*, and both are considered authoritative doctrine upon which to base organization and training.

The first thing we notice about the definitions is that they are directed only at foreign target audiences. That, of course, is a major difference from the political warfare aimed at the United States by our adversaries. The definitions do, however, leave room for targeting allied and neutral audiences, but that is seldom considered.

Another unique feature of the definitions is the separation of levels, which has caused considerable fragmentation between government agencies and is almost always the center of recommendations for new organizing and coordination procedures.

Doctrinal manuals go further in explaining the missions of Psyops when they narrow the mission statements:

Advising the supported commander through the targeting process regarding targeting restrictions, psychological actions, and psychological enabling actions to be executed by the military force.

Influencing foreign populations by expressing information through selected conduits to influence attitudes and behavior and to obtain compliance or noninterference with friendly military operations.

Providing public information to foreign populations to support humanitarian activities, ease suffering, and restore or maintain civil order.

Serving as the supported commander's voice to foreign populations by conveying the JFC's intent.

Countering adversary propaganda, misinformation, disinformation, and opposing information to correctly portray friendly intent and actions, while denying others the ability to polarize public opinion and affect the political will of the United States and its multinational partners within an operational area.

Here friendly foreign military operations become another target audience. These mission statements are not all that clear, so through examining the doctrine itself, it will be possible to gain a better understanding of what American psychological operators view as their own tasks. It will be noted that most of the focus is on the method of delivery and, to some extent, the cultural aspect of the target audience, but little effort at the larger picture of national political goals and strategies, although that is considered.

A number of principles need to be discussed in more detail. First is the notion that the "Vietnam War was won by the Communists, and lost by the United States, at the psychological-political level of conflict."* This is a profound statement and is perhaps the best argument for the United States to get better at Psyops. We often note that even though the United States never lost a battle on the battlefield, we lost the war. This statement explains why.

The terms *Polwar* and *Psyops* are used in ways that don't necessarily follow the definitions discussed above. In addition, a number of other terms are often introduced (public diplomacy, political action, coercive diplomacy, covert political warfare, black/white/gray propaganda, etc.) that are subsets of the general terms. In some cases the author is just trying to introduce a new term to explain his understanding of the phenomenon.

Perhaps a better term is *Psywar* (psychological warfare), which was the official term used by the U.S. military prior to adopting the term *Psyops*. It may be a more pertinent term because it reminds us that it is warfare with which we are concerned. The other key term is *propaganda*, but it is not too useful because it is considered pejorative by so many. Propaganda is considered "manipulated truth" and is necessarily a "dysfunctional and negative activity."† We should also subscribe to the observation that the term *propaganda* should be neutral—and can be positive or negative depending on the content and who is using it. Unfortunately, since it is so widely seen as a derogatory term, it is generally not useful.

One point made by several authors is that the message of Psyops must be based upon the truth.‡ This, of course, is a relatively idealistic, simplistic, and superficial statement. It is akin to the statement made by Rodney King after being beaten in Los Angeles in 1991: "Can't we all just get along?" But common sense tells us the world is just not black and white. There are many shades of gray that must be part of the message. There are many examples of how deliberate lies come back to haunt those who disseminated them, so when other than the truth is used, it has to be done with much thought about the consequences if they are exposed. But there will be times, perhaps in deception operations, when it is necessary to shade the truth and other times when selective facts are used that do not present the whole truth.

Almost daily examples of spinning the truth can be seen. Just examine the views of the different parties in the U.S. Congress when they are focused on the same set of facts. So in an open democracy, to find an agreed upon "truth" that can be disseminated, even to the enemy, by the Psyops organization will always be a major challenge. This is especially true when the substance of the message deals with ideological or religious topics.

* Lord and Barnett, xiii.
† Jowett and O'Donnell, xii.
‡ Lord and Barnett, 5–7.

Another principle that emerges is the effort to influence the media. In the case of Polwar there is an intense effort to influence the American media as one of the most important target audiences after its own population. In the case of Psyops the problem is different. The adversary's media is tightly controlled, so influencing them is much more difficult, but not impossible. This opens the discussion of using psychological operations in a democracy. It is considered especially unethical, if not illegal, for the military in the United States to try to influence the U.S. media by planting stories—even if the stories are true. Nonetheless, this is a critical issue to examine. It is another area that makes the battlefield uneven and gives the advantage to the adversary. This is perhaps one of the most important challenges for the future: how to set the record straight or counter opposing force psychological efforts, yet stay with the guidelines laid down by U.S. doctrine.

Much that appears in the press is on how the U.S. bureaucratic system has been and is a major obstacle to effective Psyops. In effect, as the Pogo cartoon used to say, "We have met the enemy and he is us." Although the doctrine (Joint Publication 3-53) tries to clarify organizational and coordination responsibilities, there are always challenges that render the Psyops effort more difficult. Not only has there been confusion over who is responsible for what (civilian agencies, Army, Navy, Air Force), but there has been a problem of where to fit Psyops into the Army organization. Should it be subordinated to special operations or be separate at a higher level? Where it is placed makes a big difference in funding as well as the degree to which the Psyops plans get used.

Another issue that comes up frequently is the latitude for conducting Psyops during peacetime versus wartime. Note that over the years the Psyops capability is phased out, or at least severely degraded, during peacetime. Of course, that has also been true for the military forces in general. But again, we are in a new era. Although war has not currently been formally declared, we are clearly in a war and military forces have been expanded—even Psyops organizations.

Another issue that always comes up, especially for American Psyops, is personnel. What kind of personnel should manage the Psyops organizations at the various levels? Should they include psychologists, sociologists, area studies specialists, foreign nationals, etc.? What training should they receive within the U.S. government and where? We are now dealing with adversaries that employ professionals throughout their system. They keep them in the system for a career and continue to educate them. Can you just assign smart people or good managers to the effort, or is there a professional core of knowledge that they must have? Is there a particular combination of people the organization needs? Obviously, for the technical jobs, such as running a printing plant or radio station, there are technical skills required, but how about the other portions of the organization and the decision makers within the system?

One extremely important topic is the degree to which the military effort should be subordinated to the Psyops effort. This question would not even be considered in a major conflict like Korea or World War II. But in the war on terror the environment is completely different. Col. (Ret.) Alfred Paddock is one of the few who recognize this as a possibility in his article when he talks about the "propaganda of the deed."* Although he doesn't spend much space on the subject, it is critical and could be a major part of some solutions to the Psyops problems. The U.S. does these things regularly without thinking about the Psyops message to be conveyed. Whether ship visits, joint exercises with other countries, or bombing a particular target, if the military activity were subordinated, or a secondary priority, to a larger political strategy, it could make a major difference. At the very least, it might force different military leaders to think differently in their planning.

Nearly every day, in the current conflict, someone says: "This war against terrorists cannot be solved only militarily, it must be solved politically." For the military, that statement should not mean that someone else must solve the problem; it means there must be a better integration of political and military strategies, and that is partially the role of Psyops.

Goldstein and Findley provide a very useful overview of Psyops.† They provide some general principles that should be kept in mind as detailed Psyops techniques are examined. These authors have obviously had a great deal of experience in this field and have a great deal of common sense. They make the observation that "political and military actions are critical elements in psychological operations."‡ That is the one statement that indicates that there is some potential to make military actions subordinate to psychological operations—at least in some situations.

The authors are a bit idealistic when they state: "The government must establish realistic policy goals to ensure consistent and credible operations." It would be nice, but it doesn't always happen. So Psyops officers must work around it. In many cases it is possible to refer back to current policy statements and doctrine, interpret them, and prepare our own goals. In any case, it is important that clear policy goals be included in our planning.

Some authors go back more than two thousand years to find examples of using political warfare or Psyops in conflict situations. Perhaps the strongest is from the great Chinese strategist Sun Tzu (544–496 B.C.): "To win a war without fighting is the acme of military skill."

The principal effort of political warfare or psychological operations is to change minds and behavior of those who disagree with you, and especially those who are prepared to fight you. It is as simple as that. How to do

---

* Lord and Barnett, 52.
† Goldstein and Findley, Chap. 9.
‡ Ibid., 125.

it, though, is not so simple. Ideally, then, the highest priority would be the political or psychological goals, and the military goals would be part of the effort to achieve them. In the United States, however, these priorities seem to get reversed.

Some of the most effective Psyops efforts were found in the American Revolutionary War. While they were not planned or implemented by a Psyops organization, it is clear that the fighters discovered a couple of Psyops principles early. They knew that in a revolutionary warfare situation it would be necessary to gain the loyalty of the citizen population to the cause of expelling the British—a common sense understanding. In this case the outstanding articulation of the cause and the appeal to fear prevailed. This is an example that could, however, be misleading. Certainly if a Psyops unit is to appeal to fear, as often is attempted, there must be a thorough understanding of the target audiences. One example was in Vietnam when the U.S. military prepared leaflets that appealed to fear.* In the case of Vietnam, those who read the leaflets had already been indoctrinated by the other side, so they were of little value. The examples in the Revolutionary War, however, were in a period when neither side had been prepared to resist the propaganda of the other side. The point here is that we must always consider the degree to which the target audience has been indoctrinated already, and we must be particularly aware of the substance of that indoctrination. Psyops does not work in a vacuum or equally against any target audience.

The Revolutionary War was also an example of the sensitivity to the need for assistance by allied nations—another target audience of appropriate Psyops efforts. That principle continues and has become just as important today, although perhaps a little more indirect. Public opinion in allied nations as well as nonaligned nations becomes a critical factor that must be considered in any Psyops effort. It is important to think out how an allied nation will react to a message only intended for the enemy population. Again, the Psyops effort cannot be applied in a vacuum.

American Psyops efforts have been hampered by extreme sensitivities to the U.S. Congress and the U.S. media since World War I. It is perhaps even truer today than at any time in the past. So part of the thought processes in preparing a Psyops plan must be to take those two institutions into account. The obstacles resulting from a divided Congress and media in a democratic society are formidable, but not insurmountable. It takes serious thought and analysis to find Psyops messages that can satisfy all the domestic concerns. Of course, the environment at the time also plays a major role. What could be said the week after 9/11 is quite different from what could be said five years later.

---

* Goldstein and Findley, 136.

One of the most important Psyops efforts is sometimes called propaganda of the deed. In many cases (bombing a Nazi radio station at a critical moment or the Libyan raid) the military action was designed to further a larger psychological or political goal. This is where future Psyops personnel can be creative and much more effective. A badly conceived Psyops mission can also have an out of proportion negative impact.

Political warfare techniques used to build the loyalty of one's own citizens and troops is a special issue. What we must keep in mind is that the techniques and messages used are inherent to the political warfare concept that was used by the Chinese and the Soviets and are being used by today's adversaries in the Middle East. We must understand completely the thinking behind these efforts if we are to cope with them.

Conclusion

This chapter compares the approaches of the political warfare system used by America's adversaries with the U.S. Psyops approach in the battle of ideas. It is almost like comparing apples to oranges. It seems clear that American adversaries' approaches to the battle of ideas are quite different from those of the United States. It also seems clear that the approaches used by America's adversaries are far more comprehensive. They are far more extensive and far reaching. They fall under the concept of political warfare, which includes a major structure with defined functions as well as a defined body of literature or doctrine. It includes techniques for persuading all target audiences to believe in their ideology or religion and to reject those of anyone who disagrees with them. In many cases they have been quite effective, but they too have serious weaknesses. This chapter has provided a brief introduction to what America is up against. Political warfare is a serious force that few understand in depth and is certainly a topic for future study.

American approaches to the battle of ideas have been fragmentary. While most observers recognize that conflicts must be won in the political arena as well as the military arena, there is little agreement on how to accomplish the task. Some argue that with God, history, or "right" on the American side, we will ultimately win. Others see that it is important to pay attention to the techniques and strategies used by opponents and to develop effective countermeasures. Some also make the case that America's use of Psyops must be completely renovated to cope better with the successes of adversaries. In any case, the issue of how to handle the battle of ideas between cultures or ideologies is one that should be researched in more detail and debated in depth.

United States and European Union Antiterrorism Cooperative Efforts

10

DAVID G. POPP

Contents

Cooperation between the United States and the European Union is not a recent phenomenon. Cross-Atlantic trade between the two has grown to nearly $4 trillion a year at present.* This trade has helped spread economic prosperity, but the ensuing spread of globalism that accompanies international trade invariably brings an increase in the disparity of economic classes in the trading countries. While frequent mention of Islamic fundamentalist groups' involvement in terrorism gives the mistaken inference that there are no other groups involved in terrorist activities (as the activities of groups such as the Irish Republican Army and Ulster Loyalists demonstrate), radical Muslim fundamentalist groups such as al-Qaeda are the primary focus of contemporary antiterrorist efforts. Europe is a fertile ground for the

---

* European Union website: www.europa.eu/home.

recruitment of disaffected Muslim extremists who may eventually carry out terrorist acts.*

Cooperation by the United States and the European Union is seen by many not just as well-intentioned acts by superpowers, but more as an inevitable stage of evolution in world events. Political scientists George Modelski and William Thompson have done extensive studies on global politics. In an article about global politics in the twenty-first century for the *International Studies Review Journal*,[†] they write:

> the next two to three phases of global politics, the possibilities for expanded global organization evolving around a United States-European Union nucleus are considerable but yet tempered by some likelihood of the repetition, in the coming century, of earlier patterns of intensive global conflict over leadership selection.

The authors go on to parallel the work of noted political scientist Samuel Huntington to their own notions of the inevitably close relationship between the United States and the European Union. They write:

> The key to Samuel Huntington's civilization paradigm is a distinctive interpretation of the evolution of global politics after the cold war in the context of which a new and unique situation is emerging. Bipolarity is giving way to multipolarity that gains its substance from the seven or eight different civilizations that are now in regular contact with one another.... Cultural identity will be the central force in the foreseeable future. Groups and states located within a single culture will become more highly integrated and cooperative, especially if the civilization in question clusters around a core state.... A fault line conflict between two neighboring states from antagonistic civilizations might escalate if the fighting encouraged the participation of other states rallying to the defense of one of their cultural kin. The escalation would be particularly dangerous if it brought about a confrontation of core states from civilizations.... Huntington makes a number of other fairly specific predictions. The most dangerous conflict fault line will be found between Islam and Orthodoxy (centered around Russia), ... and Islam and the West.[‡]

How prophetic for ideas written about in 1999, two years prior to the September 11 al-Qaeda attacks on the United States, five years prior to

---

* "Muslim Extremism in Europe," *Economist Magazine*, July 15, 2005, p. 24.
† Modelski, G., and Thompson, W., "The Long and Short of Global Politics in the Twenty First Century: An Evolutionary Approach," *International Studies Review*, 1(2), 109, 1999.
‡ Ibid., 112–13.

their Madrid train bombings, and six years prior to their London subway bombings.

What should make the topic of cross-Atlantic cooperation so relevant to one who studies Europe and the United States? The two shared the relatively similar events of the September 11, 2001, attacks on Washington and New York, followed by attacks in Madrid and London. These analogous memories of terrorist acts will remain embedded on the international communities' psyche and are ensured to spur action. This is coupled with the fact that much of the methodical planning, logistics, and financing took place within the confines of what the world views as two allies and preeminent superpowers, the United States and Europe.

The world's increased attention to terrorism is not a recent phenomenon. Terrorism incidents were on the increase long before the start of this millennium. The United Nations, the (then) European Commission and now European Union, NATO, and the United States all have vowed to fight terrorism. Numerous conventions, declarations, and cooperative agreements have been forged, all denouncing such acts and declaring intentions to foster relationships and practices to fight the spread of terrorism.

What have these declarations of cooperation accomplished? The intention of the author is not just to survey what these declarations say, but more importantly, what they mean to the European Union and the United States. Good intentions aside, do cooperative efforts make the respective governments look good, feel good, and most importantly, do they do any good?

In spite of all the good intentions and efforts of the United States and the European Union to foster a cooperative effort against terrorism, politics, national and international events, the countries' reaction to these events, and the news media's coverage of such events go a long way to stymie a spirit of collaboration. An example of current political commentary is an article by Peter van Ham, head of the global governance program at the Netherlands Institute of International Relations. Van Ham is also the author *of Evolution of the Trans-Atlantic Relationship: Paradise Lost?* As the title of his book implies, van Ham was not a supporter of the efforts of the Bush administration's relations with the European Union. In an editorial in the *International Herald Tribune*, he wrote:

> What has Europe done to draw America's scorn and contempt? The main reason is that Europe has proven to be an untrustworthy ally in America's hour of need.... Responses to 9/11 have been America's strategic litmus test, and most European allies are deemed to have failed miserably. Only Britain and Poland proved themselves to be good apples in a rotten barrel.... Most Europeans now look at the United States as a good friend who has turned himself away

from them, and whose arrogance may hide a deeply felt sense of insecurity, overcompensated by throwing its weight around.*

A faint view of U.S. and EU relations is not limited to the European side of the Atlantic. Numerous political commentators in the United States were critical of the lack of European cooperation in the recent Iraq war. European countries, specifically France and Germany, came under intense criticism from conservative pundits in the United States, and the world saw live on television, among other anti-European actions, how *French fries* were renamed *freedom fries* in the U.S. Senate cafeteria.

Such articles and opinions can do no good to the cause of building support for the United States in Europe. However, opinions aside, actual events may do more harm than any opinion piece, even those in internationally accepted news outlets. The following are examples of the direction the United States and the European Union do *not* want to take as they attempt to cooperate in the fight against terrorism. An environment conductive for cooperation is not possible when the United States and the European Union cannot agree on the legitimacy of measures to fight terrorism.

Recent efforts by the United States to detain and interrogate terrorism suspects located in Europe have not helped to facilitate relationships between the United States and EU. In 2003, the British Broadcasting Service[†] reported that the United States reportedly detained and removed a Muslim cleric named Abu Omar, who was identified by U.S. Intelligence Services as a suspected member of al-Qaeda. This event, commonly known as *extraordinary rendition,* took Omar from his home in Milan, Italy, to Egypt, via an Italian Air Force base shared by the United States in Aviano, Italy. A Milan, Italy, area magistrate was so incensed at the rendition that the magistrate filed European Union arrest warrants for twenty-two U.S. Central Intelligence Agency employees who were allegedly involved in the rendition.

Italian national authorities were quoted as dismissive of the arrest warrants, as well as being unaware of the rendition prior to the warrants being issued. U.S. Secretary of State Condoleezza Rice defended the use of renditions as an "established practice" and suggested that they were "often carried out without the knowledge or participation of European Governments."

As reported in the *Washington Post* and the *Economist* magazine as late as December 2005,[‡] Jack Straw, the British foreign secretary, on behalf of the EU, wrote an official demarche to the U.S. Secretary of State Condoleezza Rice demanding clarification of human rights organizations reports that

---

* van Ham, Peter, "Transatlantic Tensions," *International Herald Tribune,* February 7, 2006.
† BBC News website: www.bbc.co.uk/world/europe/45555.
‡ *Economist Magazine,* December 3, 2005, p. 48.

several al-Qaeda suspects were flown to what were alleged to be secret prisons in Europe for interrogation. This on the eve of a several-country trip by Secretary Rice to many of the countries rumored to be involved in the secret prison incidents. Prior to the secretary's departure, the goal of the trip was publicized by the U.S. Department of State to be one of fostering U.S. and European support for the "War on Terror" (the *Economist*'s quotes). Some of the countries involved in the transfers or detention are allegedly located in Eastern Europe, and were the very countries Secretary Rice was visiting, to include Poland and Romania.

As there are examples where the United States and the European Union have had their differences on antiterrorism efforts, there are also examples where the EU member countries themselves cannot agree on the enforcement of similar measures. One such example occurred in July 2005, when a German court ruled that European arrest warrants, which are utilized by EU member countries to authorize arrest of a suspect in any EU country, were not enforceable under German law. The court cited the warrant's deficiencies when allowing the release of Mamoun Darkazanli, a German-born Syrian businessman who was wanted by Spain for alleged involvement in the al-Qaeda-backed bombing of the Madrid train system. The European arrest warrant, enacted shortly after the September 11, 2001, terrorist attacks in the United States, was touted by many as a "key instrument in the E.U.'s war against terror." The warrant is also under judicial scrutiny in several other countries, to include recent EU member Poland.*

Reportedly, EU member states did not research the crimes included in the warrant to ensure that the crimes were punishable in all member states, with similar sanctions if convicted for such crimes, common elements for an extradition between countries. A survey of EU member states shows huge disparities, not just between crimes and their respective punishments, but the legal systems themselves.†

As recently as February 2006, the head of the European Union Commission for Justice, Freedom, and Security, Italy's Franco Frattini, had released a statement recording the EU's sentiment against the use of EU member countries for the alleged secret prisons for the U.S. rendition detainees and the EU's support of the basic human rights of all people. The EU has directed the commission to conduct an inquiry of the secret prisons and is in the process of identifying individuals for interview, to include U.S. Secretary of State Rice. At the same time, Frattini chided EU member countries by reminding them that only four member states of the EU have even ratified a U.S.–EU antiterrorism extradition and mutual

---

* EUPolitix website: www.eupolitix.com/EN/News/200507.
† "Germans Question Arrest Warrant," *Deutsche Welle* website: www.dw-world.de/ article.

assistance treaty, which the United States ratified in 2003. Frattini, it should be noted, was Italy's minister of foreign affairs in 2003, during the time the U.S. Central Intelligence Agency allegedly kidnapped a Muslim cleric in Milan.*

While the above incidents are hardly the way to foster cooperative relationships between the United States and EU members, many of the countries involved are aspiring EU and NATO members or have recently joined. These countries are caught between the proverbial rock and a hard place. The rock is their facing the wrath of the EU for the country's alleged participation in the alleged secret prison scheme. The countries involved are faced with no less than twelve individual investigations by member countries of the EU to determine if their airfields were used in the transfer of al-Qaeda suspects. If this is verified, the EU member countries were poised to punish the countries involved with sanctions, said Franco Frattini, the EU's justice minister.† The countries involved also face the hard place of losing U.S. support of their defense structure, enjoyed by their membership in NATO. This is a difficult position, to say the least, trying to facilitate both EU and U.S. support for their governments, balancing being an active participant in the war on terror, and being responsive to the safeguarding of human rights.

While the European Union strives to develop methods of fostering cooperation among its members, several critics point out a basic flaw in these erstwhile well-intentioned efforts. A recent EU initiative was enacted that mandated sharing of intelligence by any one member country with all other member countries. This principle is constrained by the diversity of national laws and regulations, as stated earlier. Intelligence gathering services pride themselves in the dissemination of information being guided by the time-honored need-to-know principle, and this would fly in the face of many a veteran intelligence operative.

An unnamed EU policy insider, as quoted by the German news service Deutsche Welle, said that there are structural reasons that the EU member states are fighting among themselves instead of against terrorism, the main reason being Europe itself. The source is quoted as saying:

> The E.U. is too small because we don't have (terrorism) source countries like Pakistan or Somalia. It is too big compared with the flexibility of bilateral cooperation. And it is too diverse. For (most Europeans), terrorism remains something exotic, down there in the South.‡

* European Union website: www.europarl.eu.int/news/20060214.
† Ibid., 48.
‡ "Europe's Terror Efforts under Scrutiny," *Deutsche Welle* website: www.dw-world.de/dw/article/0,1511790,00.

Past Threats to U.S. and EU Security

The catastrophic events of September 11, 2001, marked a demarcation point in the view of international trends in the fight against terrorism. While countries around the world acknowledged that terrorist groups worked across borders, most countries focused on events within their borders and were reactive, rather than proactive, in their chase of terrorist groups. Various governmental entities around the world prepare yearly reports on world terrorism trends; the U.S. State Department has done so since the late 1980s.[*] A review of those reports throughout the years prior to 2001 shows reporting of national or regional threats and what success countries had to counter such threats. Prior to the mid-1990s, no detailed reporting on the international nexus of terrorist groups appears, with the exception of state sponsorship of nonnative terrorist groups.

This is not to say that attention was not paid to international cooperation prior to 2001. For example, in the U.S. Department of State "Patterns of Global Terrorism" report for 2000[†] it is reported in the appendix that over half of the countries of the European Union signed or ratified the International Convention for the Suppression of Terrorist Financing.

While the number of terrorist incidents in Europe fell from an all-time high of almost three hundred in the early 1990s to thirty in the year 2000, this by no means should indicate a lack of terrorist activity. Nor does it insinuate a lack of the respective countries' investigation into, or actions to suppress, terrorist activity in Europe. In the year 2000, the U.S. Department of State reported the active investigations or prosecutions of twenty-eight separate terrorist organizations.[‡] While cooperation between the United States and Europe was cited in individual examples of prosecution of terrorist incidents, little to no mention exists of efforts to prevent terrorism.

The Emerging Radical Islamic Threat

One trend that continues throughout reporting during the 1980s and 1990s is the rise in the organization of Islamic extremist groups and their increased use of terrorism as a means to achieve their goals of increased instability in the West and increased exposure of their cause and beliefs.

Subsequent to the fall of the Russian-backed regime in Afghanistan, reporting emerged of the development of individual Islamic extremist groups such as al-Qaeda. A report on terrorism threats during 1999 by the Institute

---

[*] U.S. Department of State counterterrorism reports: http://www.state.gov/s/ct/rls/pgtrprt.
[†] U.S. Department of State counterterrorism reports: http://www.state.gov/s/ct/rls/pgtrprt/2000.
[‡] Ibid.

of Strategic Studies* said that the al-Qaeda terrorist group was known as an emerging terrorist organization for several years; it took significant events such as their 1996 attack on the Khobar Towers, a U.S. military facility in Saudi Arabia, and the 1998 attacks on the U.S. Embassies in Tanzania and Kenya to make al-Qaeda the subject of an international effort to suppress operatives and confiscate assets at the end of 1998.

Overview of Current Threats to U.S. and EU Security

One effect that the events of September 11, 2001 had on the perception of world terrorism was how loosely aligned terrorist groups shared ideology and methods of operation. The Islamic extremist group al-Qaeda originated in the Middle East as a result of reaction to Western beliefs, ideals, and their intrusion in their midst. However, al-Qaeda has spread virtually throughout the world, with sympathetic organizations fund-raising throughout the Middle East and Asia, and has logistical cells throughout Europe, the Middle East, and Asia, and operational cells in the Middle East, Asia, Europe, and North America. Uniquely aligned with al-Qaeda are other Islamic extremist groups, around the world, such as the Chechens in Russia, Abu Sayyaf in the Philippines, and Jemaah Islamiya in Indonesia.

In his report entitled "Europe: The New Terrorist Sanctuary?"[†] Roman Kupchinsky writes for Radio Free Europe on the proliferation of support for terrorist groups within Europe. Kupchinsky reports the growing U.S. concern that al-Qaeda's European connections have spread from individual cells of followers in Germany, Spain, and Britain to more sophisticated groups that manage training, logistics, and sanctuary for "combat-ready squads of fighters trained in the techniques of urban terrorism."

Kupchinsky goes on to say that while the vast majority of Europe's 15 million Muslims are law abiding and reject terrorism, they fully expect all of the rights and protections afforded by European countries to their citizens, including efforts by those countries to stem the social discrimination, high unemployment, and police insensitivity that make their youth targets for recruiters of Islamic extremists.

Kupchinsky cites specific suburbs of major European cities that have become the "ghettos of Europe," that have become the new sanctuaries for fundamentalist groups that glorify terrorism and are bound to bring Islamic jihad to Europe. The conditions in these ghettos, coupled with the correlation seen between the rising militancy, the discord of the conflict in Iraq, and

---

* "Transnational Trends—New Threats?" Institute for Strategic Studies, 1999.
† Kupchinsky, Roman, "Europe: The New Terrorist Sanctuary?" RFE, 4(14), 2004.

ongoing Israeli–Palestine conflict, add to the anti-Western sentiment among Europe's Muslims.

Kupchinsky goes on to say that these ghettos of Europe make an ideal place for terrorists to hide, as they are difficult for security services to infiltrate, and any unwanted intrusion by the state may be met with hostility. Coupling this fertile breeding ground with Europe's growing need for immigrants to supplant their dwindling indigenous labor supply brings what Kupchinsky calls a security gridlock of conflicting interests. When one includes this with the benefits of the ease of transit offered by the Schengen borders of the European Union (territory in member countries where border controls are not conducted at common borders) and the lack of cooperation Kupchinsky feels is present among police and intelligence services in the EU due to stringent efforts to safeguard individual countries' security, the result is an theatre of operation that benefits the terrorist.

NATO, the United States, and the EU

An agency cited that is significant to the United States and the European Union is the North Atlantic Treaty Organization (NATO). Founded at the end of World War II by the United States to counteract the threat of the Soviet Union, the original alliance of the United States, Canada, and ten European countries evolved from a defensive one to the proactive one that we see today. NATO has the original twelve members plus an additional fourteen from Central and Eastern Europe, a trend that chagrins Russia to no end, as many of the Central and Eastern European countries that are members of NATO today were once satellites of the Soviet Union.

Subsequent to the events of September 11, 2001, NATO members invoked the mutual defense clause of the NATO treaty by allowing the use of NATO assets in the war on terrorism, especially in the coalition's invasion of Afghanistan. The other antiterrorism measures that NATO initiated were enhanced intelligence sharing, overflight rights, access to ports and airfields of member countries, and deployment of naval forces. A summit in Prague, Czech Republic, in November 2002, led the NATO member states to adopt a host of measures to ensure future preparedness against terrorist acts. This "military concept," as Graham and Gunaratna explain,[*] allows for

> development of measures to act against terrorist attacks, or the threat of terrorist attacks, directed from abroad against their populations, territory, infrastructure, and forces; to provide assistance to national authorities in dealing with the consequences of a terrorist attack; to support operation by

---

[*] Ibid., 251.

the European Union or other international organizations or coalitions of allies; and to deploy forces as and where required to carry out such missions. These activities will be supported by measures to further improve intelligence sharing among allies.... NATO Operations have led to the capture of al-Qaeda operatives in the Balkans ... and led to the formation of a NATO rapid response force.

The Role of Interpol in the Combat of Terrorism in Europe

The International Criminal Police Organization (Interpol) is one of the oldest and most established entities that has international cooperation in the fight against crime as its charter. Founded as a successor to the International Criminal Police Commission in 1923, Interpol has 184 member countries that, coordinating through their central police agencies, provide a framework for mutual assistance within each country's own legal framework. Larger countries, such as the United States, with more than one predominant police agency, have representation of several agencies at Interpol's world headquarters, currently in Lyon, France. The U.S. Department of Justice and its Federal Bureau of Investigation, the U.S. Department of Homeland Security, and the U.S. Secret Service and Immigration and Customs Enforcement, and the U.S. Department of the Treasury all have representatives at Interpol.*

Interpol has member agencies in all of the countries of Europe, to include the European Union, and has a European division, currently colocated in Lyon. Interpol also has representation at the United Nations in New York and has regional offices in many member countries, to include the United States (Washington, D.C.). The bilateral cooperation that Interpol fosters goes a long way toward international cooperation in investigations. Subdivisions also exist, to include ones for Customs, finance and high-tech crime, and public safety and terrorism.

Malcolm Anderson, in his 1989 book titled *Policing the World, Interpol and the Politics of International Police Cooperation*, quotes (then) French President Françoise Mitterrand as saying, "Since terrorism is international, investigation, prevention, repression, and sanctions should also be international."† Anderson goes on to say that while terrorism in its many forms, be it acts against citizens or entire political regimes, has been around for hundreds of years, international attention to terrorism and its reach across borders did not start until the 1970s and 1980s. The spate of airliner

---

* Interpol website: http://www.interpol.int/public/icpo/default.asp.
† Anderson, Malcolm, *Policing the World, Interpol and the Politics of International Cooperation* (Oxford: Clarendon Press, 1989), 127.

hijackings in the mid-1980s was the impetus for official cooperation to begin.

As a reaction to the September 11 attacks on the United States, Interpol formed a Fusion Task Force, which takes the cooperative effort a few steps further. The Fusion Task Force collects, stores, and provides analysis of terrorist groups, methods, and incidents. The task force then creates and circulates warnings to member countries. Interpol also collects data on methods of terrorism, to include weapons of mass destruction, including nuclear, chemical, and biological. Interpol hosts international symposia to share this information in the hope of preventing such methods from being used in future terrorist attacks.

Interpol, as its charter suggests, is a framework for mutual assistance, and member countries cannot be compelled to cooperate with investigations. Interpol has no power to compel testimony or the submission of information. Since September 11, 2001, there have been several arrests of persons with ties to terrorist organizations that were the subject of Interpol alerts. One such example was the January 10, 2006, arrest of a Czech arms dealer with known ties to terrorist organizations. The arms dealer was the subject of a worldwide Interpol red notice, or notice that an individual was wanted by a member country for a crime. Unfortunately, there has been no arrest of any major terrorist, such as any al-Qaeda operative, as a result of a direct Interpol action.

As Anderson writes, almost more as an endorsement for Interpol in its current form, rather than as a conclusion about terrorism and its impact on international police cooperation, "a specialized international counter-terrorism agency would probably not improve the circulation of case related information and may well increase the difficulties of coordination between agencies."*

More to the point, as one scrutinizes Interpol's successes, Interpol's main asset is found in the bonds of the mutual cooperation it forges, not just between member states, but more importantly, between the investigators who work for the agencies tasked by the member states to fight terrorism.

United States and the European Union: Official Cooperation

NATO not withstanding, many other examples exist of cooperation between the Untied States and the European Union and its member countries. Examples of official cooperation include the following.

Founded in 1973, the Organization for Security and Cooperation in Europe (OSCE) is headquartered in Vienna, Austria. OSCE consists of fifty-five countries in Central Asia, North America, and Europe and provides

---

* Ibid., 146.

early warning of potential conflicts within Europe through programs such as crisis management, arms control, diplomacy, human rights, and security monitoring. OCSE has active programs in many areas of counterterrorism, such as police training and border control. Rather than facilitate the investigation of terrorist acts or the prosecution of terrorism, OSCE feels that a comprehensive approach to security provides comparative advantages in combating terrorism by identifying and addressing the various social, economic, and political factors that foster conditions ripe for the development of terrorist organizations.*

As mentioned previously in this report, many of the attempts of the EU to standardize its antiterrorism efforts were held back by national sovereignty concerns, so many of the European Union's efforts to improve its antiterrorism response, as well as cooperative efforts between the United States and the EU, have come about as a result of September 11.

A survey of U.S. and EU cooperative efforts was conducted in 2005 for the U.S. Congress by the Congressional Research Service of the Library of Congress.† While the ministerial or department heads for all cabinet-level entities involved in antiterrorism efforts of EU member countries and the United States meet annually, a working group of U.S. and EU senior officials meet every six months to discuss police and judicial cooperation efforts. Europol has two senior representatives stationed full-time in Washington, D.C., and the United States has an FBI liaison officer stationed at Europol at the Hague strictly for counterterrorism. Agreements were reached in 2001, 2002, 2003, and 2004 on areas such as the sharing of strategic information on terrorism investigations, personal information on terrorism suspects, extradition and mutual legal assistance, and border control and transport security. While many compromises were made in the areas of standardization of crimes related to terrorism and extraditions only for offenses with equal punishment in all countries involved, significant progress was made. Only the approval of the U.S. Senate is needed to finalize the agreement's enactment.

One of the most significant areas of discussion is directly a result of the September 11 attacks. The mutual deployment of air marshals to both Europe and the United States by all countries has long been a topic of discussion. Much discussion has taken place concerning the need for coordinated aviation security standards among the United States, the EU, and other G-8 member countries; however, until the standards are agreed to, the EU member countries will not provide U.S. air marshals concurrent

* OSCE website: www.osce.org.
† Archick, Kristin, *US-EU Cooperation against Terrorism*, CRS Report for Congress, 2005.

authority while operating in EU airspace, much less in EU countries' sovereign territory.*

Other ongoing challenges include a lack of confidence in the need for enhanced cooperation between the United States and the EU, given the excellent rapport that already exists between most individual countries' law enforcement and intelligence agencies. Also, as presented at the beginning of this paper, the aggressive posture that the U.S. government has taken in the recent war against terrorism in Iraq has alienated many European countries. Most importantly, the differences that exist in U.S. and European Union countries' legislation, punishment for similar terrorism-related offenses, and principally, the lack of consistency that continues among the EU countries' legislations and punishments will continue to hinder cooperative efforts between the United States and the EU.

Richard Aldrich, in his article in the July 2004 edition of the *Journal of International Affairs*,[†] sums up the problems that continue to be inherent in transatlantic antiterrorist cooperative efforts. Aldrich says that in spite of advances in U.S.–EU intelligence and security cooperation, significant problems remain. The 2004 Madrid train bombings have shown how terrorists continue to exploit intrinsic weaknesses in current cooperation. Tensions continue due to highly compartmentalized national intelligence gathering and dissemination. Aldrich makes an excellent point, that more advanced and elaborate information-sharing structures should be avoided and more emphasis should be placed on what information should be shared, rather than how to share it.

In 2004, the United States and the European Union held an antiterrorism summit to emphasize joint adherence to international antiterrorism conventions and protocols. Highlighted was the mutual goal to encourage the one hundred countries of the United Nations that have not ratified United Nations conventions, agreements, and resolutions. Goals of the 2004 summit that have been met to date include:[‡]

Development of joint biometric standards for travel documents
Implementation of U.S.–EU passenger name record agreement to share airline passenger information between countries
Informal dialogue on terrorism financing issues, to include investigative and prosecutorial best practices
Finalized cargo screening and inspection procedures and Customs cooperation

---

* Department of State website: http://usinfo.state.gov/ei/Archive/2005/Jul/08-410565. html.
† Aldrich, Richard J., "Transatlantic Intelligence and Security Cooperation," *International Affairs*, 80, 731, 2004.
‡ U.S. Department of State website: www.state.gov/news/06202005.

United States and the European
Union: Bilateral Cooperation

Many examples exist of unofficial cooperation between the United States and European Union countries. The vast majority of these examples of cooperation are bilateral in nature, between individual agencies that work in the cooperating countries. As mentioned earlier in this chapter, many U.S. law enforcement agencies with antiterrorism duties, to include the Federal Bureau of Investigation, the U.S. Secret Service, and U.S. Customs and Immigration, have offices in EU countries. All U.S. armed forces utilize bases in EU countries as well, and as a result have force protection as well as other ancillary intelligence duties. The U.S. Central Intelligence Agency has representation in most EU countries. None of these agencies would survive, much less thrive, in an overseas environment if it were not for the sense of the "best personal relationships" forged by their operatives with their European counterparts. The same can be said for the European police, military, and intelligence agencies with offices in the United States. An old adage in federal law enforcement goes like this: "There is more than enough work to go around to allow for competition." This is never more true in an overseas environment, where mutual force protection issues, and a plethora of investigative issues, make for a mutually agreeable relationship among U.S law enforcement and intelligence agencies operating overseas as well as among U.S. and European Union counterparts.

A specific example of bilateral cooperation between the United States and individual members of the European Union is the agreement between the U.S. and the United Kingdom to share information via a global enrollment network in which members of the U.S. Department of State and Homeland Security can share investigative and intelligence information with their counterparts in the UK in a secure manner.*

United States and the EU: Unofficial
Cooperation and Intelligence Sharing

Examples of *ad hoc* or unofficial cooperation between countries are contained in a book by Amitai Etzioni called *From Empire to Community: A New Approach to International Relations.*† The influence of the United States as the world's preeminent superpower makes it the leader of a *de facto* global antiterrorism authority formed, led, financed, and managed by the United

---

* U.S. Department of State website: http://www.state.gov/r/pa/prs/ps/2006/59242.htm.
† Etzioni, Amitai, *From Empire to Community: A New Approach to International Relations* (New York: Palgrave Macmillian, 2004), 215–51.

States. This is a result of what Etzioni calls adhesion, or other countries going along with the United States for fear of punishment if they do not, or fear of not protecting their own national interests by failing to follow suit.

The European Union countries are not the only countries to cooperate officially against terrorism. The interior ministers of seven Southeast European countries (SEE), EU members as well as prospective members, meet on a regular basis to coordinate their efforts against terrorism, organized crime, and corruption in the region. Countries represented include Bosnia and Herzegovina (BiH), Bulgaria, Croatia, Greece, Macedonia, Romania, and Turkey, as well as representatives of Montenegro and the United Nations mission in Kosovo. The SEE ministers recently agreed on joint measures aimed at preventing terror and other criminal acts through increased information exchange and mutual trust building. During these meetings, bilateral efforts also take place. The Southeastern Europe News Network recently reported that during the March 2006 SEE interior minister's meeting, BiH and Bulgaria sealed an agreement on police cooperation and readmission.*

One of the ways that governments and private industry share information to provide security and prevent terrorist incidents from occurring is through intelligence-sharing apparatuses with a single nexus. The U.S. Department of State has an excellent venue for the sharing of security information for U.S. private industry assets overseas. The venue is called the Overseas Security Advisory Council (OSAC). OSAC is a federal advisory committee operated by the U.S. government to promote security cooperation between American business and private sector interests worldwide and the U.S. Department of State. OSAC currently has over 100 country councils, and more than 3,500 constituent member organizations. The writer saw how invaluable OSAC was not just to U.S. business interests overseas, but to their host country employees and law enforcement during the 2006 Winter Olympics in Torino, Italy. OSAC provided a network for daily intelligence sharing on possible security issues during the Olympics. Ostensibly, this information was for the benefit of the U.S. business community, but the information was of great value to U.S., Italian, and international law enforcement in attendance at the Olympics.

Another intelligence-sharing center is the International Branches of Private Industry Security Concerns, such as the American Society for Industrial Security (ASIS) and the Association of Threat Assessment Professionals (ATAP). These entities have law enforcement and governmental representatives who attend meetings of the international branches, especially the European branches, as those branches have the largest concentration of

---

* Southeastern Europe News Network website: http://www.seeurope.net/en/Story.php?StoryID=58189.

U.S.-owned businesses in the world (outside the United States). These entities, as does OSAC, rely on the interchange of private industry and government to provide information concerning the safety and security of assets. This information is invaluable to government intelligence and law enforcement in their overall threat and intelligence assessments.

What U.S.–EU Pre-9/11 Antiterrorism Efforts Worked and Why?

Prior to September 11, the threat that terrorist organizations presented to the United States and Europe was more singular in focus. Events occurred in Europe and elsewhere to promote political causes, such as attacks against politicians, the hijacking of aircraft, and the bombings of places such as the Berlin disco. These events took place sporadically enough that the identification, location, apprehension, and prosecution of the perpetrators held the singular focus of the United States and Europe. Investigative and intelligence efforts that the United States and Europe were utilizing up until this point were adequate. The countries were good at this defensive or reactive method of combating terrorism. The event happens, and utilizing the available resources in the country and existing alliances internationally, one catches the persons responsible. This system worked well as long as the events were sporadic or singular in nature.

While attacks seemed to be growing in number, and terrorist groups were thought possibly to be taking their inspiration from central figures such as Osama bin Laden, no common link was established. Assumptions were made that no one group could utilize unattached cells across countries to carry out multiple terrorist attacks. Then along came events such as the shooting of employees in the CIA parking lot, the bombing of Pan Am Flight 103, the bombing of the USS *Cole* in Yemen, and the first World Trade Center bombing, and groups like al-Qaeda were identified, and the nexus was realized. Events that seemed disconnected at first were later determined to be connected, not several sporadic events but a series of coordinated attacks against a single enemy, the West, with the United States and Europe directly in their sights.

What U.S.–EU Pre-9/11 Antiterrorism Efforts Did Not Work and Why?

The 9/11 Commission, formed to study the causes of the September 11 attacks in the United States, spent several chapters discussing what went wrong in the investigation of terrorism preceding the attacks. But more importantly, the shift of terrorism, from the sporadic strikes for specific ideological causes to the long-term series of events, such as the jihad proclaimed against the West by Osama bin Laden, caught the United States and the Europe Union member countries by surprise. One of the most significant factors, as pointed out by the 9/11 Commission Report, is that the United States and Europe had to shift from a mind-set of protecting their homeland to deciding that the world was their homeland and reach across borders to cooperate and protect each other's interests as if they were their own.*

Once it is established that both the United States and Europe are bound to protect each other, then cooperation between countries is paramount. Unfortunately, this was not a jointly held position prior to September 11, either by the countries involved or the agencies involved in antiterrorism efforts within each of the countries.

The Israeli security expert Noemi Gal-Or studied international terrorism and the effectiveness of international cooperation in the combating of terrorism in his 1985 book entitled *International Cooperation to Suppress Terrorism.*† In his book, Gal-Or focuses on several less than successful attempts by Europe to cooperate against terrorism, from one of the European Commission's first acts as a commission, the European Convention on the Suppression of Terrorism, to regional and bilateral agreements. These are presented to highlight the problems that prevent effective antiterrorism measures, such as the conflicting methods and goals of the parties involved.

While most of the solutions proposed by Gal-Or are predictable, such as the standardization of antiterrorism enforcement duties for police rather than military, Gal-Or makes a unique and interesting point. Standardization of antiterrorism enforcement among regions and nations in Europe is difficult. Several European countries, such as Germany and Great Britain, see very similar terrorism offenses having very different penalties due to their unique experiences with terrorist entities. In the United Kingdom there was public support of the Irish Republican Army and Ulster Nationalists, and in Germany there was a lack of public support of the Baader-Meinhof gang. An excellent point, as without the public's support, antiterrorist efforts will have a tough go, examples of which we even see in today's multiple fronts against terrorism.

---

* 9/11 Commission Report, p. 356.
† Gal-Or, Noemi, *International Cooperation to Suppress Terrorism* (London: Croom Helm, 1985).

What U.S.–EU Post-9/11 Antiterrorism Efforts Work and Why?

The United States and European Union member countries were united in their resolve to fight terrorism subsequent to the attacks on September 11, 2001. In his book entitled *The United States of Europe: The New Superpower and the End of American Supremacy,*[*] American political scientist T. R. Reid says that the United States enjoyed an enormous amount of support in Europe after September 11. Arrests of al-Qaeda operatives were made in Germany; European intelligence services opened their files on al-Qaeda to the United States, and the vaunted American alliance in Europe supported the NATO action in Afghanistan. If anything else was not accomplished, September 11 showed Europe that the ability of a group with command two continents away could inflict serious harm on a superpower such as the United States, and Europe has made robust efforts, as detailed previously, to coordinate its own antiterrorism investigations and prosecution, as well as assist the United States.

Recent developments in U.S. efforts to locate terrorism suspects worldwide and have them extradited to the United States for prosecution in criminal courts has led to a reexamination of the U.S. role in the International Criminal Court (ICC) in the Hague. With the first official vote against cooperating with the ICC coming during the Clinton administration in 1998, the current Bush administration continued a policy of never officially ratified U.S. involvement. The ICC, seen as a hindrance to U.S. international antiterrorism efforts,[†] was avoided by the means of bilateral agreements with many countries, to include many in the EU. As recent as September 2008, the Bush administration realized that the International Criminal Court, and its wide-reaching jurisdiction and, more importantly, reputation as a fair arbiter of criminal prosecutions, can be a partner in the war against terrorism and not an obstacle, as previously thought. The Bush administration began to court collaboration with the ICC by its move to endorse *ad hoc* tribunals run by the ICC for the prosecution of terrorism. This is seen as a promising sign of cooperation with the ICC, which the entire EU has already ratified and fully endorses by its member countries' continued cooperation.[‡]

* Reid, T. R., *The United States of Europe: The New Superpower and the End of American Supremacy* (New York: Penguin Press, 2004).
† International Justice website: www.hrw.org/campaigns/icc/us/htm.
‡ International Justice website: www.hrw.org/campaigns/icc/eu/htm.

What U.S.–EU Post-9/11 Antiterrorism Efforts Do Not Work and Why?

There are many examples of how individual countries have not heeded the advice of entities such as the 9/11 Commission. One of the many best practices proposed after a thorough study of U.S. intelligence and law enforcement services' handling of al-Qaeda was coordinated and streamlined procedures for the collection and dissemination of and action on intelligence.[*] Several recent studies have shown that, in spite of a reorganization of U.S. law enforcement agencies and intelligence services, information collection about terrorist groups remains disjointed, dissemination is not complete, and elements compete for the right to act upon the information.

As recently as March 2006 the *International Herald Tribune* ran a series of articles on how the U.S. Department of Defense (DOD) has been critical of how the U.S. intelligence community is handling their antiterror operations,[†] as well as how the DOD is operating antiterrorist units out of U.S. Embassies worldwide, independent of other U.S. government entities, and sometimes without the knowledge or consent of U.S. foreign service or intelligence communities.[‡]

This is not just limited to the United States. In July 2005, the *Economist* reported[§] that Italy had enacted new measures to fight terrorism, to include broader powers for its intelligence services to obtain information, to include the easing of wiretapping within Italy. Unfortunately for Italy, its three major law enforcement agencies, each with unique antiterrorist activities, do not share information with each other or Italy's two intelligence services (domestic and foreign) efficiently.

Faltering efforts are not left just to individual countries. Recent interviews of Italian law enforcement officials, who work on antiterrorism units and liaison with other units, both in Europe and in the United States, claim that the repercussions of the recent extraordinary rendition of an al-Qaeda operative from Italy by the United States, and the resulting arrest warrants for several U.S. consulate employees in Italy, have made it difficult for the Italian government to allow its antiterrorist units to assist the United States. They also report that the ongoing investigations by the EU concerning the use of unauthorized holding facilities, and the use of European air bases to transport extraordinarily rendered al-Qaeda operatives, have made it difficult for U.S. and EU member countries to cooperate in antiterrorism investigations unless the investigations first go through a series of approvals by layers of

---

[*] *9/11 Commission Report*, p. 407.
[†] *International Herald Tribune*, March 19, 2006, p. 1.
[‡] *International Herald Tribune*, March 9, 2006, p. 6.
[§] "Italy, the Next Target?" *Economist Magazine*, July 16, 2005, p. 44.

governmental bureaucracy. Gone are the days of informal cooperation and assistance that expedited investigations and led to a high level of success of actionable intelligence gathering with a U.S. and EU nexus.

Analysis

Much has already been written on the significant amount of cooperation between the United States and the EU. The conventions, agreements, and treaties have had their maximum effectiveness. Agreements can only guarantee so much. Words must be followed by actions. The ties that bind the two together are strong, and any one incident or political row between the two will not fatally affect the relationship.

Unfortunately, a long history of what Georgetown University professor Jonathan Monten calls democratic globalism exists in the United States. This history, which is the United States acting unilaterally in world affairs, has an effect on how Europe views the United States. In his article for the *International Security Journal* entitled "The Roots of the Bush Doctrine,"* Monten outlines what the Unites States has done to hinder the goodwill built up between the United States and Europe over years of cooperation. Not just a recent phenomenon, this actually dates back to previous administrations' actions in the world in response to terrorism, as early as the Reagan administration's response to the Berlin disco bombing. Much was made of Europe's lack of enthusiasm for the Reagan administration's unilateral response to the bombing by bombing Libya, similar to how the ongoing war in Iraq is eliciting a response in Europe today.

An opposing point of view is how effective a nonaggressive or accommodating approach toward terrorist groups might be, as opposed to a more aggressive or confrontational approach. Roman Kupchinsky, in a report for Radio Free Europe on the proliferation of support for terrorist groups within Europe,† calls for less foreign policy accommodation of the Middle East by Europe. Such accommodation, when used by European countries as a shield against possible jihad in their own countries, is not seen to be productive in mollifying the indigenous radical Muslim population and only appears to be politically expedient.

A valid point is to be made in opposition to those who oppose the U.S. penchant for unilateral response to terrorist attacks. While this type of response has had mixed success (and it is hard to define what a different response would have accomplished), the opposite, which is a nonaggressive

---

* Monten, Jonathan, "The Roots of the Bush Doctrine," *International Security*, Spring 2004, p. 112.
† Kupchinsky, Roman, "Europe: The New Terrorist Sanctuary?" RFE, 4(14), 2004.

approach that the majority of Europe espouses, has had absolutely no quantifiable effect in the stemming of future terrorist attacks.

Conclusion

The writer has found that the variable that has the highest amount of impact in antiterrorism cooperation is not the interaction of the operatives and subordinates involved, but rather the actions of their policy makers. As exhibited in the months right after September 11, U.S. and European antiterrorism cooperation is at its best when the countries are also acting in a unified manner politically. While the best personal relationships will always exist between operatives of the two regions, there are direct correlations to the success of joint antiterrorism efforts when the governments of the countries are acting in concert and there are no major diplomatic rows that impede official cooperation. Governments are political animals, if you will. A government serves at the whim of the people who elect that government, and if the people or the home government is reacting adversely to a political situation, this will invariably strain relations between the two countries, no matter how necessary the actions of the government were.

As examples have shown, any act that divides the governments also impedes the operatives. If the administrations of the governments involved would give consideration to the implications of any actions that would impact the other parties involved, factor in consensus-building activity, and realize the cost-benefit consequences of actions taken unilaterally, then there may be less need for such unilateral action in the future. This will facilitate rather than impede the cooperation necessary to combat truly global terrorist entities such as al-Qaeda.

Europe and the United States have too much at stake, economically and politically, to let the divisiveness of any single political action influence their long-term relationship. Antiterrorism actions are, however, oftentimes in need of expedient measures, and these measures should not be jeopardized by any conscious action. The cooperation is too valuable to all parties to allow this to happen. In spite of all that happens politically between the United States and Europe, the functionaries on both sides of the Atlantic involved in the fight against terrorism have been insisting that the cooperation will continue. If only the policy makers would follow suit.

Trends in Strategic Security
The New Warfare

11

DALE L. JUNE

Contents

The Wu family, a clan of experts on military strategy and warfare combat, coming to us from the fifth century, brings a book and compilation of strategic tactics, arms, and fighting. This book, a collection of combat astuteness, is universally recognized as one of the world's leading and most useful books ever written on warfare and leadership wisdom. Obviously, the book is Sun Wu's (Sun Tzu or Master Sun) *The Art of War*. Sun Tzu wrote: "He who is destined to defeat first fights and afterwards looks for victory."[1]

Sun Tzu is as often quoted today in the world of business, politics, and warfare planning as he has been through the ages in matters of strategy, espionage deception, and military tactics. A sampling of Sun Tzu's quotations highlights the trueness of the strategic genius of this brilliant general/philosopher:

"The art of war is of vital importance to the State. It is a matter of life and death, a road either to safety or to ruin. Hence it is a subject of inquiry which can on no account be neglected." In the 1940s, sociologist Abraham Maslow built a pyramid of the needs of man, placing "security" as the number two requirement, slightly behind the biological needs of air, food, water, and sex. Projecting that concept to the size of a nation, one can easily visualize how important war is to the life of the state. Countries not engaged or prepared for war have been swallowed up by other, more warfaring states, reflecting on the Darwinism of "survival of the fittest" or stronger over the weaker; the most prepared over the least prepared.

> Our world has sprouted a weird concept of security and a warped sense of morality. Weapons are sheltered like treasures and children are exposed to incineration.
>
> **—Bertrand Russell**[2]

"All warfare is based on deception." This is a solid reference to the art of spying, intelligence gathering, and trickery. There are many concrete examples of the art of deception throughout the history of warfare. One of the most world-changing events characterizing this was General Dwight D. Eisenhower and the Allied forces planning the invasion of Europe at Normandy during the Second World War. The Allies worked their deception to such an extent that the Germans could not comprehend the invasion taking place at Normandy.

"There is no instance of a country having benefited from prolonged warfare." This is a very interesting comment for modern times inasmuch as the United States has been at war in Iraq and Afghanistan for nearly eight years, and from all outward appearances, little has been gained. But now the world is engaged in a global meltdown of the financial world as the banking industry and world treasuries are straining under the costs of this and other wars. It has been said that he who controls the economy (purse strings) will benefit with power. Power is the outgrowth of economic strength, with the most powerful being the wealthiest. With warfare comes the threat of diminishment of resources. The more extensive the time of war, the greater the loss even to the "winning" side. William James wrote, "War taxes are the only ones men never hesitate to pay."[3]

"Hence to fight and conquer in all your battles is not supreme excellence; supreme excellence consists in breaking the enemy's resistance without fighting." Modern-day philosopher and martial artist, the late great Lee Sai Fon (later changed to Lee Jun Fan)[4] (better known as Bruce Lee) advocated (in spite of the image portrayed in his movies) a philosophy of "fighting without fighting" by outwitting your enemy through "intimidation of the mind," or in other words, outthinking and outmaneuvering your opponent through reflex and reaction. There is a story of two great armies perched on the top of two hillsides separated by fields and a valley. The commanding generals sat on their horses for hours, staring at each other across the divide, constantly surveying the terrain, the size of the opposing force, and the preparedness of the other army. Eventually one general wheeled his horse around and called for his army to remove from the proposed battle. He had become convinced that were he to attack, he would surely be defeated by the superior force and preparedness of his enemy, thus proving Sun Tzu's admonition of "breaking the enemy's resistance without fighting" or Lee Jun Fan's philosophy of "fighting without fighting" or "don't fight force with force."

The History of Terrorism: From Antiquity to Al Qaeda[5] provides "an essential perspective on terrorism by offering a rare opportunity for analysis and reflection at a time of on-going violence, chilling threats, and renewed reprisals.... Terror long the weapon of the weak against the strong, is a tactic as old as warfare itself ... consider the emergence of modern transnational terrorism, focusing on the roots of Islamic terrorism, al Qaeda, and the rise of the contemporary suicide martyr ... dispel the widely held assumption that terrorism has no moral basis but is merely an instrument used for political gain."

"We cannot enter into alliances until we are acquainted with the designs of our neighbors." What better example than when "peace for our lifetime" came from the alliance between Great Britain and Germany in September 1938.

The following is the wording of a printed statement that Neville Chamberlain waved as he stepped off the plane on September 30, 1938, after the Munich conference had ended the day before:

> We, the German Führer and Chancellor, and the British Prime Minister, have had a further meeting today and are agreed in recognizing that the question of Anglo-German relations is of the first importance for our two countries and for Europe. We regard the agreement signed last night and the Anglo-German Naval Agreement as symbolic of the desire of our two peoples never to go to war with one another again. We are resolved that the method of consultation shall be the method adopted to deal with any other questions that may concern our two countries, and we are determined to continue our efforts to remove possible sources of difference, and thus to contribute to assure the peace of Europe.

Chamberlain read the above statement in front of 10 Downing St. and said:

> My good friends, for the second time in our history, a British Prime Minister has returned from Germany bringing peace with honour. *I believe it is peace for our time….* Go home and get a nice quiet sleep. [6] (italics added)

And the rest, as they say, is history. Germany continued the *blitzkrieg* invasion of other European countries, and England was soon engulfed in the Second World War aligned against Germany.

"Rapidity is the essence of war." In other words, take decisive action. Don't linger over decisions and vacillate, always planning, training, and preparing, yet failing to move forward. Defense never won a war; an active offense carries the day. This is a bitter lesson learned by many commanders who failed simply because they assumed a defensive strategy as opposed to attacking and being aggressive. Put more simply, "Don't just stand there; Move! Move! Move!" Union General McClellan, general of the Army of the Potomac, was relieved of duty by President Lincoln during the American Civil War; though McClellan was a brilliant general, he was always preparing for battle, but never moved forward.

"If the enemy leaves a door open, you must rush in." Spot the opening (weakness) and move forward, exploiting the opportunity the enemy has given. This is a very basic concept of every fighting method. All gates (openings) must be fortified and protected.

"Be subtle! Be subtle! And use your spies for every kind of business." Intelligence gathering and analysis is the name of the game. Know your enemy as you know yourself. This statement couldn't be truer; for how would one expect to triumph without having foreknowledge of the enemy's strengths, weaknesses, passions, and habits? This is the way to winning a contest from recreational and professional sports to national security and survival. In the sports world the term for gatherers of information about the opposing team is *scout*. In the world of warfare the word is *intelligence gathering*, often referred to as *spying*. Whatever the semantics, the ends mean knowing all you can learn about the opposition.

War is "older than dirt" and will probably remain as one of mankind's foibles until man destroys his universe as it is now known. When Pandora opened the box given to her by the king of Gods, Zeus, to be delivered as punishment to Prometheus for giving the gift of fire to mankind, war was one of the enmities released upon the world. Hope was the only remaining good left in the box. Hope maintains the wellspring of peace. More books, doctoral dissertations, and master's theses have been penned extolling, denouncing, or analyzing war than perhaps any other topic, except perhaps religion. But then of course, war and religion go very well together through the course of history. Obviously, the end goal of a war is to win. However, "in war there is no victory but only varying degrees of defeat."[7]

Hannah Arendt continues this line of rational thinking:

The technical development of the implements of violence has now reached the point where no political goal could conceivably correspond to their destructive potential or justify their actual use in armed conflict. Hence, warfare—from time immemorial, the final merciless arbiter in international disputes—has lost much of its effectiveness and nearly all its glamour.[8]

War is a howling, baying jackal. Or is it the animating storm? Suicidal madness or the purifying fire? An imperialist travesty? Or the glorious explosion of a virile nation made manifest upon the planet? In all recorded history, this debate is recent, as is the idea of peace to describe an active state happier than a mere interregnum between fisticuffs. Astounding as it may seem, war has consistently won the debate.[9]

Therein lies the issue: Is war a matter of strategic security or, as Karl Von Clausewitz in his book *Vom Krige* (On War, 1832) declared, "War is simply the expression of politics by other means"?

"... simply the expression of politics by other means," the traditional attitude of American soldiers had been that "politics and strategy are radically and fundamentally things apart. Strategy begins where politics end. All that soldiers ask is that once the policy is settled, strategy and command shall be regarded as being in a sphere apart from politics."[10]

Martin Van Creveld takes a critical look at the changing face of warfare and illustrates the "new" or "how" of maintaining a war in evolving global issues.

> The present ... also has a message—namely, that contemporary 'strategic' thought about ... these problems is fundamentally flawed; and in addition, is rooted in a 'Clausewitzian' world picture that is either obsolete or wrong. We are entering an era, not of peaceful economic competition between trading blocks, but of warfare between ethnic and religious groups. Even as familiar forms of armed conflict are sinking into the dustbin of the past, radically new ones are raising heads ready to take their place.[11]

In response to the September 11, 2001 airplane bombings in New York and Washington, D.C., the United States, with the support and cooperation of allies, assembled a large military force to invade Afghanistan and Iraq to root out and destroy terrorist training grounds, encampments and weapons of mass destruction. This became a symbol of the changing false face of war—invasion by a large force to destroy a small cadre of terrorists or insurgents. The war has proven the questionable concept of mass retaliation. Of course, one must take into consideration the possibility of faulty intelligence because no weapons of mass destruction were ever found. Unanswerable to this point is the question of what should be the correct response to attacks by a few or members of a small anonymous group.

A related question is: "How do you fight an ideology or religion?"[12] The answer to that conundrum is by awareness, information, and intelligent analysis. German physicist Max Planck is quoted as saying, "In the scientific community, when an unpopular theory is proposed, wait fifty years and those who opposed it will be dead." His remark is as true today as when he said it. In a microcosm, that is the trend of the new war. How do you combat an amorphous hydra? Certainly not with smoke and mirrors!

That hydra is the color of terrorism with the players assuming roles of independent cells, contractors, fundamentalists, the disenfranchised, and self-styled martyrs. It is of special note that in the instance of the present-day conflict or clash of civilizations identified by Samuel Huntington in *The Clash of Civilizations and the Remaking of World Order* is the collision between separation of church and state and strict adherence to canon or moral law espoused by extreme conservative religious groups. Religion could not exist without martyrs—thus the use of religiously motivated followers of fanatic leaders to execute suicide bombings in the name of God.

> Fanatical violence is found almost everywhere.... It may even increase in the future, as the result of the emergence of some new sects preaching their violent message or because of social or political upheavals. War has certainly become more brutal in many respects since the eighteenth century. Emmerich de Vattel, one of the fathers of international law, wrote in 1740: "Let us never

forget that our enemies are men." We cannot count how often that has been forgotten in the twentieth century.[13]

The fact is, unfortunately, that hatred in the public sense makes people's eyes bright, starts the adrenalin flowing, as love in the public sense does not. People feel fine when they are full of anger and hatred against someone else.[14]

Anger and hate are the twin lions of strong emotion. A charismatic political or religious leader can manipulate his followers to do his bidding, even to become suicide martyrs. Using the emotional response of anger and hatred to inflame an already emotional respondent believer, the leader can influence sufficient populations to undertake a terroristic mind-set and carry out a limited war of terroristic bombings, kidnappings, and assassinations. That, in a capsule, is the new wave of the future of warfare, small unified groups acting independently and most often without the sanction of a legitimized government.

Yes, the face of warfare has changed and will continue to evolve. Think of the weapons of warfare way back in time. Something has always replaced the "latest, most efficient killing machine" or the massed charges of screaming men "Bonzaiing" across a field with bullets thicker than bees or hornets from a nest (American Civil War and a host of other examples).

Small-scale eruptions have demonstrated new forms of warfare with a different cast of characters—guerilla armies, terrorists, and bandits [present-day Somali pirates, for example]—pursuing diverse goals by violent means with the most primitive to the most sophisticated weapons. Although these warriors and their tactics testify to the end of conventional war as we've known it, the public and the military continue to contemplate organized violence as conflict between the superpowers.[15]

Forward thinking should be definition enough to realize that superpower war would only annihilate the human race as we know it. It doesn't take a genius to realize that the coming storm will be in response to rebellious action carried out by nonnational radical fanatics grasping for individual power or, as in the case of al-Qaeda, there is a call for a single worldwide caliphate under the green banner of the star and crescent moon, i.e., fanatical and conservative Islam. However, we may place a caveat here by noting the growing power and influence of Russia and China, which only history of the future, approximately thirty to forty years from now, will tell if they become superpower threats again. In the meantime, global terrorism is a menace that must be dealt with in the present. Tactical operations and strategic planning must undergo a renaissance of thinking by nations and generals as they play their "war games" and plan for small-scale warfare, and not rehearse for war in the traditional model as carried out in the past. That past is long gone and will never return. The tide has turned away from massed forces to terrorist type raids and personal sacrifice of the individual bomber.

> Violent confrontations confirm a new model of warfare in which tribal, ethnic, and religious factions do battle without high-tech weapons or state supported armies and resources. This low-intensity conflict challenges existing distinctions between civilian and soldier, individual crime and organized violence, terrorism and war. In the present global atmosphere, practices that for three centuries have been considered uncivilized, such as capturing civilians or even entire communities for ransom, have begun to reappear.[16]

Terrorism is defined by the victim, not the perpetrator (the terrorism versus patriotism argument). The instrumental element in terrorism is to "kill one, frighten a thousand,"[17] and "the purpose of terrorism is to terrorize! It is an action the urban guerilla must execute with the greatest coldbloodedness, calmness, and decision."[18]

> Any attempt to [define terrorism] is bound to fail, for the simple reason that there is not one but many different terrorisms.... Traditional terrorism appeared in various forms: in conjunction with a civil war or guerilla warfare, in the framework of a political campaign, and also in "pure" form. It has been waged by religious and secular groups, by the left and right, by nationalists and international movements and by governments who engage in state-sponsored terrorism. Terrorists have seldom, if ever, seized power in contrast to guerilla movements.[19]

In 1957 J. Edgar Hoover, then the director of the FBI, wrote his signature book, *Masters of Deceit*. His target then was to alert America to the danger and threat posed by communism. However, by changing Hoover's word *communism* to *terrorism* we can see significant similarities.

> Every citizen has a duty to learn more about the menace that threatens his future, his home, his children, the peace of the world.... If you will take the time to inform yourself, you will find that [terrorism] holds no mysteries. Its leaders have blueprinted their objectives. The time is far too late not to recognize this 'ism' for what it is; a threat to humanity and to each of us.... There is the sobering fact that ... we have spent billions of dollars to defend ourselves from [terrorist] aggression.
> [Terrorism] is many things; an economic system, a philosophy, a political (and religious) creed, a psychological conditioning, an educational indoctrination, a directed way of life.... [Terrorists—fanatical Islamic radical conservatives] want to control everything; where you live, where you work, what you are paid, what you think, what transportation you ride—or whether you walk, how your children are educated, what you may not and must read and write.

When you read such reports, do not think of them as something happening in a far-off land. Remember, always, that "It could happen here" there are … people in this country now working in secret to make it happen here…. But also, thank God, there are millions of Americans who oppose them. If we open our eyes, inform ourselves, and work together, we can keep our country free.[20]

Communism, though a political entity, was particularly opposed to religion, yet the similarities between communism of the 1940s and 1950s and terrorism of the 1970s to the 2000s are very much twins (though perhaps fraternal twins). The end goal (was) is to destroy democracy and the free world, the communists through political conquest (Khrushchev, 1957, "We will bury you"), and religious terrorists through religious ideology domination, threats, and explosives to form a one-world caliphate (al-Qaeda manual). (Yet was not communism an ideology extended through political force and Stalin terrorism?)

In the end, organized religion is merely politicalization of a humanitarian and spiritual ideology. Politicalization of religion is simply man's word in the form of bureaucracy transmitted through the improper manipulation of the masses through power and influence. Thus, one can conclude that religious ideology is also political power in the modern sense, which can effectively lead to radicalization, fanaticism, and terrorist war.

The changing face of discord, war, and terrorism is widely recognized by observers of the world landscape. Academicians, politicians, and military advisors and wartime planners are finally agreeing that there is a continuum or globalization of low-intensity conflict in the guise of terrorism. One terrorism expert and writer, Lionel F. Stapley, sees a parallel world of globalization and global Muslim terrorism, very similar to Huntington's *Clash of Civilizations.*

[A] consequence of Western Globalization has been such as to have largely destroyed the sameness and continuity of societal cultures across the world. And this is experienced by members in both Western and non-Western societies as death of a way of life leading to a loss of identity. Faced with such unbearable experiences members of societies are unable to make sense of their environment. They respond to this experience in various ways but there are two particular responses that are constantly present in all societies. The first is dependency … the nature of the dependency is highly primitive and is in the nature of a search for a Messiah or savior. For large numbers of Western societies the object of their dependency needs is evangelical religion; while in Muslim societies nearly everyone turns to Islam, as an object of their dependency needs. The other particular response is through violent rebellion. In Western societies we see young people rioting in the streets; in Muslim societies we see suicide bombers and others engaged in global terrorism.[21]

Huntington and Stapley are only a part of the growing chorus recognizing the particulars of potential birthing of terrorism and the new battlegrounds. But they were not the first. In 1951, American philosopher Eric Hoffer understood the potential for destructiveness of vast change:

> For men to plunge headlong into an undertaking of vast change, they must be intensely discontented yet not destitute, and they must have the feeling that by possession of some potent doctrine, infallible leader or some new technique they have access to a source of irresistible power.... Finally, they must be wholly ignorant of the difficulties involved in their vast undertaking. Experience is a handicap.[22]

Essayist Audrey Kurth Cronin, writing an article in editor Michael E. Brown's collection of comprehensive essays by various writers chronicling an overview of the wide range of security issues confronting the world, argues:

> The argument here is that modern terrorism can best be seen as a power struggle: central power versus local power, big power versus small power, modern power versus traditional power. And while contemporary terrorism emanating from largely Muslim countries has more than a patina of religious inspiration, it is more useful to see it as part of a larger phenomenon—anti-globalization and the struggle between the have and have-not nations. Thus the distinguishing feature of modern terrorism is the connection between sweeping political or ideological concepts and increasing levels of terrorist activity internationally. Terrorists' broad political aims have been against empires, colonial powers, and the American-led international economic system marked by globalization.[23]

A backward look at American history by Kenneth N. Waltz[24] tells us that "[Alexander] Hamilton adds that to presume a lack of hostile motives among states is to forget that men are 'ambitious, vindictive, and rapacious.' A monarchical state may go to war because the vanity of its king leads him to seek glory in military victory; a republic may go to war because of the folly of its assembly or because of its commercial interests." If we look at the contemporary state of the world with its diverse traditional cultures, religious beliefs, and political goals, we can readily ascertain that Hamilton was correct in his assessment. In the fragmented cultures and tribal rivalries of Iraq and Afghanistan and other Muslim-dominated countries, chieftains, sheiks, and mullahs, we see individualistic struggles for control and power beyond their own boundaries—thus the invention of suicide bomber explosive vests and other horrific terrorist tactics intended to intimidate a populace beyond the immediate target and creation of a new world of warfare.

Guerrillas, rebels, and terrorists cannot operate effectively without a base of support from their constituency in the fold of common belief or acquiescence. "In order to be effective against a professional army, the rebel [terrorist] forces must have the active aid of a population not just its passive acquiescence. Only when the people provide intelligence, guides, recruits, and labor can the rebels [terrorists] set ambushes, avoid mopping-up campaigns, and exercise their extreme mobility…. Intimate, friendly relations with the civilian population allow the guerillas [terrorists] to obtain near-perfect intelligence concerning the enemy's [target's] strength and movements."[25] Thus, we can, with a great degree of certainty, conclude that the frontal war on terrorism must engage those who would support the terrorists. That will be a daunting task because as asked earlier, "How do you fight an ideology or religion?" Once an idea is formulated, it can never die. There will always be those who will pick up the staff of resistance, war, and terrorism.

> One final point that is worth reemphasizing is that terrorism is a technique available to all kinds of groups with all kinds of objectives. The fact that it is a technique rather than a defining characteristic of the organizations involved in its use is one of the factors that makes casual prediction (and resistance) so difficult.[26] … If a group has dedicated members willing to undertake suicide attacks to support the causes, the group becomes much more dangerous, instills greater fear, and is generally more effective.[27]

The imagination is a powerful force and can be a double-edged sword working for the forces of good versus the forces of evil. But, of course, the sides of good and evil are open to interpretation and viewpoint: terrorist, patriot, or freedom fighter? Whatever, one constant is important to recognize: the globalization (or Westernization versus ancient religious following) of the world has, and will continue to be, a sore spot festering in the winds of terrorism and war. It is contingent on the antiterrorist forces to imagine scenarios and plan "war games" commensurate with the imagination of terrorists and warmongers who would seek to destroy democracy, religious freedom, and the free will of man thorough their nefarious and suicidal actions. We cannot plan on fighting today's or tomorrow's war with strategy, tactics, and weapons of bygone years.

What is the prospectus of terrorism arising as homegrown in the United States? We have seen the radicalized 1960s and 1970s with rioting in the streets, bombings, arson, cities burning, and assassination. Then we have also witnessed homegrown terrorism in the form of bombings of abortion clinics, reemergence of hate-based militias, and other forms of right-wing violence. The following article from the United Kingdom newspaper *The Telegraph* reports a growing concern of terrorist experts and residents in several American cities about the possibility of second-generation American citizens with ties to Somalia becoming "mind-corrupted" and enlisting in Muslim terrorist tactics.

> Officials say a second generation of Somali immigrants is becoming increasingly radicalized and could pose a growing threat to security. U.S. law enforcement agencies are concerned young militants [who made multiple visits to radical mosques in Pakistan] could return to the U.S. to plot terror attacks.... The authorities began looking into the radicalization of Somali youths after 27-year-old Shirwa Ahmed became the first known American suicide bomber in late October [2008].
>
> The Minneapolis student blew himself up in one of five coordinated bombings in northern Somalia orchestrated by al-Shabaab, whose former leader reportedly trained at terror camps in Afghanistan before being killed in an American air strike in May, 2008.
>
> The FBI suspects the men were radicalized by classes at the Minneapolis and St. Paul mosques. The Abubakar center has denied any political activity and has condemned *"all acts of indiscriminate violence"* [Italics added]. Omar Jamal ... said Somali youth were vulnerable to recruitment because of poor job prospects, disillusionment with U.S. foreign policy in Iraq and Afghanistan, and a call to arms against a U.S.-backed Ethiopian incursion into Somalia.
>
> Andrew Liepman, a deputy director at the National Counter Terrorism Center, said: 'We are concerned that if a few Somali American youth could be motivated to engage in such activities overseas, fellow travelers could return to the U.S. and engage in terrorist activities here."
>
> "I wonder if now we are not catching up and finding that problems which are so consuming the UK are coming here," said Bruce Hoffman, a former adviser on counter-terrorism to the CIA. "al-Qaeda's aim has always been to have people inside the U.S. with U.S. passports. Here you have a cadre of susceptible individuals and you have people ready to take advantage of that."[28]

It is interesting to note that "the Abubakar Center has denied any political activity and has condemned 'all acts of indiscriminate violence.'" The key word or escape clause here is the word *indiscriminate*. It is widely known and accepted that terrorists do not operate indiscriminately! Extensive planning and resources go into every act of organized terrorism.

The many-headed hydra referred to as terrorism and the "new warfare" has taken on a personality of operating as independent cells with recruitment within the confines of the United States. To this point, the "radicalized" Somali-American youths have engaged their activities in other countries. However, the United States must be prepared for similar threats in the near future as the movement gathers momentum. Just one suicide bombing in the United States in a crowded subway, restaurant, nightclub, shopping center, recreation park, or other public place where people gather to enjoy themselves would cause psychological damage far beyond the injuries and death caused by the bomb.

So, yes, the United States is fighting a new war where the enemy is faceless and knows no boundaries. The warnings sounded in previous generations about mass movements, the growth of religious ideology, and conflicts between liberal and conservative thinking could conceivably develop into a worst-case scenario of a clash of civilizations, disintegration of society, collapse of conventional democratic government, and a fearful public.

> Our sins and our good deeds, our virtues and our vices, our good and evil qualities alike, long expended on the stupendous material of a world empire, are leading us, not to one day of reckoning or to two, but to a whole unbroken series of desperate and deadly encounters with those we have wronged.
>
> **—Francis William Lauderdale Adams, *The New Egypt: A Social Sketch*** **(London: T.F. Unwin, 1893), 252**

Endnotes

1. Tzu, 2003, xiv, xv.
2. LeShan, 1992, 33.
3. Ibid., 117.
4. Little known about the biography of Bruce Lee is that his parents raised him as a girl until the age of nine so that the "spirits" would not take away their boy— thus the feminine name *Lee Sai Fon* (later changed to the masculine *Lee Jun Fan*), which he later Americanized to *Bruce Lee*.
5. Chaliand and Blin, 2007, back cover.
6. http://eudocs.lib.byu.edu/index.php/Neville_Chamberlain's_%22Peace_For_ Our_Time%22_speech.
7. Waltz, 2001, 1.
8. Arendt, 1969/1970, 1.
9. Galvin, 2003, xiv, xv.
10. Command and General Staff School, 1936, p. 19. in Bassford, 1992.
11. Van Creveld, 1991, ix.
12. June, 2008.
13. Laqueur, 2005. 278.
14. LeShan, 1992, 21.
15. Van Creveld, 1991, cover jacket flap.
16. Ibid.
17. Chinese Communist Party leader, Mao Tse Tung.
18. Marighella.
19. Laqueur, 2005, 46.
20. Hoover, 1957, v. In quoting this material from Mr. Hoover's book, I have substituted the word *terrorist* in place of *communist*, because the contextual meaning is the same.
21. Stapley, 2006.
22. Hoffer, 1951.
23. Brown, 2003, 282.

24. Waltz, 2001, 237, quoting Alexander Hamilton and John Jay in *The Federalist*.
25. Johnson, 1966, 163.
26. Laqueur, 2005, 143, quoted in Lutz et al., 2005, 167.
27. Lutz et al., 2005.
28. Spillius, 2009, edited here for brevity.

Bibliography

Arendt, H. 1969/1970. *On violence*. New York: Harcourt, Brace & World.

Brown, M. E. 2003. *Grave new world: Security challenges in the 21st century.* Washington, DC: Georgetown University Press.

Chaliand, G., and Blin, A. 2007. *The history of terrorism: From antiquity to al Qaeda*, trans. E. Schneider, K. Pulver, and J. Browner. University of California Press.

Chamberlain, N. "Peace in our lifetime" speech. http://eudocs.lib.byu.edu/index.php/Neville_Chamberlain's_%22Peace_For_Our_Time%22_speech (accessed March 15, 2009).

Command and General Staff School. 1936. *Principles of strategy for an independent corps or army in a theater of operations.* Fort Leavenworth, KS: U.S. Army Command and General Staff School Press. In Bassford, Christopher. 1992. Clausewitz and his works. http://www.clausewitz.com/CWZHOME/CWZSUMM/CWORKHOL.htm (accessed March 11, 2009). (A very different version of this 1992 paper was published as Chapter 2 of Bassford, Christopher. *Clausewitz in English: The reception of Clausewitz in Britain and America.* New York: Oxford University Press, 1994. This version was written as courseware for the Army War College, 1996, then somewhat modified in 1998, 2000, 2002, and 2008.)

Galvin, D. 2003. *The art of war*, trans. L. Giles. New York: Barnes & Noble Classics.

Hoffer, E. 1951. *The true believer: Thoughts on the nature of mass movements.* Harper Perennial, a division of Harper-Collins Publisher.

Hoover, J. E. 1957. *Masters of deceit.* New York: Henry Holt and Company.

Johnson, C. 1966. *Revolutionary change.* Boston: Little, Brown and Company.

June, D. L. 2008. *Introduction to executive protection.* 2nd ed. Boca Raton, FL: CRC Press.

Laqueur, W. 1999. *The new terrorism.* Oxford: Oxford University Press.

Laqueur, W. 2005. *A history of terrorism*, 143. Quoted in Lutz, J. M., and Lutz, B. J. 2005. *Terrorism*, 167. New York: Palgrave-MacMillian.

LeShan, L. 1992. *The psychology of war: Comprehending its mystique and its madness.* Chicago: The Noble Press.

Lutz, J. M., and Lutz, B. J. 2005. *Terrorism.* New York: Palgrave-MacMillian.

Marighella, C. The "godfather" of urban terrorism. *The mini-manual of the urban guerilla.*

Martin, J. J. The consequences of World War Two to Great Britain: Twenty years of decline, 1939–1959. http://tmh.floonet.net/articles/britainDecline1939-59.html (accessed March 15, 2007).

Spillius, A. 2009. US facing home-grown Islamic terror threat. *Telegraph*, March 13. http://www.telegraph.co.uk/news/worldnews/africaandindianocean/somalia/4987199/US-facing-home-grown-Islamic-terror-threat.html

Stapley, L. F. 2006. *Globalization and terrorism: Death of a way of life.* London: Karnac Books.

Tzu, S. 2003. *The art of war*, trans. L. Giles. New York: Barnes & Noble Classics.

Van Creveld, M. 1991. *The transformation of war: The most radical reinterpretation of armed conflict since Clausewitz.* The Free Press.

Waltz, K. N. 2001. *Man, the state and war: A theoretical analysis.* New York: Columbia University Press.

Deprivation, Occupation, and Social Change

12

Hamas and Lebanese Hezbollah's Evolution from Bombs to Ballot Boxes

KEELY M. FAHOUM

Contents

The face of political Islam is changing. Over the last thirty years, radical Islamist groups emerged brandishing weapons and loud, angry rhetoric; some advocated widespread resistance, including suicide bombings, hijackings, and a strict code of behavior between the sexes. But within the last fifteen years, some of the most hard-core groups have drastically changed their tactics and rhetoric. What role does social change have in this dramatic shift in policies, and why are some groups choosing ballot boxes over bombs? In this essay, I will use Hamas and Lebanese Hezbollah as two cases to illustrate the changing face of resurgent Islam. I will discuss social and political factors contributing to the creation of each organization, how those factors shaped the development and nature of the groups over time, and argue that as a result of social change, these Islamist groups have softened their rhetoric, moderated their political stances, and are fast becoming alternatives to corrupt, divided governments who fail to provide security, social services, and a sense of justice for the populations they represent.

Flaws of Fundamentalism

The phrase "Islamic fundamentalism" is, in itself, a loaded concept. Scholars have debated the true definition of fundamentalism and whether or not it represents the nature of resurgent Islam. The word *fundamentalism* was coined early in the twentieth century to describe a Protestant movement against modernization and secularization of American society.* The movement aimed to reassert the fundamentals of Christianity and a literal interpretation of the Bible. The problem with this term, according to Islamic theologians, is that all Muslims believe in the literalness of the Quran, each word is the direct word of God and therefore is unchangeable and immutable. The Western (and in some cases, Eastern) application of the word has come to represent a smaller group of extremist or militant members of Islam who are not ambassadors of the religion as a whole. These groups espouse a more puritanical version of Islam, often called *salafist*. While there are groups who espouse a strict adherence to the words of the Quran, combined with the social and cultural aspects absorbed from the example of Prophet Muhammad, the word *fundamentalist* may be somewhat applicable; but on the whole, considering the subjective connotation of the term as equivalent to terrorists or extremists, it is not useful to describe the political and social role of Islam in the Middle East today. For the purposes of this essay, I will replace the term *fundamentalist* with *Islamist*, intending to present the picture of modern Islamists as a powerful force in politics and social change.

Hamas

Social and Political Factors Contributing to the Creation of Hamas

For Palestine, 1967 was a watershed year; there was the loss of the West Bank and Gaza to Israel after the Six-Day War, the refugee flight of hundreds of

---

* Aslan, Reza, *No God But God* (New York: Random House, 2005), 243.

thousands of Palestinians to neighboring Arab countries, and Israel entered and occupied both territories. For the residents who stayed behind, it became painstakingly clear that the future struggle for liberation would have to come from within; Palestinians could not depend on the surrounding Arab armies to aid in their struggle. The failure of the Arabs was not only a letdown for the Palestinians, but on a broader scale, it led to the disintegration of secular nationalism, which was reflected in a rise of Islamism.

Social conditions began to worsen significantly after the 1967 war. The West Bank, Old City of Jerusalem, and Gaza came under Israeli military control, and Palestinians were subjected to a series of brutal measures, including political suppression, economic exploitation, institutional "destructuring," and ideological and cultural repression.[*] Israel's policy intended to break up any semblance of organized resistance, institutionalization, or consolidation of national character. They attempted to fragment the Palestinians by dealing with village leaders individually in order to prevent any growth of collective identity.[†]

Israel's military control over Palestinian territories indelibly gave them power "over all aspects of Palestinian life, including: legal, civil and political rights, land and water rights, taxation, licensing, trade, services, security, health, and social welfare."[‡] The residents of the territories were at the mercy of the Israeli military bureaucracy with little oversight from the Israeli public and practically no input or control from the Palestinians. There were few significant political activities, and any physical organization or protests were banned under Israeli military rule. The "Iron Fist" policy attempted to hammer out any possibility of resistance or self-assertion, including underground organization. Israel conducted mass arrests, administrative detention, home demolitions, and deportations to curb any serious attempt at resisting colonization.[§] Political repression did not have the desired effect and only contributed to the increasing level of resistance against the Israelis. Although this oppression limited the amount of public organization for collective resistance, it did open up other channels and spaces for both secular and religious resistance groups to organize.

After 1967, the West Bank and most of the inhabitants became incorporated into the Israeli economy. The Israeli government infused Palestinian labor into their workforce, and subsequently the territories became dependent upon the prosperity and performance of the Israeli economy. In the

---

[*] Farsoun, Samih K., and Landis, Jean M., "The Sociology of an Uprising, the Roots of the Intifada," in *Intifada: Palestine at the Crossroads*, ed. Jamal R. Nasser and Roger Heacock (New York: Praeger, 1990), 19.

[†] Smith, Charles, *Palestine and the Arab-Israeli Conflict, a History with Documents*, 5th ed. (Boston: Bedford/St. Martin's, 2004), 356.

[‡] Farsoun and Landis, 19.

[§] Ibid., 21.

early 1970s, employment levels for the West Bank sat as high as 98%, but only constituted 5% of the Israeli workforce taking on mostly menial and low-wage jobs.[*] Exports and imports to the territories were subject to unfair economic practices. For example, Palestinians within the territories exported their products tax-free to Israel, while any non-Israeli products entering the region carried customs duties. Israel's absorption of Arab labor created an imperial economy that had physical control over the population, creating a "captive market" for its goods.[†]

Israeli attempts to fracture any sense of organization among the Palestinians extended into financial institutions. Destruction of formal banking and monetary institutions forced residents in the territories to resort to traditional exchange methods and the opening of Israeli banks hindered economic development within the occupied zones. By restricting and destroying institutions, Israel created insurmountable barriers to development of civil society.[‡]

The role of Islamists after the 1967 war was distinguished by passive activities and nonconfrontational resistance. There were limited amounts of guerrilla raids on Israel from the Jordan branch of the Muslim brotherhood, but education, mosque building, recruiting, and mobilization became the focus of the group at large.[§] The brotherhood's intention was to construct a large base of support that eventually would be used against the Zionist occupier. The religious groups of Gaza and the West Bank remained centered on serving the community, opening an Islamic center that provided services through a mosque with an attached health club, women's training centers, and a medical clinic.[¶] The act of opening and supporting these social centers and increasing recruitment were all part of the "upbringing of an Islamic generation."[**] Support for the brotherhood increased after the Islamic revolution in Iran, lending even further credibility to the power that lay in jihad.

The First Intifada

The first *intifada* was characterized by a rebellion against the colonization of Palestine and subsequent repression of social, political, and economic freedoms. The uprising was a struggle for national liberation and a desire for

---

[*] Smith, 357.
[†] Farsoun and Landis, 22.
[‡] Ibid., 25.
[§] Hroub, Khaled, *Hamas: Political Thought and Practice* (Washington, DC: Institute for Palestine Studies, 2000), 30.
[¶] Knudsen, Are, "Crescent and Sword, the Hamas Enigma," *Third World Quarterly*, vol. 26, no. 8 (2005) 1376.
[**] Abu-Amr, Ziad, "Hamas: A Historical and Political Background," *Journal of Palestine Studies*, vol. 22, no.4 (summer 1993) 7.

self-determination.* The intifada was not a spontaneous reaction to one cataclysmic event, but instead was a result of repeated political and legal exclusion from the overall power process controlled by the Israeli government.† Aside from oppression and occupation, there were efforts by the Israelis to dissolve the cultural and social bonds that tied the Palestinians to their historical language and values, factors that could mold the template for Palestinian nationalism to germinate.

Perhaps the most important factor contributing to the success of the first intifada was the interorganizational cooperation between political, social, and religious organizations that crossed demographic and confessional lines. The Palestinians had set up their own administrative structure and informal institutions to handle the social demands of refugees and Diaspora members uniting and motivating a movement across age, gender, ideological, and religious lines. The intifada was not dominated by one particular party, but was a concerted effort across different groups to propel and shape the movement through informal institutionalization, literature, framing, and cooperation among different factions of Palestinian groups. All organizations (committees) fell under one umbrella organization, the United National Leadership of the Uprising (UNLU). The UNLU prepared and managed distribution of communiqués that mobilized the population and articulated the stated goals, demands, and strategies of the organization.‡

The emergence of Hamas was first as a signatory to communiqués being published by the Muslim Brotherhood toward the end of the intifada. The brotherhood stayed out of the UNLU and organizational aspect of the first intifada for the most part due to the fact that they foresaw the installation of a caliphate before Palestine would be freed completely, but after reconsidering their role, they decided to issue their own messages and become more involved in the uprising.§

There were fundamental differences between Hamas and the UNLU; Hamas did not want an international peace conference or a partitioned Palestine.¶ Israel capitalized on the split between the two organizations and helped support Hamas, building and encouraging the organization.** The importance of Hamas's role in the first intifada was an opportunity to organize and pervade into every aspect of Palestinian life. The social and political realities on the ground during the uprising gave life to Hamas and the

---

* Farsoun and Landis, 16.
† Ibid.
‡ Nasser, Jamal R., and Heacock, Roger, "The Revolutionary Transformation of the Palestinians under Occupation," in *Intifada: Palestine at the Crossroads*, ed. Jamal R. Nassar and Roger Heacock (New York: Praeger, 1990), 191.
§ Ibid., 195.
¶ Ibid.
** Knudsen, 1376.

organization began creating linkages and networks with Palestinians in different social strata, which they would use to their advantage during subsequent uprisings.

Why the Resistance Went Islamist

The social change that occurred after the first intifada and Oslo peace accords, respectively, came through repressive, painful closure and economic degradation. Separation or enclavation of the West Bank and Gaza prevented any sustained economic progress and actually caused de-development when "deprived from its capacity for production, rational structural transformation, and meaningful reform, making it incapable of even distorted development."* The closure and blockage of sections of the occupied territories post-Oslo fragmented economic and territorial unity, reduced living standards, increased dependence on Israel, and increased corruption in the Palestinian Authority (PA).† Hamas's particular interest and involvement in the social dimension of Palestine can be traced back to the foundation of the movement's ideology in the Muslim Brotherhood's religious and social thought, which emphasized the priority of social development as a necessary step in the process of political change.‡

Hamas was accepted as a branch of the Muslim Brotherhood and issued a published charter in 1988. The document recognizes Palestine as an Islamic "endowment," and thus it cannot be split or given away. In addition, the charter criticizes the Palestine Liberation Organization's (PLO) secular nature and calls for unity among Palestinians.§ Due to a lack of Islamic scholarship among Hamas leadership, its message had to appeal to the popular masses and construct a mix of nationalism and Islamism within a simple and uncomplicated bureaucratic structure. The appeal of Hamas became more obvious as the stature of the PLO declined. The leadership of the PA was seen as increasingly corrupt and separated from the will of the Palestinian people. The intifada had brought about the Oslo Accords; but all the organization, the blood, sweat, and tears, brought only partial international recognition for the plight of the refugees, and the terms of the peace process were not reviewed or approved by the representatives of the UNLU. Hamas had cooperated with the UNLU, supported the unification of Palestinian efforts, and the result was more repression, cantonization of the territories, and even more pressure on

---

* Roy, Sara, "De-Development Revisited: Palestinian Economy and Society since Oslo," *Journal of Palestinian Studies*, vol. 28, no. 3 (spring 1999) 64.
† Farsakh, Leila, *Under Seige: Closure, Separation and the Palestinian Economy, Middle East Report 217*, Beyond Oslo: The New Uprising (winter 2000) 22.
‡ Hroub, 234.
§ Knudsen, 1378.

economic, social, and political efforts to unite the people of Palestine into a state.

Hamas provided an alternative to the PA, and with control over *zakat* and *waqf*, which they used to provide social services to a population suffering under Israeli colonization, they were able to gain trust among a population that was suffering from deprivation and densely populated living conditions. "The high relative deprivation experienced by generations of Palestinians is a major reason for the gradual rise of Islamism in the Occupied Territories."* The Islamic Resistance Movement benefited from a trend of "conservatism" that built up after the first intifada.† It is not surprising that the Palestinian people turned to religion in a time of desperation, hopelessness, and repression. The rise of an Islamist group among a primarily secular society was significant, and it is important to evaluate the social circumstances and motivators behind this conversion. The Hamas Charter outlines and discusses the necessity of "fortifying society" by furnishing it the Islamic grounding necessary to undertake struggle.‡

Hamas used the charity finances to build schools, nurseries, and universities, which accorded them access to families and children: 95% of the group's finances go to social services.§ Articles 20 and 21 of the charter articulate the social service responsibilities: "Part of social welfare consists of helping all who are in need of material, spiritual or collective cooperation. It is incumbent upon all members of the Islamic Resistance Movement to look after the needs of the people as they would look after their own needs."¶ The money that Hamas does provide to citizens goes directly from the group to the family; there are no intermediaries. There is some debate, however, whether or not Hamas uses its social welfare connections to recruit followers and sustain the organization.** "Social services became one of the most important sources of influence that Hamas had with broad strata of the public."††

The importance of social change with respect to the creation of Hamas lies squarely between the political, social, and economic pressures placed on the population by Israel after the first intifada, and the failure of the PA to provide adequate social welfare service and a well-organized system of communication and support. Hamas played an important role in political and social legislation building credibility, which they would capitalize on during

---

* Edwards, B. Milton, "Political Islam in Palestine in an Environment of Peace?" *Third World Quarterly*, vol. 17, no. 7 (1996) 213, in Knudsen, 1383.
† Abu-Amr, 18.
‡ Hroub, 234.
§ Knudsen, 1384.
¶ "Hamas Charter," 1988, http://www.palestinecenter.org/cpap/documents/charter.html (accessed August 28, 2006).
·· Knudsen, 1384.
††Hroub, 234.

future elections.* It was the destruction of Palestinian institutions that
fostered the most political and nationalist activism.† The group sponsored
forums, political gatherings, and Islamic exhibitions, especially on university campuses, which not only provided a public space for organization but
gave Hamas the authority to sponsor and coordinate protests, an action that
was reserved primarily for PLO factions, especially Fatah. This ability was a
testament to Hamas's popularity and willingness to reach out to the social
sphere. Political participation was an area previously shunned by the Islamic
Resistance Movement, but low-level elections were not completely avoided.
During the 1992 Ramallah Chamber of Commerce elections, Hamas representatives won more seats than Fatah, perhaps a prediction of the organization's popular support and ability to mobilize people and get them to the
polling places.‡

Hamas responded to social change by providing the services the population needed, organized tangible resistance events against Israel, and provided
a unifying theme to lean on during times of desperation and hopelessness.
Providing a network of social services enabled Hamas to stay in touch with
the concerns of the poor and working classes and an opportunity to influence their religious conduct, political choices, and beliefs.§ Although the
organization identified with strict Islamist principles, the leaders understood
the necessity of attracting a wide swath of Palestinians, some of which were
solidly behind the secular PLO. The religiously themed speeches, rallies, and
sermons were buttressed by external *muftiyeen* (official presenter of Islamic
law) in an effort to credential the movement.¶

Social justice was a second area in which Hamas was active. Sheikh Yassin
served as an arbitrator during disputes, and as a result of the inefficiency of
Israeli courts with even small civil cases, many people turned to an informal but reputable judicial system. Providing judicial services also gave the
movement moral authority within the territory.** After the arrest of Yassin,
there was a gap in the judicial process primarily because there were no other
Hamas members who had the religious credentials to fill his shoes.

Hamas also administered guidance regarding social behavior and education. They encouraged modesty in women's dress, restraint on interpersonal
and social relationships, condemning corruption, and encouraged religious
education as a strategy to fortify the population against the Israeli occupation. Some scholars have argued that this strategy was helpful in "instilling

---

* Taraki, Lisa, *The Islamic Resistance Movement in the Palestinian Uprising, Middle
  East Report 156, Iran's Revolution Turns Ten* (January–February 1989) 32.
† Farsoun and Landis, 26.
‡ Abu-Amr, 16.
§ Hroub, 235.
¶ Ibid., 186.
** Ibid., 236.

religious values that extolled sacrifice and martyrdom"; however, these religious education principles were in place before Hamas was created.*

The Second Intifada

Although religion did not have a front seat during the first uprising, it certainly did during the second. During the second intifada, "religion played a major mobilizing and symbolic role."† Targets of violence became religiously motivated and came to characterize the nature of the uprising. Ariel Sharon's visit to the Haram al-Sharif created significant tension and sparked demonstrations that took on a decidedly religious tone. The PA was not immune from the transformation; communiqués and press releases became more religious, and they took advantage of the wave of religiosity sweeping through the territories. Support for Hamas also came as a response to the disorganization of the PA. There was little knowledge of who was running the show, what were the objectives, how were they going to get things done, and especially what safety nets were in place for when Israel would inevitably shut critical services such as food or water off. The mosque and further religious networks had preestablished channels of communication, legitimacy, and gathering places, and had already entrenched themselves within the social service circles of the community. It seems fitting that some of the Palestinian civilians turned to the most organized, credible group that could project and sustain the movement; that group just happened to be Islamist.

The major difference between the first and second intifada was the absence of a large civil rebellion. PA rule and the effects of Oslo had demobilized the population and deepened their alienation from political action.‡ The PA was unable to provide basic logistical support to the population—another reason why Hamas gained credibility on the street. The second uprising was characterized by its disorganization, lack of strategic clarity, and tactical inconsistency.§ The violence that characterized the second intifada was not only an effort to strike at Israel, but a competition for credibility between Fatah and Hamas. Fatah confined its attacks primarily to the occupied territories, while Hamas attacked inside Israel, gaining support from Palestinians who were "enraged by the actions of the Israeli military, devastated by the tightening siege and left in the lurch by its own leaders and the international community."¶ Hamas's use of violence was also strategic,

* Hroub, 241.
† Hammami, Rema, and Tamari, Salim, *Anatomy of Another Rebellion, Middle East Report 217, Beyond Oslo: The New Uprising* (winter 2000) 9.
‡ Ibid., 12.
§ Rabbani, Mouin, *The Costs of Chaos in Palestine*, Middle East Report 224 (autumn 2002) 6.
¶ Ibid., 7.

attempting to subvert efforts at peace by the PA that would strengthen the organization and work against the goals of the Islamist organization. One particularly disastrous result for the PA was a crackdown by Israel on its civil and military infrastructure and its reoccupying the West Bank, which had previously been subject to the PA's jurisdiction. The violent attacks on Israel were not necessarily born of frustration and anger; they were tactical maneuvers in an overall strategy to destabilize and discredit the PA and subsequent peace process that could all but minimize the importance of Hamas.

Some researchers argue that bombings play a strategic "spoiler role" to the peace process.[*] The Palestinian Authority released a statement saying,

> The suicide bombings are a key element in the arena of struggle between the Israelis and Palestinians and an analysis of the circumstances of the timing and execution of the vast majority of the bombings, particularly the major ones conducted by Hamas and the Islamic Jihad had agents who provided information on political developments, including inside information about negotiations with Israel, and the United States, thus enabling Hamas and Islamic Jihad to respond accordingly.[†]

The purpose of the bombings was to create and amplify doubts on the target side that the moderates could be trusted with a peace plan, and that they would not go back on the agreement later on.[‡] Much of the suicide bombing campaigns and everyday violence became retaliatory in nature.

Societal factors within the Palestinian territories included a deep sense of widespread and frequent victimization by external enemies conducted through the course of political conflict and legitimate authorities promoting extreme violence.[§] Palestinian society went through a large shift in strategic violence between the first intifada and the second. The second resistance was hallmarked by a move to suicide terror. The Palestinian society (including women) could embrace the extreme violence primarily because they perceived overwhelming threats to their security, identity, and national aspirations, and because they saw themselves solely as the victims.[¶] The social changes that occurred during the second intifada created a wider support base for Hamas. There was concrete and tangible evidence that they were doing *something* to thwart Israeli control over the territories. After hearing

---

[*] Bloom, Mia, *Dying to Kill: The Allure of Suicide Terrorism* (New York: Columbia University Press, 2005), 20.
[†] Ibid.
[‡] Kydd, Andrew, and Walter, Barbara F., "Sabotaging the Peace: The Politics of Extremist Violence," *International Organizations*, vol. 56, no. 2 (spring 2002) 264.
[§] Hafez, Mohammed, *Manufacturing Human Bombs, the Making of Palestinian Suicide Bombers* (Washington, D.C.: U.S. Institute of Peace, 2006), 53.
[¶] Ibid.

about one female suicide (Wafa Idris) bomber's success, young girls from within her same refugee camp iconized her and desired to emulate her actions. One young sixteen-year old girl cried out emotionally, "When you see people killed in their houses, when you see blood every day and your sister, brother or father is killed in front of you, what are you going to do? Nothing?! Of course you're going to do something, even give your soul!"* Although there were strategic, ideological, and systemic reasons for the use of suicide bombings, these are at the most fundamental level acts of desperation. Society was demanding action, and Hamas was delivering.

Post-Intifada and Elections: A New Face for Hamas

During the self-rule elections in 1996, Hamas debated inside the organization whether or not to participate. Some members saw it as a way to demonstrate the presence of the group and an opportunity to publicly campaign against Oslo. Ismail Haniyeh argued that participation in elections would guarantee a legitimate political presence for the movement after the voting and could introduce badly needed reforms in domestic institutions that could combat corruption.† In addition, Hamas had long desired participation in the creation of official institutions, to participate in civil society and to promote internal development without being subjected to arrest and harassment, enjoying parliamentary immunity; but most importantly, Hamas saw political participation as a way to provide an alternative to the secular, corrupt government run by the PA.‡

The high number of registered voters and voter turnout was particularly surprising for Hamas, but it also sent the group a message: political participation may be an option to consider for the future. Social participation in the electoral process influenced Hamas to consider democratic participation for power within the territories.

It was another ten years before Hamas had a second chance to participate in major elections within the territories. Hamas saw the 2006 elections as an opportunity to illustrate their power through elections and to fulfill the recommendations made by Haniyeh in 1996. In order to run for office, Hamas had to balance several issues, and promote themselves as a corruption-free, forward-thinking party, which differed significantly from earlier efforts to restrict involvement to social services and religious education. Smaller elections for community offices indicated a strong and widespread support base for Hamas. This added confidence to the Islamic Resistance Movement that

---

* "Female Suicide Bombers," National Geographic Explorer television report, aired April 14, 2006.
† Hroub, 226.
‡ Ibid.

they could obtain a large number of seats within the Palestinian parliament.* The decision to participate in the January 2006 elections was a sign of the group's moderation and appeal to non-Muslim Palestinians. The elections were a turning point for the organization and placed them in charge of myriad political, social, and economic issues that have plagued the Palestinian refugees for decades. The victory gave Hamas the chance to flex its muscles politically instead of violently.

The face of Hamas has changed significantly. Early in the movement they grew out of the shadow of the Muslim Brotherhood, whose social participation was limited to aid, guidance, and providing services for the public. Over time, the group gained popularity, influence, and served as an alternative to the corrupt and secular PA. After violent confrontations with Israeli military members and the use of suicide bombings as political instruments, Hamas has realized that their future is not in bombs, but in ballots. The political victory of the movement has saddled Hamas with social, political, and economic responsibilities on a grand scale and subjected the group to intense international scrutiny of such a level that violence would only undermine the organization. As a result, they have, after much consternation, opted to work with the PA and operationalize their vision of Islamic nationalism.

Lebanese Hezbollah

Social and Political Factors Contributing to the Creation of the Lebanese Hezbollah

The social and political factors that set the foundation for the creation of Hezbollah can be traced back to the early political organization of Lebanon itself. After political consolidation under confessional divisions, religious identities were solidified and sharpened and reinforced traditional patron-client relationships.† The Christians dominated the international trade system, and the poorer regions of the country suffered under feudal conditions. Separate and rigid identity systems created a barrier to the formation of an overall national identity. Various religious groups had different goals for Lebanon and the population. The influx of Palestinian refugees and the subsequent relocation of the PLO to Lebanon in the early 1970s only added fodder to the sectarian divisions within the country, and eventually sparked a civil war that would rage for many years. The lack of equality and develop-

* Zweiri, Mahjoob, "The Hamas Victory: Shifting Sands or Major Earthquake?" *Third World Quarterly*, vol. 27, no. 4 (2006) 278.
† Harik, Judith Palmer, "Between Islam and the System: Sources and Implications of Popular Support for Lebanon's Hizbollah," *Journal of Conflict Resolution*, vol. 40, no. 1 (March 1996) 42.

ment along with a shortage of food aggravated the political factors surrounding the start of the war.

Social factors contributing to the creation of Hezbollah grew out of unequal social status for the Shi'a, who populated the southern area of Lebanon. The community was dominated by a few notable families who were unwilling to deal with problems of economic and social development that could have led to the loss of any political authority.* Many Shi'a were dissatisfied that they did not have equal access to the political system as other religious groups. For Shi'a, property destruction, death, and dislocation endured during the civil war and Arab-Israeli conflict within southern Lebanon created even more resentment toward the Christian regime.†

While the Lebanese civil war was raging and sociopolitical issues within the different cantons were beginning to bubble up, there was a massive revolution that turned the secular resistance efforts on their head. In 1979, a revolution in Iran, orchestrated and represented by Ayatollah Ruhollah Khomeini, overturned the secular, U.S.-supported shah. A circle of Lebanese mullahs formed Hezbollah and patterned it after Iran's Islamic revolutionary ideology, pledging complete loyalty to Khomeini.‡ The fighters were primarily locals, and this fact would later provide the foundation for the stability and indigenous nature of the group, which makes the job of routing out militants next to impossible. The newly created Hezbollah addressed social concerns such as dirty water, sewer networks, and social justice systems. The political domination of the Christians created resentment among the Shi'a population, who knew they were in the majority of the population; this caused much consternation because the Lebanese constitution held power in reserve for the largest population within the country. The amount of deprivation suffered by the people of southern Lebanon created a desire for change, and because the state was absent, a space was created that would be filled by Hezbollah. "In Lebanon's case, it is widely believed that the low standard of living endured by many Shiites compared with members of other societal groups has encouraged their political mobilization and offered fundamentalists broad opportunities for recruitment."§ The feeling of deprivation is a common theme among populations, which feel resentment and estrangement from their respective governments. In addition, some political theorists have suggested the deprived and embittered Muslims are open to promises made by militant Muslim groups

---

* Harik, 43.
† Ibid., 46.
‡ Harik, Judith Palmer, *Hezbollah, the Changing Face of Terrorism* (New York: I.B. Tauris, 2004).
§ Picard, Elizabeth, "Political Identities and Communal Identities: Shifting Mobilization among the Lebanese Shi'a through Ten Years of War, 1975–1985," in *Ethnicity, Politics and Development*, ed. Dennis L. Thompson and Dov Ronen (Boulder, CO: Lynne Riener, 1986), 161, in Harik, 46.

who promote Islamic governments as an alternative.* Interviews conducted with families of Hezbollah fighters asserted that young men didn't join as fighters out of necessity, but because it suited their ideals.†

The emergence of Hezbollah was also in response to regional forces impacting the Middle East: colonialism, secularism, corruption, regional conflict, and resentment of Israel.‡ Hezbollah provided both Iran and Syria the opportunity to fight the Western powers of colonialism and occupation against a common enemy. Syria's desire to regain the Golan Heights would be the penultimate goal in their support of Hezbollah. For Iran, Hezbollah offered a way to fight the Israelis by proxy as well as to promote the expansion of Shi'a Islam in Lebanon.§ The first years of Hezbollah were marred by acts of resistance against Israeli, American, and Lebanese interests. The strike against U.S. military forces was both a success and a failure. The violence met short-term goals, expelling the American forces, but the act placed a black mark on the organization and facilitated its placement on the U.S. State Department's terror list. This action has hindered Hezbollah's efforts to be an internationally recognized political group who represented the interests of all Lebanese, not just the Shi'a.

After the civil war ended, Hezbollah's fight against forces occupying Lebanese soil continued. The political grievances of the Lebanese Muslims were addressed, but there were no significant changes in the type of government ruling Lebanon; it was still a confessional government with no foreseeable solution to unequal or nonexistent social services for the rural areas of the country. Hezbollah's role became twofold: assist in providing relief to the poor communities regardless of religious affiliation, and serve as a militia force working to expel Israeli forces still occupying southern Lebanon. The peace accords, which helped broker the end of the civil war, also established a timetable for parliamentary elections.¶

The last hurdle for Hezbollah to address as a military organization was the remaining Israeli forces in the southern zone· of Lebanon. After eighteen years of occupation and harassment by Hezbollah guerrillas, the Israelis withdrew from the area. Seen as a victory by Arab countries and lauded by Iran, Hezbollah earned great credibility as a military force. It was on the political front that they had to prove themselves. Although the Israelis withdrew, Hezbollah maintained their military posture because there was no viable Lebanese army to replace them. The reaction of the Lebanese in the south to the Israeli withdrawal was one of pride and victory. Hezbollah had

---

* Harik, 47.
† Norton, Augustus Richard, "Hizballah and the Israeli Withdrawal from Southern Lebanon," *Journal of Palestine Studies*, vol. 30, no. 1 (autumn 2000).
‡ Harik, 11.
§ Ibid., 39.
¶ Harik, 45.

achieved the one thing no other Arab nation had been able to do: defeat Israel. Some politicians claimed that if Israel withdrew, Hezbollah would continue attacking Israel on a regular basis, and while some attacks did occur following withdrawal, Hezbollah avoided major conflict with Israel.* This was the first indication that perhaps the movement had changed and that emphasis would now be placed on engaging the Lebanese government on a political playing field.

Hezbollah as a Political Party: Changing Faces?

Measured against Hezbollah's success as a terrorist organization turned political party is the unique ability of its political leaders to recognize and adapt to the sociopolitical environment of the time. Hezbollah has altered its two faces (revolutionary and political) to suit the desires of the Lebanese population, their most important support system. The political chameleons of Hezbollah's leadership have been able to master the most important aspects of Lebanon's political game and exploit them in their favor. They have evolved with and through the political system, not in opposition to it.

In order to be elected into office, Hezbollah adjusted their original vision for an Islamist state, and by providing social services, regulations on fair economic interaction (such as measuring octane levels in gas tanks to ensure customers were receiving the quality of products they were paying for), agricultural advice to farmers in the Biqa'a Valley, and even snow removal, they have amassed popular support across demographic, religious, and sectarian lines.† Hezbollah has made use of the kinship and tribe system within Lebanon. During the 1998 elections, they were able to manipulate the Lebanese electoral system by using "family politics" to entice voters to elect their organization into power via key clan members in the local areas, regardless of their religious affiliation.‡ In addition, they were meticulous on election days, keeping lists of those that had or had not voted and working to transport the sick and elderly to the polls to ensure everyone that could vote did.

Hezbollah has worked hard to shed the label "terrorist organization," and they've had help in doing so. Holding up their part of the agreement to passively allow Hezbollah to act as a militia, protecting the southern border of Lebanon against Israeli incursions, the Lebanese government participated in numerous international debates arguing for Hezbollah's role as a resistance organization and not a terror group. Citing UN Security Council Resolution 425, the Lebanese government set out to prove that Hezbollah

---

* Norton, 22.
† Harik, 54.
‡ Harik, 102, 109.

was simply a resistance force and not a terrorist group. Even after 9/11, the Lebanese government struggled to keep themselves out of the "against us" column in President Bush's "with us or against us" classification. Hezbollah has also tried to keep its proverbial nose clean by refusing to participate in any attacks directly targeting civilians.* They have also attempted to get out from underneath the Iran surrogate label. "If Hezbollah had acted as a cat's paw of foreign interests in Lebanon, its primary agenda was very much its own; liberating Lebanon of the Israeli occupation."† The resistance group sees itself as a branch of the resistance from the "American-Zionist project," which threatens to upset the entire region, imposing its hegemony, and ultimately destroy Palestine.‡

In addition to the political adroitness of Hezbollah's leadership, Hezbollah has cornered the market on effective public relations. By running its own television channel, publishing literature, and orchestrating protests, the organization has been able to get the word out about its cause and garner support from the committed and uncommitted populace. In addition to the persuasive political speeches given by charismatic Hezbollah leadership, the organization has worked to ease the fears of non-Muslim supporters. In an open letter to the public, published in a Beirut daily newspaper in 1985, they defended and promoted their efforts to liberate Lebanon and Palestine. Hezbollah was honest about their relationship with Iran and attempted to market the fight against Israel as the duty of every Muslim.§ They also used themes of democracy and the right of the public to freely choose their leaders, and commit to staying within the legal boundaries of the Lebanese political and electoral system.

The two major factors that have fostered the organization's triumph have been a powerful regional support network (namely, Syria, Iran, and reluctantly, the Lebanese government) and the political adroitness, combined with the public relations savvy of Hezbollah's leadership. The current public leader of Hezbollah, Hassan Nasrallah, has effectively mastered the "know your audience" mantra during his political speeches. Instead of the usual fiery rhetoric that is so often used by Islamist organizations, Nasrallah picks and chooses his words carefully based on the desires of his audience.¶ Although he may sugarcoat the goals of the organization, he stays true to Hezbollah's core identifier as an Islamist group with Islamist goals. The spiritual leadership of the group, Sayyid Muhammad Husayn Fadlallah, is an unconventional, poetically gifted individual with

* Ibid., 2–3.
† Norton, 26.
‡ Harb, Mona, and Leenders, Reinoud, "Know Thy Enemy: Hizbullah, 'Terrorism' and the Politics of Perception," *Third World Quarterly*, vol. 26, no. 1 (2005) 181.
§ Ibid., 66–67.
¶ Ibid., 71.

words of action and dreams of change.* He saw Lebanon as an opportunity to develop his ideas and to help redeem the lost youth of Beirut. His speeches combined themes of traditional Islamic concepts and anticolonial nationalism. "For the Arabs, Fadlallah substituted the Muslims, and for Arabism, he substituted Islam."† Nasrallah and Fadlallah have worked to change Hezbollah from an Islamist group bent on installing an Islamic government in Lebanon into a fair and democratic country that supports all Lebanese regardless of ethnicity, religion, or gender. By focusing on the social needs and wants of the population, by involving themselves in the political process, Hezbollah has moved away from violence and toward engagement.

Social Change as a Moderator for Hezbollah

Although Hezbollah started out as a strict Islamist organization announcing its intentions to create an Islamist government, its leaders understood that the people of Lebanon did not necessarily want a strict religious theocracy. They were able to adjust their vision and, if the opportunity ever arrived, accept an Islamic government, but without the strict moral and behavioral codes they so desired. Hezbollah has always maintained its Islamist roots and has never denied its tie with Khomeini's vision of a pan-Islamic Middle East, but its key to survival in a multireligious Lebanon was a willingness to negotiate on the Lebanese government's end state. In addition, Hezbollah has provided social services and welfare to the Shi'a minority, but did not limit that aid strictly to Muslims. Creating a support network built from poor and less fortunate Lebanese citizens otherwise ignored by the government was a strategy used by other Islamist organizations. Citing their aid as Islamic charity, Hezbollah's goal may have been aimed more at fostering popular support for their cause by winning over the minorities of Lebanon. Hezbollah's aid to the poor Shi'a and Christian communities was truly a win–win for the country. They provided services to those that may have otherwise not received it, improved their living conditions, gave them hope, and unified them behind a common goal. This benefited the Lebanese government by creating an environment less likely to foster rebellion. The moderation of Hezbollah has been a change from previous principles of "rejection and violence" toward "domestic courtesy and accommodation."‡

---

* Kramer, Martin, "The Oracle of Hizbullah: Sayyid Muhammad Husayn Fadlallah," in *Spokesmen for the Despised: Fundamentalist Leaders of the Middle East*, ed. R. Scott Appleby (Chicago: University of Chicago Press, 1997), 89, 91.
† Ibid., 93.
‡ Harb, 183.

The latest conflict between Israel and Hezbollah has reinforced the fact that the organization's standing within the Shi'a fabric of Lebanese society is as strong as ever. Hezbollah used its social network to provide fighters to resist the Israeli invasion. The group used classic guerrilla hit-and-run tactics, which have proven effective on overwhelming conventionally superior enemies; however, it was Hezbollah's cemented link with the social networks within southern Lebanon that allowed the fighters to appear and disappear at will, absorbing back into the population. This is classic guerrilla tactics, and as one Lebanese man proudly remarked, when asked why it was so hard to find and beat Hezbollah, "*We* are Hezbollah"* (referring to the population at large).

Hezbollah has evolved from a small Islamic extremist group with visions of an Islamicized Lebanon to a politically savvy resistance group that has been able to capture, for the most part, the hearts and minds of the Lebanese people. They have been able to avoid the pitfalls of authority while simultaneously leading the charge against Israeli occupation in the Middle East. Without their support network, Hezbollah could not survive, but with it, it has become one of the most influential political forces in the Levant today.

Conclusion: Common Causes and Common Solutions

In this essay, I presented the case of two terrorist-turned-political Islamist organizations. I discussed the social and political circumstances that influenced the creation of both organizations. I find value in pointing out similarities between the two groups' creation and evolution toward political entities. First, both organizations were created as a response to Israel's occupation and aggression within their geographical area. As a result of Israel's presence, social, economic, and political repression became a daily fact of life, and both organizations resisted violently against the occupation. Both countries, Palestine and Lebanon, were subscribing to the secular nationalist form of resistance against the West, but eventually found that by bringing religion back in, they could marshal a great deal of support for their cause. Social circumstances were similar in both cases; the affected population was dispossessed, humiliated, deprived, and economically restricted. In addition, there was little institutional opportunity to change the circumstances in their favor and no alternative to government rule. Both organizations filled the vacuum created when the state apparatus evacuated the social spaces within each country. The Shi'a of Lebanon and the Palestinians in the territories suffered

---

* CNN television news coverage of the war, July/August 2006.

similar social ills and depended heavily on the quality of life provided at the hands of the Islamists.

The face of these two Islamist organizations changed dramatically. They saw value in political participation and were able to work out their grievances appropriately so that violence does not seem to be an attractive or viable alternative. In fact, violence at this point would undermine their goals. Hezbollah has taken a significant beating from the Western press for its actions in 1983 of kidnappings and attacks on U.S. military members, but the willingness of the organization and its leader, Hassan Nasrallah, to compromise their own Islamist goals, enter the political field, and offer negotiations should be evidence that the group is looking to survive any military confrontations or absorption into the Lebanese Army and remain a viable force in Lebanese politics and society. Hamas and Hezbollah have evolved significantly; they have offered negotiations with Israel and the West, and emphasized their social service programs to needy citizens. If the movements continue on the same trajectory, it is possible that both groups could disarm and become absorbed into the political fabric of their respective countries. This would require, however, a level of independence and freedom to make the system work.

The Diminution of the Citizen in the Age of Homeland Security

13

DEBRA D. BURRINGTON

Contents

> See yourself in others. Then whom can you hurt? What harm can you do?
>
> **—Buddha, *The Dhammapada***

Introduction

As I write this essay, from my vantage point in Los Angeles, the United States has just inaugurated its first mixed-race president. Widely regarded as "African American," born in Hawaii of a black Kenyan father and a white mother from Kansas, Mr. Obama has publicly referred to himself as a "mutt." Though this self-referential description was uttered in the context of the short-lived American obsession with selection of a puppy for the presidential offspring as the family prepared for its move into the White House (and might therefore be regarded as inconsequential), the metacontext of multiraciality that surrounds the new president instead marks this comment as significant. To be clear, I believe Mr. Obama understands full well that borders and boundaries bleed in what is inarguably the beginning of our first postmodern presidency. His worldview cannot be pinned down to an overly simplistic black and white where matters of either race or politics and policy are concerned, and referring to himself in ways that recognize his mixed-race heritage asks that we think beyond either-or categories as well. I begin this essay by making these observations in part to contextualize the historical moment in which I write, but also because Mr. Obama's worldview, to the extent that it is represented in his historic speech on race delivered in Philadelphia during the primary campaign, as well as through his perspectives on race, religion, politics, the Constitution, etc., in *The Audacity of Hope*, offers us an opportunity to grasp on a national level the imperative to problematize politics and our debates about it in order to craft a conciliatory, pragmatic, and consensus-oriented political culture. As odd as it may seem at first glance, there is indeed a connection between homeland security and building this type of political culture.

My central argument in this essay is that as we worry about Homeland Security, we must also be concerned about *homeland security*. Despite its inclusion in the present volume, this is not an essay about the Department of Homeland Security (DHS), or the Homeland Security Act of 2002. It does not explore the functions of the DHS or the logic behind the particular combination of the multitude of federal agencies brought together under the umbrella of this single cabinet-level department. It does not debate whether the DHS should or should not include major investigative agencies such as the FBI and CIA, or whether its rather wide-ranging mission enables its incursion into territory ostensibly governed by the U.S. Department of Defense. Importantly, though, this essay also does not attempt to minimize very legitimate concerns about potential terrorist activity by rogue nation-states or terrorist organizations. In other words, I do not want my argument here to be regarded as an attempt to minimize very real concerns about the potential for international or domestic terrorism on U.S. soil and the need to guard against it. Rather, my emphasis here is placed upon what we miss if we look always or only to "the outside" or to "the foreign" as we try to understand how to live together and govern in a post-9/11 world where we—by which I mean those of us who are subjects of this "American experiment" called the United States—may actually be our own worst enemies. However, this is also not an essay about the threat of domestic terrorism in the sense that was experienced, for example, by the attack on the Murrah Federal Building in Oklahoma City. Instead, in this essay I concentrate on the extent to which the United States is being weakened from within by two things: (1) culture wars and (2) greed. In the first case I discuss the so-called culture wars using examples from recent debates about gay rights. In the second instance I draw from the recent financial meltdown and what we now (finally) admit is a deep economic recession.

Both of these examples allow us to wonder about the nature of citizenship in our present moment, and both also allow us to reflect upon the state of our values and our ability as a nation to find places where we can live together productively and respectfully without destroying ourselves from within. In ways we do not normally reflect upon as we articulate strategies for addressing the notion of terrorist threat, I suggest a secure homeland is built upon a bedrock that enables a kind of inclusiveness and even generosity that we have yet to attain as a nation. I argue in this rather personal essay that we live at a time where the meaning of the term *citizen* as well as what the word itself makes possible has been diminished, perhaps irreparably. Furthermore, I suggest that our penchant to blame "outsiders" and "foreign others" for our ill fortune is at times a distraction that may contribute to a weakening rather than a strengthening of our nation at a very dangerous time. In fact, one could even speculate that both known and heretofore unknown terrorist factions might very well regard this as a time to sit back and watch the United States to see how much damage we can do to ourselves as a nation from within. Perhaps we have become the ultimate "reality show," a kind of ethnographic adventure playing itself out via Internet news sources and cable TV news.

The Political Geography of Citizenship

The homeland cannot be secure from without if it is also not secure from within, and this condition pertains if some individuals are denied the meaning of citizen in its most fundamental sense. This denial manifests itself through marginalization, the mechanics of which may include stigmatization, psychic and emotional abuse (such as street harassment), isolation or ghettoization, and demonization and physical violence that are used by majorities as a way to regulate access to public spaces by minorities or "feared others." I made this argument in a 1998 article published in the political science journal *Polity* titled "The Public Square and Citizen Queer: Toward a New Political Geography" and continued by suggesting that "free and equal access to the public square is a fundamental prerequisite to the exercise of democratic citizenship." If I were to ask a random group of individuals to name activities that illustrate the rights of citizenship, it is likely that the right to vote would be named by most. Others might cite the ability to put pressure on legislative bodies or to join with groups hoping to influence policy through activities such as lobbying, letter writing, protests, or demonstrations. Indeed, all of these are indicators of citizenship in a democracy. There are other prerequisite conditions, however, that must exist in order not only for these activities to occur, but also for them to be meaningful in a broader sense and to be exercised thoughtfully. In this same article I asserted that a political geography of citizenship demands that one of the most important of these prerequisites "is the ability to occupy—literally to exist as an element of—the public landscape. Without free and equal access to the public square, an individual cannot exercise formal political rights to their fullest extent." In other words, there is a strong nexus between the less formal ability to circulate freely among one's peers (indeed even to be regarded as a peer), to interact with those individuals and institutions that represent state (or economic) power, and the perception that one can actually influence political or policy outcomes.

In the late 1990s while living in Salt Lake City I worried about attempts to marginalize sexual minorities that were rooted in attempts by gay and gay-supportive high school students to carve out a physical and psychic safe space for themselves in their schools. The young organizers hoped that by creating "gay-straight alliances" they could support one another and find safety from both psychological and physical violence perpetrated by members of the majority. They expected that these alliances would be recognized as official school clubs and that a faculty sponsor would be assigned, just as it would with something like a Spanish club. When they were not so recognized, the turmoil that erupted in the wake of the denial of official status was surprising to many observers looking into Utah from other parts of the country. National organizations such as the American Civil Liberties Union and those dedicated specifically to the rights of sexual minorities (Gay Lesbian Straight Transgendered Education Network, National Gay and Lesbian Task Force, Human Rights Campaign) weighed in, as did newspapers such as the *New York Times,* the *Los Angeles Times*, and the *Washington Post.* Religious and political conservatives in the state preferred that sexual minorities remain silent and invisible, and even that the category of "the homosexual" cease to exist. The editors of the *Deseret News* (a historically Mormon-leaning newspaper) suggested that prohibiting the so-called "gay clubs" from existing within the public schools was where a "line in the sand" must finally be drawn to limit what was perceived to be the growing quest of sexual minorities to obtain political visibility.

A little more than a decade later and a bit more to the west, the line in the sand being drawn in California, again by religious and political conservatives (and perhaps ironically with the Mormons once again at the helm in many respects), was around same-sex marriage. A ballot initiative made its way into the presidential election in 2008 only months after the California Supreme Court recognized the right of same-sex couples legally to marry as an aspect of equal protection under the California Constitution. In the tradition of race and gender, sexual orientation was determined by the court to be what is known as a suspect classification, so that any legislation or policy seeking to limit the rights of same-sex individuals to enter into civil contracts such as marriage (among other rights) would have to undergo the heightened, strictest scrutiny of the courts. Furthermore, it would be the burden of the state to prove that the discrimination is necessary and justified rather than the citizen to prove that neither is the case. Outraged by the action of the California high court, conservatives obtained enough signatures to get a measure on the ballot. In what for many was a heartbreaking outcome, the ballot initiative, known as Proposition 8, passed narrowly, thus eliminating the right of same-sex couples to marry. The rhetoric was eerily similar to the 1996 scenario in Utah, in which gay men and lesbians were demonized as predators seeking to recruit young minds, and television commercials broadcast concerns to California voters that same-sex marriage would be required to be discussed and taught about—given voice and visibility to—in California public school classrooms. Churches announced (erroneously) to their congregants that all religions would be forced to conduct same-sex marriages. When Proposition 8 won, the outrage was national in scope. Large demonstrations occurred in every major U.S. city and in many small towns over the course of at least a week. The euphoria of progressives from an Obama landslide was muted by the stunning passage of Proposition 8. One photo from a demonstration in Los Angeles shows a mixed-race young woman holding a bright yellow sign reflecting on the outcomes of several ballot propositions and reads: "CA elected a Black Prez, protected the rights of women, pigs, chickens and cows ... BUT NOT THE RIGHTS OF GAY PEOPLE?" At the time of this writing Proposition 8 has been declared unconstitutional by the U.S. District Court for the Northern District of California, and same sex marriages may resume in the state shortly. In the meantime, supporters of a ban on same-sex marriage promise to appeal this decision. Regardless of the outcome in a court of appeals, the issue is expected to be heard by the U.S. Supreme Court within the next few years.

While it can be argued with some justification that political battles such as these indeed foster a kind of awareness and activity that are part of a political education, and therefore a precursor to informed citizenship, it can be suggested with at least as much merit that the repetition over time of defeat has a significant wearing effect on members of a group. Indeed, members of these particular minority groups hear the message over and over again that they are not regarded as equal to other citizens. It may even be the case that informed awareness and the desire to participate as a voting citizen are muted as a result of repeated marginalization, except for the increased activism of vocal and typically more affluent subgroups. Continued marginalization, demonization, and silencing of a minority may contribute to withdrawal from political participation. Or, a high level of disaffection caused by repeated marginalization may result in the desire to work against the status quo in ways that obfuscate the building of consensus.

Greed Is Good—Greed Is Right

As 2008 came to an end it was announced that the United States had been in a recession for about a year. Commentators compared the situation to the 1980s when the nation underwent another recession that was not nearly as bad. In 1987 a popular film titled *Wall Street* hit the big screen. The film is emblematic of what has been called an era of excess, though one which pales in comparison with the current crisis. One of the most enduring moments in the film occurs when Michael Douglas (as the character Gordon Gekko, a corporate raider) gives a speech in which he utters the line "greed, for lack of a better word, is good." Although Gekko's character is widely regarded to be a composite of several big Wall Street movers and shakers of the period, it is important to note that his "greed is good" line is reminiscent of a similar one spoken by Ivan Boesky, one of a group of players caught in a $20 million insider trading scandal. Boesky also gave a speech in which he asserted "greed is right." Two decades later we have come full circle, but the circle is larger, and the hole we are digging for ourselves is deeper.

The homeland cannot be secure from without if it is also not secure from within. Similarly to the case of marginalization, isolation, violence, and silencing discussed in the previous section of this essay, I similarly argue that some are denied the full meaning of citizen in its most robust sense through the kind of marginalization that occurs through mechanisms allowing for continual growth in the gap between the wealthiest and the poorest among us. In the twenty-first century, perhaps more than before, our status as consumer is in some senses arguably more important than our status as citizen. Or perhaps we are citizen-consumers, but to the extent that some can never hope to rise to the levels of participation necessary to claim full title to either label, as a nation we risk a level of disaffection from within that may result in levels of unrest that make us less secure.

I am not going to take the time and space here to rehearse the dollar figures involved in what has become known as the "crash of 2008." The news continues to be dominated by stories on a daily basis that bring more and more bad news our way. Anyone can access any news source—print, TV, or Internet—and find stories about what is obviously a worldwide recession of historic proportions. Globalization has indeed spread the pain all over the world. At the end of 2008 the combined stocks at all of the exchanges were down an average of about 40%. According to the *New York Times* (December 31, 2008) investor gains of the last six years were virtually wiped out, to the tune of $7 trillion in shareholder wealth. One of the most scandalous stories of 2008 ended up being the discovery that Bernard Madoff, one of the "golden boys" of Wall Street (and former chair of the NASDAQ Exchange) had allegedly bilked investors out of $50 billion (*Wall Street Journal*, December 12, 2008). According to a more recent article in the *Wall Street Journal* (February 9, 2009), Madoff and the Securities and Exchange Commission have apparently reached an agreement for Madoff to pay off the defrauded investors. The housing bubble burst and the subprime mortgage scandal fueled the largest home foreclosure problem in American history. According to one news source (*U.S. News and World Report*, January 15, 2009), 2008 foreclosure filings increased 81% over 2007, and 225% over 2006. As 2009 got shakily under way the unemployment rate skyrocketed to the highest rate in forty years according to the Economic Policy Institute, and states (including two of the biggest—New York and California) scurry to prevent their unemployment insurance funds from running out of money. In the nation's capital Congress struggles to find a solution, what most economists of every political stripe agree must be an economic stimulus package of a size never before seen, per-haps as large as $800 billion. As of this writing the bill has passed and we wait earnestly to see whether it will have the desired effects.

How is all of this related to homeland security? The simple, if trite, answer echoes the words of a popular song from a bygone era: "the rich get rich while the poor get poorer." During the 1970s the difference between the compensation of executives compared to the average worker was about 35%. According to the Economic Policy Institute, today top executives earn about 275% more than the average worker. Put another way, for every $1 the average worker makes, a top executive makes $275. This does not include the gargantuan bonuses that have become a scandal. It was reported in early 2009 by every major news source that at the same time U.S. taxpayers are footing the bill for a financial bailout package of approximately $700 billion (passed in the waning hours of the Bush admin-istration) to keep failed financial institutions in business, and while massive lay-offs in virtually every industry put the number of lost jobs at 3.5 million since the recession began and 600,000 in January 2009, Wall Street executives took home performance bonuses amounting to $20 billion. One news source (ABC News, January 29, 2009) reported that this is in the range of what was paid in bonuses in 2004 when performance was indeed strong, but the difference in 2009 is that these institutions are on the verge of financial collapse.

One of the classic understandings of politics is that it is a view into who gets what, when, and how. This is politics as concerned with how power cir-culates in a society such that some people gain advantages while others do not. Politics is not simply about how the formal institutions of government work, but rather it also includes an understanding of how opportunities are distributed for all citizens to take part in helping to give shape to a politi-cal society. This sort of understanding of politics requires that we examine who has a chance to help decide how we live together, and who gets to ben-efit from the life we create as a people. Those who do not enjoy equal access to the public sphere and to the institutions that comprise it—including economic ones—cannot enact the rights of citizenship in its most robust meaning. No nation can be safe and secure when economic marginaliza-tion occurs and when economic turmoil exists at the level we are currently experiencing. Let me illustrate using a few examples from the city where I live, Los Angeles. According to data from the Economic Policy Institute and reported by the Liberty Hill Foundation, in Los Angeles the wealthiest fifty Los Angelenos have a combined net worth of $60 billion, more than the net worth of the bottom 2 million people combined. Between 1979 and 1997 real family income in Los Angeles County declined 7% for the bot-tom 20% of the population, while it increased 106% for the top 1% of the population. Thirty-five percent of Los Angelenos live in situations where the combined household income is under $25,000, in a city where it is esti-mated that it takes at least $38,780 to live. The differences are stark and the picture grows darker as the recession deepens. This is a story repeated nationwide, though the income gap in Los Angeles is among the worst in the nation.

Summary and Conclusions

The forms of marginalization discussed in this essay function together to create a dynamic that threatens to weaken our nation from within in ways that negatively affect our security in an already unstable world where our image has already been substantially tarnished. The feared other is held at a distance—as shown through the two examples in this essay of sexual minorities and the financially disadvantaged—and the "othering" reflects the relative importance of our designation as citizens or consumers. In theory each of us is both citizen and consumer, but in a crisis such as the one we currently face, perhaps the importance of identity as citizen will take a backseat to identity as consumer. The cynic might suggest that concern for the economically disadvantaged is more about boosting their ability to stimulate the economy and less about them having food in their stomachs and roofs over their heads. One might ask, "What difference do motivations make?" and perhaps the only good citizen is also a good consumer, or perhaps that is a bit too cynical. At any rate, we stand at a defining moment in history, and how we resolve our crisis as a nation will either set us on a path where a reexamination of our consumerist values occurs and guides us to becoming a more inclusive society, or where it does not occur and thereby blinds us to our larger possibilities. Our standing in the world already has been seriously weakened, and perhaps, as I alluded earlier, our enemies wait in the dark, watching to see if we can right our ship. Perhaps our emphasis on Homeland Security (capital H and capital S) has indeed made us more secure from terrorist attack, or perhaps we are once again deluded in our sense of self-importance. Criticisms already abound about how an ill-considered emphasis on security above all else has shredded our civil liberties, that the war on terror has been allowed to justify the curtailment of dissent, the limiting of access to the public square by those who wish to protest, and the belief that such curtailment is justified on the theory that where protest occurs terrorists may be lurking. To reiterate where I began, I do not want this essay to be read as suggesting that the threat of terrorism is imagined. I simply ask that we step back and take a breath and think, just a little. To that end, I conclude with a single, but very long, sentence I wrote in New York City when I lived there for a year about nine months after the tragedy of 9/11 had happened:

Rot

This city will bury itself under the bags of garbage that pile up on the curbs every day it will drown under its own filth succumb to the cancer that rots it from within ... shit is sprayed on the wall behind the toilet a few stray specks adorn the seat there are no paper liners the wall-mounted container long empty there is no toilet paper to fabricate a makeshift liner or wipe one's ass and who would want to sit here anyway no matter how full the bladder or bowel the floor into the stall is black with dirt as if a downpour has brought everyone inside with wet muddy feet but there has been no rain today or for weeks the empty toilet paper holder lies open but not really empty it is filled with balled up bits of paper used sanitary napkins and torn open tampon wrappers ... the sidewalk before me runs with reddish orange grease and bits of rotted lettuce thrown there from the back doorway of the restaurant the stench is so bad I nearly gag and my feet slide as my shoes contact the greasy surface once I've seen them clean it with bleach too late the concrete now per-manently impregnated smell and black greasiness linger ... the man across the subway aisle looks dead and probably is who could tell if the stench from his filthy clothes and skin is that of death encroaching or merely from his nights of sleep beneath the city beneath the subway platform beneath our feet forgot-ten the line of clear snot that comes from his nose dribbles onto his forearm a good two feet below his bent face the amazing thing is that it is huge and unbroken so unbelievable it is hard not to stare a bubble forms in the snot and grows but does not pop and then as the train bursts into the morning sun it is caught in the light glows with rainbow colors for a moment and then disap-pears back into the thick stream of mucous: has he exhaled a living breath or have his lungs simply expelled the last air of his death rattle in a half hour's time he has not moved has not appeared to breathe perhaps even the mole people are driven to the surface of the city to die in the sunlight no one will go near him people stand on the train as far away from him as they can while he thus enjoys a whole bench to himself if he is alive to enjoy how long will he remain unmoving in this spot so still before someone determines if he is dead and then what will happen to him ... on the street in the broad daylight of mid-day a homeless person accosts the young woman reaches out to touch her rambling incoherencies foaming at the mouth she must strike his arm away as it closes in on her forearm ... at ten in the morning the woman is already so drunk as she pays for her big bottle of beer that the man at the newsstand has to run after her to give her the $10 in change she has coming ... the man reaches into the nearly overflowing trash can to retrieve a soda bottle with some liquid still in it finishes it off and returns the bottle to the can reaches next into the paper bag that once contained someone's meal finishes off the bagel and returns the bag to the can ... the teenage girl sits in a crumpled heap but manages to lean against the building for a bit of rest head in hands what can be seen of her face tired beyond her years long past any look of despair her hand-lettered cardboard sign says she is a stranded traveler without money will anyone help her get home her dirty paper coffee container in front of the sign nowhere near to filling with the needed funds ... and then alongside all of this are the sights and sounds and smells of privilege the stench of it nearly overwhelming the money flowing invisibly down the middle of the streets a tidal wave of capitalist excess fucking everyone in its way up the ass ... I don't want to be anywhere near this place when it all comes crashing down the attitude of indifference barely masking the rage that exists just below the skin and that will boil to the surface of this cesspool when the rebellion begins.

Chemical, Biological, Radiological, and Nuclear Terrorism
14
Weapons of Mass Terror

RICHARD J. NIEMANN

Contents

Introduction

Twenty years has passed since terrorism expert Brian Jenkins made the observation that "terrorists want a lot of people watching and a lot of people listening and not a lot of people dead."[1] However, since the September 11, 2001 attacks on the United States that brought down the World Trade Center, this has all changed. Terrorists are moving in a direction where increased violence has its place in helping terrorists to accomplish their goals. They are willing to kill and murder masses, including sacrificing themselves in order to accomplish their task. Terrorist have adapted their tactics and utilize those tactics that can be delivered through small clandestine groups that generate a collective effect from the fear of never knowing who they are or where they might strike next. Therefore, the use and dissemination of weapons of mass destruction (WMD) has such a far-reaching effect on not only the target, but the population it affects as well. With the increased use of WMDs, particularly chemical, biological, radiological, and nuclear weapons (CBRN), we need to have a historical understanding of how we got to this point, and by examining past uses of CBRN, I hope to give the reader a better idea of how unconventional weapons have been used and why they are so attractive to terrorist groups. We must consider that there are precautions that must be met in preparation of a CBRN attack at the most rudimentary level. The three points that must be considered relative to biological agent and preparation are as follows: First, biological agents are easy to conceal. The amount needed to harm large populations and cause an epidemic over a relatively large region is very small. Second, once persons are exposed and infected, they continue to spread the disease to others unknowingly due to the contagious nature of the disease. The contagious nature of a biological weapon makes it a force multiplier, which continues to multiply the casualties silently and without detection over a significant time span. Third, in the event of a surreptitious attack, the most likely scenario will target first responders, who most likely will make up health care professionals in emergency rooms, outpatient facilities, public health care settings and other health care organizations, rather than the traditional first responders, such as police and fire.[2]

One thing is clear, the longer the terrorist-induced epidemic continues unrecognized and undiagnosed, the more those infected will continue to flood the health care system and drain resources. Therefore, the ability to identify a chemical, biological, radiological, or nuclear weapon is paramount so as not to cause a delay in initiating treatment and containment while preventing further infectious outbreaks and contamination from occurring to the population.

Which terrorists or terrorist groups are most likely to resort to the use of CBRN? In order to better understand just which groups are most likely to be involved in either manufacturing or utilizing CBRN, I will examine the secular right-wing terrorists, Islamic terrorists, and cults and extremist sects that have many attributes that make them prime candidates that either have or will utilize WMDs.

Just how will a terrorist group disseminate such an agent to accomplish their goals is played out in some thought-provoking scenarios for the reader to examine.

Next, I will examine some attributes associated with the use and dissemination of chemical, biological, radiological, and nuclear weapons to give the reader a better understanding of the real implications associated with their use.

What effects will a CBRN attack have on the population? The effects of an attack on the population will be examined in order to explain the fear and chaos associated with an attack of this nature and give first responders a better idea of just what they will encounter in order to better prepare them to deal with just such a situation.

Recent Attacks

The most recent example of such an incident was demonstrated in March 1995, when the nerve agent sarin (GB) was released in an indiscriminate attack in the Tokyo subway system, causing over 5,500 people to seek medical attention.[3] A previous incident occurred in June 1993 in the city of Matsomoto;[4] however, the agent was released in an apartment complex and the attack was specifically aimed at a small population living in the building and not on the general population.

The terrorist group responsible for the above incidents is the cult Aum Shinrikyo. This cult has a significant following and membership with assets totaling in the billions of dollars. The cult attracted members from throughout the European countries, including Germany and Russia, and the United States.

Aum Shinrikyo, with its vast financial resources, has acquired large facilities where members of the cult trained as chemists were able to manufacture and experiment with chemical and biological warfare agents, which they ultimately produced and released.[5]

A skilled chemist can readily synthesize chemical weapons if he or she has access to the precursors needed, and even those less familiar with the process can readily obtain this information through various websites on the Internet and can acquire precursors via the same way through intracountry shipments.[6]

To understand just how a lone terrorist or terrorist cell would employ such a chemical or biological attack, it must first be understood that most chemical agents are in the form of a liquid. Since each agent has different properties, they each have a different rate at which they evaporate and produce vapor. While the agent could be used in its liquid form by spreading droplets of the agent on locations that would most likely come into contact with people, it is very unlikely that that agent would be very effective. The most effective way to disperse an agent is by making the agent into an aerosol[6] that can be released into the environment targeted. If an agent is released outside, the agent is not stagnant and will move based on the wind direction; the wind dilutes and moves the agent based on other environmental conditions. However, when used indoors, such as in a building, the agent's vapor remains stagnant and the concentration builds, at least until the agent can be filtered out through a ventilation system. However, this could also be the source that a terrorist may choose to disseminate such an agent into an infrastructure that would reach and infect the largest population at all levels within that infrastructure.

One thing that is clear is that the risk of domestic and international terrorists using CBRN has escalated over the last ten years. According to the Federal Bureau of Investigation (FBI) and the Central Intelligence Agency (CIA), terrorists based in the Middle East or elsewhere have the propensity to use chemical or biological weapons against U.S. targets. Former defense secretary William Cohen warned, "This scenario of nuclear, biological, or chemical weapons in the hands of a terrorist cell or rogue nation is not only plausible, it's ... quite real."[7]

A Historical Perspective of Biological and Chemical Weapons

The prospect that someone would actually manufacture, much less use, a chemical or biological weapon against any civilization is appalling. However, the use of these weapons has been recognized for their deadly value to conquer one's enemies throughout history. Some historical events where CBRN were used include the following.

In 1346, the Tartars, who were infected with bubonic plague during their siege at Kaffa[7] on the Crimean Coast, used catapults to throw their dead into the city and spread disease to Genoan defenders, who became infected, taking the black death with them when they fled to Italy. In 1763, Lord Jeffery Amherst, the British commander of the American colonies, infected American Indians by giving them "gifts" of blankets infected with smallpox.[7] In World War I, about 1.3 million men (including Adolf Hitler) were wounded by gas, and of them, 91,000 died as a result of the exposure.[7] In the 1930s, the Ethiopians were repeatedly gassed by the Italian army.[7] Japan launched a series of over eight hundred gas attacks in attempts to conquer Manchuria and is alleged to have used biological agents to attack the Chinese.[7] The Japanese also are said to have used agents to conduct experiments by infecting Chinese prisoners of war.[7] During WWII, the prospect of the use of chemical and biological weapons was far more feared than used on the battlefield.[7]

The Germans developed tabun and sarin; they also developed the extremely potent cholinesterase inhibitors, which were manufactured in German factories, where they are believed to have produced around 12,000 tons of poison gas a month. From this incredible production, the Luftwaffe accumulated a half-million gas bombs. During this same time the British had a biological program that was years ahead of the Germans in every aspect except for their research on nerve gas, which was not as sophisticated. The British produced 5 million cattle cakes filled with anthrax that were part of a contingency plan between the United States and Britain to deploy against Germany.[6-8]

Nations, including the United States, have continued to develop offensive chemical, biological, radiological, and nuclear weapons. However, none of these has ever won wars. Their use appears to have been strictly tactical. With the advent of stockpiling these weapons since the WWI era, it was only a matter of time before a terrorist or terrorist organization would possess these "poor man's nuclear weapons." The reasons possession of these weapons is so attractive to terrorists and their organizations include:

Inexpensive to manufacture
Hard to detect
Easy to disperse
Lack warning attributes, such as odor, color, and irritancy
Not detected until the victim exhibits symptoms of exposure
Psychological terror of the unknown generates fear[7,10,11]

The very fact that most Americans are unfamiliar and have not been exposed to CBRN brings about the thought of injury, infection, or death from an invisible weapon that generates fear and loss of personal safety, increased stress and terror, not only in victims but the public as well. The potential to employ CBRN in the United States was realized in February 1993, when Ramzi Youessef, a member of a group called Shaykh Umar Abd-al Rahman, drove a truck containing an unknown amount of sodium cyanide packed with explosives, and the bomb was detonated in the garage level of the World Trade Center in New York. The terrorist and cell are liked to Iran, who is alleged to be responsible for sponsoring the terrorist act. This incident marked the first of international terrorism on American soil.

In April 1995, Timothy McVeigh and Terry Nicholas drove a Ryder truck containing 5,000 pounds of ammonium nitrate into the Murrah Federal Building in Okalahoma City, killing 168 people and 19 children, leveling the nine-story building.

In April 1995, the Justice Department foiled what was going to be an attack by the cult Aum Shinrikyo. The plot was to release the agent sarin in the park at Disneyland in Anaheim, California, Easter weekend.

In October 2001, anthrax spores were sent through the mail to American media at NBC and ABC and to the offices of Senators Tom Daschle and Patrick Leahy.[12] The contaminated letters continued through the postal system, contaminating other mail as they came in contact with postal sorting machines and postal workers. The contaminated mail continued to show up in many other places, including the Supreme Court and the State Department. These incidents caused widespread fear and panic throughout society. Citizens everywhere were stockpiling supplies like duct tape, kits to seal windows, gas masks, and other supplies. The perception by the American public of the ability of the government to secure the public from any further attacks was severely questioned by these attacks.[9,10]

Terrorist Groups Most Likely to Use CBRN

It is clear that chemical weapons lie within the grasp of terrorist groups, and that technology is allowing the development of CBRN to become increasingly easier. According to Nadine Gurr and Benajimine Cole in their book *The New Face of Terrorism*,[13] the terrorist groups that are most likely to use CBRN include the following.

Secular right-wing terrorist groups have as their goal to replace the liberal democratic state with some form of national socialist or fascist regime. They utilize violence as a catalyst to achieve their goals, often creating chaos that might lead to civil war or uprising. These groups are racist and tend to use racist slogans to fuel their ideology, and tend to be very violent in nature, harboring genocidal fantasies. These groups see the government as the main enemy and tend to target government buildings and figures through various terrorist and guerrilla strategies and tactics to achieve their goals.

The Okalahoma bombing was a watershed for their activities since it was the first time it signaled a willingness to perpetrate acts of indiscriminate mass killing. It seems that these groups have the motivation to use CBRN, through preaching of their leadership that espoused the use of such tactics to achieve the group's goals, as well as preaching that it is "a divine duty to destroy their enemy, leaving them to fulfill their objective of creating a new white state as God's kingdom on Earth, establishing a powerful religious imperative to conduct terrorist attacks involving mass casualties." This theological underpinning of their belief system will make it easier for these groups to engage in mass casualties.[13,14]

Islamic terrorist groups have been associated with CBRN since the emergence of the network of terrorist groups that are financed by UBL; the network is the International Islamic Front for the Jihad against the Jews and the Crusaders and the al-Qaeda organization, which are anti-Christian and anti-Western in orientation. While this front relies heavily on the use of conventional terrorist strategies and tactics, UBL has said that it is "the duty of the Jihad not only to acquire these chemicals and develop them, but to kill 4 million Americans, 2 million of them woman and children." UBL has made it perfectly clear that he and his organization are trying to acquire and develop these weapons to be used against their enemies. UBL and his followers, in no uncertain terms, blame the United States and its allies for the support of Israel and its presence in the Saudi region.[6,13]

Islamic extremist groups' major strategic goal is to target Western targets around the world. Islamic states see the West as invading their culture and threatening their very way of life. Islamic groups are driven by rage and revenge and seem to cite the West as responsible for all the problems associated with the Middle East; therefore, it is their position to force the United States out through all conceivable means available to them, including the use of NBC weapons at their disposal.[13] The utilization of attacking the United States on its own soil in bringing down the World Trade Center on 9/11 is an example of just how far an organization is willing to go to make its point. It is also an indication of the will of the group to utilize indiscriminate mass killings on their targets.

It is particularly clear that cults and extremist sects have a wide range of belief systems, which incorporate phenomena such as the resurrection of the dead; the second coming of Christ, or their particular religious leader; a war of Armageddon; or the end of the world and the appearance of the antichrist. These types of mentalities and ideologies are the reason that these terrorist groups are so dangerous and more apt to develop and use chemical weapons. It is feared that groups such as these are more volatile in their beliefs and may take matters into their own hands and initiate their own Armageddon through acts of terrorism. Another reason why groups of this nature would develop or acquire CBRN is that the group has a large financial resource to pull from in its membership. The mixture of motivation and potential capabilities to acquire and use CBRN has groups such as these at the forefront of concern.[13]

Despite the particularly stronger political motivations of religious orientated groups to use CBRN, it would be unwise to rigidly differentiate between the groups that are predominantly religious in character and those that are predominantly secular in nature. Some of the secular groups have goals that are as revolutionary as the goals of these predominantly religious groups and could therefore be subject to similar motivations to use CBRN.[13,14] Another characteristic rising is the lone terrorist or amateur that acts on his or her own behalf for the group. These amateur actors are on the rise. Examples of these domestically motivated persons are Ted Kaczynski and Timothy McVeigh, who acted outside the group and killed indiscriminately. This class of terrorists seems to be the fastest-rising group today, and a group that needs to be tracked and monitored since the likelihood that they will use CBRN is increasing.

How CBRN Agents Will Most Likely Be Disseminated

The deliberate introduction of CBRN into the infrastructure of American lives has resulted in a significant alarm concerning how to best handle and respond to just such a threat concerning our health and safety. The response to a CBRN threat can be broken down into two different scenarios: overt and covert disseminations.[7,8] The nature in which the agent is released will dictate the response by first responders. Despite the consequences of an agent being released, either overtly or covertly, the primary mission by first responders is the preservation of life.

A scenario involving the introduction of an agent in an overt attack would involve an agent released following an articulated threat like a note in a package or a letter forewarning of the impending attack. Past threats like the letters mailed to NBC, ABC, and the offices of Senators Tom Daschle and Patrick Leahy, as well as subsequent letters that reached the Supreme Court, all articulated that the recipient had just been exposed to anthrax.[3,7,11] In this scenario, law enforcement would be notified to respond along with the Fire department and emergency medical services (EMS) personnel. An initial assessment of the threat by first responders would determine the level of the attack and to notify the Federal Beau of Investigation (FBI) weapons of mass destruction (WMD) coordinator, who would assign an agent to further investigate the incident. Under Presidential Directives 39 and 62, the FBI is given the authority to investigate incidents in matters that involve a domestic threat such as bioterrorism, where a threat is articulated and includes a biological weapon that is used as an instrument in the attack.

The FBI's Counterterrorism Division, located in Quantico, Virginia, coordinates and determines threats based on their creditability, including the manner in which the threat is received and the significance that the threat will impose upon the safety of the public. Once the threat is identified, the FBI determines the appropriate response level, including manpower and equipment needed to enter the "hot" zone. In the event of an attack, CBRN threat representatives from the Centers for Disease Control and Prevention (CDC), Department of Health and Human Services (DHHS), U.S. Department of Agriculture (USDA), and the Food and Drug Administration (FDA) would participate based on the threat and the nature of how the agent was deployed or initiated into society. The method of isolating and collecting a biological or chemical agent is left up to the protocols set by the FBI's Hazardous Material Response Unit (HMRU). State and local response teams would follow the protocols set up by the FBI's HMRU team as well in order to ensure that the safest precautions are taken in collecting the specimens used, to determine the agent used and preserve the evidence to criminally prosecute those responsible. Laboratory response networks (LRNs) are set up in more than eighty-five state health laboratories and perform analysis of the substance or chemical or biological substance and provide a resource for complete test results to be disseminated to FBI officials in order to effectively handle the necessary decontamination of the area, as well as provide information to medical facilities so that victims can receive the most prompt response and effective treatment for those exposed to a chemical or biological agent.

A covert release of a biological agent would not be known for several days or even longer. The way in which a covert release would initially be detected would be through health care facilities and hospitals when the discovery of the disease's presence would surface through the presentation of unusual signs or symptoms manifesting in individuals requesting medical aid. In the initial stages, people showing up in emergency rooms and public health care facilities would report symptoms of fever, back pain, headache, nausea, and other symptoms that would appear to indicate the patient had an ordinary viral infection. In the case of smallpox, a small rash would develop several days later, and the symptoms might be dismissed by the time the rash becomes pustule and patients started dying. Terrorists responsible for the release could be long gone, the person-to-person contact would continue, and more and more casualties would begin to accumulate.[12,14]

In a scenario like this, there is initially no crime scene for police, and they probably will not even be notified of such an event. An act of this nature will probably take days or longer to discover and would follow the identification of the agent used in the attacks from lab reports of epidemiological inquiries sent from public health systems. In this case, the law enforcement community would be notified by the public health community of such an incident, not the other way around, like in an overt scenario.

According to the FBI, in 1999 during testimony before the House Energy and Commerce Subcommittee on Oversight and Investigations, the need for improved federal statutes was tackled and adequately addressed the threatened use and possession of biological weapons. The FBI strengthened its case by providing the following statistical evidence of opening 181 cases for investigation in 1998 alone related to WMD events, of which 112 were related to biological weapons. Since then, the numbers have continued to increase following September 11, 2001. The FBI Joint Terrorism Task Force responded to approximately 7,089 suspicious letters where the suspicious material found resembled or had trace amounts of anthrax. Nine hundred fifty other incidents involved other WMD material or bombs, and the FBI estimates having received about 29,331 telephone calls from the public in response to suspicious packages.[8,15] While many of the calls to the FBI were prompted out of civil panic in the wake of the events of 9/11, establishing a public awareness campaign and disseminating that information to the public would have been invaluable based on the data derived from the FBI statistics on the need to educate the public and quell the publics fears early on.

To stress just how important the government and the Department of Homeland Security in the United States feel about the likelihood that terrorists are planning to make CBRN attacks part of their *modus operandi*, the Department of Homeland Security has outlined the most likely methods of attack by a terrorist group operating in the United States and the implications of what the consequence and outcomes will most likely be.

The document, known simply as the National Planning Scenarios, lists the most likely scenarios that first responders are likely to encounter, offering estimates of the probable death tolls and economic damage caused by such an attack.

The scenarios include blowing up a chlorine tank, killing 17,500 people and injuring more than 100,000; spreading pneumonic plague in the bathrooms of an airport, sports arena, and train station, killing 2,500 and sickening 8,000 worldwide; and infecting cattle with foot-and-mouth disease at various locations, costing hundreds of millions of dollars in losses. Since the events could unfold in any major metropolitan community or rural area, the scenarios are based on events and not specifics.

The Department of Homeland Security is trying to identify just what prepared means by compiling such a list of scenarios and identifying possible attack scenarios and specifying just what state and local governments should do to prevent, respond to, and recover from such an attack. Matt Meyer, then the acting executive director of the Office of State and Local Government Coordination and Preparedness at the Department of Homeland Security, which is in charge of this effort, was quoted in the *New York Times* on March 19, 2003, as saying, "We live in a world of finite resources, whether they be personnel or funding."[16] He plans on outlining just how resources are distributed in the event of such an attack occurring and where resources are earmarked to go immediately to prevent future attacks.

I have outlined the fifteen scenarios that are most likely to occur in the event of a terrorist attack from the report, and the possible outcomes of such attacks in the appendix of this chapter, along with the web address of the location of the actual document.

Chemical Weapons

Today, a few pounds of an agent can cause thousands or hundreds of thousands of deaths, crippling society through the release of a CW poisoning or spreading disease affecting thousands. Recently, the capabilities to produce these weapons have moved from the sole possession of governments to being within the means of terrorist organizations and even in some cases an individual. The migration of this technology has raised the threat that the average citizen may be exposed to these weapons to a level unprecedented in history. While there is a considerable amount of uncertainty about likely casualty levels from a CW attack and overestimates are common, CW attacks involving third-order WMD in optimal weather conditions have the potential and capacity to kill hundreds or thousands and injure even more.[17,19]

Biological weapons are weapons such as pathogens (disease-causing organisms) or a toxin (a poison of biological origin).[7,11] One way a terrorist group could use such a biological weapon could come in the form of a preemptive strike against massed military troops. This would require a fast-acting, easily transmitted agent, one that need not be potentially lethal. The fact that a wounded soldier requires two or three soldiers out of the battle to care for him or her is a major incentive to use and acquire biological agents.

The use of an agent like anthrax could deny advancement by first responders such as police or military units, if the chemical was deployed against an advancing line.

The deployment of chemicals at logistic choke points would have a significant effect on first responders and military forces if utilized properly.

Contaminating milk or produce with botulism could possibly contaminate and kill enough people to paralyze a significant population, depending on the deployment of the biological pathogens.

Infecting one person with smallpox could conceivable cause twenty more to become affected, and those twenty could multiply to four hundred people infected in a significantly short time. This would cause a considerable drain on manpower, labs, the ability to inoculate and treat the population affected, as well as quarantining a sufficient area to stop the spread of such a disease.[7,9,11,15]

Chemical weapons achieve their desired effects through the result of their chemistry and not their physical effects, such as fragments or a blast, as an example.

CW agents come in varied forms, such as nerve agents, blister agents, mustard gas, blood agents, vomiting agents, incapacitating agents, and other poisons. Due to their nature, these weapons can be delivered in a variety of physical forms, including vapor, gas, liquid, or solid. Today, we have a better understanding of how and why such chemicals can be used against humans and animals to cause mass casualties.

The major routes in which chemical agents affect people are:

Absorption into mucous membranes
Inhalation into the lungs, which can interfere with breathing and then
     enter the circulation
Intravenous (IV), the direct ingesting of the agent into the system
Orally (or by ingestion), eating or drinking contaminated foods or drinks
Percutaneously, through the skin and directly into the system
Parenterally, directly into the digestive system (not a common method)[7,11]

The delivery system used to disseminate a CW can come in many forms; however, the easiest way to deliver the CW would be pumping a CW into a relatively closed-in area, like a building that has limited access points, and then delivering the CW through the system's vents or AC system. This would ensure delivery of a contaminant throughout an entire capsulated area such as a building.[4,7] The CW is sure to remain stagnant inside without adequate ventilation to minimize the chemical's effect, and it would have a significant effect on everyone being exposed to the chemical. While more sophisticated delivery systems include bombs and shells that could package the CW with a small explosive charge, CWs are most effective when held in the air, and thus keeping the CW in the air proves to be the hardest problem for terrorists to overcome in order to successfully use CWs. In one exercise in 1998, the U.S. government estimated that the release of sarin gas into a corridor of the Pentagon would result in twenty-six deaths and one hundred others being exposed to the agent.[4]

The OTA[20] estimates that 1 kilogram of VX released inside a large building could kill five hundred people of the one thousand exposed; tens of kilograms of phosgene would have the same effect; while hundreds of grams of VX in a subway car could kill fifty to one hundred passengers. The OTA estimates fatalities between sixty and two hundred from a release of 300 kilogram of sarin in a normal urban area in moderate wind conditions. Therefore, the numbers of deaths from a CW attack are likely to be equivalent to some of the most destructive attacks using conventional weapons, and even this would require amounts of a CW beyond that which could be produced in a basement lab.

Biological Weapons

No explosions will be heard as death is disseminated throughout the population, affecting each person from the inside out. The new threat is a disease that is spread from person to person, once infected, from the inside out, contaminating the population by spreading person to person without a trace, killing hundreds, even hundreds of thousands.

The effects of BW can be more variable and more lethal. Only a few pathogens are known to have the potential to cause deaths exceeding those that could be caused by CW and nuclear weapons. Some agents such as anthrax kill 100% of untreated victims, but brucellosis kills only 5% of untreated victims. Neil Livingston states that half an ounce of type A botulinum toxin, properly distributed, can kill everyone in North America.[7,22] And 130 grams of ricin, effectively dispersed, can kill thousands of people. The Advanced Concepts Research Corporation calculates an attack with anthrax spores on New York City could kill over six hundred thousand. Representative figures for multiple points of attack using 100 kilograms of dry anthrax powder are 1 to 3 million deaths, and from a single source, using 30 kilograms of dry powder, 30,000 to 100,000 deaths.[22] Indoors, the OTA estimates that an attack

with 1 to 100 liters of anthrax would cause 8,000 to 40,000 deaths, and brucellosis would cause 160 to 800 deaths.[7,22] As is the case with CW, the precise
way that the BW is administered, including the delivery method, the pathogen, whether a single or multiple attack points are used, effects such as time
of day, weather, and other factors. The ability of the medical personnel to
identify, isolate, and treat those exposed while at the same time determining
the origin and proper response that is needed to restrict the pathogen from
further infecting beyond the initial contacts.[7,17]

Radiological Weapons

The effect of radioactive material contaminating emerges from an incident
in Brazil in 1987, where a caesium source was found in a clinic and broke
open and 17 grams of a powder was released. Four people were killed and
thousands of cubic meters of soil had to be decontaminated and removed.[9,23]
From this example, it is realistic to see that the effects of a radioactive attack
have consequences that stretch much further than the immediate casualties,
and the need to cordon off an area to prevent any further contamination. The
amount of people and resources needed to clean up such an attack would
have a catastrophic effect on draining the resources of many states.[20,23]

It is probably impossible to prevent such an incident; however, this new
awareness of the prospect of terrorists acquiring and using CW has prompted
LEO to examine these instances and respond to these threats in order to
interrupt such plans while they are still in the production stage to counter
this new threat.

Nuclear Weapons

The potential number of casualties caused by nuclear weapons is less sensitive
to the method of delivery and is more dependent on the explosion yield, along
with the area in which the blast occurs. Currently, there is no empirical evidence
available that suggests the amount of death associated with such an explosion
from a nuclear device. The nearest comparative figures and evidence we have to
examine are based on the 20 kt weapon dropped on Japan that killed between
90,000 and 120,000, and caused another 90,000 injuries. Theodore Taylor estimates that the detonation of a crude nuclear weapon with a yield of .05 kt in
New York could kill up to fifty thousand.[20,23] CBRN have the potential to cause
large amounts of indiscriminate casualties and are capable of being exploited in
a number of operational roles.[19,20] Keeping this in mind, it is extremely important to search out and find competent advisors whom you can consult in training the populace of first responders to handle just such an event.

Psychological Effects from a CBRN Attack

The psychological effect that a terrorist group could have through the release of CBRN on a population would be of great strategic importance in spreading fear, panic, and possibly civil uprising against one's own government for fear that the government could not protect the population. Therefore, CBRN terrorism is the highest on the priority list to most terrorist groups because of its higher psychological impact value. One would argue that CBRN confer a decisive advantage for only one type of attack, indiscriminate mass casualties.

CBRN terrorism creates the political conditions in which governments must be able to respond immediately and effectively to look competent in the eyes of society and diminish any thoughts of incompetence on the part of the government as looking ill prepared.[23]

Whether or not CBRN would further terrorist objectives is primarily dependent upon the consequence of their use by the group. The immediate impact would be the damage and casualties that would stem from such an attack, but also the repercussions that such an attack would have on the economy of the state, its internal politics, and even the effects felt on society itself. The consequences of such an attack will vary according to the weapon used. Richard Falkenrath[23,24] states that there are seven consequences of a WMD attack. They are:

Casualties. The primary consequence from any category of NBC weapon will be the number of casualties, based on the quality of the weapon and the environmental conditions at the time of detonation.

Contamination. The area contaminated by third-order WMDs could be substantial, reaching hundreds of miles farther than the release point and contaminating very large areas, dependent upon environmental conditions. The area contaminated from a nuclear device will vary dependent upon its yield.

Panic. Fear and panic from being contaminated or living within the immediate radius will have a major consequence, disrupting personal, social, and economic way of life for many.

Degraded response capabilities. Those, including first responders, that become contaminated will have a substantial effect on the response of those trained to deal with an NBC attack since those contaminated will need to be removed and dealt with; those contaminated will degrade the resources of many governmental bodies in handling such an attack.

Economic damage. The consequences from such an attack would render many businesses, governmental buildings, etc., destroyed or unusable from such an attack.

Loss of a strategic position. The victim state (country) may be reluctant to sponsor any further international interests for fear that it would provoke continued terrorist attacks. Being intimidated by a terrorist (clandestine) group would help the terrorists achieve their political objectives.

Social-psychological damage and political change. The continued risk that a subsequent attack would follow immediately has a demoralizing effect on the victim state. Richard Falkenrath states "that public expression of paranoia, xenophobia, isolationism, and vengeful fury become powerful influences on foreign policy." This would be devastating to most governments because society would lose confidence in their government to protect them and could incite civil uprising.[22–24]

With all this in mind, we need to remember that many variables exist, and while a state can experience any or all of these consequences, the implication and intensity of such an attack will define the intensity experienced by the victim state.

Many analysts agree that the majority of CBRN attacks will consist of attacks involving first-order weapons and a small incidence of second-order weapons, where the consequences can be properly managed by most states' resources.[24] However, in very rare occasions, terrorists could possibly acquire third-order WMD. A state may not be able to handle the consequences from an incident involving this type of munitions. And since all CBRN have short- and long-term effects that are much more damaging than those achieved with conventional weapons, this would certainly create a long-term issue for the victim state. For this reason, CBRN will be the choice for some terrorist groups in order to achieve their political, social, or religious objectives.[24,25]

It is clear that terrorists seek targets that have specific political, religious, or social objectives conducive to the terrorist group's beliefs, for which the terrorist group is willing to employ and use violence to achieve certain objectives. Propaganda is achieved by the terrorist group through the use of violence to generate a message to their constituents and enemies to illustrate that the group, as well as the cause, is still alive. Propaganda is then needed by the terrorist organization to build support and keep political pressure on states that they are in conflict with as they continue to use violence to generate continual propaganda and group support for their cause. Thus, a terrorist attack serves this interest and achieves an objective of the group at the same time. Terrorists need to choose the level of violence that is necessary to achieve the level of propaganda that will result in the desired effect.[25] Terrorists assess the desired level of violence that is needed to achieve their objectives without alienating their constituency; however, a terrorist group may justify a higher level of violence, such as the use of WMDs, to achieve their goals if the terrorist organization believed that an indiscriminate attack against an institutional target would achieve the group's objectives.

Terrorists utilize many strategies and tactics in order to achieve their objectives, and while some are more desirable than others, what is certain is that many strategies involving CBRN can have more of an effect than those absent such a threat. Therefore, examining terrorist strategies and tactics, where the real possibility exists that CBRN may be used against a target of opportunity, is essential to understanding instances where such weapons may be used in discriminate and indiscriminate attacks against targets of opportunity. CBRN could be used in the following ways in order to achieve a desired effect.

Defeating a security force. The use of CBRN to defeat such a force would have a desirable effect since it would level the playing field in a terrorist group's favor; however, a more desirable effect arising from such an attack would be weakening the will of a government that supplies such a force. The truck bomb that was driven into the Marine barracks in Beirut in 1983, where 241 soldiers were killed, and the bombing of the French barracks and the U.S. Embassies are examples of such a tactic. This attack led to the withdrawal of troops and legitimized the objective since the attack was aimed at soldiers.

Attacking economic targets. A strategy of terrorists is to strike at economic targets in order to bankrupt a state by attacking property and economic infrastructures in order to raise the cost of war and force concessions from the government. Islamic terrorist organizations have used this tactic to attack the tourist industry by attacking foreign tourists.

Polarizing communities. The theory behind the concept of polarization is that these attacks will trigger a government to respond with ruthless countermeasures that increase the campaign of violence against the entire society, dividing them and pushing one half toward support for the terrorist group generating the violence.

Breaking the will of the government. All of the strategies mentioned can be part of a much broader strategy to use terror as a means of weakening the will of a government while allowing the terrorist organization to continue in its struggle. There are many ways that such a strategy like this might be accomplished: using violence against large numbers in discriminate attacks on a population, acts that lead to large numbers of indiscriminate casualties, and using the act of assassination to kill both discriminate and indiscriminate individuals and small groups from a population. It is clear that killing that occurs in unlikely places on one or two individuals at a time casts the largest cloud of fear and uncertainty, since these acts are generally harder to explain.[23-25]

There are innumerable targets that exist in any state that are of high value to a terrorist organization. While past history has shown that certain terrorist groups are ready to use NBC weapons to achieve certain goals through indiscriminate mass casualties attacks, while other organizations select CBRN to attack their targets discriminately, it is uncertain whether terrorists are sophisticated enough to deploy CBRN. And while CBRN and WMDs in particular are the optimum choice of weapons for a terrorist organization in achieving some goals and attacking some targets, and their use on some targets is questioned, one thing is sure: the ways in which a terrorist organization might use CBRN will be determined by the technical characteristics of the weapon that the organization proves capable of producing. While terrorism cannot be stopped, neither will the terrorists, who will continue to further explore their options in utilizing CBRN.

Medical Response to an Incident

In preparation of an incident involving a high number of casualties, the CDC, in cooperation with other federal agencies, has been testing various procedures in planning, preparing, and preventing the risk of a CBRN attack. One part of the equation is the response package, which enables health care professionals to respond to an incident location and begin administering treatment to those infected by a biological virus. In order for these teams to be effective, they must have the medicine available in great quantities to treat the population affected. To make sure that the required medical supplies are available, the federal government awarded a $428 million contract to two pharmaceutical companies to produce and strategically stockpile antidotes vital to preventing and preparing for a chemical or biological attack. The event of an attack by chemical or biological means on U.S. soil would have an overwhelming effect on the health care system, depleting medical resources quickly. The CDC has set up strategic stockpiles in eight guarded warehouses nationwide and is ready to respond should they be called upon. In the event the CDC is called upon, they would activate a "push"—a push package would be deployed to the location of need. The push package contains stockpiled drugs, vaccines, and medical supplies that are loaded into cargo containers and then delivered by a Boeing 747. Landing at a military or commercial airport, the packages can be safely unloaded and delivered via Federal Express or UPS to the destination. State and local officials have the burden of tracking and ensuring that the supplies reach the required locations and balancing the needs of each location. In the event more supplies are needed, it is also their responsibility to notify the CDC to activate another push.

Another strategy of the CDC in responding to a national response where a medical response is required is its ring containment strategy. The ring containment strategy is modeled after the World Health Organization's method that was used to eliminate smallpox around the globe. The plan is to create mobile teams of health care professionals that can respond to outbreak locations and quickly contain, identify, and treat these chemical or biological health issues. The response team is made up of a physician leader, a senior public health advisor, two epidemiologists, lab specialists, a commutations specialist, a community liaison, and technical support personnel. The team would coordinate its movements with state and local officials to isolate the patients, vaccinate all in the area that may or could be contaminated by the outbreak, and then vaccinate the second ring of individuals that may have come into contact at some point with those infected.

The ring containment strategy[26] has been validated in many areas of the world when responding to and treating natural outbreaks; however, whether this strategy would be successful against a bioterrorist attack has many doubting. Many in the medical community think that the strategy is designed with public health in mind and not in terms of national security. The CDC has been working with federal, state, and local authorities, as well as the medical community, to test and retest many of the strengths and weaknesses of their current strategy, and they are moving in the direction of national security to address how the CDC will operate in the future. (For more updates, visit http://www.cdc.gov.)

Conclusion

In preparation of this chapter, I discovered that my own situational awareness grew about the days since September 11 and just how the world we live in has changed. However, I often wonder if people really remember what took place that day, or have we all but forgotten the sacrifices made? Have we supported our troops overseas? Do we remember that they are at the tip of the sword, fighting an enemy that is not immediately recognizable by the brand of their state's uniform? We have these terrorists on the run unlike any other time in our history; however, we need to stay the course and know that this war on terror is going to be long and require much sacrifice. As the men and women are fighting overseas, they look to those holding the shield back home, the federal, state, and local police, to keep the homeland safe. These individuals know that it is really the beat cop, more than anyone else, that will have the first contact with these terrorists. Officers like Diane Dean, an alert Customs official,[27] stopped the millennium plot and subsequently captured North African–born Ahmed Rassan, an al-Qaeda operative. Or patrol trooper Charles Hanger, who is responsible for locating and arresting Timothy McVeigh, carrying a concealed handgun. Or the Salt Lake City, Utah, police officers that located Elizabeth Smart. Or the rookie police officer in North Carolina that is responsible for arresting and bringing to justice serial bomber Eric Rudolph,[28] who had eluded authorities for five years. It is men and women like those previously described that are protecting the homeland; it is they that are the shield of protection in your streets and in your neighborhood.

It will be these men and women that will prevent, contain, and respond in national or state emergencies, because for them the threat is real and guarding against it is real. They realize we are vulnerable. They realize the sacrifice needed to continue the momentum in containing and preventing further terrorist attacks. The information contained in this chapter is short and hopefully to the point on a wide range of issues that pertain to CBRN attacks and the health and well-being of every American, and while each section could fill a library, this is not my intention. The information contained in this chapter is a primer to fuel thought about just how vulnerable the United States really is. All the prevention will not stop those motivated enough to carry out their plans. However, if we don't fall into the head-in-the-sand philosophy, and if we realistically look at steps to prevention, then we can build an infrastructure that will make those that want to hurt us unable to reach us. The simple theme of this chapter is: "If it's predictable, it's preventable." I hope that this is the message conveyed, and I hope I have stirred your awareness of how vulnerable our society is to just such a terrorist attack.

Endnotes

1. Jenkins, Brian Michael, "International Terrorism: A New Mode of Conflict," in Carlton, David, and Schaerf, Carlo, eds., *International Terrorism and World Security* (London: Croom Helm, 1975), 15.
2. Statements made to the U.S. Department of Health and Human Services on the topic of bioterrorism preparedness by Tommy G. Thompson before the Subcommittee on Labor and Human Services, Education and Related Agencies Committee on Appropriations. The U.S. Senate, October 3, 2001, http://www.hhs.gov/asl/testify/t011003.htm.
3. Ibid.
4. Gurr, Nadine, and Cole, Benjamin, *The New Face of Terrorism: Threats from Weapons of Mass Destruction* (New York: St. Martins Press, 2002), 287.
5. Ibid., 273.
6. Ibid., 135–38
7. Sidell, F. R., *Chemical Agent Terrorism*. http://www.nbc-med.org/SiteContent/MedRef/OnlineRef/Other/Chagter.html p.1. (accessed February 2, 2005).

8. Testimony of J. T. Caruso, deputy assistant director of the Counterterrorism Division, FBI before the Senate Judiciary Committee on Technology, Terrorism and Government Information, November 6, 2001, "Bioterrorism."

9. Orient, J. M., Chemical and Biological Warfare: Should Defenses Be Researched and Deployed? Doctors for Disaster Preparedness, http://oism.org/ddp/cbw-jama.htm (accessed February 2, 2002).

10. Sullivan, John B., Jr., *Toxic and Biological Terrorism*.

11. Chem-Bio Frequently Asked Questions, in *Guide to Better Understanding Chem-Bio*, Tempest Publishing, P.O. Box 22572, Alexandria, VA 22304-9257, http://www.tempestco.com.

12. Gurr and Benjamin, xi. The introduction has some thought-provoking thoughts on just how vulnerable a society we really are.

13. Ibid., 116–18.

14. Ibid., 105–24.

15. www.cdc.gov/mmwr/preview/mmwrhtml/rr4904a1.htm.

16. http://www.nytimes.com/2005/03/16/politics/16home.html).

17. http://www.fbi.gov/terrorinfo/counterrorism/waronterrorhome.htm.

18. Guillemin, J., *Biological Weapons. From The Invention of State-Sponsored Programs to Contemporary Bioterrorism* (New York: Columbia Press, 2005), 3, 159, 175.

19. Gurr and Benjamin, 49.

20. Ibid., 47–48.

21. Ibid., 51–56.

22. Ibid., 42–46.

23. Ibid., 80–86.

24. Ibid., 87–98.

25. Ibid., 98–104.

26. de Rugy, Veronique, and Pena, Charles V., *Responding to the Threat of Smallpox Bioterrorism: An Ounce of Prevention Is Best Approach*, Policy Analysis 434, April 18, 2002. The authors are policy analysts at the Cato Institute.

27. Gertz, Bill, *Breakdown. How America's Intelligence Failure Led to September 11* (Washington, DC: Regency Publishers, 2002), 61.

28. *Chicago Tribune*, March 11, 2005. Editorial on how the street cop is making a difference in the war on terrorism and how basic policing skills are having an impact on locating and stopping terrorists and their organizations.

Selected Bibliography

Books

Gertz, B. 2002. *Breakdown: How America's intelligence failures led to September 11.* Washington, DC: Regency Publishers.

Gram, T. 2004. *Common sense on weapons of mass destruction.* Seattle, WA: University of Washington Press.

Guillemin, J. 2005. *Biological weapons: From the invention of state-sponsored programs to contemporary bioterrorism.* New York: Columbia University Press.

Gurr, N., and Cole, B. 2002. *The new face of terrorism: Threats from weapons of mass destruction.* London: I B Tauris.

Keegan, J. 2003. *Intelligence in war: Knowledge of the enemy from Napoleon to al-Qaeda.* New York: Random House.

Laqueur, W. 2004. *No end to war: Terrorism in the twenty-first century.* London: The Continuum International Publishing Group.

Internet Resources

Chemical Agent Terrorism, by Fredrick R. Sidell: http://www.nbc-med.org/Site Content/MedRef/OnlineRef/Other/Chagter.html (accessed February 2, 2005).

FBI war on terror website: http://www.fbi.gov/terrorinfo/counterrorism/waronter-rorhome.htm.

Monterey Institute of International Studies: http://www.miis.edu/.

Chemical and biological effects as well as other terrorism information: http://www.tempestco.com/publishing.

National Planning Scenario: http://132.160.230.113:8080/revize/repository/CSS Prototype/simplelist/Planning_ScenariosExec_Summary_.pdf (accessed March 20, 2005).

"Office of State and Local Government Coordination and Preparedness at the Homeland Security Department," *New York Times*: http://www.nytimes.com/2005/03/16/politics/16/home.html (accessed March 19, 2003).

U.S. Department of Health and Human Services: http://www.hhs.gov/asl/testify/t011003.html (accessed October 3, 2001).

Apocalypse
Courage and Commitment

15

DALE L. JUNE

Contents

> Apocalypse—the destruction or devastation of something, or an instance of this; disaster, catastrophe, day of reckoning.

For over 600 years the western hemisphere, in general, and for nearly 250 years the United States, in particular, have been beacons for people seeking a refuge for relief from poverty and political and religious persecution. There have been other reasons, of course, for example, to avoid criminal prosecution in their homeland, to escape war and invasion, adventure seeking, and a host of other motivations, including forced slavery and indentured servitude. However, it's not always for purposes of establishing oneself for the greater good that some people migrate to the "free world." Sometimes their intentions and motivations are to destroy the freedoms and opportunities others have worked so hard and sacrificed so much to build.

People sleep peaceably in their beds at night only because rough men stand ready to do violence on their behalf.

—**George Orwell**

The Blackhawks are the last of the free men of the conquered countries—we fight for the freedom of men rather than for profit or politics!

—*Blackhawk* **comics, 1944**

It is September 11, 2001; the officer jumps into his patrol car and races to the scene of the twin towers burning in his beloved New York City, where he has passionately served for twelve years. As he starts his engine he takes and swallows a deep breath, and his partner and he are on the way. The show has just begun, as he rushes through the busy streets of New York thinking of what could possibly go wrong on such a lovely day. But what he is about to experience is going to change American society and the world forever.

As he arrives at the scene he sees people running, trying to escape the bombed and burning buildings. The carnage reminds him of devastation he has seen on the evening news showing crumpled metal and torn, shattered bodies at the scene of suicide bombings of markets and public transportation in the Middle East. The scene here is not on videotape, nor is it halfway across the world. It is here, in the United States, in his city, where he has lived all his life. The reality of the dead bodies is just getting to him as he smells the corpses on the ground. His eyes widen, and he cannot believe that this is happening. He cannot convince himself that this is real. His mind cannot grasp the enormity of the scene before him. His heart pounds and his pulse and blood pressure race to maximum levels with the adrenalin his brain is ordering up and shooting throughout his body as he leaps out of the car and tries to help a woman who is bleeding and struggling to get up. This is no routine traffic stop or patrol contact; he just follows what his eyes and heart tell him to do. Nothing could have prepared him for the reality of this nightmare.

As he turns around to carry the wounded woman to his car he sees a building crumbling, falling onto the patrol car, killing his partner, who is helping a stricken and terrified man. He collapses with the woman: she is dead. He is holding her in his hands and he is crying; his emotions starting to come out. For a minute they might seem to comfort him, but in reality he is dying inside. His partner, with whom he had been friends since high school, is now dead and lying under a pile of debris. But he doesn't stop; he feels that if he saves one life, just one, he will retire after this horrendous day knowing that he has seen and smelled evil up close and personal.

His wishes were granted and he saved a little girl from the burning build-ing, but unfortunately he did not get to see the day of his retirement. As he grabbed the little girl his body became hot, and as he put her down on the ground, he realized his body had caught flames from the explosion. That was his final realization as his body turned into ash. But there were remains. Remains of him and his badge, his gun, and the memory of what a great officer and family man he was. This girl is alive somewhere, and she knows she will remember him. He will always mean something to her. Many other officers and firefighters were killed that day in their line of duty and will never be forgotten.*

Protection and Bravery Have a Long History

> Many a Lord gathered in council considering long in what way brave men could struggle against ... terrors of sudden attack.
>
> **—Beowulf**

Knights, the original "soldiers of fortune," sold the services of their particu-lar martial arts and skill to anyone who could afford them to protect them and their property, usually in the name of their ruler, their king, or in service to the Church and religion. Knights, similar to samurai in medieval Japan, roamed the countryside seeking employment as "protectors of the realm." Sworn to duty and loyalty of their employer, knights engaged enemies and fought to the death often against overwhelming odds, even knowing they were about to die. Better to die in the line of duty than to flee the battlefield in cowardly disgrace.

In time of combat, soldiers, since the earliest American wars, are awarded medals for displaying courage under fire. The most prestigious medal of all, the Congressional Medal of Honor, awarded in every war since the American Civil War, is bestowed upon those who exhibit "courage above and beyond the call of duty." Police officers also receive medals for valor and bravery. Most medals are awarded posthumously, for with that badge of courage comes a call to make the greatest sacrifice of all. Standing in the line of fire so others may live is the grandest calling of all for soldiers, police, and firefighters. Fear rides with a police officer when the "chips are down," but it is that little extra bit of courage that pushes fear aside, allowing him to react in an appropriate and heroic final stand.

---

* From an essay by Elizaveta Kirillova, a senior criminal justice student at American Intercontinental University–Los Angeles (2008).

Live Life So You Will Have No Regrets When You Die!

Police and firefighters are of a different mold. Some call it the "police mentality" or subculture; others see it as "dedicated to the values of serving mankind." Police and firefighters rush to the fire, the source of shooting, the scene of disaster, and impending injury or death. There is no hesitation. They are the "angels who rush in where others fear to tread." There is certainly fear, yet it is the motivator that spurs them. When all is said and done, they are willing to take a bullet or fall through a burning floor so that someone else will live.

Dedication of being charged with the responsibility for the security, safety, and well-being of another human being is in keeping with a pledge of their honor, reputation, even their life to accept obligations that by mere definition mean danger and potentially life-threatening circumstances. Professionals of this nature can be characterized as physically fit, expertly trained, and confident, willing to provide security to those who can't protect or save themselves.

A college graduate who would be an outstanding candidate as a U.S. Secret Service special agent was heavily encouraged to apply for a position as an agent. She was smart, carrying a perfect four-point scholastic average, had sound judgment, was athletic and physically fit, outwardly self-confident, and fit the image expected of a Secret Service agent with a professional demeanor and attitude. She had one drawback that prevented her from applying to the service; she was afraid that what if, somehow during a moment of crisis, she failed to react as expected. Knowing the well-earned reputation of agents who have stood in the line of fire, even taking a bullet meant for the president, she was not willing to risk that scenario of failing to respond properly. It was interesting to note that she had no concern for the potential danger of placing herself between a shooter and the person she was assigned to protect. Her major, and only, concern was that she was afraid she wouldn't (couldn't) react to neutralize the danger.

Therein may be a particle of a clue to the question of what drives a police officer to run toward the sound and danger of shooting, and perhaps what drives a fireman to run into a burning building while others are fleeing. When they are sworn in as officers, they take an oath to help those who can't help themselves, and that oath is something they become dedicated and loyal to.

That oath of dedication and loyalty is buttressed by a value system of ideological (religious, ethical, and moral), social, aesthetic, and doctrinal (political) beliefs, and more. Values influenced by personal experiences and culture affect the way people think about the world and the way they live their lives. There are other important values, like honesty, humor, kindness, courage, strength, intelligence, family, love, education, trust, choice of religious beliefs, freedom, and memories. These are all things worth dying for if they are preserved for fellow man.

You Can't Be Neutral in the Combat Range

Aristotle described courage as the mid-point between "foolhardiness" and cowardice. Cowardice, naturally, is the antithesis of bravery, wherein foolhardiness is disregarding all caution, leading to actions that imperil the fool. Life and death happen in hundredths of a second. An officer seldom has the opportunity to think of consequences that may or may not occur as a result of his actions. He acts or reacts as his training, education, and experience take him. As Brasidas of Sparta once said, "Fear makes men forget, and skill that cannot fight is useless."

In one police action, officers received a call of a domestic violence situation with a gun involved. As the officers arrived at the house, a man came running out with a shotgun in hand. He ran to the rear of the house, where he was stopped by a tall fence in the backyard. The chasing officer pointed his .357 magnum at the man but did not shoot. The man was holding the shotgun in an upward position but not pointing it at the officer. Suddenly he dropped the gun and began sobbing. Upon disarming the man and questioning him, it was found that the man and his wife were going through a difficult divorce. The man had gone to the house to retrieve the gun that had been passed to him by his grandfather, and his wife was trying to keep from him. The shotgun was empty. The officer was forever grateful that he did not shoot, though it would have easily been justified. The object lesson to be learned was that sometimes things do not bear out what appearances indicate, but can officers afford to hesitate? In this instance the officer was in a combat zone, knowing that a slightest movement within a thousandth of a second could spell his death or the death of the man with the shotgun. Yet he hesitated. Not for fear, but for the knowledge of the value of human life. As Ralph Waldo Emerson once said, "Nothing can bring you peace but yourself. Nothing can bring you peace but the triumph of principles."

Through the Looking Glass

He woke up in the morning feeling good about himself. Today was the day they would bring damage upon the United States. There would be no second guessing, no looking back. He had his orders and he had sworn to follow instructions to the letter.

> Somewhere a True Believer is training to kill you. He is training with minimum food or water, in austere conditions, day and night. The only thing clean on him is his weapon. He doesn't worry about what workout to do—his rucksack weighs what it weighs, and he runs until the enemy stops chasing him.

The True Believer doesn't care "how hard it is"; he knows he either wins or he dies. He doesn't go home at 1700; he is home. He knows only the "Cause."*

The knowledge he possessed was above average because his parents had educated him and sent him to many schools. He also learned a lot from the streets and his bosses, or the "main men," as they were called. He was also a devoted follower of the Islamic religion and a believer of Osama bin Laden. He believed in Osama and relied on every one of his words. Why would Osama lie to him? He was treated like one of Osama's sons, so why would Osama hurt his own member? Whether this was true or not, this soon to be airplane hijacking suicide bomber had extraordinary training on how to induce considerable damage in one fell swoop. He knew exactly what he was supposed to do, and for that he would be regarded as a true hero. He would not receive a medal for his exploits, but his picture and story would soon grace a wall of martyrs and heroes. He would be celebrated as brave and daring, courageous beyond the call of duty or patriotism. His family would bask in the glory of the honor he brought to them for giving up his life for his religion and the rewards in paradise. To sacrifice his life "in the line of duty" was actually a privilege to him and to everyone else.

He had had training classes, just like the police officer who was to die in the fiery blast that September morning. However, instead of classes on how to protect people and how to use instincts to save lives, he had classes on how to destroy people and how to use horrific tactics to instill fear into people. His training was long and arduous, and he absorbed it very well. He felt he was born to serve Osama bin Laden and the cause of worldwide Islamic domination.

All his life he had been a good citizen of Islamic causes, and joining al-Qaeda, where Osama offered him this opportunity to serve Allah, gave him cause to live—and die gloriously. With the doctrine of bin Laden, he found the mission for which he felt he was destined. Being chosen for this one opportunity to strike at the United States because of all the "unholy" things he had been told about the decadent United States, he agreed to make a great sacrifice and do as he was told in the name of Osama bin Laden and the glory of God. Today he would change American society as nothing before. He would take his place on a commercial airline flight from Boston along with co-conspirators and at a certain point take control of the plane and pilot it into the World Trade Center. He did this knowing there was no turning back once the plan was initiated, and his death in a fiery explosion was only a short flight away. He did not consider that he had been manipulated and

* NCOIC of the Special Forces Assessment and Selection Course in a welcome speech to new SF candidates, www.rivervet.com/images/followmethese%20are%20my20creden-tial (accessed December 20, 2009).

perhaps brainwashed with the ideology of al-Qaeda. He saw it only as doing his duty he had sworn to fulfill for God.

Heavenly Rewards to Gain

"You will do great things. God will reward you with heavenly bliss to be gained in Paradise." Osama taught all of his followers one thing: that they had nothing to lose and the heavenly rewards to gain. People who have nothing to lose will risk and do anything, while people who have something to lose will usually avoid risks. Osama taught his followers that they already had enjoyed life and that it was time for them to enjoy something better: paradise in heaven. If they were to engage in terrorist attacks and end up dying, they would go to paradise where Allah awaited them with their rewards.

Standing in the cockpit of the plane, the controls locked, the building looming larger as the plane rushes toward it on a deadly and fiery collision course, his excitement growing with each passing thousandth of a second, anticipating his entrance to paradise and glory, shouting, "Allah Akbar! Allah Akbar!" (God is great! God is great!), he raises his arms over his head, his crazed joy exceeding everything he has ever experienced, he sees the look of fright, alarm, and panic on the faces of the people in the building just that hundredth of a thousandth of a second before impact. It is the last thing he ever sees. Death is instant. And the American people's nightmare is just beginning.

People who have nothing to lose believe. And what they believe in is the idea that if they do everything that they are supposed to do, according to the will of God, they will be in a better place. It is beyond difficult proportions to fight a war where people who have everything to lose fight people who have nothing to lose. It is terrible to say, but the truth is, the individuals who have nothing to lose are more likely to win. Although most of the time these individuals die in their courageous and committed acts of destruction, they send a message that death, while serving the wishes of God, is the purist form of living even while taking away hundreds, if not thousands of innocent lives.

Terrorists were not born the horrible destructors of peace that the world has come to know. Terrorists are made, they are shaped, and they are molded by circumstances of their lives and by other ideological individuals who have taught them to believe in the same fanatical idealism of how they believe a society should be controlled. Behavior, ideas, beliefs, values, and principles of terrorists come from societal sources and conditions, morals and norms, preached by powerful speakers and powerful individuals who can change a person's view on life to fundamental radicalism.*

---

* From an essay by Elizaveta Kirillova.

Police do what they do because they have everything to lose: family, freedom, love, joy, civil rights and liberty, and principles of a well-lived life. That is the main difference between living in a free and democratic secular world, and living in a religiously fanatic terroristic society that breeds suicide bombers.* An act of sacrificial bravery is unselfish if done in the name of preservation of life, but to take lives "in the name of God" hoping to gain entrance to paradise and to reap its rewards is extremely selfish and shortsighted.

The terrorist attacks of September 11, 2001, unleashed an epidemic of stress-related problems upon the American people. Those and other incidents (including domestic or homegrown terrorism) have affected all of us. Many people are afraid to fly. Many don't use public transportation because they are scared that it might blow up. Whenever a tragic incident occurs—a car explodes, an airplane crashes, or a café is blown up—persons automatically start thinking that it was possibly a terrorist attack. Terrorism is so ingrained in all of our citizens that we automatically assume that an incident where something blows up and people die must be a terrorist attack. One goal of terrorism is to disrupt a society by causing widespread psychological damage and social disruption. But even before the horrendous attacks of 9/11, American citizens were struggling with stress-related problems. The attacks of 9/11 (similar and reminiscent of the Japanese attack on Pearl Harbor on December 7, 1941) just raised the stress to a higher level and made life extremely more difficult.

Standing for Opportunity, Freedom, and Democracy

I do not love the bright sword for its sharpness, nor the arrow for its swiftness, nor the warrior for his glory. I love only that which they defend.

—**J. R. R. Tolkien**

Nothing symbolizes the concept of freedom as much as the lady standing in the Harbor of New York. The Statue of Liberty, a gift to the American people from the people of France in recognition of the principles of freedom, liberty, and justice for which the United States stands, looks outward to welcome everyone to the shores of freedom, liberty, and opportunity. And nothing summarizes the concept of Lady Liberty more than the sonnet "The New Colossus," by American poet Emma Lazarus, inscribed in bronze at the base of the statue in 1903, enhancing the Statue of Liberty's image as a symbol of freedom and opportunity.

* Ibid.

Not like the brazen giant of Greek fame,
With conquering limbs astride from land to land;
Here at our sea-washed, sunset gates shall stand
A mighty woman with a torch, whose flame
Is the imprisoned lightning, and her name
Mother of Exiles. From her beacon-hand
Glows world-wide welcome; her mild eyes command
The air-bridged harbor that twin cities frame.
"Keep, ancient lands, your storied pomp!" cries she
With silent lips. "Give me your tired, your poor,
Your huddled masses yearning to breathe free,
The wretched refuse of your teeming shore.
Send these, the homeless, tempest-tost to me,
I lift my lamp beside the golden door!"

This "golden door," this lamp being lifted and held high by the "Mother of Exiles," shines for everyone regardless of their origin, social standing, skin color, or religion. Nowhere in the history of the world has there ever been a more open invitation to a land made of more than mere promises of "rewards in paradise." This land, this America, vilified and defiled by usurpers who seek nothing more than to destroy what they see as decadent and against "God's wishes" is the "paradise" they seek. Only they are blinded by the four horsemen of the apocalypse*—often referred to as Conquest, War, Famine, and Death.

* Background to the four horsemen: After taking the scroll from God and being worshiped by all creation, the Lamb (Jesus, the Lamb of God) now opens the seven seals of the scroll to reveal its contents. The seals, as with the trumpets, are in a group of four, two, and one. The opening of the first four seals reveals the four horsemen of the apocalypse. The opening of the first four seals is introduced by each of the four living creatures in turn. Each one of the four living creatures reveals a horseman; the first three horsemen are summed up by the fourth horseman: "They were given power over a fourth of the earth to kill by sword, famine and plague, and by the wild beasts of the earth." These are popularly known as the four horsemen of the apocalypse. The power of these horsemen is limited to a quarter, and with the trumpets later it is limited to a third. The fifth seal reveals those who had been slain because of the word of God and their testimony, that is, the persecuted church. The sixth seal reveals the day of the Lord, which brings the Lamb's wrath to those on the earth. The opening of the seventh seal reveals silence. The seven seals sum up human history from the viewpoint of heaven and the Church. There is war, famine, and pestilence in general, and on the Church in particular there is persecution; then the end will come, bringing terror to the world, this probably accounts for the silence of the seventh seal. http://www.apocalipsis.org/fourhorsemen.htm (accessed December 7, 2009).

Horses and Their Riders*

The white horse and rider—Pestilence, conquest, righteousness, evil;
   meaning to go forth in conquest.
The red horse and rider—War—to take peace from the earth and make
   men kill each other.
The black horse and rider—Famine—to kill with hunger.
The pale horse and rider—Death—followed by Hades (the lord of the
   dead and ruler of the nether world), kills with the scythe, with famine, disease, and the beasts of the earth.

Freemen in a Free Land

"It is the moral right and duty for every government to protect its own citizens, especially innocent civilians, from harm's way in every conflict."[†]

> We the People of the United States, in Order to form a more perfect Union,
> establish Justice, insure domestic Tranquility, provide for the common
> defence, promote the general Welfare, and secure the Blessings of Liberty to
> ourselves and our Posterity, do ordain and establish this Constitution for the
> United States of America.

For over two hundred years this great living document has been the cen-
terpiece of democracy and the great golden key to living in a land where the
government has guaranteed the rights of every man. There is no exception
to the law, and even the most heinous of crimes is dealt with in a manner of
justice and fairness. The United States is a land ruled by law as adopted by representatives of all the people. No man is above the law, and any demagoguery
and promises made by man in the name of his God are the ramblings of a mis-
creant bent upon his own troublemaking and self-centered lust for power.
   Let us take a moment to closely examine this preamble to the U.S.
Constitution phrase by phrase:

"We the People"—We the people, meaning us, everyone—common man,
   from beggar and thief to the highest in honesty and social standing.
"... of the United States"—All the states united in one great country and
   a federalized government devoted to the people of the United States
   living the slogan of *E Pluribus Unum* (out of many, one).

---

* http://en.wikipedia.org/wiki/Four_Horsemen_of_the_Apocalypse (accessed December
   7, 2009).
† Decker,   David   N.,   www.haaretz,com/hasen/objects/pagesResponseDetails.jhtml?
   (accessed December 7, 2009).

"... in Order to form a more perfect Union"—The Constitution was formed to replace the weak Articles of Confederation, which originally bound the states together as a confederation. The intent of the Constitution was to strengthen those bonds and to guarantee certain rights and liberties to people while establishing the basis and foundation of a strong and stable government.

"... establish Justice"—To establish a means for every man to be treated equally, without prejudice or bias, and to found a means of creating a lawful redress for wrongs committed against another person.

"... insure domestic Tranquility"—Authorization of a legal means of keeping the peace and restorative order when it is threatened by crime, riots, and disorder.

"... provide for the common defence"—A strong military and militia are the backbones of defense against any who would seek to overthrow the established government of the United States and to conquer its people.

"... promote the general Welfare"—Provide an environment of caring and concern for all the people of the United States and to use the power of the government to ensure that everyone has equal opportunity for life, liberty, and happiness.

"... and secure the Blessings of Liberty to ourselves and our Posterity"—As stated, liberty is a valued blessing and must be preserved for us, the present, but also for generations to follow.

"... do ordain and establish this Constitution for the United States of America"—To proclaim that the document so described is the foundation and basis for life, liberty, justice, and freedom for all in these, the United States of America.

Good versus Evil—Fighting an Ideological War

There is a need to realize that the struggle against terrorism is a conflict of fighting ideas and beliefs of faith. This is not a war in the traditional model of fighting a nationalistic or imperialistic country or a race that is "evil." It is extremely hard to fight an idea because these ideas become beliefs, values, and principles by which certain individuals (terrorists) live. By killing insurgent soldiers, these ideas are not going to go away. Ideas are being reborn each and every day and are taught to children at an early age. Deaths in Iraq are not going to solve the problems that America is facing. This is because deaths do not stop ideas. There are individuals being born every day with fundamentalist, even puritan, beliefs, values, and principles contrary to the idealism of democracy and freedom.

Some ideas may stem from the Islam religion, but the main issue is how a group of men decades and centuries ago decided to interpret these ideas and beliefs in their own way. After interpreting these ideas and beliefs in their own way (because of their personal thinking, feelings, and leanings), these groups of men came up with amendments (rules) that most of their descendents now grow up believing are "God's truths." Individuals aren't born evil or born with hate in their body and soul: they were born empty slates and molded into terrorists.

Modern terrorism is the result of conflicting ideologies. Modern terrorists bring with them an odd attraction of infusing religious beliefs with violence. They are fighting to spread their brand of religious dogma and morals through thought control and physical endangerment, such as suicidal bombings. It is a doctrine of "spreading God's word" as interpreted by fanatical religious zealots who are myopically absorbed in their way being the only way in the "sight of God." Anyone not practicing Islam according to strict interpretation of the Quran as preached by ultra-conservatives is considered a nonbeliever and deserving of death. Interestingly, the current thinking of Islamic radicals is reminiscent of medieval Christianity. During that era, anyone not practicing the religion as formulated, interpreted, and commanded by the Church was considered a heretic and subject to imprisonment, torture, and death—death usually coming in the form of burning at the stake.

Religion and ethnicity have become driving forces toward the goals of terrorists, with politics taking a back-row seat. Of course religion and politics have an unusual, often symbiotic, relationship. Isn't religion, in some ways, political? Hiding behind the veil of religion, terrorists have a certain given immunity in the United States, for instance, invoking their Constitutional first amendment right of freedom of religious expression. Accordingly, if certain religious practices are not followed, fanatics can cite religious dogma to rationalize, perhaps justify, actions deemed to be against the laws of man. The mantra is "God has said to destroy evil. My god is better and stronger than your god [though in monotheism, there is but one God, as major religions teach] and if you do not follow my beliefs, you must be a nonbeliever. If you are a nonbeliever you must be evil and a follower of Satan and must be destroyed." Thus, violence is justified to eradicate evil as seen through the eyes of radicalized religious zealots.

Suicide Bombing as a Terrorist Ideology

During the Algerian fight for independence from France during the late 1950s, a pattern of placing bombs in public places was established by the freedom fighters. Most often, the bombs were placed in restaurants or markets by women who simply placed the bomb under a counter and quietly walked away and were far from the location when the bomb exploded. This method was found to be very effective and eventually led to independence for Algeria. In the natural evolution of warfare and bombing tactics, the next step was the concept of suicidal bombing.

Suicide bombers, such as the 9/11 terrorists, do not identify themselves as suicide bombers, but rather as courageous soldiers seeking self-chosen martyrdom. They see themselves as victims, not aggressors, in their war against nonbelievers, and view themselves as being at war. They may even see a suicide bombing as the next last great adventure in the name of their religion and for their God. But they are wrong; death is everlasting and cannot be considered an adventure, especially by the victims who stand face-to-face with it. In one bombing in Pakistan, the only thing remaining of the bomber was his head, which was still recognizable enough for identification and photographing for a newspaper. Was it possible he went to paradise headless, if he went at all? There are those who will say he went to paradise; others, especially the friends and family of the victims, say he was from hell and was returned there. All a matter of ideological belief.

Police Protect from Harm

"The United States is a nation free from the notion of George Orwell's 'thought crime.' In America, one may think whatever one likes, however bigoted, misinformed, or absurd it may be. However, it is not a nation free from 'action crime.' In the United States, it is still against the law to do things to harm another person."*

Call it duty, honor, courage, or commitment, but police officers, the front line against those who would bring harm to others, including terrorism of all stripes, will knowingly and willingly take head-on the dangers that threaten their community, their country, and their values and principles. Former British prime minister, the late Winston Churchill, noted, "The truly great aspects of the human condition are fundamentally simple—freedom, justice, honor and duty. And the most defining human quality … courage." And as Agis said in 427 B.C., *"The Spartans do not inquire how many the enemy are, but where they are."*

Commitment in Response

The best response to a terrorist threat—real, potential, or threatened—is preemptive or proactive. The primary responsibility for terrorist attack

---

* Sweeny, Amanda, www.cavalierdaily.com/2009/11/12/freedom-from-harm (accessed December 6, 2009).

prevention lies with policy makers, law enforcement, intelligence agencies, and first responders. Policy makers are positioned to address issues confronting them by terrorists and are responsible for decisions laying the groundwork for conditions spawning terrorism. Policy makers must be more pragmatic than dogmatic when dealing with questions of culture, religion, politics, and economic practices.

Law enforcement at all levels of political jurisdiction must continue to investigate activities that may be linked to terrorist movements, training, and planning. A large question looming over a violent incident is: Is this merely an accident, a criminal act, or the result of a planned terrorist strike? One answer to that question is to determine the intent or motive of the person(s) responsible for the act. Other aspects to be determined are the means of the carrying out of the act, and how was the opportunity afforded?

Often the smallest clue or incident will lead to a major terrorist arrest or provide information that will derail a terrorist objective. Three cases in point: Timothy McVeigh, the Oklahoma City federal building bomber, was caught as result of a traffic violation. The 2001 airplane bomb attacks in New York and Washington, D.C., could have been prevented if the clues had been given proper attention. A series of common service station robberies in Southern California were later determined to be linked to a terrorist organization.

Intelligence agencies have a responsibility to assemble and decipher information and data usable to law enforcement agencies and policy makers to provide them with the latest assessments and conclusions for strategic and tactical planning.

First responders to a terrorist incident are normally police patrol officers, medical personnel, and hazardous material handlers. They must be trained to recognize evidence of terrorist participation in a crime scene, accident, or hazardous material conditions that have the potential for immediate harmful consequences or long-range planning for a future terrorist attack.

Border Security

Even prior to 2001 it was recognized that the United States had over ten thousand very porous miles of border. Smuggling of commodities (mostly drugs and people) could easily be accomplished by airplane and boat, or simply sneaking past checkpoints in car or on foot through tunnels, across deserts, or over mountains. Immigration (especially from the south) was such that the U.S. Customs and Immigration Services plus the Border Patrol were in a state of merely "sticking a finger in the dike" to slow the trend.

After the 2001 terrorist attacks on the homeland, America reacted with broader and stricter enforcement of the immigration laws and demanded a more secure border against the alarming stream of illegal entry. Not only did the federal and state governments rush to reinforce the men, women, and technology guarding the peaks, valleys, deserts, oceans, roads, streets, air travel, and railways along the borders, but American citizens in a form of *posse commitatus* formed citizen groups to help stem the tide of illegal entry.

The question of immigration and illegal entry into the United States is a major issue facing American politicians on all governmental levels. The impact is felt by people in nearly every aspect of daily life: social programs, education, employment, and infrastructure services such as medical and health care, law enforcement, utility power, traffic congestion and other necessities provided by the government and the American taxpayer for quality of life matters.

With literally hundreds of thousands of people legally entering and exiting the United States on a daily basis, the task of sorting out the terrorists, saboteurs, and others who would wreak destruction and havoc on the nation has become monumental. In addition, taking into consideration the potential of crossing into the United States through illegal means, the potential for plotters to engage in destructive activities grows by exponential numbers. A project costing millions of dollars was the building of a border fence and the installation of bright lights along the U.S.-Mexico border, similar in concept to the building of the Great Wall of China to keep out the Mongols.

A wall was built separating East and West Berlin, Germany, in 1962 to keep the East Berliners from crossing into West Berlin. That fence kept out only those unable to find a way around, under, or over the wall. Though it stood as a great deterrent, those with a strong enough will and body were able to find ways to compromise the intent of the Soviet communists and escaped to West Berlin in spite of all efforts and obstacles against them, including shooting those attempting to cross the line to freedom and a better life. The Great Wall of China still stands, but the Mongols invaded anyway through various methods; the Berlin wall came down in a flurry of freedom and enthusiastic liberty. The same will, perhaps, be said in the future about the border fence between the United States and Mexico.

It has been said that a good fence makes for good neighbors. This may be true in small neighborhoods, but between nations a fence is intended to keep out unwanted people. The U.S.-Mexico border fence has been successful in some ways, in that it keeps out the less than daring and strong and funnels a great majority of border crossers to official border crossing points where their papers and credentials are examined.

The Border Patrol, on horseback, on foot, in helicopters, and on all-terrain vehicles, maintain a rigorous watch through the back country of the mountains and deserts and have detected and captured high numbers of individuals (led by people smugglers known as coyotes). However, an unofficial guessed estimate would say that well over 99% of the people caught in this law enforcement effort are the job seekers and "the tired, the poor, the huddled masses." But the web is closing, so that anyone intending to enter the United States with a motive of causing death and destruction faces very limited opportunities.

Criminals and terrorists have been deterred and captured at legal border crossing checkpoints, as well as the illegal routes used by smugglers for generations. The highly successful endeavors of the Border Patrol (greatly increased in manpower, but still inadequately staffed) and the U.S. Customs and Immigration Service have been in the forefront of homeland security with many far-reaching and beneficial consequences.

Travel Restrictions

Historically, travel between the United States, Canada, and Mexico has been open for citizens of the United States. Effective in May 2009, passports became required documents that all travelers between these countries must possess.

Since immediately after the bombings of 2001, travel restrictions include airline passenger screening consisting of removal of shoes, belts, jewelry, jackets, and everything else falling just short of strip searches and examination of body cavities. Everything and everyone must pass through metal detectors and are subject to questioning by security monitors. Items considered for passenger cosmetic use, such as makeup, toothpaste, shampoo, and other liquids (not exceeding 3 ounces), must be in one zip-locked type baggie.

The U.S. Department of State has established various websites providing travelers with the latest in travel alerts and information to make their trips successful and safe. These sites include traffic regulations and criminal laws, medical care facility protocols, and various other avenues that will be of concern to the American traveler in various countries. The State Department also sponsors information that a traveler must know in the event of emergencies while abroad, for example, medical insurance coverage and medical evacuation, should it become necessary, locations of embassies, procedures and policies in the event of a terrorist attack, etc.

Borders, airports, and seaports have become security lockdowns with extreme Customs inspections of persons and commodities entering the United States. Inspections of cargo destined for the United States from foreign ports are carried out prior to shipment.

Homegrown Terrorists

Unfortunately, however, "the number, variety and scale of recent U.S. cases suggest 2009 has been the most dangerous year domestically since 2001."* This *Los Angeles Times* article of December 7, 2009, highlighted several instances wherein the number of major arrests of Americans accused of plotting with al-Qaeda and allies to deploy bombs in New York and elsewhere showed a steady increase. Homeland Security Secretary Janet Napolitano provided some insight in a strongly worded speech about the threat of radicalized homegrown terrorism. "We've seen an increased number of arrests here in the U.S. of individuals suspected of plotting terrorist attacks or supporting terror groups abroad such as Al Qaeda.... Home-based terrorism is here. And, like violent extremism abroad, it will be part of the threat picture that we must now confront."†

One page of the *Los Angeles Times* (May 13, 2009, p. A-10) carried two stories. In "5 Convicted in Terrorism Trial" (dateline: Miami), five Florida men were convicted of trying to join an al-Qaeda plot to blow up the Chicago Sears Tower and to place bombs in government buildings. The second story, with a dateline from New York, convicted a man on twelve counts of attempting to set up an al-Qaeda weapons training camp in Oregon.

In New Jersey, Americans were convicted of plotting to attack the military base at Fort Dix. In Minnesota it is believed that young adventure-seeking Somali boys living in Minnesota are being recruited to join terrorist groups in Somalia. In October 2008, an American Somali boy from Minnesota was the first American terrorist to be engaged as a suicide bomber. The bomb he carried killed thirty people in Somalia.

Timothy McVeigh, Theodore Kaczynski, and Jose Padilla are possibly the three most well-known American citizen terrorists. But they do not have a monopoly on being the only homegrown terrorists in America. In the United States there are quasi-military groups known as militias who train with explosives and firearms in anticipation of "restoring" America's freedom. We also have hate groups such as the Ku Klux Klan and the neo-Nazi movements. A certain militant brand of environmentalists has been classified as ecoterrorist for their methods, including the use of arson and explosives. On the same list of "single issue" terrorists are the antiabortion militant movements.

---

* Rotella, Sebastian, "A U.S. Strain of Extremism May Be Rising," *Los Angeles Times*, December 7, 2009, p. A-1.
† Ibid., pp. A-1, A-12.

Conclusion

Terrorist issues in contemporary America have shown a very wide spectrum of colors, from immigration concerns to the recruitment of suicide bombers. As long as there are people harboring emotions of hate, revenge, or fundamentalist ideology to force upon someone else, there will be those who will take it upon themselves to be the sword that delivers their message in body count and fear. They are the apocalyptic horsemen who will deliver death to all who are not in strict compliance with their own dark-sided version of life, death, and death thereafter. And there will be those who bravely are committed to stand for freedom and choice, and will place themselves between the danger and innocent noninvolved citizens, the victims of the hate-mongering jackals of terrorism.

On that early September morning in 2001, as the flames engulfed him, the police officer answered his last call to duty, honor, and commitment. On that day, which will live forever in the minds of freemen everywhere, that officer and many others gave their lives so that the truly great aspects of humanity will forever be shining.

> If one seeks peace and can be fiercely honest with oneself and the reality of life, one will undoubtedly find the place of strength, courage, and wisdom to live the life one seeks.
>
> **—Leslie Moses**

Homeland Security
What Everyone Can Do. Deter! Detect! Disrupt!

16

BART BECHTEL

Contents

Surveillance: The Weakest Link

> … that the personal security and order that is usually a basic assumption of public life cannot in fact be taken for granted in a world where terrorist acts exist.
>
> —**Mark Juergensmeyer,** *Terror in the Mind of God: The Global Rise of Religious Violence*

While most of the following is in the context of terrorist activity, it pertains equally to nonterrorist criminal acts, such as street crime, drugs, and gang activities. Securing the homeland is everyone's responsibility. There are not enough law enforcement personnel at any levels to accomplish this gigantean task. Each of us must contribute as much as we can. Frequently, ordinary citizens ask, "What can I do?" The answer may seem obvious, but to many it is not.

Consider the fact that the majority of crimes are solved not through investigation, but rather from information provided by ordinary citizens. That is right, the average person on the street. Have you ever thought about the frequency with which law enforcement reaches out to the community for information and tips? Hotlines are established and rewards offered. Think also about various crime-solving and prevention methods embraced across the country: community policing, law enforcement citizen academies, Drug Abuse Resistance Education (DARE), Neighborhood Watch™ programs, amber alerts, crime solver telephone tip lines, etc. In virtually every community, there is one program or another that involves citizens supporting law enforcement. A common thread that runs through many of the programs is vigilance.

This chapter will concentrate on that one aspect of what citizens can contribute, even without special training. As noted above, vigilance is a key ingredient. We will explore what vigilance means, why we need it, and how we achieve it.

The price of freedom is eternal vigilance.

—Thomas Jefferson, third president of the United States (1743–1826)

The *Random House Webster's College Dictionary* defines *vigilance* as "the state or quality of being vigilant; watchful." The same dictionary defines vigilant as: "1. keenly watchful to detect trouble, wary. 2. ever awake and alert." Reality is that none of us can be "ever awake." But, in the aggregate, we can keep many eyes and ears open around the clock.

First, let us take a look at a program most everyone is familiar with or has heard of, Neighborhood Watch. Simply put, Neighborhood Watch is a nationwide program of groups of neighbors looking out for each other, not snooping or spying on each other. These groups gather, meet with local law enforcement, get training, and keep a watch over each other, their homes, and property. It does not mean being nosey. It means staying vigilant for trouble in its many forms.

Now, imagine every neighborhood (residential, commercial, industrial, and recreational) doing the same thing. This would greatly assist law enforcement and help secure the homeland. Think of the millions of pairs of eyes and ears that could aid in the fight against terrorism and crime.

> As we face one of the most serious challenges to the American way of life, law enforcement agencies across the country are prepared to meet the challenge, and do their part in the fight against terrorism. We have transformed Neighborhood Watch by giving it a new mission—secure the homeland by encouraging, promoting, and empowering people, to get involved in their communities, through Neighborhood Watch....
>
> The Neighborhood Watch™ Program is an excellent way for all the residents of our country to become involved in the fight against terrorism and help law enforcement. We are counting on your help to succeed, please join the effort.
>
> **—Aaron Kennard, Executive Director, National Sheriff's Association[1]**

Why must we be vigilant? To answer this question, I will illustrate the terrorist and criminal planning methodology. Though I will illustrate it in a structured fashion, you must understand that is fluid and dynamic. The steps are not always linear and can actually be occurring simultaneously.

Terrorist/Criminal Planning Phases

1. Preliminary target selection
2. Initial surveillance
3. Final target selection
4. Preattack surveillance
5. Operational planning
6. Rehearsal and practice
7. Execution
8. Escape and exploitation

As noted above, some of these phases may be concurrent, but they exist. Even a petty street criminal plans his criminal act. He may have decided on an operational site, with which he is already very familiar, waiting until his victim (target) appears in the operational zone, then attacking and escaping. In the foregoing, the rehearsal may be mental or could have been a previous attack.

In testimony before the House of Representatives Committee on International Relations in May 2000, Assistant Secretary of State for Diplomatic Security David Carpenter remarked about protective measures under way for U.S. diplomatic facilities abroad:

The newest addition to our programs and of major significance has been the establishment, in less than one year, of surveillance detection programs at almost all of our overseas posts. *A critical lesson learned from the bombings is that there is intense surveillance conducted against our facilities prior to an attack.* Since going operational in January 1999, surveillance detection teams, most of which work with host government's security services, have observed over 700 suspected incidents of surveillance against our personnel and facilities. It has, in a sense, expanded our security perimeter and zone of control beyond our previous limitations. (italics added)

In another instance, Missouri Homeland Security Coordinator Paul Fennewald stated:

In every terrorist attack that I have either responded to, or are familiar with, terrorists have conducted extensive surveillance of their targets prior to the terrorist attack.... This surveillance activity is one of the few easily recognized, but often overlooked indicators that terrorists are planning an attack. The ability for both law enforcement and our critical infrastructure partners to recognize this activity is key to preventing terrorism.[2]

How do we know this? Simply, we asked criminals and terrorists. Also, we have terrorist training manuals. Below are excerpts from the translated al-Qaeda training manual. The manual was located by the Manchester (England) Metropolitan Police during a search of an al-Qaeda member's home. The manual was found in a computer file described as "the military series" related to the "Declaration of Jihad" (see Chapter 3).

Methods of Gathering Information Using Covert Means

The Military Organization may obtain secret information using:

1. Surveillance, intelligence, and observation
2. Theft
3. Interrogation
4. Excitement
5. Drugging
6. Recruitment

A. Surveillance, Intelligence, and Observation

Civilian and military targets (personalities). The monitoring may be done on foot or by car.

Goals of an Agent:

1. find a place for a secret meeting
2. locate a 'dead box'
3. carry out "secret watching" [surveillance]
4. destroy the target

Instructions/tips on how to go after target and not get caught: how to observe a house and Perticular [*sic*] Target[3]

Criminals and terrorists conduct surveillance to gather information about a target to determine if in fact the target is a viable one. Unlike common criminals, terrorists are less hurried. Time is on their side. They are patient. Surveillance may occur over extended periods, sometimes years. While patience and extended careful surveillance may be advantageous, it may work against them. There is more of a chance that they will make mistakes, exposing the surveillance and making them vulnerable to detection. Keep in mind that if a surveillant can see its target, the surveillant can be seen. It is just a matter of knowing when and where to look.[4]

Now, what does surveillance mean to you and your contribution to homeland security? More than you might imagine. Actually, what it means is you need to conduct *surveillance detection*. This is a proactive undertaking where you, as an individual, or as part of a group/team, look for people conducting surveillance. You are looking for people gathering information/intelligence, to plan for an attack against a person, place, or thing. That is it, in a nutshell.

Surveillance detection is critical to identifying hostile acts in the planning. If you look back at the planning phases, you will see that there are at least two and usually three opportunities to detect surveillance. The first and usually the easiest to detect is the initial surveillance. The second is the preattack surveillance, which occurs when the terrorist or criminal wants to verify that little or nothing has changed since the initial surveillance. The third opportunity to impede an attack is to detect the rehearsal for the operation. Failing this, if the operation moves into the actual attack phase, there is a very high chance it will succeed, or put another way, there is a low percentage chance the victim will survive. The odds are not good.

> It is very unlikely that you will see clearly what you take no trouble to look for.
>
> **—J.-J. Rousseau,** *Émile*

How does the average citizen conduct surveillance detection? Many people already do so without knowing it. Most people are generally familiar with their neighborhood. They know who lives next door, what cars belong to which residences, and what the daily routines are for many of the residents. If not, this is the starting point. If you do not know your neighbors, introduce yourself. You do not need to be nosey, just become acquainted. Observe who drives which vehicles. Note license plates. You may even want to photograph or video record your neighborhood. Doing even one of these things will make it easier for you to spot when something is out of the norm. Learn which of your neighbors work away from their residence during the day or night. The same goes for those who stay at home during the day.

When an unfamiliar person or vehicle enters or traverses your neighborhood, pay attention! Get a good description. Write it down, or at least make a good mental note and include the date and time of the sighting. This may be useful information for law enforcement should some crime or disturbance take place that requires investigation. If you observe something strange or troubling, report it to law enforcement. *Unless it is an emergency, do not use 911.* Call the regular business number, which you should have handy by your telephone. *Do not confront a suspicious person or persons.*

As you drive in and out of your neighborhood, pay attention to things along the routes you travel. Learn alternate routes, in case of some form of traffic disruption (construction, roadwork, emergency services operations, etc.). Make note of the conditions of yards and upkeep of properties, especially any unexplained deterioration. Learn which properties are owner occupied, rentals, vacation, or seasonally occupied homes. If you notice a broken window or open door in a property, consider whether it may be accidental, weather related, or perhaps the result of vandalism or crime. If the latter, notify your local law enforcement so they can investigate. Keep an eye out for people loitering or congregating in an area that is out of the norm. If you see this, especially if cars drive by slowly or stop for a short period and someone approaches the car, then the car drives off, it could be an indication of drug dealing. *Do not follow the car.*

If you jog or take walks around your neighborhood or walk your dog, consider varying the times of these activities, if possible. It will give you different snapshots of your area. What cars are in the driveways at what time of day? You will be able to observe when people leave their homes and return. By consciously observing your surroundings, you will quickly learn what is ordinary and what is extraordinary. When you observe the latter, think about it, ask: Why is it different. Is there a reasonable and nonthreatening explanation? If you cannot come up with a good answer, call law enforcement and explain your concern. The worst thing that can happen by doing this is that there is nothing wrong. The best thing that can happen is that there is nothing wrong.

History has shown that terrorist attacks do not occur in a vacuum. Attacks are organized and planned weeks, months, or sometimes years in advance. *The planning stage is the best opportunity to prevent attacks.*

Many domestic terrorists/extremists are relatively easy to detect. Warning signs include distinctive dress, such as uniforms and insignias, speeches, writings and videos, tattoos, and actions. Remote or guarded compounds used for assemblies and training are another indicator.

International terrorists may be more difficult to detect and may exhibit fewer warning signs than domestic groups and individuals.

Potential Indicators of Terrorist Preparations

Civilians, like law enforcement, should be alert to many other indicators, including potential indicators that an individual may be planning, may be aware of others who are planning, or may be motivated to assist in conducting a terrorist attack:

Talking knowingly about a future terrorist event, as though the person has inside information about what is going to happen. Statement of intent to commit or threatening to commit a terrorist act, whether serious or supposedly a joke, and regardless of whether or not you think the person intends to carry out the action. (All threats must be taken seriously.) Statements about having a bomb or biological or chemical weapon, about having or getting the materials to make such a device, or about learning how to make or use any such device—when this is unrelated to the person's job duties. Handling, storing, or tracking hazardous materials in a manner that puts these materials at risk. Collection of unclassified information that might be useful to someone planning a terrorist attack, e.g., pipeline locations, airport control procedures, building plans, etc., when this is unrelated to the person's job or other known interests. Physical surveillance (photography, videotaping, taking notes on patterns of activity at various times) of any site that is a potential target for terrorist attack (including but not limited to any building of symbolic importance to the government or economy, large public gathering, transportation center, bridge, power plant or line, communication center). Deliberate probing of security responses, such as deliberately causing a false alarm, faked accidental entry to an unauthorized area, or other suspicious activity designed to test security responses without prior authorization. Possessing or seeking items that may be useful for a terrorist but are inconsistent with the person's known hobbies or job requirements, such as explosives, uniforms (to pose as a police officer, security guard, airline employee), high-powered weapons, books and literature on how to make explosive, biological, chemical, or nuclear devices, multiple or fraudulent identification documents. Statements of support for suicide bombers who have attacked the United States or U.S. personnel or interests abroad. [5]

Repeated use of "God" not coupled with profanity.

Use of foreign terms/phrases not in context.

Misstatements of common American terminology.

Persons seen near potential targets carrying video cameras or observation equipment with high-magnification lenses.

Persons observed with maps, photos, or diagram sketches with facilities highlighted.

Persons observed using night vision devices without logical explanation.

People observed parking, standing, or loitering in the same areas over extended periods or days.

A pattern or series of false alarms requiring law enforcement or an emergency response.

Reported thefts of military, law enforcement, or fire ID cards, license plates, uniforms, etc.

Nonmilitary persons wearing or transporting military-style weapons, clothing, or equipment.

Reports of computer hackers attempting to access sites with personal identification, maps, or other targeting examples.

Theft or unusual sale of large numbers of semiautomatic weapons.

Theft or large sale of ammunition.

Reports of automatic weapons firing.

Theft or sale of protective body armor to non-law-enforcement persons.

Paramilitary groups carrying out training scenarios.

Explosive theft or sale of large amounts of explosive powder, blasting caps, or high-velocity explosives.

Purchasing/possessing large quantities of ammonium nitrate fertilizer.

Theft or sale of containers (i.e., propane bottles, propane tanks, etc.).

Theft of explosives, explosive materials, or chemicals.

Unexplained weapons fire explosions in rural or wooded areas.

Treatment of chemical burns or missing hands/fingers.

Untreated chemical burns or missing hands/fingers.

Rental of self-storage space (for chemicals, etc.).

Delivery of chemicals to self-storage facility.

Chemical fires, toxic odors, brightly colored stains, or rusted metal fixtures in apartments, hotel/motel rooms, or self-storage units.

Rental, theft, or purchase of a 1-ton (or larger) truck or van.

Modification of truck/van with heavy-duty springs to handle heavier loads.

Physical surveillance of a potential target multiple times.

Purchase of or illegal access to target blueprints.

Theft or burglaries at army surplus stores or state surplus stores.

Rental of storage units for storage of nontraditional items (i.e., fertilizer, fuel oil, propane, etc.).

Claims of conspiracy or attacks.

Jail intelligence.

Presence of pamphlets, communiqués, flyers, etc.

Terrorist literature and manuals.

Bomb-making manuals.

Law enforcement training manuals.

Evidence of drug proceeds going to support terrorist organizations.

Large-scale drug-for-gun/explosive exchanges.

Recruiting drug dealers for political causes.

Illegally obtaining bomb-making materials.

Document fraud.

Counterfeit or altered driver's licenses.

Altered vehicle registrations and license plates.

Suspicious identification cards (all types).

Numerous places of residence that may not exist.

Possession of forged documents.[6]

With the head of the U.S. Department of Homeland Security's "gut feeling" that the country could face another terrorist attack, the Miami Police Department, on July 13, 2007, unveiled its seven signs of terrorism to educate the public about how to properly identify a potential threat. The seven signs of potential terrorism are:

Surveillance: Someone recording or monitoring activities. This may include the use of cameras—either still or video—note taking, drawing diagrams, annotating on maps, or using binoculars or other vision-enhancing devices.

Intelligence gathering (elicitation): People or organizations attempting to gain information about an important place, critical structure, its operation, or workers. An important place might be a power or water plant, bridge, school, stadium, or shopping mall. Terrorists may ask what the building is used for, about building operations, deliveries, and security-related information. Elicitation attempts may be made by mail, fax, telephone, or in person.

Tests of security: Any attempts to measure reaction times to security breaches or procedures in order to assess strengths and weaknesses.

Acquiring supplies: Purchasing or stealing explosives, weapons, chemicals, ammunition, etc. Also includes acquiring military uniforms, decals, flight manuals, passes or badges, or the equipment to manufacture such items, or any other controlled items.

Suspicious persons out of place: People who don't seem to belong in the workplace, neighborhood, business establishment, or anywhere else. Includes people wearing conspicuous clothing such as jackets or sweaters in hot weather. Also includes stowaways aboard ships or people jumping ship in port and suspicious border crossings.

Dry run/trial run: Before carrying out the final operation or plan, terrorists typically conduct a dry or trial run. A trial run consists of putting people into position and moving them around according to the plan without actually committing the terrorist act. It could also include mapping out a route to determine traffic flow.

Deploying assets: People and supplies getting into position to commit the act. This could be a person's last chance to alert authorities before the terrorist act occurs.

The list of seven signs was distributed widely throughout the United States by numerous law enforcement and homeland security elements.

On May 26, 2004, FBI Director Mueller said: "We need the support of the American people. First to cooperate when called upon, as agents will be reaching out to many across the nation to help gather information and intelligence. Second, to be aware of your surroundings and report anything suspicious."

There is no more difficult art to acquire than the art of observation, and for some men it is quite as difficult to record an observation in brief and plain language.

—William Osler, MD, *Aphorisms from His Bedside Teachings and Writings*

Developing and Enhancing Community and Private Sector Partnerships

One example of community outreach by law enforcement is a community-based counterterrorism training program launched by the Teaneck, New Jersey Police Department to empower residents to be proactive in the fight against terrorism.

The curriculum was developed by the Community Anti-Terrorism Training Institute and is titled the Community Anti-Terrorism Training Initiative (known as Cat Eyes). It is designed to help communities combat terrorism by enhancing neighborhood security, heightening the community's powers of observation, and encouraging mutual assistance and concern among neighbors. It instructs residents to watch for terrorist indicators that do not include a person's race or religion, teaches average citizens about terrorism, educates and empowers citizens, establishes a neighborhood block watch program, and educates schoolchildren. The program involves the joint efforts of federal, state, and local governments along with community residents and private companies who donate time, money, and resources. Specifically, the training provides tips on the main forms of terrorist surveillance, the profile of terrorists, and what constitutes suspicious activity. The program teaches residents to be analytical about identifying suspicious activity and to be precise and detailed in reporting any activity deemed suspicious. The reaction of those trained in the program has been consistent with the department's desired result of empowering the community to be effective participants in counterterrorism efforts at the grassroots level.

These partnerships have traditionally played a fundamental role in all facets of policing and problem solving. Enhanced community trust and cooperation can greatly assist an agency, in both identifying and addressing terrorism-related issues. Most of these systems are already in place through years of practicing community policing and neighborhood policing principles. Additionally, we can enhance overall community awareness by providing general Homeland Security training for our community members.

By working hand in hand with the community and providing this general awareness training, our citizens represent force multipliers, hence drastically increasing the volume of eyes and ears on our streets. Private sector partnerships are also extremely valuable for all law enforcement agencies for the same reasons.[7]

In the field of observation, chance favors only the prepared mind.

—Pasteur

The vigilance of all New Yorkers has kept MTA buses, subways, and railroads safe. The MTA reminds them to:

Be alert to unattended packages.
Be wary of suspicious behavior.
Take notice of people in bulky or inappropriate clothing.
Report exposed wiring or other irregularities.
Report anyone tampering with surveillance cameras or entering unauthorized areas. (http://www.mta.info/mta/security/index.html)

Following the attacks of 9/11, the Washoe County Sheriff's Office in Nevada formed a Citizen's Homeland Security Council (CHSC). This volunteer organization of over four hundred citizens studied and attended classes in a number of subjects, including, but not limited to:

Introduction to weapons of mass destruction
Hazardous materials
Acts of terrorism
Threat recognition and observation skills

Following the extensive education, the CHSC members are ready to assist the sheriff during natural or man-made disasters and special events.

The following reiterates and reinforces much of the foregoing.

Suspicious Behavior Could Indicate Terror Plotting

Anthony L. Kimery[8]

"... being able to distinguish the ordinary from the extraordinary."

Coinciding with concerns among some intelligence services that suspected Hezbollah "sleeper cells" in Canada have been activated, Canadian law enforcement authorities increasingly are training for spotting potentially suspicious activity and behavior that may indicate terrorists are conducting surveillance or other goings-on in preparation for targeting a specific structure or location for attack.

Several years ago, Robert David Steele, an outspoken veteran intelligence officer, told HSToday.us that "50 percent of the 'dots' that prevent the next 9/11 will come from bottom-up [local] level observation" and unconventional intelligence from "private sector parties."

Since 9/11, the Department of Homeland Security (DHS) and law enforcement in the Washington, DC capital region have actively urged citizens to report "suspicious activity." Mobile electronic signs urging people to report suspicious activity are routinely placed at strategic locations throughout the metro area for periods of time. The last one of these portable warnings I saw was at the convergence of Key Bridge and George Washington Memorial Parkway on the Virginia side of the Potomac River just across from Georgetown.

Lynda Howes, a civilian member of the emergency event and management unit of the Calgary (Canada) Police Service, told attendees of the "Trilateral Security Conference" in Calgary that law enforcement must learn how terrorists operate in order to prevent attacks. She said counterterrorism is only manageable if it is tackled at the grass roots level. She explained that it is vital that everyone—including the public, the police, government, and private industry—recognizes the potential indicators of terrorism and what actions to take if, and when, they are encountered.

Howes said terrorists must recruit members, research their targets, procure resources, receive, transfer and conceal money, and provide transportation and communication. And "each one of those phases represents an activity" that can be identified if a person is trained to know what to be on the look-out for. "Those activities are associated with a behavior. Once we have that behavior, those are things you and I will be witnessing every single day and are things we can pick up on as potential indicators."

In late 2002, The Air Force's Office of Special Investigations launched "Eagle Eyes," a program to "deter terrorism by recognizing and reporting pre-attack activities," according an OSI memo.

"Every terrorist act is preceded by observable planning activities," according to the OSI memo. "When troops and citizens know what to look for and how to report suspicious activity, terrorist acts can be prevented."

Department of Defense personnel have routinely been advised to report suspicious reconnoitering of military facilities, people asking detailed information about specific sites, and any other activity which could indicate a "dry run" attack. The Department of Homeland Security (DHS) says "knowing what to look for and being able to distinguish the ordinary from the extraordinary are the key elements to successful surveillance detection." ... "A persistent stream of reported suspicious incidents requires an understanding of the purpose of terrorist surveillance, to know what terrorists look for, and how they conduct surveillance operations."

DHS's advice states: "Terrorists conduct surveillance to determine a target's suitability for attack by assessing the capabilities of existing security and discerning weaknesses in the facility. After identifying weaknesses, they plan their attack at the point of greatest vulnerability." ... "Because terrorists must conduct surveillance—often over a period of weeks, months, or years—detection of their activities is possible," ... "regardless of their level of expertise, terrorists invariably make mistakes. The emphasis of surveillance detection is to key in on indicators of terrorist surveillance activities." ... "successful surveillance detection efforts require immediate reporting of incidents similar to the following:

Multiple sightings of the same suspicious person, vehicle, or activity, separated by time, distance, or direction;

Individuals who stay at bus or train stops for extended periods while buses and trains come and go;

Individuals who carry on long conversations on pay or cellular telephones;

Individuals who order food at a restaurant and leave before the food arrives or who order without eating;

Joggers who stand and stretch for an inordinate amount of time;

Individuals sitting in a parked car for an extended period of time;

Individuals who don't fit into the surrounding environment because they are wearing improper attire for the location or season;

Individuals drawing pictures or taking notes in an area not normally of interest to a tourist or showing unusual interest in or photographing security cameras, guard locations, or watching security reaction drills and procedures; and

Individuals who exhibit suspicious behavior, such as staring or quickly looking away from individuals or vehicles as they enter or leave facilities or parking areas

Other activity which should cause a heightened sense of suspicion includes:

Suspicious or unusual interest
Surveillance (suspicious in nature)
Inappropriate photographs or videos
Note-taking
Drawing of diagrams
Annotating maps
Using binoculars or night vision devices

"Terrorists may also employ aggressive surveillance techniques, such as making false phone threats, approaching security checkpoints to ask for directions, or 'innocently' attempting to smuggle nonlethal contraband through checkpoints," DHS's advice states. "The terrorists intend to determine firsthand the effectiveness of search procedures and to gauge the alertness and reaction of security personnel."

In 2004, RAND developed the book, *"Mapping the Risks: Assessing Homeland Security Implications of Publicly Available Geospatial Information,"* for the National Geospatial-Intelligence Agency, and determined that "potential attackers, such as terrorist groups or hostile governments, are more likely to [utilize] reliable and timely information … such as through direct access or observation. In addition, many types of attacks, such as those by ground parties, are likely to require detailed information for attack planning purposes (depending on the target type and mode of attack). This type of information, which mostly comes from such nongeospatial sources as engineering textbooks or human expertise on the operations of a particular type of industrial complex, is essential for attackers to have a high confidence in their plan."

But according to John Bumgarner, an 18-year veteran of special operations who has worked with most of the intelligence agencies at one time or another, and is now research director for security technology at the U.S. Cyber Consequences Unit, a non-profit research institute, it has become more and more difficult for terrorists to physically recon targets, especially in the US.

"To actually start planning very detailed reconnaissance of a building, and all the streets that go into it, and all the alleyways and everything else, that could require a lot of physical reconnaissance on the ground—it's not something that you can actually just easily do anymore," Bumgarner stressed, "especially in the post-9/11 environment where conspicuous photographing, videoing and other apparent physical surveillance can, and has—repeatedly across the nation—caused people to be detained and questioned about their activities."

"In other words," said Bumgarner, "it's gotten a whole lot harder for a terrorist to conduct the kind of conspicuous physical surveillance of a target that's necessary for conducting a large-scale or mass casualty attack."

Endnotes

1. www.usaonwatch.org/Messages/AMessageFromTheNationalSheriffsAssociation. php (accessed November 1, 2007).
2. Missouri's Office of Homeland Security, news release, May 22, 2007, www.dps. mo.gov/dps/NEWS/Releases07/May/HSSurveillanceDetectionTraining.htm (accessed November 2, 2007).
3. Al-Qaeda training manual, UK translation.
4. Critical incident solutions. (2005.) http://www.ci-solutions.net/implementation/survdetect.php (accessed November 2, 2007).
5. http://rf-web.tamu.edu/security/Security%20Guide/S5improp/Terrorism.htm (accessed August 3, 2008).
6. The list of potential indicators is by no means all-inclusive. Numerous unsuccessful attempts were made to identify original sources for the list. Sources included USDOJ material, DHS material, various law enforcement notices, and training material. The author makes no claims as to originality.
7. Christano, Bob. 2006, August. Counterterrorism and the line-level officer: Our first line of defense (pdf).
8. Kimery, Anthony L., Every eye a spy, March 30, 2008, http://hstoday.us/index.php?option=com_content&task=view&id=3932&Itemid=128.

The HUMINT Side of Competitive Intelligence

17

WAYNE TAYLOR

One of the oldest documented professions in the world is not only considered a profession but is considered an art as well. The art of espionage has been documented in the Bible, manuscripts of the Byzantine Empire, and *The Art of War* by Sun Tzu. This profession has developed over centuries, ranging from myriad clandestine collections to subtle debriefings through skillful elicitation to Internet-based spy-tech. Collection activities focused on both tactical and strategic operations providing the world-renowned chess game of cloak-and-dagger activities, pitting one intelligence service against another. Yet as capitalism began to flourish, there was no surprise that intelligence collection began to intermingle among the corporate world. As *corporate espionage* became a taboo term, the suggestion of competitive intelligence, competitor intelligence, and business intelligence began to find mild acceptance throughout the battlefields of the boardrooms, industrial complexes, and social networking events.

Before exploring the true essence of human intelligence (HUMINT) in correlation to competitive intelligence (CI), one must gain an understanding of the various forms of business-related information collection and how each may be related. The most widely referred explanation of competitive intelligence is the acquisition of publicly available information of the competitors of an individual's company to gain a distinct advantage in business. The acquisition of a competitor's critical information, such as strategic decisions, financial performance, and productivity, to name a few, is referred to as competitor intelligence. Additional information acquired that is not considered competitive in nature is referred to as business intelligence. The information acquired, no matter the title given, has strategic implications in the business environment and is considered a strategic necessity in the corporate world.

The acquisition of the information in the realm of competitive intelligence is often acquired from publicly available resources. Oftentimes, many individuals believe that competitive intelligence is collected solely from journals, articles, employment notices, Internet pages, and other written publications that may provide data points for analysis. What many fail to realize is that although collection from written publications may occur, this collection may only equal 10 to 20% of the information that exists. The other 80 to 90% is acquired through verbal communication—from interviews, lectures, webinars, and even conversations at the local coffee shop. Yes, the local coffee shop near the company headquarters is a prime collection opportunity for the HUMINT competitive intelligence collector. Whether the information is derived from written publication or HUMINT collection, the data points or information acquired is only one piece of the larger puzzle.

The analysis of the information collected and that which is unknown may oftentimes be deduced in an effort to develop an overall picture of the situation. But to understand truly how competitive intelligence works, and how HUMINT may be interwoven, one must recognize the elements of the intelligence cycle. Though controversy may exist in some circles regarding how many steps or elements may exist in the intelligence cycle, for this article we will use the following five as our accepted measure:

1. Planning
2. Data collection
3. Analysis
4. Communication
5. Decision/feedback

No matter the type of collection, the initial planning stage must be developed to guide the collection emphasis to place one ahead of his or her competition. During the planning phase, a business or organization must identify the intelligence needs and requirements one directly has of his or her competition. These intelligence gaps an organization has in turn develop the collection emphasis, which will assist in guiding the remaining elements of the intelligence cycle. In an effort to ensure success, one may desire to outline the specific requirement in detail to ensure the collection effort has the potential for success.

As the planning stage is the initial development of requirements, the data collection element is often considered the most interesting and challenging of the group. Oftentimes an individual who is collecting the information will find the necessary information in print or through electronic media. These collectors may range from professional researchers to executives to sales and independent information research specialists—all individuals who have a vested interest in collecting the competition's information and using the information to surpass the competition. As society becomes more technologically dependent, collectors are able to explore the vulnerabilities of technology and collect raw data needed for the next element of analysis.

The collection of raw information may develop piecemeal; therefore, the element of analysis is essential in understanding how the information may benefit one's business or organization. The analysis phase is able to dissect information into financial, economic, trend, risk, pattern, event, and opportunity analysis, which will assist in the strategic decision-making process. Once the information is analyzed, the information is shared with the appropriate decision makers, which will allow one to move ahead of his or her competition.

The communication of the processed or analyzed information must be packaged in a clear and concise manner, which will allow the decision makers to process the data quickly. The flow of information, the manner in which it may be presented, and the intended audience all must be considering factors while communicating the competition's information. This information will then allow the appropriate decision makers to determine the next step an organization or business must take to remain one step ahead of the competition. But one question may still remain, one question that may be asked by those in the corporate world, the tactical battlefield, or the strategic political realms: How does one know the information or the analysis of the information is truly accurate? This question opens the door for the element of HUMINT collection of competitive intelligence.

When one first thinks of competitive intelligence, an individual first thinks to rush out and attempt to acquire as much information as he or she can about his or her rival or competition. This is the first true misconception many managers have regarding the purpose of competitive intelligence. Competitive intelligence requires the collector to know his or her sources and to develop accurate assessments of both the sources and the information shared. Interesting enough is the fact that those two requirements are the same that exist for HUMINT collectors when dealing with tactical and strategic collection to support the actions and policies of a country. And just as a true intelligence professional considers two specific factors, so must a HUMINT competitive intelligence collector consider the same two factors.

In intelligence collection, time and focus are two key ingredients that must be considered prior to conducting or even accepting any collection operation. True intelligence officers do not appear as the cinema may portray. Intelligence officers use time-honed techniques to develop and acquire sources that will provide the desired raw data, which become analyzed and eventually turn into intelligence. In competitive intelligence one must determine how much time he or she is willing to spend on a project. When considering the time, a collector must identify how he or she will spend his or her time in terms of collecting raw data, how much time will be spent developing an assessment of the source and data, and how he or she will justify his or her time to the appropriate managers. In order for an individual to effectively use his or her time appropriately, the collector must develop a focused approach to the operation. When developing focus, the collector identifies exactly what he or she desires to collect. The focus allows the collector to ask the right questions while attempting to collect the raw data. The focus further allows an individual to focus on the correct sources, so that the time is used adequately.

The validation of the information collected and analyzed may be reverified through the careful art of elicitation of individuals who have either direct or indirect access to the desired information. Those who are or have been involved in HUMINT collection may have recently discovered that the advances of technology have opened vast opportunities for the HUMINT collector. Just as the aforementioned intelligence cycle had a number of elements that explain the intelligence process, the HUMINT cycle has similar elements:

1. Spot
2. Assess
3. Develop
4. Recruit
5. Manage
6. Dismiss

To best describe these steps, one must look at why this is the greatest time for the HUMINT collector. On any given day, one may find a secretary, personal assistant, office manager, or information technology professional who may go the majority of the day with little to no true human interaction. Individuals in today's society find that communication through e-mail, Internet chat, Internet dating, text messaging, and even the telephone has replaced previous face-to-face personal communication. These same individuals could go to the gas pump and never have to interact with another human being; they can go to the grocery store and use self-checkout to avoid interaction with a sales associate; and they can either do their banking online or through the automatic teller machine. The avoidance of the personal interaction leaves an unrealized psychological desire that allows the HUMINT collector an advantage against his or her unwitting subject.

Previously mentioned was the fact that the majority of information to be collected was accessible through verbal communication. At every exchange of information, or every transaction that occurs, some type of information is exchanged. Although one may not consider acquiring information during this specific time, the HUMINT collector realizes that this will soon be the environment that he or she has been patiently waiting for. The HUMINT collector will latch on to each and every word stated and each networking opportunity as an opportunity to acquire additional sources. As the HUMINT collector begins adding names and numbers to his or her Rolodex, this individual must return to identify the precise requirements in an effort to choose the correct source in which to invest time.

The HUMINT collector begins by identifying the intelligence requirements that an organization may be lacking against its competition. As with the planning phase, the individual must plan and identify the specific individual who may have the placement and access to obtain the desired information. Once an individual is identified as having the proper placement and access, the HUMINT collector may now use myriad techniques to meet and elicit a desired response from the intended target. Those involved with HUMINT understand that most individuals have a unique desire for human interaction, especially when the individual is able to speak about himself of herself or is able to speak about a subject in which he or she has a distinct interest. As the relationship develops, so does the freedom of information through skillful elicitation of conversational gates, which lead the individual into sharing information either wittingly or unwittingly. Often people consider this a form of treachery, especially because true elicitation is a serious activity that is considered a professional activity by those who understand how to employ this activity in their occupational duties. Many unsuspecting individuals find talking about themselves is self-gratifying, as they feel a sense of pride or accomplishment. Others feel they are subject matter experts in their respected fields and wish to impart their knowledge to others. And yet, there are still those who find the necessity to share information with others and gossip about situations in which they may not be actively involved.

Once the HUMINT collector is able to engage a person in conversation, he or she is able to begin developing an assessment of what makes the individual tick. This assessment explores the motivations and vulnerabilities of an individual, as well as further exploring his or her placement and access to the desired information that one is attempting to acquire. Though many desire to place a specific profile or scientific equation on how long or what measures should be used to develop assessment, the time-honored tradition of developing a friendship has continued to work throughout the world. Other techniques, such as bribery or coercion, push the collector into the realm of corporate espionage, and should be avoided.

The use of human intelligence techniques to acquire information is considered a fine line to walk by those who misinterpret the actions as corporate espionage. Corporate espionage crosses both the legal and ethical boundaries that exist in the world of competitive intelligence. For this reason, many individuals believe that HUMINT collection is the same as corporate espionage. Corporate or industrial espionage refers to the stealing of trade secrets or information, blackmail activities, bribery, and even surveillance of equipment and computer media through various technological surveillance and collection activities. As one can obviously identify, the differences between industrial espionage and HUMINT collection are often misconstrued since a well-defined line exists between these two disciplines. As a result of the blurred lanes in the road and the misinterpreted definition, many collectors have steered clear from HUMINT collection in competitive intelligence. What one must remember is that a collector is only having what some may consider an innocent conversation, and is not asking the individual to do any activity that may be construed as illegal.

As *corporate espionage* has become a taboo term among the business community, the suggestion of competitive intelligence, competitor intelligence, and business intelligence has found acceptance throughout the battlefields of the boardrooms, industrial complexes, and social networking events. This acceptance has further led to a path of human intelligence collection of competitive intelligence among our modern technologically advanced society. The time has arrived once again for HUMINT collectors to use their distinct skills, their art, their unique trade, to answer the intelligence gaps or requirements that are unknown and will place their organization ahead of the competition.

Terrorist Threats South of the Border
18

DR. JUAN A. BACIGALUPI

Contents

On the morning of September 11, 2001, America suffered a well-coordinated terrorist attack. On that morning, close to three thousand people died. While we consider the threat from Middle Eastern organizations and are vigilant against this threat, we have other threats against not only the American homeland, but against Americans worldwide. This threat originates from some of our neighbors to the south. Our country has seen attacks from Puerto Rican nationals, anti-Castro organizations, and other groups.

This chapter looks at organizations that have been involved in terrorist activities in the Americas in the past. The State Department reports, "The threat of a major terrorist attack remains low for most countries in the hemisphere. Overall, governments took modest steps to improve their counterterrorism (CT) capabilities and tighten border security, but corruption, weak government institutions, ineffective or lack of interagency cooperation, weak or non-existent legislation, and reluctance to allocate sufficient resources limited progress."[*]

In a news story published on March 31, 2008, Admiral James Stavridis, then commander of the United States Southern Command, and current commander of the U.S. European Command and NATO's supreme allied commander, Europe, stated: "We consider Latin America and the Caribbean to be potential bases for future terrorist threats to the United States and others in the Americas."[†] Part of the reason for this threat is the outlaw nature found in the hemisphere. There is extreme poverty, economic systems that rely on no-official markets, and government and law enforcement corruption. This permits terrorist organizations to thrive and establish bases within Latin America.

Foreign terrorism is not new to our country. In 1950, two members of the Puerto Rican Nationalist Party attempted to assassinate President Truman. Several years later, four Puerto Ricans entered the visitor's gallery of the House of Representatives firing numerous shots, injuring several members of Congress.[‡] Another Puerto Rican organization, the Fuerzas Armadas de Liberación Nacional (FALN), has "claimed responsibility for more than 120 bombings of military and government buildings, financial institutions, and corporate headquarters in Chicago, New York, and Washington DC, which killed six people and injured dozens more."[§] More recently, Cubans residing in the United States have been involved in bombings and assassinations, including the firing of a bazooka at the United Nations building and the car bombing of a former member of the Chilean government.[¶]

Argentina

Argentina remains a stable country. However, a recent shift toward the left suggests the possibility of increased activity. Several terrorist events in the

---

[*] Office of the Coordinator for Counterterrorism, U.S. Department of State, "Country Reports on Terrorism," April 30, 2007, Chap. 2, http://www.state.gov/s/ct/rls/crt/2006/82735.htm.

[†] "US Admiral Says Caribbean Possible Terrorist Threat," http://www.caribbean360.com/News/Caribbean/Stories/2008/03/31/NEWS0000005643.html.

[‡] Roig-Franzia, Manuel, "A Terrorist in the House," *The Washington Post Magazine*, February 22, 2004, p. W12, http://www.latinamericanstudies.org/puertorico/lolita-house.htm.

[§] Pérez, Gina M., "Fuerzas Armadas de Liberación Nacional (FALN)," *The Electronic Encyclopedia of Chicago*, http://www.encyclopedia.chicagohistory.org/pages/489.html retrieved on 2008-01-15.

[¶] Franklin, Jane, "Terrorist Network Operating Openly in the United States," *Znet Daily Commentary*, April 30, 2005, http://www.zmag.org/Sustainers/Content/2005-04/30franklin_.cfm.

past (prior to 2005) resulted in property damage and casualties. Since then, American businesses have received e-mail and bomb threats, and were at times the focus of protests and demonstrations, but actual reporting and confirmation of these types of incidents declined. Intelligence and news reports suggest that there are Hezbollah supporters and members within the immigrant Syrian and Lebanese communities of the triborder area between Brazil and Argentina.* Hezbollah and Iran remained the chief suspects for the July 18, 1994, terrorist bombing of the Argentine-Israeli Mutual Association (AMIA) that killed eighty-five and injured over two hundred people.[†] However, some news reports suggest that the perpetrators were not members of Hezbollah.

Bolivia

Bolivia is one of the poorest countries in South America. Lack of resources, corruption, and the infiltration of terrorist organizations from neighboring Peru plague Bolivia's fight against terrorist organizations. In the 1970s, Bolivia was the victim of organized terror attacks on its population. According to the U.S. State Department, "The Bolivian government released Francisco 'Pacho' Cortez, a member of the National Liberation Army (ELN), who was arrested in Bolivia after the statute of limitations on his case expired. Bolivian authorities also arrested Aida Ochoa, a suspected member of the Tupac Amaru Revolutionary Movement (MRTA), in October 2005, but then released her in early 2006."[‡] The arrest of Ochoa suggests that Peruvian terrorist organizations are extending their influence to Bolivia. The Bolivian district attorney prosecuting a gang leader allegedly responsible for the murders of three foreign tourists in Bolivia said the gang had received training from Sendero Luminoso (Shining Path). The *Global Politician* endorses the involvement of organized crime with terror organizations, stating that in "some countries of Latin America, such as Peru, Bolivia and Columbia, activity of terrorist organizations is closely tied to the Mafia."[§]

---

* Office of the Coordinator for Counterterrorism, U.S. Department of State, "Country Reports on Terrorism," *Western Hemisphere Overview*, http://www.state.gov/s/ct/rls/crt/2006/82735.htm.

† Loyola, Mario, "All along the Watchtower: The War on Terror Has Arrived in Latin America, and Is Headed Our Way," *National Review Online*, http://article.nationalreview.com/?q=MjVjMDFjMTY3MzI4M2E2YjE5MzE0YmY2MzRmOTQ1ZTY=.

‡ Office of the Coordinator for Counterterrorism, U.S. Department of State, "Country Reports: Western Hemisphere Overview," April 30, 2007, Chap. 2, http://www.state.gov/s/ct/rls/crt/2006/82735.htm.

§ Rzayev, Aliheydar, "Financing of Terror: Interconnection of Criminals and Terrorists," *Global Politician*, September 11, 2007, http://www.globalpolitician.com/23428-terror-sponsors. Retrieved 2009-03-27.

Brazil

Brazil is the largest country in South America. "Political and labor strikes and demonstrations occur sporadically in urban areas and may cause temporary disruption to public transportation." As in other countries, these demonstrations may evolve into violent confrontations between law enforcement and the perpetrators. Intelligence reports suggest that Colombian terrorist groups operate in border areas of Brazil. However, the State Department knows "of no specific threat directed against U.S. citizens across the border in Brazil at this time."*

Triborder Area (Argentina, Brazil, and Paraguay)

The governments of the triborder area have long been concerned with arms and drugs smuggling, document fraud, money laundering, and the manufacture and movement of contraband goods through this region. Hezbollah and Hamas appear to use the triborder region to raise funds by participating in illegal activities and by the participation of the numerous immigrants in the area. In "August 2008, the U.S. Southern Command and the DEA, in coordination with host nations, targeted a Hezbollah drug trafficking ring in the Tri-Border region of Argentina, Brazil and Paraguay."†

Chile

The State Department considers the potential for terrorist activity in Chile to be low. There has been some politically motivated violence among indigenous communities in southern Chile. None has affected Americans. Potential for civil disturbance is low, although demonstrations, sometimes violent, do occur.‡ A recent terrorist-related incident occurred when police arrested Miguel Tapia Huenulef for an alleged "arson attack on a private estate" and for an attack on the public defender's office in Temuco. During the arrest, the police "claim they found a stash of dangerous weapons," including "a submachine gun, ammunition clips, two grenades and bomb-making materials."§

---

* U.S. State Department, "Brazil, Country Specific Information," http://travel.state.gov/travel/cis_pa_tw/cis/cis_1072.html#country.
† Levitt, Mathew, "Hezbollah: Narco-Islamism," The Washington Institute for Near East Policy, March 22, 2009, http://www.washingtoninstitute.org/templateC06.php?CID=1257.
‡ U.S. State Department, "Chile, Country Specific Information," http://travel.state.gov/travel/cis_pa_tw/cis/cis_1088.html.
§ Witte, Benjamin, "Chile: State Seizes Mapuche 'Terrorist,'" The Patagonia Times, March 16, 2009, http://www.patagoniatimes.cl/index.php/20090316769/News/Human-Rights-Indigenous-News/CHILE-STATE-SEIZES-MAPUCHE-TERRORIST.html.

Colombia

Colombia faces a continuing terrorist threat from the Fuerzas Armadas Revolucionarias de Colombia (Revolutionary Armed Forces of Colombia—FARC), the Ejercito de Liberación Nacional (National Liberation Army—ELN), and remaining elements of the former Autodefensas Unidas de Colombia (United Self-Defense Forces of Colombia—AUC). Government action weakened Colombian-based terrorist groups. However, these groups continue their terrorist activities of murder, kidnapping, and terror. Recently, the FARC has resumed active military operations against primarily police and government targets.

The Department of State "continues to warn U.S. citizens of the dangers of travel to Colombia. While security in Colombia has improved significantly in recent years, violence by narco-terrorist groups continues to affect some rural areas as well as large cities. The potential for violence by terrorists and other criminal elements exists in all parts of the country."*

The FARC's military operations consist mostly of tactical-level encounters and the use of kidnapping and extortion. "The FARC is a terrorist group dedicated to the violent overthrow of Colombia's government. It consists of approximately 10,000-armed guerillas organized into 77 'fronts' and four urban militias. The FARC has also evolved into the world's largest supplier of cocaine.

The FARC's 10th Front is responsible for attempting to obtain control, by military force, of the Arauca Department of Colombia, an area bordering Venezuela. To support its terrorist activities, the FARC's 10th Front supplies and arranges cocaine shipments from airstrips in Venezuela and the Colombian border with Venezuela."†

The FARC suffered several significant losses in its military leadership in the last few years, resulting in a loss of members. While some reports place the group's strength at ten thousand, other estimates place the FARC's strength at only about three thousand armed combatants. They operate primarily in rural areas, but occasionally conduct operations at urban centers. During March 2009, the FARC increased attacks against government and infrastructure, causing some casualties and damage.

According to the ELN web page,‡ they first appeared in January 1965, claiming to fight against oppression from the government. This organization

---

* U.S. Department of State, Bureau of Consular Affairs, "Travel Warning," March 25, 2009, http://travel.state.gov/travel/cis_pa_tw/tw/tw_941.html.
† U.S. Department of Justice, "Associates of Colombian Terrorist Organization Charged with Conspiracy to Import Ton-Quantities of Cocaine," http://news.prnewswire.com/DisplayReleaseContent.aspx?ACCT=104&STORY=/www/story/03-20-2009/0004992200&EDATE=.
‡ http://www.eln-voces.com/index.php?option=com_content&task=view&id=131&Itemid=63.

appears to have minimal conventional military forces. Its main operations include kidnapping for ransom and attacks on petrochemical infrastructure for protection "taxes."

The AUC, known as the paramilitary forces, was formed to retaliate against the leftist guerrillas. The AUC was an elite paramilitary force, heavily armed, well organized, and of course, illegal; it was created to protect its sponsors from the threats of the guerrillas using terror. Supposedly demobilized in 2006, recent reports suggest a resumption of activities of the right-wing paramilitary forces. Included in AUC's protection methods are homicides, mutilation, and dismembering of agricultural leaders, supposedly linked to the FARC, as well as massacres designed to act as an example.

Cuba

The State Department claims that the Cuban government continued to permit U.S. fugitives to live legally in Cuba and is unlikely to satisfy U.S. extradition requests for terrorists harbored in the country. Likewise, Cuba contends that the United States does not honor extradition requests, specifically for Luis Posada Carriles, accused of being the mastermind of several assassination attempts against Castro and being involved in the mid-flight destruction of a Cubana de Aviacion aircraft with seventy passengers and crew on board.* There does not appear to be any factual basis for active participation of Cuba with terrorist organizations, and there are no guerrilla or terrorist organizations based in Cuba. However, Cuba's relationship with Iran, Venezuela, and other countries opposed to the United States suggests the possibility of links to some terrorist organizations.

Ecuador

Ecuador's greatest counterterrorism and security challenge was the presence of Colombian foreign terrorist organizations, frequently linked with narcotics trafficking organizations, along its northern border. Members of the Revolutionary Armed Forces of Colombia (FARC) and the National Liberation Army (ELN) were widely present on the Colombian side of the border and regularly entered Ecuadorian territory (generally as unarmed civilians) for rest and resupply. The Ecuadoran government discovered several training

---

* Office of the Coordinator for Counterterrorism, U.S. Department of State, "Country Reports on Terrorism," April 30, 2007, Chap. 3, http://www.stae.gov/s/ct/rls/crt/2006/82736.htm.

camps for these groups on the Ecuadorian side of the border.* During 2008, Colombia conducted an armed military incursion into Ecuadoran territory to attack a FARC military camp, resulting in the capture of several members of the guerrilla group as well as a laptop computer with substantial information of terrorist links to other countries and organizations. This incursion caused a breach in the relations between Ecuador and Colombia, as well as between Venezuela and Colombia.

Ecuadorian police suspected several small Ecuadorian groups of domestic subversion and involvement in terrorism. Of greatest concern was the estimated two-hundred-member Popular Combatants Group (GCP), a faction of the Marxist-Leninist Communist Party of Ecuador. Its members are mainly students trained in the use of firearms and low-yield pamphlet bombs, which they deployed in major cities without casualties. Also of concern were the Political Military Organization (OPM) and Alfarista Liberation Army (ELA), which were reputed to have ties with and support from Colombian narcoterrorists.† However, with a leftist president at the helm of the country, these leftist organizations will probably wither and disappear.

El Salvador

El Salvador was the only Latin American country with troops serving alongside U.S. forces in Iraq. While it continued supporting the U.S.-led coalition, the election of a leftist president will present a shift in its policies. The main terrorist organization in the country, the Frente Farabundo Marti para la Liberación Nacional (Farabundo Marti National Liberation Front—FMLN), reorganized itself after a long civil war and became a formal political party. As time passed, the FMLN candidates achieved substantial success, and in the recent presidential elections, the FMLN candidate won the presidency. The main threat faced in the cities and countryside of El Salvador is organized crime. Currently, there are no known terrorist organizations based in El Salvador.

Guatemala

Severe resource constraints of both technology and manpower, corruption, and an ineffective criminal justice system hindered efforts against

---

* Office of the Coordinator for Counterterrorism, U.S. Department of State, "Country Reports: Western Hemisphere Overview," April 30, 2007, Chap. 2, http://www.state. gov/s/ct/rls/crt/2006/82735.htm.
† Ibid.

transnational crime threats, such as drug trafficking and alien smuggling, especially through remote areas of the country.* The country remains relatively free of terror activity. In 1968, a rebel faction assassinated "Gordon Mein, ambassador to Guatemala."[†] During the 1980s numerous death squads operated in Guatemala, mainly kidnapping dissidents, torturing, and then killing them. Currently, the main threat against U.S. nationals comes from traditional criminal activity linked to the poor economic situation found in the country.

Mexico

Mexico continually works with the United States in combating illicit drug traffic. It has worked in the past on the war on terror, by trying to prevent terrorist entry into the United States through the common border. However, in recent years, the increased operations by drug cartels have resulted in numerous deaths to visitors and law enforcement officers. The U.S. State Department continued a travel advisory for Mexico due to the Mexican drug cartels engaging in an "increasingly violent conflict—both among themselves and with Mexican security services—for control of narcotics trafficking routes along the U.S.-Mexico border. Some recent Mexican army and police confrontations with drug cartels have resembled small-unit combat, with cartels employing automatic weapons and grenades. Large firefights have taken place in many towns and cities across Mexico but most recently in northern Mexico, including Tijuana, Chihuahua City, Monterrey, and Ciudad Juarez."[‡]

According to the Federal Research Division of the Library of Congress, "Mexico's government officially recognizes the existence of just three insurgent groups." Mexico's military, however, "has identified as many as 16 guerrilla bands. The best known is the Zapatista National Liberation Army (Ejército Zapatista de Liberación Nacional—EZLN), with which the government has had an uneasy truce since the insurgents staged a violent, short-lived 1994 revolt in the southern state of Chiapas. The other two are the People's Revolutionary Army (Ejército Popular Revolucionario—EPR), which operates mainly in Guerrero and Oaxaca states, and an EPR offshoot formed in 1998 called the Revolutionary Army of the Insurgent People (Ejército Revolucionario del Pueblo Insurgente—ERPI). Media reports indicate that

* Ibid.
† "List of US Diplomats Killed Abroad," *USA Today,* http://www.usatoday.com/news/world/2008-01-01-2036205597_x.htm.
‡ U.S. Department of State, Bureau of Consular Affairs, Travel alert, Mexico, February 20, 2009, http://travel.state.gov/travel/cis_pa_tw/pa/pa_3028.html (accessed March 29, 2009).

as many as 25 insurgent groups may be active in the country. Except for the EZLN, most of the insurgent groups number no more than a few dozen to a few hundred militants. Several of the guerilla bands are recent offshoots of the Popular Revolutionary Army (EPR), a leftist insurgency based in the mountainous state of Guerrero."* These organizations probably pose no threat to the United States, but could pose a threat to U.S. nationals traveling in Mexico.

Nicaragua

Nicaragua has seen a former guerrilla organization, accused of numerous terrorist acts, assume the presidency of the country in free and open elections. The Frente Farabundo Marti para Liberación Nacional (Farabundo Marti Liberation Front—FMLN) participated in a guerrilla war that resulted in thousands of deaths and damages to property during the long civil war. Since the signing of a peace agreement between the government and the FMLN, the former guerrillas used the ballot box to gain access to the government. They held mayoral positions in a many large cities, including the capital (which they lost in the 2008 election), and have done a credible job according to world observers. Many analysts consider the country may shift further left with the election of the FMLN's president.

As in other developing countries, with the decline of world economic markets, there has been an increase in petty and violent crimes in major urban centers. The State Department warns that violent crime "is increasing and petty street crimes are very common. Gang activity also is increasing, though not at levels found in neighboring Central American countries. Pickpocketing and occasional armed robberies occur on crowded buses, at bus stops and in open markets."†

Panama

The Panama Canal, as Panama's principal economic asset, could be a lucrative terrorist target that would influence world economies. FARC rebels from neighboring Colombia, as they do in Ecuador, use border areas to hide and conduct base camp operations. The State Department warns U.S. citizens that "travel to Darien Province" is dangerous. It further states that while "no

---

* Federal Research Division, Library of Congress, "Organized Crime and Terrorist Activity in Mexico, 1999–2002," p. 34, www.loc.gov/rr/frd/pdf-files/OrgCrime_Mexico.pdf.
† U.S. Department of State, Bureau of Consular Affairs, "Country Specific Information: Nicaragua," http://travel.state.gov/travel/cis_pa_tw/cis/cis_985.html.

incidents have occurred at [resorts in the Darien Province], U.S. citizens, other foreign nationals and Panamanian citizens have been the victims of violent crime, kidnapping and murder in this general area."*

Paraguay

Paraguay faces a difficult task in its triborder region. Because of the difficult terrain and isolation, it is difficult for the central or regional governments to provide adequate security within the area. Additionally, the presence of an immigrant community in the region contributed to the possible presence of Islamic terrorists using this area as a base of operations for terrorist activities. The State Department states that United States "citizens have on occasion been the victims of assaults, kidnappings, robberies, and rapes."†

The recent election of Fernando Lugo, a former Roman Catholic Bishop and strong advocate of liberation theology, shifted the political landscape of Paraguay to the left. While there are no national terrorist organizations, the fear of Islamic terrorist organizations in the triborder area continues to face the nation.

Peru

The main terrorist threat in Peru is Sendero Luminoso (Shining Path—SL). This organization's goal is to establish a leftist revolutionary government similar to those found in Cuba and other leftist countries. This organization had its heyday in the 1980s and 1990s, costing over sixty-nine thousand lives. The group suffered its major setback when the government arrested its leader, Abimael Guzman, and sentenced him to life in prison. Additionally, the number two military leader, Hector Aponte Sinarahua "Clay," also died. During the 1990s, SL suffered many setbacks and almost disappeared. However, with the growth of narcotics traffic and the decline of the world economy, the organization has reemerged.

Another revolutionary organization that in the past used terrorist tactics is the Movimiento Revolucionary Tupac Amaru (Tupac Amaru Revolutionary Movement—MRTA). Military operations of this organization decreased since 1996. It is possible that MRTA members, following the lead of the FMLN in Nicaragua, began entering legitimate political organizations of

. U.S. Department of State, Bureau of Consular Affairs, "Country Specific Information: Panama," http://travel.state.gov/travel/cis_pa_tw/cis/cis_994.html.
† U.S. Department of State, Bureau of Consular Affairs, "Country Specific Information: Paraguay," http://travel.state.gov/travel/cis_pa_tw/cis/cis_997.html.

the left. "MRTA members decided the best way to fight the war was to attack the holdings of Peru's wealthy elite, but sought to cause the least amount of injuries possible by frequently warning of its attacks in advance. Experts say Tupac Amaru has been less violent, in general, than Shining Path."* An interesting finding in this organization is the presence of U.S. citizens as part of the group. In 2000, the Peruvian judicial system found Lori Berenson guilty of conspiring to attack the Peruvian National Congress and sentenced her to twenty years in prison.†

In addition to these threats, the FARC uses remote areas of the joint Peru-Colombian borders to establish base camps and purchase weapons.‡

Suriname

Suriname's minister of justice and police claimed, in December 2007, that criminal organizations were planning attacks in Suriname. "According to the minister, there were arrests over a two-week period late in the year, and investigations had pointed to involvement of the FARC and unspecified African crime organizations."§

Trinidad and Tobago

This Caribbean island, one of the world's producers of natural gas, is the "home of one of the first attempts at violently establishing a modern Islamic extremist state in the region after the attempted Islamic coup in July 1990." The group responsible, Jama'at al Muslimeen, under the control of Imam Yasin Abu Bakr, is alive and thriving in Trinidad. Major General Gary D. Speer, former acting commander in chief of the U.S. Southern Command, in April 2002, stated: "The recent bombing outside the U.S Embassy in Peru preceding President Bush's visit is indicative that other domestic terrorist groups pose threats to the United States elsewhere in the hemisphere. These include, but are not limited to, the Sendero Luminoso (Shining Path) and

---

* Gregory, Kathryn, "Shining Path, Tupac Amaru (Peru, Leftists)," Council on Foreign Relations, September 25, 2008, http://www.cfr.org/publication/9276/.
† "Descartan modificación de condena a Lori Berenson por estado de gestación," 24 Horas Libre, September 17, 2008, http://www.24horaslibre.com/politica/1221644078.php.
‡ Office of the Coordinator for Counterterrorism, U.S. Department of State, "Country Reports on Terrorism," April 30, 2007, chap 6, http://www.state.gov/s/ct/rls/crt/2006/82738.htm.
§ "Caribbean Nations Make U.S. Terror Report," CaribbeanWorldNews, May 1, 2008, http://www.caribbeanworldnews.com/middle_top_news_detail.php?mid=692.

Tupac Amaru Revolutionary Movement (MRTA) in Peru and the Jama'at al Muslimeen (JAM) in Trinidad and Tobago."*

Venezuela

With President Hugo Chavez in power, Venezuela has distanced itself from the United States. During the Bush administration, the secretary of state identified Venezuela as a state "not fully cooperating with U.S. antiterrorism efforts. In light of Venezuela's actions, the United States imposed an arms ban." This resulted in Venezuela's contracting with Russia for the purchase of advanced aircraft and combat systems.

An individual claiming to be a member of an Islamic extremist group in Venezuela placed two pipe bombs outside the American Embassy in Caracas on October 23, 2006. Venezuelan police safely disposed of the two pipe bombs and immediately made one arrest. The investigation by Venezuelan authorities resulted in the additional arrest of the alleged ideological leader of the group. At year's end, both suspects remained in jail and prosecutors were pressing terrorism charges against them.[†]

While some in the Bush administration claimed there was a strong link between terrorist organizations and Venezuela, Organization of American States (OAS) head Jose Miguel Insulza, testifying before the U.S. Congress, stated: "There is no evidence, and no member country, including this one [United States] has provided the OAS with any such proof.[‡]

Conclusion

We must remain vigilant against all threats to our nation and to the citizens of our nation. As Admiral Stavridis said, "We consider Latin America and the Caribbean to be potential bases for future terrorist threats to the United States and others in the Americas." We must remain ever vigilant so other acts, such as those that occurred on September 11, or those acts that occurred in 1954, do not reoccur.

---

[*] Kelshall, Candyce, "Radical Islam and LNG in Trinidad and Tobago," Institute for the Analysis of Global Security, November 15, 2004, http://www.iags.org/n1115045.htm.
[†] "Country Reports on Terrorism," Chap 2, http://www.state.gov/s/ct/rls/crt/2006/82735. htm.
[‡] AFP, "OAS Chief to US CONGRESS: No Venezuela-Terrorist Link," April 10, 2008, http://afp.google.com/article/ALeqM5ipNXwHOq34tlujMqpPj9OZVXwznw.

Mexico Violence That Threatens Our Southern Border

19

Ripening Conditions for Escalated Terrorism Domestically and Internationally Immediately South of the United States

AUGUSTO D'AVILA

Contents

There are no better conditions and timing than the next five years for terrorist organizations such as al-Qaeda to take advantage of a well-planned strike against the United States or its allies. While the United States is tied down with Iraq, Afghanistan, Iran, Pakistan, and fighting al-Qaeda, people around the world watch as the United States slowly shifts its attention to a transitioning president, a nonpartisan Congress, and divisions in and among the governments of American continents. Time seems to stand still as not much of anything is being done or can be done to curb the problems and issues that plague the Americas when you consider al-Qaeda's ideology, exploitation of weakened governments, corruption, and draining governments economically through military spending. You may begin to see that we live in fragile times. Add a little more stress to the United States across its borders and you have a problem of immeasurable proportions.

If you were worried about al-Qaeda, what about drug cartels in Mexico? How could current conditions affect Mexico? Central America? South America? We will take a look at some factors involved to answer questions. We live in a world with unstable economies, high unemployment, divisive governments, corruption, anti-U.S. opinion worldwide, violent crimes and beheadings, drug cartel takeovers, a slumbering border region in South America, and the development of dictatorial governments in Central and South America with ties to communist and hostile regimes in the Middle East.

Mexico is well known for its drug production and is a main supplier of marijuana and methamphetamine to the United States, with sales estimates ranging from $13.6 billion to $48.4 billion yearly. There are about seven main cartels or organizations operating in Mexico. The Gulf, Sinaloa, and Juarez cartels are the three main players. They have about thirteen, seventeen, and twenty-one Mexican states, respectively, that they have a presence and bases in. The Tijuana cartel and Gulf cartel have merged to form the "Federation" to gain a bigger portion or territory for profit.[1] These Mexican cartels are increasing their involvement with gangs in the United States, such as the Latin Kings and Mara Salvatrucha (MS-13) for distribution in the southwest. The cartels do not care which gangs they sell to or what rivalries may come between them. They also use corruption or intimidation of law enforcement officials to make progress in their operations. Reports suggest that as many as 1,500 of 7,000 of Mexico's Investigative Agency are or have been under investigation for working for the Sinaloa cartel. Competing cartels fight for influence over law enforcement and the media, and use intimidation and murder. Murders have been on the increase in Nuevo Laredo, at approximately six hundred since 2003. Between 1800 and 1900 Mexicans were killed in related violence in the first thirty-six weeks of 2007.

Los Zetas

The Gulf cartel employs groups such as Los Zetas, Negros, MS-13, and Guatemalan Kaibiles (special forces). The Zetas, as reported, were formed by deserters of the Mexican military's Special Air Mobile Force Group (GAFES) in 1990. The Zetas are more highly trained militarily, are able to use sophisticated weapons, and conduct more complex operations. It has been reported that these soldiers were trained in the United States (unconfirmed) and then were bribed/bought to join the cartel. The Zetas membership initially included special forces, but they have recently been recruiting military, paramilitary, and civilians due to shortages. The Zetas perform assassinations, kidnappings, weapons trafficking, drug dealing, money laundering, and money collection for the Gulf cartel. They also control trafficking routes along the eastern edge of the U.S.-Mexico border. The Zetas have also trained smaller groups such as La Familia, who have carried out numerous executions in Michoacan.

Negros and Pelones

The Sinaloa cartel has its less trained but heavily armed groups also, the Negros and Pelones. The Negros have escalated attacks against police in Nuevo Laredo and are at battle with Los Zetas.

Violence on the Rise

One of the major battlegrounds for the drug cartels has been across the border from El Paso, Texas, in Juarez. The situation has increasingly gotten worse. As for intimidation, its police chief was forced to resign after receiving a threat that one policeman per day would die if he did not resign.[2] Plaguing the battle to disrupt the cartel is the level of corruption found among Mexico's military and paramilitary forces, making it all the more difficult to control the cartels and eliminate the violence and murders. Deaths related to drug trafficking have doubled from 2,275 in 2007 to 5,207 in 2008, mostly attributed to La Familia. La Familia left its calling card at a nightclub after decapitating and tossing five heads on the dance floor, claiming, "The family doesn't kill for money. It doesn't kill women. It doesn't kill innocent people, only those who deserve to die. Know that this is divine justice."[3] La Familia uses decapitations with messages in an intense propaganda campaign to intimidate, terrorize, and inhibit action by the local authorities. News of its activities has appeared on national news, Internet videos, and half-page advertisements in newspapers.

Mexican drug cartels are sending assassins into the United States to kill Americans to the point that Phoenix, Arizona, has now become the kidnapping capital of America, with 370 in 2008.[4] Already there is a list published of Americans and law enforcement who are targeted for assassination. Killings, kidnappings, firefights, and home invasions are happening more frequently here and across the border from Texas to California. No longer is the threat across the ocean, or across the border, it has arrived at our doorstep.

References

1. Cook, C. W. 2007. *Mexico's Drug Cartels*. CRS Report for Congress.
2. Cuevas, M. 2009. Nine bodies found in common grave near Ciudad Juarez, Mexico. CNN. www.cnn.com/2009/WORLD/americas/03/14/mexico.bodies.found/
3. Grayson, G. W. 2009. La familia: Another deadly Mexican syndicate.
4. Webster, M. 2009. Phoenix and Tucson police report over 400 kidnappings of Americans by Mexicans.
5. Anderson, C. 2008. *U.S. officials fear terrorist links with drug lords*. Associated Press Writer.

Common Chemicals as Precursors in Constructing Improvised Explosive Devices

Tools for Locating Bomb Makers and Their Clandestine Labs

20

RICHARD J. NIEMANN

Contents

Introduction

Bombings account for more than 75% of terrorist activities.[1] Explosives are the single most common weapon used by terrorists. The world has witnessed an increase in the loss of life and property as a result of terrorists who have demonstrated their intentions to generate devastation upon a populace that disagrees with their schema or ideology. Evidence of their acts, with the use of improvised explosive devices (IEDs) as a common theme among terrorists

Figure 20.1 Common houehold products can be used to manufacture explosive material.

causing death, wide destruction, and fear, is played nightly on television, over the Internet, and in newspapers and magazines.

In the United States, typically there are only three venues to obtain or exert control over explosive materials: military magazines, commercial blasting companies, and the construction of the IED (utilized most often by the criminal terrorist). The acquisition of materials to build IEDs can be found among household items commonly available at every hardware, grocery, or drug store in the nation. All that is needed is a basic understanding of chemistry and electricity, some basic tools to formulate and construct the device, and a recipe book that outlines the process of combining the proper mixtures of materials (Figure 20.2).

The Internet offers the terrorist a virtual university in which to obtain his bomb-making degree. Information can be obtained that covers all aspects of building improvised explosives as well as lists of the materials needed. The Internet provides terrorists with forums in which to meet and exchange ideas as well as venues to ask questions and trade manuals, articles, and movies showing the proper method of constructing IEDs.[2]

An improvised explosive device can be constructed to look like almost anything since the devices are constructed from everyday materials as nonconventional devices. IEDs are used to harass, incapacitate, injure, or kill enemy combatants or a civilian population by using explosives or a combination of weapons of mass destruction (WMD) compounds to achieve mass casualties. The strength of the device is in the shape, size, container, and

Figure 20.2 Easily purchased materials and common products found in most homes can be combined to make flammable and improvised explosive devices (IEDs).

functioning method that distinguish one device from another, as well as the abundant array of delivery methods. The more sophisticated and experienced the builder, the harder it is to detect these devices, and therefore they become extremely deadly.[3] The availability of precursors found in common chemicals and the vast amounts of material that illustrate how to construct IEDs make the ability to fabricate such a device easily obtainable by a terrorist. The only missing ingredient is imagination on the builder's part.

The intention of this chapter is to address the availability of common chemicals as precursors to IEDs in a manner that will increase the awareness of public safety personnel and first responders to an acceptable level of recognition and will assist in detecting a clandestine bomb-making facility. The basis of this chapter is aimed at securing the homeland from further attacks by terrorists through recognition, early detection, awareness, and understanding of terrorist tactics and methods.

Terrorist Cells

Modern terrorist organizations are formed with all the planning and organization that can be found in some of the most successful businesses; these terrorist organizations have rules and regulations as well as financial investors that facilitate the life of the organization. Within the organizational structure of the terrorist organization are two sections: (1) an operations section, where leadership and active terrorists are responsible for planning and carrying out attacks, and (2) the support section, which is responsible for recruiting new members from the pools of sympathizers along with the raising of financial resources to fund activities. Additionally, the support section is responsible for disseminating the group's ideological information (propaganda) through venues like the Internet and other news media outlets.

The structure of an operational terrorist organization is considered a cell and usually consists of no more than three to five operatives. The cellular design (similar to the communist party cells of the 1950s) eliminates the extent of damage to the overall organization, which their exposure by a counterterrorist unit would cause if they were infiltrated. The compartmental design, while not an accident, ensures that no person can identify more than a few fellow terrorists should the cell become compromised. This in turn eliminates a certain amount of damage should the cell become compromised, disrupted in any fashion, or arrested by the authorities.

Currently the military has seen an increase in multifunctional cells[4] found in antigovernment and extremist movements. These member cells, having skilled operatives among their ranks, are trained in and have resorted to guerrilla warfare; they operate independently in small cohesive units, move undetected, and conduct violent attacks with no warning or detection, in hit-and-run operations, and then slip back among the populace.

Counterterrorism analysts base classification of terrorist attacks on the objectives of the terrorists. Common objectives of terrorist groups are recognition, corrosion, intimidation and provocation, and insurgency support operations, like most of the operations currently being conducted in Iraq and surrounding areas. Terrorist organizations have very clear-cut objectives and goals; however, they must utilize tactics that they can successfully accomplish within their financial limitations. In order to achieve the maximum "bang for the buck," terrorists and terrorist organizations often choose explosives and bombings. Bomb attacks offer the terrorist a tremendous amount of options since bombs can be detonated in a number of ways, from exploding on impact to time-delayed or even remote detonations. Bombs offer the terrorist a number of ways to make their political or religious statement. Terrorists utilize bombs for various reasons, including:

- Explosives can be acquired at very low costs, and device manufacturing and construction require little technical expertise.
- Precursors are readily available in every hardware and drug store in the nation.
- "How to" manuals are easily attainable over the Internet and in various jihadist forums, including print.

- There is a little chance of getting caught since bombings are attacks that are clandestine in nature. A sophisticated device offers anonymity to the bomber if detonated by time delay or remotely.
- Bombings as a tactic guarantee terrorists and their organization the greatest chance of media coverage from an explosion.[5]

Acquiring Precursors

Precursors are chemicals that are available in many forms and have a wide variety of uses when used as sold; however, they also serve a dual role as primary or secondary ingredients in the construction of improvised explosive devices. Most precursor chemicals are regularly found around residential homes and can be acquired legally through a variety of stores, including hardware stores, drug stores, beauty supply chains, and big box stores like Sally Beauty Supply®, Home Depot®, and Radio Shack®.

Common, everyday chemicals, when used as designed, have a legitimate purpose and offer many conveniences; however, when utilized in a manner to manufacture improvised explosives devices, which they were not designed for, they become precursors and quickly become an immediate threat to the homeland and everyone's community. Table 20.1 represents a list of precursors that are commonly acquired by terrorist bomb makers to build improvised explosive devices.

Table 20.1 represents a list of precursor chemicals used in making improvised explosive devices. Law enforcement officers should utilize the list as a reference from which to draw additional information during investigations.

Being aware that these chemicals, when acquired by terrorist bomb makers, can represent a hazard since they are chemicals needed to construct

Table 20.1 Precursor Chemicals

Acetone	Glycern	Perchloric acid
Ammonia	Iodine	Peroxide
Benzene	Lead	Silver
Butane	Mercury	Sulfuric acid
Ethylene	Methane	Toluene
Ether	Nitric acid	Urea
Glycol		

Note: This chart represents a list of precursor chemicals used in making Improvised Explosive Devices. Law Enforcement officers should utilize the list as a reference from which to draw additional information during investigations.

improvised explosive devices should immediately send up a red flag to first responders, law enforcement, and public safety personnel that terrorist activity is occurring or that the location is a possible clandestine bomb-making laboratory. First responders coming into contact with subjects that have a sufficient quantity of any of the items or materials previously identified for which there is no logical explanation for their legitimate possession or use should raise a red flag that will assist law enforcement first responders in developing a reasonable suspicion to make further inquiry as to their possession.[6] Law enforcement officers understanding the basic components needed to construct and assemble an IED, as well as materials that can be construed as precursors, will produce a starting point to further investigate what the legitimate need is for a particular person or persons to be in possession of such items like the chemicals in the table above, or tools, electrical wire, circuit boards, cannon fuse, soldering tools and flux, liquid nails, pipes and end caps, ball bearings or nails, and manuals that detail how to construct explosive devices.

Timothy McVeigh manufactured a vehicle-borne explosive device (VBIED) from a product called ANFO, which is ammonium nitrate and fuel oil; ammonium nitrate is used extensively in the farming community. ANFO was the main ingredient used in fabricating an explosive device that caused significant property damage and death to the occupants of the Murrah building in Oklahoma City.[7]

Improvised explosive manuals like the *The Mujahideen Explosives Handbook: Organization for the Preparation of the Mujahideen* covers various aspects of where, how, and what precursor material is required to build an assortment of improvised explosive devices, from military to commercial explosives, by combining several mixtures that include two main ingredients, an oxidizer and a fuel.[8] The manual compiled by Abdel-Aziz, aka *Sanna 'Al Qannabel* ("Bomb Maker") offers the untrained terrorist and explosive maker a concisely articulated method of what is required to build an IED, as we can see from the following quote taken from the manual:

1. Theory of Explosives
    2.8 The theory of mixes
        A good mixture must contain 2 main substances. The first must be rich in Oxygen and the second must be able to react very fast so that it changes and multiplies its volume. This is what we call explosives.
        2.8.1 Good producers of Oxygen (O)
            1. Potassium Chlorate (KClO3).
            2. Potassium Nitrate (KNO3)
            3. Ammonium Nitrate (N2H4O3)
            4. Potassium Permanganate (KMNo4)
            5. Sodium Chlorate (NaCio3)

2.8.2 Makers of good reaction with Oxygen (O)
1. Aluminum (Al) powder
2. Magnesium (Mg) powder
3. Mixture of Carbon (C) and Sulphur (S)
4. Mixture of Carbon (C) and Sugar
5. Mixture of Carbon (C) and Wood
6. Mixture of Flour and Starch[9]

What is apparently clear from the manual is that the author understands the basic chemical process needed to create an explosive. Three components are necessary to create a fire: fuel, heat, and oxygen. To sustain the fire we need to add one component, and that is a chemical-exothermic reaction to occur after the ignition process is completed. An oxidizer, fuel, and heat are the three components required for an explosion to detonate; a chemical reaction occurs when all three elements are present and we introduce an insult—the result is an explosion.[10] The difference between the combustion of a fire and that of an explosive is the speed at which the chemical reaction occurs.[11]

If we look at the list above, under 2.8.1.3 we find the chemical ammonium nitrate. While this chemical has a legitimate purpose as a fertilizer, we can quickly determine from the material presented thus far that this chemical is the main ingredient in manufacturing an IED explosive.

Constructing an improvised explosive device from the materials listed in Table 20.2 can be accomplished with very limited knowledge of chemistry. The only thing a terrorist needs is access to a computer or manual like *The Mujahideen Explosives Handbook*, as well as access to any host of precursor chemicals from the list in Table 20.2, to fabricate an improvised explosive device. To further define the ease of obtaining such items like precursors and the knowledge to fabricate them, we can take a direct quote from the *Pakistani Training Manual*, which says:

> This is the kind of course that teaches us how to make deadly explosives and lethal poisons from easily available substances anywhere on the market or anywhere across the globe.

One thing is clear: when it comes to defining terrorists activities such as the creation and use of such tactics as vehicle-borne explosive devices (VBIEDs), suicide-borne explosives (SBIEDs), and improvised explosive devices (IEDs), the United States has had a very limited experience in dealing with such items, probably due to the tight regulatory compliance that is required from governmental agencies in order to obtain items such as explosives. The material presented thus far shows that explosives are by no means out of the reach of any terrorist or terrorist organization. We need only to look to past experiences where an IED was assembled and utilized as

Table 20.2 Chemicals Categorized as Fuels and Oxidizers

Fuel + Oxidizer = Energetic material, or explosion occurs

Fuels		Oxidizers	
Aluminum powder (Al)	Nitromethane (CH_3NO_2)	Ammonium nitrate $(H_4N_2O_3)$	Barium peroxide
Charcoal	Polyvinylchloride	Sodium nitrate	Lead tetroxide
Diesel fuel #2	Silicon	Iron oxide	Potassium chlorate $(KCLNO_3)$ "hot"
Flour	Sugar $(C_{12}H_{22}O_{11})$	Lead dioxide	Potassium perchlorate "hot"
Iron	Sulfur	Ammonium perchlorate "hot"	Potassium nitrate
Magnesium (Mg)	Titanium	Barium nitrate	Sodium perchlorate "hot"
Petroleum	Nitrobenzene $(C_6H_5NO_2)$	Ammonium triiodide (dry iodine)	Potassium permanganate
Turpentine	Ethyl nitrate $(C_2H_5NO_3)$	Calcium hypochorite (HTH or cholorine prills) "hot"	Peroxide Hot oxidizer extreme hypergolic reaction
Castor oil	Wax, paraffin	Nitric acid	
Vaseline	Shellac		
Glycerin $(C_3H_8O_3)$	Sawdust		
Antimony (Sb)	Phosphine (Ph_3)		
Hydrogen sulfide (H_2S)			

Note: This chart represents a list of commonly found fuels and oxidizers. The names of oxidizer components end in either *ate*, *ite*, or *ide*. "Hot" identifies chlorates and peroxides.

an explosive and played a significant role, for instance, at the Murrah Federal Building and the first World Trade Center. These bombings illustrate the significance that explosives have had on our population; they are evidenced from the death and devastation that these explosions created by the significant loss of life and the destruction of property.

Building the Improvised Explosive Device

The availability of products needed to construct an IED is abundant; however, without an understanding of the dual use of such chemicals, most first responders, public safety, and law enforcement personnel would not recognize the preincident indicators that the construction of an IED was occurring. Every day, first responders, public safety, and law enforcement personnel come into contact with suspicious materials and persons in a variety of circumstances. Being able to recognize IED components is critical in securing the homeland.

Terrorist cells use safe houses to plan, store materials, and build IEDs, and these locations are vital to their operation. Locating such places will most likely come from suspicious circumstances occurring at odd hours of the night or calls from neighbors that might lead law enforcement to just such a location nestled among the populace. However, since law enforcement makes arrests based on two standards of evidence—eye witnesses and physical evidence—even if we are able to locate the safe house, we falter if we are unable to identify the components for the building of IEDs when conducting investigations into suspicious matters.

Clandestine IED factories require the handling and use of a number of chemicals, much like meth labs. However, IED factories are clean and orderly, keeping the major components needed to build an IED separate from each other so that items like chemicals are not in close proximity to a power source, which could be catastrophic to a terrorist operation.

Sanna 'Al Qannabel assembles the IED in an orderly fashion and will require clean work space to build a device in an area that offers enough room to accomplish such a task. In order for explosives to be effective, they need to be assembled in a proper explosive chain. Therefore, the need to have an organized location where components can be separate is imperative. Fuse assemblies, chemicals, containers, detonators, electronic activators, switches, and explosive material all need to be stored separately.[12]

Triacetone triperoxide (TATP), aka the mother of Satan, is a chemical IED that made the news when it was used in London. This IED explosive was developed over a hundred years ago; however, it was too unstable and abandoned for safer explosives. This chemical cocktail has been used as a method of initiation and as a main explosive charge by various terrorist organizations. The process of fabricating this explosive requires three readily available chemicals: acetone (fingernail polish remover), hydrogen peroxide (found at beauty supplies for hair dyes), and sulfuric acid (drain cleaner or battery acid). The explosive hexamethylene triperoxide diamine (HMTD) is similar in nature and composed of peroxide, usually with a concentration of over 30% citric acid and hexamine tabs used as a heating source for campers and military personnel.

Urea nitrate is the most used form of IED and is available from the agricultural industry, and the two main components in the composition are nitric acid and urea. Urea prills* can be found in common products such as de-icing compounds for sidewalks, and require the use of a grinder to be

---

* Prill or prilling is to make a solid into granules or pellets that flow freely and do not clump together (Encarta Dictionary).

made into a paste. Most often an industrial coffee grinder will be used to accomplish this task. By saving a quantity of concentrated urine in containers, one can process the liquid and then extract the urea; mixing sulfuric acid with the urea begins the chemical transformation. The extraction requires an ice bath to assist in the chemical conversion.[13] Large steel pots are usually acquired to mix the chemicals in.

Manufacturing plastic explosives is easily accomplished when potassium chlorate, which is readily available, is mixed with several over-the-counter materials; the result is a deadly and highly unpredictable explosive. The manufacturing of such a substance is accomplished by mixing solidox, a welding oxidizer compound, and sugar or glucose into a putty or thick paste. The completed product of potassium chlorate will appear as a white crystal powder.[14]

Chemicals like ammonium nitrate can be found in everyday items like cold packs. Aluminum powder is available from sources like professional paint stores or filed from an ingot. When the two substances are combined, they yield an explosive that is comparable to 75% the explosive power of TNT.

Heat- or shock-sensitive IEDs are usually fabricated from mercury or mercury filaments. Mercury filaments or switches can be found in thermometers, or switches; even children's shoes that light up when the child walks contain mercury switches. Mercury is composed of nitric acid, ethyl alcohol, and distilled water. The items are often assembled and used as an initiation device to set the main explosive charge off. All the necessary items can be bought at any drug store.

From the list of chemical cocktails identified above, we can see that a dual use exists between items we use for legitimate purposes and those needed to construct an IED or explosive device.

Law enforcement officers that have come into contact with TATP have found that its appearance is very similar to crack cocaine, and that HMTD is very similar in appearance to powered cocaine. Drug test kits to test for the probable presence of cocaine contain two chemicals used in the testing process of crack cocaine: methanol sodium hydroxide, which gives off a winter-green odor, and cobalt thiocyanate, which gives a visual indication that narcotics are present by turning blue. Methanol sodium hydroxide and cobalt thiocyanate are oxidizers and will cause a violent reaction when TATP or HMTD are introduced into a drug test kit. The results to an unsuspecting officer can be deadly.

The availability of the precursors can easily be obtained without much effort by almost anyone, and tracking such sales of these items is not practiced among retailers in our consumer markets. Only through training and awareness in recognizing precursor chemicals will first responders, public safety, and law enforcement have an understanding of the difference between those that acquire such items with a legitimate purpose versus those that are evidence that an IED fabrication facility (safe house) is manufacturing explosive devices.[15]

Awareness for First Responders

In the tactical community, phrases that operators live by are "situations dictate tactics" and "events drive responses." These are the mantras that members of the special operations community adhere to when confronting tasks that require authoritarian intervention, and the same is true for first responders in the public safety community. The ability to formulate plans as circumstances change and then revise them as information is updated about a situation affects what your response to the given situation will be. The type of incident and whether the incident involves a crime against persons or property will also have a significant effect on the tactics chosen by a first responder in restoring order from chaos. However, without an awareness of what is occurring in the time and space you occupy, you may miss important clues that signify criminal or terrorist activities. Without the proper awareness training we may gloss over items we don't understand.

In order to understand the significance of the contribution that can be made in this area, the following case study is presented to solidify the value of understanding the material presented thus far. On April 12, 1988, a New Jersey state trooper conducted a traffic stop on a vehicle for a traffic infraction. While speaking with the driver, the trooper noticed several canisters of gunpowder as well as several bags of lead shot on the backseat of the subject's vehicle. There was a cardboard box with three red fire extinguishers that had black electrical tape with wires protruding from them. After a brief conversation between the trooper and the driver in this case, the driver consented to an examination by the trooper of the contents located in the rear of the vehicle. The trooper, after careful examination, concluded that the items based on his observation were associated with the fabrication of IEDs and/or an explosive device, and the driver was taken into custody. The driver was identified as Yu Kikumura, a member of the Japanese Red Army, a terrorist organization. Yu Kikumura had been trained by the Japanese Red Army as an explosives expert.

Yu Kikumura had in his possession several forged passports, a quantity of smokeless gunpowder, ammonium nitrate prills, and wadding material, lead BB shot, and a flashbulb connected to several wires as a makeshift detonator. Among the items discovered by the trooper were electric timers, toggle switches, some batteries, and jack connectors. Not only was this traffic stop a monumental interdiction of a member of a terrorist organization, but the trooper was able to interdict a terrorist act before it occurred. The trooper in turn was able to take several bombs of the street that might have lead to death and destruction.

Understanding the materials that go into the construction of explosive devices as well as maintaining situational awareness alerted this trooper to understand the gravity of his situation. Law enforcement officers can continue to make interdiction stops like this one by remaining alert and asking inquisitive questions that lead to uncovering those suspected of terrorist activity. The goal of any law enforcement officer or first responder should be interdicting a terrorist attack by locating the bombs, bomb components, or bomb maker prior to the initiation of an attack.[16]

Business Awareness Project, Homeland Security Initiative

The following initiative explains suspicious threat indications that may unveil the possibility of criminal activity being planned through the purchase of dual-use items commonly available throughout stores within the community.

Many businesses within our community, both retail and commercial, sell and distribute items considered dual-use items. Dual-use items are items that when used as designed are perfectly safe and provide a legitimate function within our lives. However, when these items are used for purposes other than that for which the item was designed, the results can be hazardous. An example of such an item is a 4-inch pipe, threaded on both ends, which can be easily sealed by an identical pair of threaded end caps. Although perfectly safe for its intended purpose, when such an item is filled with gunpowder, the result is the manufacture of an IED or bomb. The devastation such an item can have on a community is enormous.

Without the help of the business community in sharing information about suspicious circumstances, it is extremely difficult to discover criminal behavior associated with acquiring dual-use items to commit criminal acts. The availability of chemicals at a hardware store provides legitimate purpose; however, if acquired for other intentions, they can be potentially lethal in the proper quantities. Therefore, the [insert your organization's name] focus is on what a criminal's intentions are to successfully disrupt their plans before they become reality. It is equally important to focus on the suspicious activity that has occurred; many times this information may indicate a criminal's intentions.

When a criminal attempts to or actually purchases items such as chemicals while making suspicious inquiries, this might indicate a criminal's attempt to build an explosive device or collect the proper chemicals necessary to manufacture illicit drugs, such as methamphetamine.

In the interest of the community, in order to create a safer homeland, we are asking the businesses in the area to report any and all suspicious encounters. Businesses need to communicate to their staff that if a high level of suspicion exists that the product being purchased may be employed in a manner other than intended, the business has the right to refuse to sell the items being purchased. Training your staff in security measures is essential and should be an integral part of your business training program.

In order to assist businesses and their staff in determining what suspicion indicators are, we have compiled the following list as a guide. It was assembled to assist in making a determination as to whether a subject's behavior is indicative of attempts to conceal his real motives in purchasing certain dual-use items.

One way of making this determination is to directly confront a person with specific questions about the intended use of the item(s) purchased. Persons with evil intentions will display nervousness and become irritable and openly evasive.

Indications in Making a Determination

- Does this person insist on paying in cash? The customer is willing to pay cash for a very expensive item when the terms of sale would normally call for financing.
- Does this person have an out-of-state driver's license?
- Does this person have a temporary address or use a motel address?
- Does this person ask for deliveries to be made to a storage address?
- Does this person seem too young, especially to purchase a quantity of small pipes and end cap(s) or pipe nipple(s) without any explanation for their use?
- The person is evasive in answering "What are you doing with the materials?"
- The customer or purchasing agent is reluctant to offer information about the end use of the item.
- The product's capabilities do not fit the buyer's line of business, such as an order for sophisticated computers for a small bakery.
- The item ordered is incompatible with the technical level of the person.
- The customer has little or no business background.
- The customer is unfamiliar with the product's performance characteristics but still wants the product.
- Routine installation, training, or maintenance services are declined by the customer.
- Delivery dates are vague, or deliveries are planned for out-of-the-way destinations.
- A freight-forwarding firm is listed as the product's final destination.
- The shipping route is abnormal for the product and destination.

- Packaging is inconsistent with the stated method of shipment or destination.
- When questioned, the buyer is evasive and especially unclear about whether the purchased product is for domestic use.

Identify Anyone That Seems Suspicious

In order to help identify possible subjects that display suspicious behavior in making purchases of dual-use items, we suggest the following:

- Require a driver's license for cash sales of all pipe(s), end cap(s), and chemical or propane materials sold.
- Copy a subject's information into a standard log book and make it a policy to log information such as name, driver's license number, address, and the items purchased.

Remember that accuracy and timeliness are the key elements to thwarting attacks to our community before they happen.

What to Report

If you can answer yes to the above questions and believe that suspicious activity exists to warrant further investigation, you can help greatly by acquiring as much information as possible, including:

- Vehicle description
- License plate number
- Physical description
- Driver's license number
- Other items observed within the subject's vehicle
- Anything overheard by the subjects talking to each other
- Who, what, where, when, and how

The overall goal of this initiative is to secure the approval and compliance of all senior management staff of businesses within the community that sell or have items that are considered dual-use items. Our ability to secure compliance within the business community through the senior management is essential to contributing to the success of securing our community and making it safer.

This project is aimed at taking a proactive approach to homeland security through establishing a two-way method of communication between our business community in establishing additional eyes and ears that would otherwise go unheard and unseen. The amount of information gained through such a cooperative homeland security initiative is unparalleled when the community is moving in the same direction toward a common goal of securing a better homeland.

Summary and Conclusion

Today's first responder, public safety, or law enforcement officer has a very limited amount of knowledge when it comes to identifying explosives or explosive materials. Law enforcement, public safety, and first responders come into contact with many people in a variety of locations throughout their normal course of business on a daily basis, either through investigations, calls for service, traffic stops, or a host of other reasons. Having the knowledge to ascertain what constitutes a bomb-making component, what precursor chemicals are, and what, if any, additional items make up the construction of an IED component are essential in identifying dual-use items.

Only through training in the identification of explosive materials will first responders, public safety, and law enforcement personnel be able to act in a manner aimed at identifying crucial material and chemicals used to construct IEDs. Only then can we begin to stop terrorist bomb-making facilities and secure a safer tomorrow.

Glossary of Terms

This is a standard glossary of terms of the ATF.

Ammonium nitrate: Classified as an oxidizer. An oxidizer is a substance that readily yields oxygen or other oxidizing substances to promote the combustion of organic matter or other fuel. Ammonium nitrate alone is not an explosive material. However, federal explosives storage regulations require the separation of explosive magazines from nearby stores of ammonium nitrate by certain minimum distances.

ANFO: An explosive material consisting of ammonium nitrate and fuel oil.

Black powder: A deflagrating or low-explosive compound of an intimate mixture of sulfur, charcoal, and an alkali nitrate (usually potassium or sodium nitrate). *See* low explosives.

Blasting agent: Any material or mixture consisting of fuel and oxidizer intended for blasting, not otherwise defined as an explosive, provided that the finished product, as mixed for use or shipment, cannot be detonated by means of a no. 8 test blasting cap when unconfined.

Booster: An explosive charge, usually a high explosive used to initiate a less sensitive explosive. A booster can be either cast, pressed, or extruded.

Bulk mix: A mass of explosive material prepared for use in bulk form without packaging.

C4: A military plastic/moldable high explosive.

Commercial explosives: Explosives designed, produced, and used for commercial or industrial applications, rather than for military purposes.

Common chemicals: Any chemical compound or element that, as part of a physical mixture, would be necessary for that mixture to be considered an explosive mixture, or any chemical compound or element that could be classified as an oxidizer or as a readily available fuel.

Dealer (federal): Any person engaged in the business of distributing explosive materials at wholesale or retail.

Detection taggants: A marker or taggant placed into an explosive material that has utility before a bomb explodes.

Detection taggants with identification capabilities: A marker or taggant placed into an explosive material that has both preblast and postblast utility.

Detonating cord: A flexible cord containing a center core of high explosive and used to initiate other explosives.

Detonation: An explosive reaction that moves through an explosive material at a velocity greater than the speed of sound.

Detonator: Any device containing an initiating or primary explosive that is used for initiating a detonation. A detonator may not contain more that 10 g of total explosives by weight, excluding ignition or delay charges. The term includes, but is not limited to, electric blasting caps of instantaneous and delay types, blasting caps for use with safety fuses, detonating cord delay connectors, and nonelectric instantaneous and delay blasting caps that use detonating cord, shock tube, or any other replacement for electric leg wires.

Dynamite: A high explosive used for blasting, consisting essentially of a mixture of, but not limited to, nitroglycerin, nitrocellulose, ammonium nitrate, sodium nitrate, and carbonaceous materials.

Emulsions: An explosive material containing substantial amounts of oxidizers dissolved in water droplets surrounded by an immiscible fuel.

Explosive: Any chemical compound, mixture, or device, the primary or common purpose of which is to function by explosion.

Explosive incidents: Actual and attempted explosives/incendiary bombings, stolen and recovered explosives, hoax devices, and accidental explosions, as defined in the ATF's Explosive Incidents Report (EIR).

Explosive materials: Explosives, blasting agents, and detonators. Explosive materials include, but are not limited to, all items in the list of explosive materials (see Appendix C-1).

ExploTracer taggant: ExploTracer is based on synthetic granules dyed with fluorescent pigments and iron particles. To ensure that each particle has a distinctive code of its own, rare earth elements are added.

Fertilizer: A substance used to make soil more fertile, such as ammonium nitrate.

Filler: A type of explosive/incendiary/chemical substance that, in combination with a fusing or firing system, constitutes an improvised explosive device (e.g., dynamite, match heads, gasoline).

Flammable liquid: Combustible. A flammable material is one that is ignited easily and burns readily, i.e., gasoline, charcoal lighter fluid, diesel fuel, and paint thinners.

Fuel: Any substance that reacts with the oxygen in the air or with the oxygen yielded by an oxidizer to produce combustion.

HF-6 taggant: HF-6 is similar to the 3M (Microtaggant) and is coded according to its several layers of color. The HF-6 taggant was developed by Swiss Blasting, and is used exclusively in its own products.

High explosives: Explosives that are characterized by a very high rate of reaction, high-pressure development, and the presence of a detonation wave in the explosive, and which can be caused to detonate by means of a blasting cap when unconfined.

HMTD: An abbreviation for the name of the explosive hexamethylene triperoxide diamine.

Identification taggants: A marker or taggant placed into an explosive material that has utility after an explosion to identify the manufacturer, date, and shift when it was manufactured. Once this type taggant is located and identified, the information it provides would allow law enforcement to trace all of the same type explosives manufactured on that specific date and shift to all of the legal purchasers.

Importer: Any person engaged in the business of importing or bringing explosive materials into the United States for purposes of sale or distribution.

Interstate: Pertaining to or existing within the boundaries of a state of residence.

Interstate or foreign commerce: Commerce between any place in a state and any place outside of that state, or within any possession of the United States (not including the canal zone) or the District of Columbia, and commerce between places within the same state but through any place outside of that state.

ISOTAG: A readily identifiable, mass-enhanced, nonradioactive molecular marker that employs the unique chemical structure of the host product without harm to the quality of the product or the environment.

License (federal): Required if a person is intending to engage in the business as an explosive materials manufacturer, importer, or dealer, and allows a person to transport, ship, and receive explosive materials in interstate or foreign commerce.

Licensee: Any importer, manufacturer, or dealer licensed under the federal explosives laws.

Low explosives: Explosives that are characterized by deflagration (a rapid combustion that moves through an explosive material at a velocity less than the speed of sound).

Marker: *See* taggant.

Metric ton: 2,204.6 pounds or 1,000 kilograms.

Microtaggant: Color-coded polymer microchip consisting of ten layers, including a magnetic layer and a fluorescent layer, which is intended to function as an identification taggant. The chip was developed by the 3M Company, but is now manufactured by Microtrace, Minneapolis, Minnesota, which acquired the rights to production in 1984.

Nitrogen (N): One of the three primary plant nutrients, together with phosphorus (P) and potassium (K).

Other: For purposes of the EIR, the category of other includes match heads, military explosives (excluding C4 and TNT), improvised mixtures, flares, boosters, detonator cord, gases, blasting caps, PETN, RDX, HMTD, model rocket propellant, and smoke grenades.

Oxidizer or oxidizing material: A substance, such as a nitrate, that readily yields oxygen or other oxidizing substances to stimulate the combustion of organic matter or other fuel.

Permit: Required if any person intends to acquire or use explosive materials from a licensee in a state other than the state in which he or she resides, or from a foreign country, or who intends to transport explosive materials in interstate or foreign commerce.

Permittee: Any person who has obtained a federal user permit to acquire, ship, or transport explosive materials in interstate or foreign commerce.

Person: Any individual, corporation, company, association, firm, partnership, society, or joint stock company.

PETN: Abbreviation for the name of the explosive pentaerythritol tetranitrate.

Photoflash and fireworks powder: An explosive material intended to produce an audible report and a flash of light when ignited, and typically containing potassium perchlorate, sulfur or antimony sulfide, and aluminum metal.

Precursor chemicals: Any chemical compound or element that can be subjected to a chemical reaction or series of reactions in order to synthesize the chemical compound or element into an explosive compound.

Pyrotechnic: A chemical mixture that, upon burning, produces visible, brilliant displays, bright lights, or sounds.

RDX: An abbreviation for the name of the explosive cyclonite, hexogen, T4, cyclo-1,3,5,-trimethylene-2,4,6- trinitramine; hexahydro-1,3,5,-trinitro S-triazine.

Reworked explosives: Any residual or off-specification material that can be recycled within the manufacturing process.

Slurry: An explosive material containing substantial portions of a liquid, oxidizer, and fuel, plus a thickener.

Smokeless powder: Any of a class of explosive propellants that produce comparatively little smoke on explosion and consist mostly of gelatinized cellulose nitrates.

Specialty explosives: Any specialty tool used for a particular purpose other than blasting, such as explosive-actuated device (jet tappers, jet perforators), propellant-actuated power device (construction nail guns), commercial C4, detasheet, oil well perforating guns, etc.

Taggant: A solid-, liquid-, or vapor-emitting substance put into an explosive material for the purposes of detection or identification. Also known as a marker or tracer element. (For purposes of this report, tagging is the act of marking or adding a taggant to an explosive material.)

TNT: An abbreviation for the name of the explosive trinitrotoluene.

Ton: 2,000 pounds or 0.907 metric ton.

Tracer element: *See* taggant.

Undetermined: For purposes of the EIR, the category of undetermined captures incidents in which fillers could not be identified through laboratory analysis or incomplete data that were reported.

Urea ammonium nitrate (UAN): UAN solution is a popular liquid fertilizer in the United States and other industrialized areas.

Users: Any persons who purchase and use explosives within their state of residence and are not federal licensees or permittees.

Water gel: An explosive material containing substantial portions of water, oxidizers, and fuel, plus a cross-linking agent that may be a high explosive or blasting agent.

Endnotes

1. FBI Bomb Data Center, http://library.sau.edu/bestinfo/Majors/Criminal/Bomb.pdf (accessed January 10, 2007).

2. The Jamestown Foundation, *Terrorism Focus* II(15), 2005, www.jamestown.org (accessed January 10, 2007).
3. IED Construction, http://www.globalsecurity.org/military/intro/ied.htm.
4. Kozlow, C., and J. Sullivan, *Jane's Facility Security Handbook* (Alexandria, VA: 2000), 12–13.
5. Ibid. Nance, M., *The Terrorist Recognition Handbook: A Manual for Predicting and Identifying Terrorist Activities* (Guilford, CT: 2003), 121–24.
6. Reasonable suspicion is a less demanding standard than probable cause. Klotter, J., *Legal Guide for Police: Constitutional Issues*, 6th ed. (Cincinnati, OH: 2002), 30.
7. Department of Homeland Security, *Incident Response to Terrorist Bombings* (Energetic Materials Research Course, New Mexico Institute of Mining and Technology, August 2006), 4–43, 48.
8. Ibid.
9. Abdel-Aziz, *The Mujahideen Explosives Handbook: For the Preparation of the Mujahideen*, 1996, www.exet.nu/html.download/ovrigt/mujahideen_explosives_book.pdf (accessed September 2005).
10. Ibid., 86.
11. Department of Homeland Security, 2006, pp. 3–12, 17.
12. Ibid.
13. Nance, 2003, 98.
14. Abdel-Aziz, 1996.
15. Ibid., 86.
16. Ibid., 87–88. *NMT Manual*, 4–29.
17. Nance, 2003, 251–52. Adopted from Nance's telling of a traffic stop that resulted in the arrest of a terrorist and a substantial amount of IEDs. This example illustrates that being vigilant is necessary when it comes to performing one's daily duties in law enforcement, and that just such an encounter may yield results of terrorist activity occurring in close proximity to your jurisdiction.

Bibliography

Abdel-Aziz. 1996. *The Mujahideen Explosive Handbook*. Organization of the Preparation of Mujahideen. http://wwwexet.nu/html/download/ovrigt/mujahideen_explosives_book.pdf. (accessed September 5, 2005).
Ansari, M. 2004. *JTIC exclusive: A bomber's A-Z notes from Pakistani terrorist training manual*. Jane's Terrorism and Insurgency Center.
Anti-Defamanation League. 2002. *Countering suicide terrorism*. Herzliya, Israel: International Policy Institute for Counter-Terrorism at the Interdisciplinary Center.
Arquilla, J., and Ronfeldt, D. 2001. *Networks and netwars: The future of terror, crime, and militancy*. Santa Monica, CA: RAND Corp.
Bell, D. 1960. *The end of ideology*. Cambridge, MA: Harvard University Press.
Bergen, P. 2002. *Holy war inc. Inside the secret world of Osama Bin Laden*. New York.
Bjorgo, T. 2005. *Root causes of terrorism: Myths, reality and ways forward*. New York.
Bloom, M. 2005. *Dying to kill: The allure of suicide terror*. New York: Columbia University Press.
Boaz, G. 2005. *The counter-terrorism puzzle: A guide for decisions makers*. Israel: ICT, The Institute.

Boobytraps. 1965. FM-5-31. Department of the Army.

Castle, M. M. 2004. Drano bombs. http://mlcastle.net/raisethefist/draino.html (accessed March 7, 2005).

Davis, C. 2003. *The Middle East for dummies.* Hoboken, NJ.

Department of Health and Human Services. *Health and medical response to chemical/ biological terrorism.*

Emerson, S. 2002. *American Jihad: The terrorist living among us.* New York.

Emerson, S. 2006. *Jihad incorporated: A guide to militant Islam in the US.* Amherst, NY.

Federal response plan (FRP) terrorism annex. 1999.

Ganor, B. 2000. *Suicide terrorism: An overview.* ICT, The Institute.

Gertz, B. 2002. *Breakdown: How America's intelligence failures led to September 11.* Washington, DC.

Gundry, C. 2003. *Chemical plant bomb threat planning handbook.* 1st ed. Clearwater, FL: Critical Intervention Services.

Hazardous materials handbook, 471–473. 3rd ed. NFPA.

Hoffer, E. 2002. *The true believer: Thoughts on the nature of mass movements.* New York.

Hoffman, B. 2006. *Inside terrorism.* 2nd ed. New York: Columbia Press.

Katz, S. M. 2005. *Jihad in Brooklyn: the NYPD raid that stopped the first suicide bombers.* New York.

Kean, T., and Hamilton, L. 2004. *The 9-11 report.* New York.

Khosrokhavar, F. 2005. *Suicide bombers: Allah's new martyrs.* London.

Klotter, J. C. 2002. *Legal guide for police: Constitutional issues.* 6th ed. Cincinnati, OH.

Klotter, J. C., and Kanovitz, K. 2002. *Constitutional law.* 9th ed. Cincinnati, OH.

Kozlow, C., and Sullivan, J. 2000. *Jane's facility security handbook.* Alexandria VA.

Kushner, H. 1996. *Suicide bombers: Business as usual.* Studies in Conflict and Terrorism.

Laqueur, W. 1996. Postmodern terrorism: New rules for an old game. *Foreign Affairs.*

Nance, M. 2003. *The terrorist recognition handbook: A manual for predicting and identifying terrorist activities.* Guilford, CT.

Pedahzur, A. 2005. *Suicide terrorism.* Malden, MA: Polty Press.

Pickett, M. 1998. *Explosives identification guide for first responders.* New York: Delmar.

Poole J. 2005. *Militant tricks: Battlefield ruses of the Islamic insurgent.* Emerald Isle, NC.

Reuter, C. 2004. *My life is a weapon: A modern history of suicide bombings.* Princeton, NJ.

Rostberg, J. 2005. *Common chemicals as precursors of improvised explosive devices: The challenge of defeating domestic terrorism.* Monterey CA: Naval Postgraduate School.

Schweitzer, Y. 2000. *Suicide terrorism: Development & characteristics.* New Brunswick, NJ: ICT, The Institute.

Shay, S. 2004. *The Shahids: Islam and suicide attacks.* New Brunswick, NJ: ICT, The Institute.

Taylor, M., and Horgan, J. 2000. *The future of terrorism.* London: Frank Cass & Co.

Venzke, B., and Ibrahim, A. 2003. *The al-Qaeda threat: An analytical guide to al-Qaeda's tactics & targets.* 1st ed. Alexandria, VA: Tempest Publishing Company.

Weapons of mass destruction (civil support team) operations handbook. 2000.

White, J. 2004. *Defending the homeland: Domestic intelligence, law enforcement, and security.* Belmont, CA: Thomas Wadsworth.

White, J. 2005. *Terrorism and homeland security.* Belmont, CA: Thomas Wadsworth.

Internet Sources

Conversing with the Adversary. http://www.labat.co.il/ (accessed November 5, 2006).

EPA National Contingency Plan. www.epa.gov/oilspill/ncpover.htm (accessed November 6, 2006).

IED—A weapon's profile. http://www.defense-update.com/features/du-3-04/IED. htm (accessed November 5, 2006).

Israel Insider. What makes a bomber tick. http://www.israelinsider.com/channels/ security/articles/sec_0049.htm (accessed November 4, 2006).

Vulnerabilities in the terrorist cycle. *On Point: A Counterterrorism Journal.* http://www. uscav.com/uscavonpoint/Print.aspx?id=140 (accessed November 1, 2006).

Who 'outed' Mohammad Naeem Noor Khan? *Behind the Lines.* http://www.antiwar. com/justin/?articleid=3271 (accessed November 4, 2006).

Zedalis, D. *Female suicide bombers.* http://www.carisle.army.mil/ssi (accessed November 1, 2006).

Panopti(con)
Art and the Aesthetics of Dissent

21

CLAUDIA M. HUIZA

Contents

Almost two hundred years after Jeremy Bentham proposed the concept of the Panopticon architectural structure as a way of monitoring convicts in prison, it has been debunked by the technological advancement of maximum surveillance power: satellites and video cameras positioned in public places to monitor and spy on the everyday actions of ordinary citizens going about their business. A voyeur's delight, Martin Durazo's recent multimedia curatorial effort, encompassing the work of seventeen well-known American artists, issued a solemn, if not aesthetically satisfying, gossamer-like spread showcased at the Bank Gallery in downtown Los Angeles. The works featured, from painting, photography, drawing, and video to collage and installation pieces, engage in theories centered around power structures. The artists take literal and metaphorical cues from the interpretation of Bentham's panoptic theory and imagery. The work debates systems of power and control, security and surveillance for a public audience that rarely encounters such over-the-top controversial themes (Figure 21.1).

The tiny incline leading into the foyer-like interior gallery space, made of little bricks that seem to leap out of their weathered mortar encasings upon resting one's feet on them, provides an initial unbalanced feeling of entry into a different kind of space. Indeed, with its intensely high-ceiling walls notably dressed for the occasion with five of LA-based Chris Tallon's unique paper 3D surveillance cameras, the show has the effect of a larger-than-life presentation, where the participants in this journey of awareness building and reflection are immediately offered a variety of works to sink their imagination and thoughts into (Figure 21.2).

Figure 21.1 Inside foyer gallery shot. (From Bank Gallery, downtown Los Angeles.)

Show curator Martin Durazo, known for creating enormous life-size installations that offer ingenious self-reflective commentaries on subculture explorations of life, death, and everything in between, offers a sociospatial investigation of the modern jail cell. His in-your-face style is never tongue in cheek, confronting controversial and difficult themes such as the

Figure 21.2 Wide-angle gallery shot. (From Bank Gallery, downtown Los Angeles.)

Figure 21.3 Plexiglas, plywood, steel, rubber glove, license plate. Dimensions variable. (From Martin Durazo, Made in U.S.A., 2008.)

dehumanization that occurs once a person is relegated to the system of incarceration where surveillance becomes a tool to be (ab)used by institutional forces at will (Figure 21.3).

Thus, it is fitting that the current work, "Made in U.S.A." (2008), a maquette meant to signify an actual life-size jail cell, evokes the way in which prisoners are "always already" spied upon at all times, their actions open to the scrutiny of the jailers, wardens, and ironically, even the reality and YouTube TV audience who watch the videos of prisoners being processed from the safety of their own homes on any given night. But within this "open-cell structure" sits a vice-clamp holding a used medical examination glove, alluding to the psychological and physical trauma prisoners are exposed to despite, and no doubt within, full view of their "caretakers" (Figure 21.4).

Durazo's maquette is a type of structural symbolism evoking without apology the rawness of the psychosexual allusions contained within the 2 × 2 open-ended cell, paired with an obvious suggestive nod to the omniscient "other" that is always already present in the subculture of the incarcerated. Made up of found objects, including a piece of dark, reflective acrylic and cardboard on one wall; found wood, and a sliver of transparent, yellow acrylic on another, its purpose, it seems, is to negotiate the never-neutral space between the realm of reflection, in the form of the acrylic "wall" and reality, in the form of the concrete-color painted wood "wall." Calling attention to the constraints found in a typical jail cell, the focus here goes beyond the mere casualness of such constraints, and moves on to the affirmation that indeed, nothing is typical in such a structure. This is nowhere more obvious

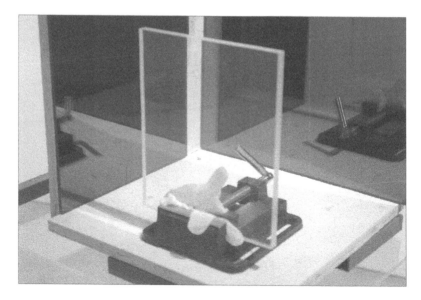

Figure 21.4 Plexiglas, plywood, steel, rubber glove, license plate. Dimensions variable. (From Martin Durazo, Made in U.S.A., 2008.)

than, when upon closer examination of the piece, one finds attached to the northwest side of the maquette a confederate flag license plate, thus charging the piece with a particularly controversial historical context (Figure 21.5).

But the piece doesn't stop there, for floating between the floor of the structure and clear acrylic pedestal stand one finds a semirusted, graffiti-red steel form of a swastika, hailing a variety of levels of interpretation and meaning. A metaphor for the Althusserian concept of the injustice of modern relations of ruling gone awry, the installation forces the audience to literally lower themselves on all fours in order to catch a glimpse of the steel-rod shape that underscores the jail cell structure, a shape wrought through fascist stigma from its original meaning of good luck.

Mike Dee's Love Constraints

Situated a few steps from the Durazo piece are two semibiographical sculptures by LA-based multimedia artist Mike Dee titled "heartsmelt, (the panopticon)" (2008) and "heartsmelt (tower of …)" (2008), in which he investigates the themes of vulnerability, sensuality, and touch through an exploration of what happens to love in prison. Notice the positioning of the *heartsmelts* in relation to the two paper security cameras by artist Chris Tallon. Tallon's installation is an illustration of the domestic terrorist mode that has engulfed post-9/11 United States, and catapulted us to a previously unknown level of what cultural critic William Staples calls "power seeing." The cameras do not

Figure 21.5 Plexiglas, plywood, steel, rubber glove, license plate. Dimensions variable. (From Martin Durazo, Made in U.S.A., 2008.)

have to be operable to operate. They are fakes but do appear to be watching. Just as in any surveillance, it works when detected but best when it is not detected. Here there is no freedom of movement, no freedom of expression, one's location is readily available to the authorities, to those in control at the current moment. Here, the surveillance cameras are positioned in a way that make us immediately aware that in our society nothing is private any longer, everyone is always being watched and scrutinized by the formless, unnamed "omniscient others," the agents of the state.

The significance of the cardboard box pedestal in lieu of traditional materials such as white-painted wood or acrylic pedestals is twofold: to invoke the need to protect a person's privacy in an environment that voids any such

Figure 21.6 Melted plastic, hot glue. (From Mike Dee, "heartsmelt (the panop-ticon)," 2008. With permission.)

possibility, and the fact that matters of the heart must be stashed away deep inside a type of emotional storage space of the soul for self-protection. The cardboard containers meant to house the beautiful charges are disposable, breakable, frail, and upon the touch, the entire sculpture gives and rocks, alluding to its fragility and vulnerability. Constructed from melted metal-lic plastic heart-shaped wall hangings and hot glue, the attractively shiny red-metallic forms at first appear to be a kind of anodized aluminum-fused metal with a high production finish, but instead, are very fragile inexpensive 99-cent store type material (Figure 21.6).

Themes of access, deception, and disillusion abound in these works. The figures consist of a visual trick, becoming a metaphor for disappointment and fragility. In their simple construction and presentation, the sensually melted shapes invite the public to touch and "feel" them, thus letting the audience take pleasure in doing what is usually prohibited in a traditional high-art gallery space. Furthermore, upon the touch, they provide yet another layer of meaning, revealing that things are not what they seem, that our eyes can be deceived. What at first appears to be a stable, solid structure turns out to be an easily crushable form, a flimsy fake. The reality is that the pieces are not really created at a metal smelting factory but simply with a home-based hot air gun that easily melts the thin, delicate, mylar-like plastic material. Thus, the deliberate placement seeks to make the work accessible to all. And the composition, especially the reflective material luminosity of the *heartsmelts*, encourages the audience to engage in a deeply internal meditation and reflection about what it means to love, or be in love, under the constraints of indoctrination or institutionalization of any kind.

Conforming Constraint: The Works of Master Artist Sherin Guirguis

In the initial announcement for the 11th Cairo Biennale, we are told that "since its inception in 1984, the Cairo Biennale is considered one of the most important cultural events in the Middle East. Conceived and initially designed to explore contemporary art in the Arab world, the concepts of the successive artistic directors expanded the interest to the global international arena. The biennale is produced by the fine arts sector of the Egyptian ministry of culture.... The success in sustaining the event had a direct impact on the contemporary art practices arising from Egypt as well as from the Middle East region in the past two decades."* It is fitting that one of the most prominent artists featured in this year's Cairo Biennale, Sherin Guirguis, is also one of two female contributors to the Panopti(con) exhibition, pushing the boundaries of societal norms.

Guirguis, an LA-based multimedia artist of Egyptian descent, takes no shortcuts in the breath of her luminous cutting-edge work. Harmoniously merging sculpture, collage, painting, paper cutting, and carving in creating delicate, superbly polished artistic gestures, she surely places at the forefront of a new wave of feminism worldwide. Her works explore the status of the female "other" in the postmodern media-dominated spectacle that is grounded in fundamentalist doctrine, thus pitting the public against the domestic realms. Her sociospatial cartographies explore themes of control

* See http://www.cairobiennale.gov.eg/default.aspx

Figure 21.7 Untitled collage, 10 × 12 inches, 2008. (From Sherin Guirguis.)

and punishment, the tension between fear and desire, and the inherent contradictions that arise in sociocultural constraints and restraints. Guirguis's intricately hand-cut neon-color collages draw attention to the repetitive star-and-flower patterns that inhabit the dense mushroom clouds reminiscent of the atomic bomb explosions in Hiroshima and Nagasaki (Figure 21.7).

Residing upon a study of the deadly human and moral holocaust that the atomic bombing comprised, the sheer beauty of the delicate cut paper, whose patterns are derived from none other than Middle Eastern harem screens, are an alluring draw to a voyeur's untrained eye. According to Middle Eastern culture, the intent of the decorative harem screens is to hide the female figure from the male gaze. The female body should not only be covered in its entirety when in the public eye, but it must also remain hidden even in the domestic space of the harem. Thus, the desired object of the female body is protected from the gaze by the allure of the hypnotic screen patterns. Guirguis's small hand-carved architectural designs transform the intended use of the harem screen into a commentary on the status of feminism in the Middle East. They suggest the possibility that the push to keep women hidden behind "protective" screens is motivated by the fear of that which cannot be controlled—in this case, intelligent women. At the same time, the harem screens have a twofold purpose, for they both contain and hide the women's desire and need for control and protection of their own space. They can see out, whereas the men on the other side of the screen cannot see in. In this game of peek-a-boo, the never-ending loops that comprise the geometric patterns represent the omniscient, divine eye of God, always watching.

The earliest fragments of harem screens date back to the fourth-century Islamic culture, with notable examples to be found in Algeria, Morocco, and Spain, as well as throughout the rest of the Middle East. From its very beginnings, the parameters for making Islamic art forbade the representation of images of anything living. Representations of living beings were and are still encoded today within these endless patterns and writings in the form of calligraphy, thus pointing to the fundamental idea of restricting creativity. It is this continuous contradiction and constraint that is investigated in Sherin Guirguis's work.

Vibing the Fine Line

Skip Arnold is known for his provocative multimedia and performance art. His work engages the themes of power, self-awareness, place and time, aggression, risk, and brutality. The two photographs included in the Panopti(con) show are no exception. These photographs are striking for their physicality and simplicity—the subject of which seems to be emotionally perturbed and alienated by the social confines of ordinary life in the present moment. Making an unwilling voyeur of the viewer, these "portraits," like the rest of his *ouvre*, uncover a powerful commentary on life, death, socialization, and all its mores and taboos, challenges and constraints. Arnold, who is notorious for utilizing his own body as sculpture and art object, exposes the constructiveness of societal norms in the image within an image that comprises his c-print photographs titled "Study for Doorstop" and "Mirror—Mirror" (Figure 21.8).

In "Mirror—Mirror," the angle from which this photograph is taken lures the audience into the otherwise uncomfortable act of "looking up" into the backside of Arnold's naked, seemingly headless body. Although there is a face in the picture, it is only visible through the image on the mirror, adding an interesting layer of meaning to the piece. Standing statuesquely on a ledge suspended above an elegant clock, the subject of "Mirror—Mirror" appears to be engaged in deep meditation while looking at his reflection in the mirror. Actively positioned with his flexed arms bent at the sides, hands resting at the sides of his waist, he strikes a semierotic pose and seems to be taking stock of his lower body, lost in self-reflection. By the sheer positioning of the arms, we are led to think that this figure is an active agent in his story, that despite the nudity, there is no vulnerability here. Indeed, the subject is not aware of, nor would seem to care much about, the myriad sets of eyes that could be scrutinizing him, for he seems to be intensely involved in the intimate world of self-scrutiny. Positioned high above, he is the personification

Figure 21.8 Study for "doorstop" Brussels, Skip Arnold, C-Print, 30 × 22" ed. 2 of 3. Mirror-Mirror, Skip Arnold, 2006 C-Print, 30 × 14.5 ed. 2 of 3.

of what, in our hypersexualized society, might seem to be an inaccessible or unobtainable realization of oneself as "other."

The clock, with its Roman numerals, is symbolic of the emotional preoccupation with the way in which health, beauty, and youth trickle away with time. And the way in which the subject is facing away from the viewer and transfixed upon his own life-size mirror image underscores the powerlessness of the audience to see all and know all about this precariously positioned subject. The challenge is to begin to regard our world and our position in it in a whole new, radical way.

However, in "Doorstop," the perspective is that of a person looking down toward the intended subject, a naked man who seems to be lost in the act of self-comfort in an otherwise ordinary-looking sideways glance at an artist's studio. Far from a figure of strength, this vulnerable man has turned away from the mirror in the photograph; as if he cannot bear even his own eyes, much less those of the audience.

To live in the present, conscious of our every imperfection, is likened to balancing oneself upon a perfectly elevated tiny white pedestal, teeter-tottering at the mercy of an unforgiving, perilous abyss. Arnold seems to be saying that to recognize the "other" in ourselves, to really take a good look at everything we are, naked, uncovered, with all our imperfections for everyone to see, may result, at any moment, in a pitfall that is nonetheless worth taking the risk and flexing our strength.

Thus, it is the aim of the Panopti(con) exhibition to offer a set of creative interpretations of the impact that the oversaturation of surveillance and control systems has on the human psyche. It is no surprise that in this postmodern time of global crisis encompassing both the cultural and economic, the domestic and the public, and even the material and psychological realms, we look to artists to relieve anxiety and inspire optimism through their visions. As curator Martin Durazo puts it, "It is in this vein that the artists collected here are given the task of channeling clarity for the viewer and themselves." Through an uninhibited exploration of their respective concerns and hopes, the artists featured in Panopti(con) allow us to arrive at a greater understanding, a more informed understanding, of ourselves and our world.

Policing the Future
Homeland Security and Terrorism: *Nineteen Eighty-Four* and the *Terminator*

22

DALE L. JUNE

In may not be a stretch of the imagination to suggest that the police role of the future will no longer be involved with citizen services or complaints. Those aspects of current policing will be conducted by private neighborhood security patrols who can respond more quickly and cheaply to calls for service and investigation of minor complaints.

Police will be involved only as investigators in the most serious crimes (against the state), terrorism, and threats or endangerment to public officials and national security. Not only will the patrol function of police become a responsibility of private patrols, but the police will have the capability of monitoring street and neighborhood activity through a network of cameras as we move more and more toward a society of surveillance. Technology has already placed a "sky watch" program in orbit around the planet capable of photographing exact up-close locations, maps, and grids instantly viewable by any curious seeker, police agency, or subversive group at the click of a computer mouse.

There may be a movement toward further surveillance, scrutiny, and militarization of the police with greater powers of arrest, search, and seizure. Movements are afoot to repeal the Second Amendment of the Constitution (the right of citizens to bear arms). Once that slippery slope gains strength, what can we say about the erosion of other constitutional rights, such as provided in Amendments 1, 4, 5, 6, 7, 8, and 14?

Civil rights are those rights granted to the people by the government and guaranteed by the Constitution. For the sake of security against the tyrants, fanatical fringes, and megalomaniacs, it is not inconceivable that "the people" will voluntarily forsake their civil rights and forfeit freedoms for increased police and government power to provide the desired level of homeland security.

With the movement away from traditional police service, police of the future will be highly trained in the areas of intelligence gathering and analysis, personal protection of public figures, and counterterrorism. More simply stated, police will no longer police but will become symbols of the government mandated to prevent terrorist acts of horror, sabotage, and assassinations or murder.

One doesn't have to look very far to see the indicators. Colleges and universities are scurrying to forge partnerships with police and law enforcement agencies to bring working relationships that will focus more and more on antiterrorist research, training, and modeling. Agencies with enforcement, protective, investigation, and intelligence gathering mandates and responsibilities are forming elite special units ranging from SWAT to covert intelligence gathering and analysis as the patrol functions are slowly being relegated to the less motivated and undereducated, whose primary role is becoming less important in the evolving global war on crime and terrorism. Perhaps there will come a day when uniformed officers are used primarily for making arrests, seizing property, and controlling the masses.

That is what this book has been all about—the recognition that warfare has changed from state versus state to the weak and powerless against the rich and powerful. A small and determined organized group following an ideology and a charismatic leader, utilizing methods such as intentionally targeting and attacking citizen populations, public decapitations, and methods heretofore believed to be against the rules of war, conventions, and treaties, can "awaken a sleeping giant" and bring him to his knees.

This all sounds very much like George Orwell's prophetic novel *1984* and the science fiction movie series *Terminator,* but the indicators are beginning to fall into place where the "out of the ordinary" is becoming very commonplace and accepted. When we look at the changes in the world since World War II, or even the last twenty years, we can see Orwell was a futurist before his time and the *Terminator* may not be science fiction after all as it comes to reality.

Index

Milton Keynes UK
Ingram Content Group UK Ltd.
UKHW031126141024
449569UK00006B/414